NO ONE WOULD
LISTEN

NO ONE WOULD LISTEN

A True Financial Thriller

HARRY MARKOPOLOS

with

Frank Casey, Neil Chelo,
Gaytri Kachroo, and Michael Ocrant

WILEY

John Wiley & Sons, Inc.

Published by John Wiley & Sons, Inc., Hoboken, New Jersey.
Published simultaneously in Canada.

For general information on our other products and services or for technical support, please
contact our Customer Care Department within the United States at (800) 762-2974,
outside the United States at (317) 572-3993 or fax (317) 572-4002.

Wiley also publishes its books in a variety of electronic formats. Some content that appears
in print may not be available in electronic books. For more information about Wiley
products, visit our web site at www.wiley.com.

Library of Congress Cataloging-in-Publication Data:
Markopolos, Harry.
   No one would listen : a true financial thriller / Harry Markopolos.
     p.   cm.
   Includes index.
   ISBN 978-0-470-55373-2 (cloth)
     1. Madoff, Bernard L.   2. Ponzi schemes—United States.   3. Investment
advisors—Corrupt practices—United States.   4. Hedge funds—United States.
5. Securities fraud—United States—Prevention.   6. United States. Securities and
Exchange Commission—Rules and practice.   I. Title.
   HV6697.M37 2010
   364.16'3092—dc22
                                                                              2009049433

Printed in the United States of America
10 9 8 7 6 5 4 3 2 1

To all the victims—you above all others deserve
to know the truth.

Contents

Foreword

Harry Markopolos is a hero.

But not for anything he meant to do. He did not stop Bernie Madoff from creating the largest Ponzi scheme of all time; nor did he save Madoff's investors any money.

What he did do was create a clearly documented record of his warnings so that *when* Madoff's scheme eventually toppled under its own weight, the Securities and Exchange Commission (SEC), which *was* charged with stopping fraud and protecting investors, could not assume an ostrich defense.

Ponzi schemes exist in stable disequilibrium. This means that while they can't ultimately succeed, they can persist indefinitely—until they don't. Just the fact that something has gone on for a very long time doesn't mean it's legitimate. Madoff's story shows that investors are attracted to too-good-to-be-true situations despite the red flags. How statistically different was Bernie Madoff's track record from General Electric's 100-quarter record of continual earnings growth or Cisco's 13-quarter record of beating analysts' quarterly estimates by exactly one penny per share between 1998 and 2001? Madoff's record was clearly implausible and, therefore, raised the question of what was wrong. The question is: Do we draw the line at Ponzi schemes or do we do something about less clear-cut manipulations as well?

One time I pointed out to a Wall Street analyst that a certain company was cooking the books. The analyst responded that it made him more confident in his bullish recommendation because such a company would never disappoint Wall Street.

For years, I observed and experienced the SEC protecting large perpetrators of abuse at the expense of the investors whom the SEC is supposed to protect. The SEC has been very tough, and usually appropriately so, on small-time cons, promoters, insider traders, and, yes, hedge funds. But when it comes to large corporations and institutionalized Wall Street, the SEC uses kid gloves, imposes meaningless nondeterring fines, and emphasizes relatively unimportant things like record keeping rather than the substance of important things — like investors being swindled.

Bernie Madoff epitomized the problem. When he was legit, Madoff was a large broker-dealer and the former chairman of NASDAQ. He was not famous as a money manager, let alone as a hedge fund manager, because he wasn't one. After his scheme collapsed and he became known as a crook, he was rechristened as a hedge fund operator — even though, to this day, his was the only so-called hedge fund I've heard of that didn't charge a management fee or an incentive fee. I doubt he would have fooled the SEC had he been known as a hedge fund manager, as the SEC would've been predisposed to catch him if they had known him with that title.

Warren Buffett said, "You only find out who is swimming naked when the tide goes out." The financial crisis of 2008 revealed many, including Madoff, to be inappropriately attired. Effective regulation must mean that the skinny-dippers are stopped while the tide is still in.

As you will see, the SEC has taken some steps toward reform, and Harry Markopolos is optimistic that the agency will do better. I'd hold off judgment until the SEC brings cases that matter against large corporations that haven't gone bankrupt (taking action before the money is lost) and against institutionalized Wall Street.

The silver lining in the Madoff collapse, if there could be such a thing, is that for at least one moment in time, the SEC has been exposed. And for his role in making that happen, Harry Markopolos deserves all of our thanks.

DAVID EINHORN
December 2009

Who's Who

Investigation Team and Advisers

Frank Casey
Neil Chelo CFA, CAIA, FRM
Gaytri Kachroo, personal attorney
Harry Markopolos CFA, CFE
Phil Michael, *qui tam* (whistleblower) attorney
Michael Ocrant

Madoff and Advisers

Nicole DeBello, Madoff's attorney
Bernard Madoff, founder, Madoff Investment Securities LLC
Ira Lee Sorkin, Madoff's attorney

Wall Street Feeder Funds

Access International Advisors and Marketers
Francois de Flaghac, marketing
Patrick Littaye, Founder
Prince Michel of Yugoslavia, marketing
Tim Ng, junior partner (and husband of Debbi Hootman)
Rene-Thierry Magon de la Villehuchet, Chief Executive Officer

Fairfield Greenwich Group
Douglas Reid, Managing Director
Amit Vijayvergiya, Chief Risk Officer

Financial Wizards and Wall Street Brains

Dan DiBartolomeo, Founder, Northfield Information Services
Jeff Fritz, Oxford Trading Associates
Leon Gross, Head of Equity Derivatives Research, CitiGroup
Andre Mehta, CFA, super-quant and Managing Director of
    Alternative Investments at Cambridge Associates
Chuck Werner, math wizard from MIT

Markopolos's Friends and Colleagues

Harry Bates, sergeant, Whitman, Massachusetts, Police Department
Pat Burns, Director of Communications, Taxpayers Against Fraud
    (whistleblower organization)
Boyd Cook, major general in the National Guard, Maryland dairy farmer
George Devoe, CFA, Chief Investment Officer, Rampart Investment
    Management Company
Elaine Drosos and family, owners of the Venus Cafe in Whitman,
    Massachusetts
Dave Fraley, managing partner, Rampart Investment Management
    Company
Scott Franzblau, Principal, Benchmark Plus
Bud Haslett, CFA, Chief Option Strategist, Miller Tabak Securities
Dave Henry, CFA, Chief Investment Officer, DKH Investments in
    Boston, Massachusetts
Chuck Hill, CFA, succeeded Markopolos as president of the Boston
    Security Analysts Society
Daniel E. Holland III, Managing Director, Goldman Sachs in Boston
Debbi Hootman, Darien Capital Management
Greg Hryb, CFA, Darien Capital Management
Louie Markopolos, Harry's younger brother
Matt Moran, Vice President of Marketing, Chicago Board Options
    Exchange
Peter Scannell, Putnam Investments' Quincy employee who filed a
    claim with the Securities and Exchange Commission
Rudi Schadt, PhD, Director of Risk Management, Oppenheimer Funds
Diane Schulman, False Claims Act fraud investigator
Jeb White, President, Taxpayers Against Fraud

Burt Winnick, Managing Partner, McCarter & English in Boston
Bill Zucker, attorney, McCarter & English

Journalists

Erin Arvedlund, *Barron's* magazine reporter
Reuben Heyman-Kantor, *60 Minutes*
Andy Court, *60 Minutes*
John "Front Page" Wilke, *Wall Street Journal* reporter
Greg Zuckerman, *Wall Street Journal* reporter

Government Officials

Securities and Exchange Commission (SEC)
David Becker, General Counsel
Steve Cohen, attorney
Christopher Cox, former Chairman
David Fielder, Assistant Inspector General
Noelle Frangipane, Deputy Inspector General
Robert Khuzami, current Director of Enforcement
David Kotz, Inspector General
Lori Richards, former Director, Office of Compliance, Inspections and
 Examinations
Mary Schapiro, current Chairman
Jonathan Sokobin, Deputy Chief Economist, Office of Economic
 Analysis, and Director of Risk Management
Heidi Steiber, Senior Counsel
Linda Thomsen, former Director of Enforcement
Andrew Vollmer, former Acting General Counsel
John Walsh, Chief Counsel, Office of Compliance, Inspections and
 Examinations
Chris Wilson, Senior Counsel
David Witherspoon, Senior Counsel

Boston Regional Office
Jim Adelman, former senior enforcement attorney
David Bergers, former New England Regional Director of Enforcement,
 who replaced Grant Ward, current Regional Administrator

Michael Garrity, Assistant Regional Director
Edward Manion, Senior Staff Accountant
Juan Marcelino, former Regional Administrator
Joseph Mick, Assistant Regional Director
Walter Ricciardi, former Regional Administrator
Grant Ward, former New England Regional Director of Enforcement

Northeast Regional Office in New York
Doria Bachenheimer, Assistant Director of Enforcement
Meaghan Cheung, Branch Chief
Peter Lamoure
Simona Suh, enforcement attorney

Senate
Jeff Merkley (D-OR)
Chuck Schumer (D-NY)

House of Representatives
Gary Ackerman (D-NY)
Shelly Capito (R-WV)
Joe Donnelly (D-IN)
Barney Frank (D-MA), Chairman of the House Financial Services
    Committee
Scott Garrett (R-NJ), Ranking Member, House Capital Markets
    Subcommittee
Al Green (D-TX)
Paul Kanjorski (D-PA), Chairman of the House Capital Markets
    Subcommittee
Carolyn Maloney (D-NY)
James Segel, Special Counsel to the House Financial Services
    Committee
Brad Sherman (D-CA)

Other
Andrew Cuomo, current New York State Attorney General
William Galvin, Massachusetts Secretary of the Commonwealth
Eliot Spitzer, former New York State Attorney General
Kathleen Teahan (D, Plymouth), Markopolos's former local
    Massachusetts state representative

Introduction to the Paperback Edition

I lead a very busy life. I'm involved in several investigations of the financial industry that will shock people when, and if, they become public. The "if," of course, is the result of my experience in the Madoff case, when so many individuals and institutions simply chose to ignore the facts in front of them. However, these investigations are what matter to me now. I have made several speeches about our Madoff investigation, mostly to professional organizations, but it has reached the point where I really don't enjoy talking about it anymore. Fortunately, it is in my rearview mirror. Unfortunately, that's not true for most of us.

We're going to be living with Bernie Madoff for the rest of our lives. He has become so much a part of our culture that he has achieved a certain kind of infamy—his name has become a metaphor for a brilliant and heartless criminal, while his face has become a popular and instantly recognizable Halloween mask. This is a story that will have an impact for generations and still produces frequent headlines in the news: Madoff got beaten up in prison; Madoff's son commits suicide and his body goes unclaimed; the victims' trustee, Irving Picard, files another lawsuit; another formerly exclusive golf club has been put up for sale because too many of its members lost too much money; an auction of Madoff's personal belongings grosses $2 million—including $6,100 for slippers with his initials embroidered in gold thread. But for me, of course, and the Fox Hounds, Bernie Madoff will always be the one who got away.

In the months since the initial publication of this book there have been substantial and significant actions. On paper, Madoff defrauded an estimated three million investors of $64.8 billion, although his records included only 5,000 direct accounts. Obviously, $64.8 billion is an arbitrary number, as there are several different ways of calculating the losses. But any conversation about Madoff has to begin with the fates of the victims. I've come to believe that there are far more victims than anyone has speculated. I actually didn't appreciate how depraved a human being Bernie Madoff was until I began meeting a few of those victims. I've been invited to make many speeches, and each time I do I meet victims. I've heard too many stories about people who have committed or attempted suicide, or who died of heartbreak or stress, after losing much or all of their life savings to Madoff. In addition to the 339 funds of funds in more than 40 countries we know about, I've learned of consolidators who put together large groups of small investors and delivered their money to established funds that invested with Madoff. After one TV interview, the host of a major news program whispered to me, "Harry, there are a lot of victims here." It turned out that almost all of the camera operators had lost their life savings.

That surprised me. Madoff almost exclusively accepted large investors and, while technicians make a comfortable salary, they don't have millions of dollars to invest. The host explained that they had been approached by a consolidator who pooled their savings and gave it to a fund of funds. They'd lost everything—but only the name of the consolidator appeared on the long list of victims. I heard similar stories several different times, meaning at least some of the names on the victims list actually represented multiple investors.

■ ■ ■

It's clear now that some people will get some money back. Who and how much is another question. Initially one investor who had lost several million dollars was offered 10 percent of the value of his loss by a syndicate trying to buy debt in the event there is money returned. Recently that same person was offered as much as 35 percent of his claim, so obviously there are people who believe that eventually there will be a significant payout. In fact, by the end of 2010 it appeared investors whose claims had been approved might receive as much as half of their investments minus what they already had received.

European victims have fared much better than Americans. According to reports, a group of European banks that sold Madoff-linked financial products to their clients have agreed to pay $15.5 billion to an estimated 720,000 Madoff investors. Supposedly that represents the entire amount those clients had invested, but not the profits Madoff had reported to them. About 20 percent of all European investors have chosen to file their own lawsuits. Not all European banks or funds of funds are participating, but it's still a much better settlement than anything offered thus far to American investors. The fact that the banks settled isn't surprising; the European investors included the wealthiest and most powerful citizens in those countries—among them some royals—and they had a lot of clout with those banks.

It also seems clear at least some of those banks had doubts about Madoff. ABC News reported that JP Morgan's London office filed a "Suspicious Activity Report" with UK authorities two months prior to Madoff's arrest claiming his returns were most likely fraudulent. Morgan already had begun withdrawing investments from feeder funds dealing with Madoff, which caused an advisor to one of those funds to threaten a Morgan representative that the fund's "Colombian friends" could "create havoc."

These "friends," obviously drug lords, as well as Russian Mafia and other criminals who had invested tens of millions of dollars, were precisely the people I was so concerned about when we began blowing the whistle on Madoff.

In this country the court-appointed trustee, Irving Picard, has reviewed more than 16,000 claims for repayment of losses. Picard is in a very difficult situation but he is doing an extraordinary job. He's decided that profits on paper aren't legitimate and has rejected all those claims. He's also decided that those people who took out an amount equal to or greater than the money they actually put in won't receive any funds. Taking everything into consideration, he has found that only about 2,300 of the claims, worth $5.58 billion, are valid.

The question is how much money Picard will eventually be able to claw back or recover. By the end of 2010 he had recovered about $3 billion, and had reached an additional $7.2 billion settlement with the estate of the late investor Jeffrey Picower. Picower was one of Madoff's largest investors and had received those funds in excess of his investments. Picard also had filed civil suits against Madoff's family, investment funds, and wealthy investors, seeking an additional $48 billion. In November he brought a $2 billion lawsuit against UBS AG, accusing that bank and its related entities of 23 counts of financial fraud, pointing out, "Madoff's scheme could not have been accomplished unless UBS had agreed not only to look the other way, but also to pretend that they were truly ensuring the existence of assets and trades when in fact they were not and never did." In early December, he sued JPMorgan Chase for $6.4 billion, and Sonja Kohn's Bank Medici for $19.6 billion—but asking the courts to treble the Kohn figure under racketeering statutes. When filing those charges he referred to Kohn as Madoff's "criminal soul mate."

All of these entities have denied his charges. For example, Morgan's spokesperson said the lawsuit "blatantly distorts both the facts and the law in an attempt to grab headlines," and the bank will defend itself vigorously." But it does seem clear that many of these banks and funds knew Madoff was a fraud, if not a Ponzi scheme. The *Financial Times* reported in December that several banks, as well as Access International, had been warned of serious problems. A specialist brought in by that fund warned after four days of investigation, "If this were a new investment product not only would it fail to meet due dil standards you would likely shove it out the door . . . EITHER extremely sloppy errors OR serious omissions in tickets." By the time Picard is done, he estimates he could end up filing lawsuits against as many as 1,000 investors he describes as "net winners." Those are "the people who made money, who got more, have made money at the expense of the people who didn't."

Unfortunately, at least some of those net winners are elderly people who were duped by Madoff or investment funds, people who were dependent on the returns they got from him and are now living on whatever they have left. So what do you do about those people? Do you take their remaining money and leave them destitute? It's difficult not to be sympathetic; I've met several people who have already lost most of their life savings and are terrified the trustee will be able to claw back what they have left.

It's a lot easier to go after those people who walked away from Madoff with a fortune. The question that I have been asked more often than any other is: Do I think Madoff's family knew what he was doing? Certainly Irving Picard does, claiming that the family used

Madoff's Ponzi scheme as "a family piggy bank." In July 2010 he sued three businesses controlled by Madoff's sons and other family members to recover more than $30 million. In his court papers Picard wrote that Madoff family members spent as much as $200 million for their own purposes. "Foremost. among the recipients of Madoff's gifts of customer funds were his closest family members, including his wife Ruth Madoff, his brother Peter, his two sons Andrew and Mark, and his niece Shana." In November 2010 Picard filed 40 lawsuits against family members and former employees of the firm seeking to recover $69 million that was fraudently transferred to these people. In addition, Madoff's former secretary and the woman who handled daily cash balances were arrested and charged with conspiracy, securities fraud, and falsifying records.

And in December 2010 Mark Madoff committed suicide in his $6 million apartment, writing despairingly that "No one wants to hear the truth," as his two-year-old child slept in the next room. Unfortunately, I suspect this will not be the last death directly attributable to Bernie Madoff.

■ ■ ■

In response to the public outrage, and perhaps to my testimony, the government has taken steps to encourage whistleblowers. The Dodd-Frank Wall Street Reform and Consumer Protection Act, which was part of the regulatory overhaul signed into law by President Obama in July 2010, specifically increased the potential reward to whistleblowers who provide "original information" from 10 percent up to 30 percent of any successful enforcement action that exceeds $1 million. Even while the precise details of the program were still being hammered out in Congress, plaintiff law firms began advertising on radio and in the newspapers for whistleblowers. While it is still rare for a bounty to be paid, with fines in the tens of millions of dollars these cases can be far more lucrative than the normal slip-and-falls many of these firms handle. As one Washington firm offered, "If you are aware of any securities or tax law violations and would like to discuss the SEC [Securities and Exchange Commission], CFTC [Commodity Futures Trading Commission], or IRS whistleblower programs with a [name of firm] attorney at no charge, please contact us."

Obviously a lot of major corporations are nervous about this new regulation, as perhaps they should be. In October 2010, attorneys representing several major financial, pharmaceutical, and big-box companies asked the SEC to force employees to bring any accusations to the firm before taking them to the agency. In addition, they asked the SEC to refuse to accept charges from those people with "fiduciary responsibility" to the company, basically executives and directors.

It's actually pretty funny: The SEC is finally ready to show some teeth—and these firms are asking the agency to have those teeth pulled. Until the final regulations are promulgated, it's impossible to know how weak or strong they will be. A lot of people are watching.

The only member of the Fox Hounds still actively working on the Madoff case is Gaytri Kachroo. She was invited to speak in front of the World Legal Forum in The Hague about the problems facing investors trying to make claims concerning financial frauds across national borders. She has served as the vice-chair of the Global Alliance on the Madoff case (a civil society of about 5,000 lawyers from 28 countries), which has led to international discussions about how to deal with multinational financial frauds. She also is actively representing many Madoff investors in their negotiations with Irving Picard, and in their potential lawsuits against the SEC. It's an extraordinarily complex situation, and it isn't going to be resolved quickly or to the satisfaction of most of the people who have suffered damages.

For the rest of Fox Hounds—Neil, Frank, Mike, and me—the Madoff case remains the superglue that bonded us together, but it long ago ceased to be part of our daily or weekly lives. Unless there is a story in the papers, we rarely even discuss it. We get up in the morning and, unlike Madoff or many of his victims, we simply move forward with our normal lives. And having once been so close to pure evil, we are enjoying every minute of normality.

Introduction

On the rainy afternoon of June 17, 2009, David Kotz sat patiently in a small room with a single barred window at the Metropolitan Correction Center, a prison in lower Manhattan, waiting to interview Bernard Madoff, the mastermind behind the greatest financial crime in history. Kotz, the Securities and Exchange Commission (SEC) inspector general, was investigating the total failure of his agency to expose Madoff's $65 billion Ponzi scheme—even after I'd warned the SEC about it in five separate submissions over a nine-year period.

Kotz and his deputy, Noelle Frangipane, sat across from an empty chair, and on either side of it sat Madoff's two attorneys, Ira Lee Sorkin and Nicole DeBello. Eventually Madoff was escorted into the room by a guard, who carefully unlocked and removed his handcuffs. Bernie Madoff had been a king of the financial industry, the widely respected cofounder and former chairman of NASDAQ, the owner of one of Wall Street's most successful broker-dealers, and a prominent New York philanthropist. Now, wearing a bright orange prison jumpsuit that glared against the drab gray walls of the room, he sat down between his impeccably dressed lawyers.

Madoff had agreed to this interview with the single stipulation that it not be taped or transcribed. Kotz began by explaining to Madoff that he had a legal obligation to tell the truth. The fact that he was to be sentenced a week later may have influenced his decision to talk openly to Kotz. Or it may simply have been his ego making a last grasp for attention. When it comes to assigning motives to Madoff's actions, who can really say? His motives make him an enigma, even to this day.

As Kotz later recalled, Madoff was overly polite and seemed forthcoming. "I guess we were concerned that all the answers to our questions would be one or two words or he wouldn't provide much information or his lawyer would cut him off every time he tried to say something, but there was none of that. He answered all of our questions expansively. It seemed like he didn't hold anything back."

Over a three-hour period, Kotz and Frangipane took copious, nearly verbatim notes as Madoff revealed for the first time the whole story of his Ponzi scheme, claiming it had been started almost by accident and that he admittedly was astonished that he hadn't been caught by the SEC. He was extremely critical of that agency, calling its investigators idiots, assholes, and blowhards. Kotz noted how frequently Madoff boasted of his connections in the financial industry. "He claimed to know so many important people—'I knew this one,' that one 'was a good friend,' this one he 'knows very well,' that one he 'had a special relationship with.'"

But it was about halfway through this interview, when Kotz asked him about me, that his attitude changed. "So let me ask you," Kotz said, consulting his notepad, "How much do you know about Harry Markopolos?"

Madoff immediately waved his arm dismissively. He bristled. I was nothing, he told Kotz. "This guy is getting all this press, all this attention. He thinks he's some kind of seer. But believe me, it's all overblown. You know what? He's really a joke in the industry."

Madoff continued, explaining that I was "a guy who was just jealous" of his business success. As Kotz listened to him, he began to realize that Madoff considered me a competitor and appeared to be bothered by the fact that I was getting attention that rightfully belonged to him. He wouldn't let it go. Later in the interview he defended his investment strategy, which I had ripped apart, telling Kotz, "All you have to do is look at the type of people I was doing this for to know it was a credible strategy. They knew the strategy was doable. They knew a lot more than this guy Harry."

No, they didn't. They just saw the money. And they could not see through the dangerously charming exterior of a man who labeled me a "joke."

■ ■ ■

Let me say first that I take no pride in having the last laugh. I'm Harry Markopolos, and this is the true account of my first case as a whistleblower to the SEC.

How did I become a whistleblower? It all began in 1999 when my friend Frank Casey first brought Madoff to my attention. I was confounded by the Wall Street mogul's financial successes, and had to know more. I tried but couldn't replicate his results. I later concluded it was impossible. One red flag led to another, until there were simply too many to ignore.

In May 2000, I turned over everything I knew to the SEC. Five times I reported my concerns, and no one would listen until it was far too late. I was a whistleblower taking on one of the most powerful men on Wall Street, and at some points through the nightmarish journey, I feared for both my safety and that of my family. I was convinced the crime he was committing was going to be the worst in market history. Ten years later, Madoff is now behind bars and we all know why.

My investigation team, as it came to be known, was comprised of four honest people with the shared belief that good ethics demands action. The four of us were the last and unfortunately only functioning line of defense between Madoff, his global organization of feeder funds, and their victims. We tried mightily to stop what we knew was wrong. As a result of our work the SEC—if it continues to exist—will be a different agency, and the way we police and regulate our markets will have been changed completely.

This is our story.

Chapter 1

A Red Wagon in a Field of Snow

On the morning of December 11, 2008, a New York real estate developer on a JetBlue flight from New York to Los Angeles was watching CNBC on the small seat-back television. A crawl across the bottom of the screen reported that Bernard Madoff, a legendary Wall Street figure and the former chairman of NASDAQ had been arrested for running the largest Ponzi scheme in history. The developer sat silently for several seconds, absorbing that news. *No, that couldn't be right*, he thought, but the message streamed across the screen again. Turning to his wife, he said that he knew that she wasn't going to believe what he was about to tell her, but apparently Bernie Madoff was a crook and the millions of dollars that they had invested with him were lost. He was right—she didn't believe him. Instead, she waved off the thought. "That's not possible," she said, and returned to the magazine she was reading.

The stunned developer stood up and walked to the rear of the plane, where the flight attendants had gathered in the galley. "Excuse me," he said politely, "but I'm going to be leaving now. So would you please open the door for me? And don't worry—I won't need a parachute."

■ ■ ■

At about 5:15 that December afternoon, I was at the local dojo in my small New England town watching my five-year-old twin boys trying to master the basic movements of karate. It had been a gloomy

5

day. Rain continued intermittently, and there was a storm in the air.
I noticed there were several voice mails on my cell phone. *That's curious*, I thought; I hadn't felt it vibrate. I stepped into the foyer to retrieve
the messages. The first one was from a good friend named Dave Henry,
who was managing a considerable amount of money as chief investment officer of DKH Investments in Boston. "Harry," his message said
clearly, "Madoff is in federal custody for running a Ponzi scheme. He's
under arrest in New York. Call me." My heart started racing. The second message was also from a close friend, Andre Mehta, a super-quant
who is a managing director of alternative investments at Cambridge
Associates, a consultant to pension plans and endowments. I could hear
the excitement in Andre's voice as he said, "You were right. The news
is hitting. Madoff's under arrest. It looks like he was running a huge
Ponzi scheme. It's all over Bloomberg. Call me and I'll read it to you.
Congratulations."

I was staggered. For several years I'd been living under a death sentence, terrified that my pursuit of Madoff would put my family and
me in jeopardy. Billions of dollars were at stake, and apparently some
of that money belonged to the Russian mafia and the drug cartels—
people who would kill to protect their investments. And I knew all
about Peter Scannell, a Boston whistleblower who had been beaten
nearly to death with a brick simply for complaining about a million-
dollar market-timing scam. So I wouldn't start my car without first
checking under the chassis and in the wheel wells. At night I walked
away from shadows and I slept with a loaded gun nearby; and suddenly,
instantly and unexpectedly, it was over. Finally, it was over. They'd
gotten Madoff. I raised my fist high in the air and screamed to myself,
"Yes!" My family was safe. Then I collapsed over a wooden railing.
I had to grab hold of it to prevent myself from falling. I could barely
breathe. In less time than the snap of my fingers I had gone from being
supercharged with energy to being completely drained.

The first thing I wanted to do was return those calls. I needed to
know every detail. It was only when I tried to punch in the numbers
that I discovered how badly my hand was shaking. I called Dave back
and he told me that the media was reporting that Bernie Madoff had
confessed to his two sons that his multibillion-dollar investment firm
was a complete fraud. There were no investments, he had told them;

there never had been. Instead, for more than two decades, he had been running the largest Ponzi scheme in history. His sons had immediately informed the Federal Bureau of Investigation (FBI), and agents had shown up at Madoff's apartment early that morning and arrested him. They'd taken him out in handcuffs. It looked like many thousands of people had lost billions of dollars.

It was exactly as I had warned the government of the United States approximately $55 billion earlier. And as I stood in the lobby of that dojo, my sense of relief was replaced by a new concern. The piles of documents I had in my possession would destroy reputations, end careers, and perhaps even bring down the entire Securities and Exchange Commission (SEC), the government's Wall Street watchdog—unless, of course, the government got to those documents before I could get them published. I grabbed my kids and raced home.

My name is Harry Markopolos. It's Greek. I'm a Chartered Financial Analyst and Certified Fraud Examiner, which makes me a proud Greek geek. And this, then, is the complete story of how my team failed to stop the greatest financial crime in history, Bernie Madoff's Ponzi scheme. For the previous nine years I had been working secretly with three highly motivated men who worked in various positions in the financial industry to bring the Bernie Madoff fraud to the attention of the SEC. We had invested countless hours and risked our lives, and had saved no one—although eventually, after Madoff's collapse, we would succeed in exposing the SEC as one of this nation's most incompetent financial regulators.

For example, it was well known that Madoff operated his legitimate broker-dealer business on the 18th and 19th floors of the Lipstick Building on New York's East Side. But what was not generally known was that his money management company, the fraud, was located on the 17th floor of that building. Months after Madoff's collapse, the FBI would reveal to my team that based on our 2005 submission providing evidence that Madoff was running a Ponzi scheme, the SEC finally launched an investigation—but that its crack investigative team during the two-year-long investigation "never even figured out there was a 17th floor." I had provided all the evidence they needed to close down Madoff—and they couldn't find an entire floor. Instead they issued three technical deficiency notices of minor violations to Madoff's broker-dealer arm. Now, that really is setting a pretty low bar for other government agencies to beat. But sadly, all of this nation's financial regulators—the Federal Reserve Bank, the Federal Deposit Insurance Corporation, the Office of the Comptroller of the Currency, and the Office of Thrift Supervision—are at best incompetent and at worst captive to the companies they are supposed to regulate.

As I would later testify before Congress, "The SEC roars like a mouse and bites like a flea." In retrospect, considering how much I have learned since then, and how much my team has learned, that probably was inaccurate: I was being too kind. Tens of thousands of lives have been changed forever because of the SEC's failure. Countless people who relied on that agency for the promised protection have lost more than can ever be recovered. In some cases people lost everything they owned. And truthfully, the SEC didn't even need to conduct an extensive investigation. My team had given them everything they needed. With the materials we submitted, it would have taken investigators no more than the time it took to ask Madoff three questions for his fraud to be discovered and his operation to be shut down. The magnitude of this Ponzi scheme is matched only by the willful blindness of the SEC to investigate Madoff.

■ ■ ■

This was not my first fraud investigation. My first investigation, which had a much more satisfying conclusion, concerned stolen fish. At one time my dad and two uncles owned a chain of 12 Arthur Treacher's Fish & Chips restaurants in Maryland and Delaware. Eventually I became the assistant controller, which was basically a glorified bookkeeper. Then I became the manager of four units in Baltimore County. If you own a chain of restaurants, you will learn more about retail theft than you care to know. We had one manager who was using the restaurant as a front for his major income activity, which was selling drugs out of the drive-through window. Customers would place their order with him and find something other than fish and chips in their bags. We had another manager we knew was stealing from the restaurant, but we couldn't figure out how he was doing it. Finally my uncle parked across the highway in the International House of Pancakes parking lot and watched him through a pair of binoculars. He discovered that when the cashier took her break, this manager would literally bring in another cash register from his car, and for the next hour he would ring up sales for himself. He had a nice business going; unfortunately, it was my family's business.

We had a limited number of family members; so to eliminate fraud we had to rely on professional management, using the most advanced computers available at that time, to manage inventory. We had formulas for the components that went into every order: the amount of fish, chicken, shrimp, and clams. Every portion was controlled by size. I learned accounting in those restaurants. We continually matched our inventory to our sales and in that way could determine where our shortfalls were. Our goal was 3 percent waste. We wanted some waste, and some leftovers, because at the end of the night if you don't have waste it means you've given your customers cold fish or spoiled shrimp that should have been thrown out. Too little waste meant you were not providing a quality product; too much waste meant there was theft.

When I discovered more than 5 percent waste in my district, I began examining the numbers. The numbers told me that something was fishy in one of our fish and chips stores. I appreciate mathematics, and I knew the answer was in front of me; I just had to be smart enough to find it. I enjoy watching the choreography of the numbers. There is a certain satisfaction I get from it. I wasn't always that way; in seventh and eighth grades I struggled with math and needed a tutor to lead me through algebra. In high school I excelled in math and enjoyed it. I studied finance in college and had terrible calculus teachers. They were PhD's who didn't know how to teach. I couldn't understand them, and I dropped the subject three times. I finally hired a PhD student in physics to tutor me, and eventually I was doing differential equations. I turned out to be a natural in math.

More than a natural, in fact. I'm a quant, which is the slang term for a quantitative analyst. Basically, that means I speak the language of numbers. Numbers can tell an entire story. I can see the beauty, the humor, and sometimes the tragedy in the numbers. Neil Chelo, a member of my Madoff team and a close friend, describes quants as people who conceptualize things in the form of numbers. As he says, quants look at numbers and see associations that other people aren't even aware exist, and then understand the meaning of those associations in a unique way.

A lot of my friends are quants. Neil is a quant; he can be obsessive about balancing not only his monthly bank statements, but even his credit card bills—to the penny. Quants are nerds and proud of it.

I look at numbers the way other people read books. For example, obviously computers are pretty darn fast doing math and calculating the value of derivatives, but even today there are certain calculations that are so math intensive that even a computer can choke on them. Occasionally a situation arises in which there is a second derivative, called gamma, which is the rate of change in the first derivative, delta. Don't try to understand this calculation, unless you intend to trade options. You'll never need to know how to do it and there is no test at the end. And you certainly won't need to know it to understand how Bernie Madoff successfully ran his worldwide Ponzi scheme for decades. Bernie's fraud was much less sophisticated than that. But in those situations prices can move literally at an infinite rate. A computer can't track it very quickly. I can. After working in the financial industry for several years I could calculate those prices faster than a computer. Generally there were a couple of times every year when I had to throw out the computer and look at the price of a stock or the market and calculate my own option prices in a few seconds. In one of those situations, my ability to do the calculations rapidly and correctly could salvage our investment or even allow us to make a lot of money. Actually, it was that same combination of ability and experience that enabled me to look at the returns of Bernie Madoff and know almost instantly that his claims were impossible.

It was my ability to understand the numbers that allowed me to catch the thief in my fish and chips store. I started by inventorying every shift for a week or two, which allowed me to pinpoint those shifts on which the thefts were occurring. That allowed me to identify the suspects. Finally I determined that there was only one person working all those shifts. Once I knew who the thief was, I was careful not to catch him. He was putting food in a shopping bag and carrying it out to his car. If I had caught him doing it I would have had to fire him, which probably would have meant paying unemployment. The amount of money involved was too small for law enforcement to become involved, but significant for my business. So rather than firing him, I didn't say a word. Over time I just cut back his hours until he was working only one shift a week—not enough to survive on—and he quit.

Bernie Madoff was a much bigger fish, but oddly enough not much more difficult to catch.

Actually, it was another fraud that first brought me into the financial industry. My father's former banker, the man who got the family into fast food, was working as a registered representative, a salesman, at a firm called Yardley Financial Services. It was shut down after the CEO was caught selling fake London gold options. The former banker joined several other former Yardley employees and opened Makefield Securities. My dad bought a 25 percent interest in the firm, and I went to work there in 1987.

I began by doing oil and gas partnership accounting, completing depreciation schedules, matching trade confirms—all relatively basic and often very boring work. I probably was underpaid for the work I was doing, but whenever you work for family you're going to be underpaid. Look at Bernie Madoff's two sons. Their father was running the most successful fraud in history and—at least according to Bernie—he wouldn't let them participate.

My first day as a licensed broker was October 19, 1987. I remember it well because that was the day the stock market crashed. Makefield was an over-the-counter market marker that traded between 12 and 25 stocks. We relied on Harris terminals—dumb terminals I called them because they did not automatically update prices. They simply provided the quote at the moment you hit the stock ticker. But they showed who was bidding and asking on shares at different prices. I came in to work that morning ready to begin my career as a broker, and instead walked into chaos.

We had only four phone lines coming in. They started ringing at 9 A.M. and never stopped. Not for a second. I knew that it was unusual, but I hadn't been in the market long enough to understand it was unprecedented. I did know that it wasn't good. We were one of the few companies buying that day, because we were short; we had been betting that the market would go down, and needed to cover our positions. For much of the time we didn't even know where the market was—our computers couldn't keep up with the price declines. The New York Stock Exchange tape was delayed about three hours, so at

1 o'clock in the afternoon we were still getting trades from 10 A.M. There wasn't a moment of calm the entire day. Everybody in the office was shell-shocked. They were trading every step down. I had been trained, but I wasn't ready to be thrown into the battle. I was so junior that they certainly weren't going to trust me. I spent the day running errands and setting up trading calls so that our traders could handle their calls more efficiently. We knew the market was crashing, but we didn't have enough information to understand how bad it was. The end of the day was the ugliest close anybody would ever want to see. We worked through much of the night processing trades, trying to get some understanding of where we were. The market had fallen almost 23 percent.

So much for my first day as a licensed broker.

What surprised me from the very beginning of my career was the level of corruption that was simply an accepted way of doing business. Bernie Madoff wasn't a complete aberration; he was an extension of the cutthroat culture that was prevalent from the day I started. This is not an indictment of the whole industry. The great majority of people I've met in this industry are honest and ethical, but in a business where money is the scoreboard there is a certain level of ingrained dishonesty that is tolerated. I became disillusioned very quickly. I learned that the industry is based on predator-prey relationships. The equation is simple: If you don't know who the predator is, then you are the prey. Frank Casey, who discovered Madoff for our team, referred to those elements on Wall Street that conduct their business for bottom-line profits rather than serving their clients as "rip your face off financing." I don't know where my education went wrong, but my brother and I had been taught that there was no such thing as a minor lapse of ethics. Either you were honest or you were not. It was not possible to be partly honest. I learned that at Cathedral Prep in Erie, Pennsylvania. It was the kind of Catholic school that had a very strict rule that every teacher followed: Once a teacher knocked you down he had to stop beating you.

I was one of the better-behaved students and was knocked out cold only once. At the beginning of the year we had to turn in two bars of soap to use in the showers after gym. I brought two bars of Pet'um Dog Soap, which leaves your coat shiny, clean, and tick-free. It had a nice drawing of a Scottish terrier on the wrapper, which I showed to my classmates. That was my mistake. The teacher called us individually to drop our soap in a box at the front of the room. When my name was called, the rest of the class started laughing loudly. The teacher looked in the box and found my Pet'ums. "Come here, Meathead," he commanded. He grabbed a thick textbook and beat me with it until I went down. He followed the rules! When I got a beating like that I couldn't go home and tell my parents, because my father would then give me another beating for causing a problem in school.

A prank I did get away with was infesting the school with fruit flies. In 10th-grade biology class we were breeding fruit flies for a series of experiments. I managed to sneak a vial home and secretly bred two complete cycles, so I had tens of thousands of fruit flies in a five-gallon jar. I explained to my mother that I was breeding them for a special science project. One morning I convinced her to bring me to school early. I slipped into the school through an open door by the cafeteria and released them all. It took them three days to infest the entire building, which had to be fumigated over the weekend.

More often, though, I got caught. Detention was held on Saturday mornings, when our job was to clean the school. I was a regular in detention. My parents never knew, though; I managed to convince my mother that I was in a special honors program that met on Saturday mornings. She would brag to her friends that her son Harry was so smart he was invited to attend honors classes on Saturdays!

At Cathedral Prep the difference between right and wrong was demonstrated to me on a daily basis. I learned there that actions had consequences. When I began working in the financial industry I learned very quickly that dishonest actions also had consequences—often you ended up making a lot more money. The most valuable commodity in the financial industry is information. Manipulating the market in any way that gives an individual access to information not available to other people on an equal basis is illegal. In early 1988 I was promoted to over-the-counter trader. I was making a market in about 18 NASDAQ stocks. One of the companies with which I traded regularly was Madoff Securities. That was the first time I had ever heard the name. All I knew was that it was a large and well-respected company at the other end of the phone. Madoff was a market maker—the middle-man between buyers and sellers of stocks—and if you were dealing in over-the-counter stocks, eventually you had to do business with Madoff. It was soon after I started trading that I encountered massive violations taking place on an hourly basis. This was not true at Madoff specifically; in fact, I don't remember a single incident in which its brokers were dishonest. But I had just learned all the regulations, and I saw them broken every day, every hour; and everybody knew about it and nobody seemed to care. The regulations were quite clear. The sellers in a deal have 90 seconds to report a trade. By not reporting it they were allowing the price to stay at levels different from those that would have resulted if the trading volume had been reported. Basically, it meant they were trading on inside information, which is a felony. It causes a lack of the transparency that is necessary to maintain fair and orderly markets.

This happened in my trades every day. It was an accepted way of doing business, although I couldn't accept it. I would report it regularly to the district office of the National Association of Securities Dealers (NASD) in Philadelphia, and they never did a thing about it.

My younger brother had similar experiences. At one point he was hired by a respected brokerage firm in New Jersey to run its trading desk. On his first morning there he walked into the office and discovered that the Bloomberg terminals that supposedly had been ordered hadn't arrived. Then he found out that the traders didn't have their Series 7 licenses, meaning they weren't allowed to trade. And then he learned that the CEO had some Regulation 144 private placement stock, which legally is not allowed to be sold. But the CEO had inside information that bad news was coming and he wanted to sell the stock. My brother explained to the CEO, "You can't sell this stock. It's a felony." The CEO assured him he understood.

My brother went out to lunch with the Bloomberg rep to try to get the terminals installed that he needed to start trading. By the time he returned to the office, the unlicensed traders had illegally sold the private placement stock based on insider information. My brother had walked into a perfect Wall Street storm.

He called me in a panic. "What do I do?"

I said, "These are felonies. The first thing to do is write your resignation letter. The second thing you do is get copies of all the trade tickets; get all the evidence you can on your way out the door. And the third thing you do is go home and type up everything and send it to the NASD." That's exactly what he did. The NASD did absolutely nothing. These were clear felonies and the NASD didn't even respond to his complaint.

When I started at Makefield in 1987, the industry was just beginning to become computerized, so most of the business was still done on the phone. I would spend all day with a phone hanging from my ear. I spoke with many of the same people every day and often got to know them well—even though I never met them in person. Among the people I most enjoyed speaking with was a client named Greg Hryb, who was with Kidder Peabody's asset management arm, Webster Capital. Greg was nice enough to take time during those calls to teach me the business. When he started his own asset management firm, Darien Capital Management, in June 1988, he hired me as an assistant portfolio manager and an asset manager trainee. I moved to Darien, Connecticut, that August, and it was there that my education really began.

■ ■ ■

Darien Capital Management was a small firm; there were only four or five of us working there. But in the early 1990s we were managing slightly more than a billion dollars. And that's when a billion dollars was a lot of money. We considered ourselves an asset management firm, but we operated as a hedge fund. Because we were so small, each of us had to wear many hats, which was a great opportunity for me. I did everything there from routine correspondence, monthly client statements, and handling of compliance issues to assisting a very good fixed-income portfolio manager. It was a lot of grunt work, but I was in on all the action. I got to learn the business of being a money manager by being an assistant portfolio manager. I learned more there in three years than I might have learned elsewhere in a decade.

Certainly one of the more important things I learned was that the numbers can be deceiving. There is a logic to mathematics, but there is also the underlying human element that must be considered. Numbers can't lie, but the people who create those numbers can and do. As so many people have learned, forgetting to include human nature in an equation can be devastating. Greg Hryb showed me the value of networking; he helped me build the wide spectrum of friends and associates I was able to call upon during the nine years of our investigation.

I stayed at Darien Capital for three years. One of the people who marketed our products was a woman named Debbi Hootman. Eventually I became friendly with Debbi and her future husband, Tim Ng, who was working at Smith Barney at that time. Eventually Tim recommended me to Dave Fraley, the managing partner at Rampart Investment Management Company, in Boston, who hired me as a derivatives portfolio manager.

Rampart was an eight- or nine-person institutional asset management firm that ran almost nine billion dollars, the majority of it for state pension plans. When I began working there it had a suit-and-tie, kind of starchy New England atmosphere. It exemplified the conservative Wall Street firm. Gradually, though, just like in the industry itself, standards were relaxed and we evolved into a more casual dress-down-Fridays place to do business. It was at Rampart that I began my pursuit of Madoff and my battle with the SEC.

The relentless quest pursued by just about every person working in the financial industry is to discover inefficiencies in the market that can be exploited. It's sort of like trying to find a small crack in a wall—and then driving a truck through it. At one time, the business of Wall Street consisted almost entirely of selling stocks and bonds; it was a staid, predictable business. Stocks went up; stocks went down. But then some very smart people began developing an array of creative investment products, among them indexed annuities, exchange-traded funds, structured products, and mortgage-backed securities. The business of basic investments became extraordinarily complicated, far too complicated for the casual investor to understand. Every firm in the industry and practically every person in the business had a theory and developed their own niche product in which they became expert. Everybody. These products were created to take advantage of every move the market made. Up, down—that didn't matter anymore. So rather than simply picking stocks in companies whose names they recognized and whose products they used, investors suddenly had a supermarket of esoteric—meaning sometimes speculative and risky—investment opportunities from which to choose. Rampart's investment strategy was called the Rampart Options Management System. It's not important that you understand what we did, but simply that Rampart sold call options against client portfolios in a highly disciplined fashion, which would generate cash flow while reducing the overall risk. We were writing covered calls on big stock portfolios for institutions. It was a strategy that over an entire market cycle increased income while decreasing risk—as long as our client didn't panic at the top. Unfortunately, as I learned, too many clients panicked right before the market topped and pulled out just before the strategy was about to become highly profitable.

Each summer Rampart would bring in an unpaid intern from a local college and I would mentor him or her. In the summer of 1993 that intern was Neil Chelo, a confident, wiry young man from Bentley College, a business school in Waltham, Massachusetts. Several years later Neil was to become a member of my Madoff team. Neil almost didn't take the intern job. Although his father encouraged him to work for the experience, telling him that Wall Street people were smart and that if he got down in the trenches with them, eventually he would make a lot of money, his mother was strongly against it. "Be something respectable," she told him. "Be a doctor or a lawyer." He pointed out to her that they were Turkish-Albanian, not Jewish. But what really upset her was the fact that her Turkish-Albanian son was going to work for a Greek! She told him, "Oh, my God, Neil. That's why you're not getting paid. The Greeks always take advantage of the Turks!"

Of course, as I would occasionally point out to Neil, that's not exactly the way Greeks interpret the Greek-Turkish relationship.

When Neil began his internship, he assumed he was going to sit down at the trading desk and learn by participating in the business. Instead, I handed him a reading list of about 14 books and told him his job that summer was to read all of them so we could discuss them. Among the books on my list were *Market Wizards* by Jack Schwager (New York Institute of Finance, 1989); Justin Mamis's *The Nature of Risk* (Addison-Wesley, 1991); and *Minding Mr. Market* (Farrar Straus & Giroux, 1993) by James Grant. My objective was to provide him with the education he wasn't going to get in an academic curriculum. Although I don't dislike business schools, I believe half of what they teach students will be obsolete within five years and the other half is just outright false. Generally, they teach formulas that no one uses, case studies that no longer apply in the real world, and concepts that are just going to get people into trouble if they try to apply them. These formulas are an attempt to model the financial world in a simplified form, but they can't possibly take into account the extraordinary complexity of the markets. It's important to know these formulas, though; once you've mastered them you can begin to make the necessary adjustments for the real world.

Neil spent about half his time helping prepare monthly statements, confirming trades, tracking dividends, downloading reports, and doing all the other work done in the back office. The other half was spent reading books on my list. He sat across the desk from me, and I literally would quiz him. If he didn't know the answer, I'd expect him to find it. And I insisted he do all the math by hand. Neil remembers (I don't) that one afternoon I gave him the Dow Jones Industrial Average for 30 stocks and their price fluctuations for a day and asked him to calculate the actual point change in the Dow. It was not difficult to pull it up on a calculator, but I insisted he do the math.

Neil was obviously smart, but even as an intern, he was headstrong and opinionated. If he disagreed with something I said, he would not hesitate to let me know quickly and forcefully. And like a pit bull, once he got his teeth into an argument he wouldn't let it go. Now, I had spent 17 years in the military. Among the lessons I had learned was that you can raise an objection once, maybe twice; but once a command decision was made, you didn't continue to question it. Neil hadn't learned that lesson, so when he believed he was right he wouldn't let go. But these weren't frivolous arguments; he knew his stuff. That's what made him so valuable when we began to analyze Madoff's numbers.

Math came naturally to Neil. Like me, maybe even more than me, he could glance at numbers and draw meaningful conclusions from them. At Bentley College, he played a lot of poker, ran a small bookie operation, and came to believe firmly in the efficient markets hypothesis. Believing that concept was where Neil and I differed most. The efficient markets hypothesis, which was first suggested by French mathematician Louis Bachelier in 1900 and was applied to the modern financial markets by Professor Eugene Fama at the University of Chicago in 1965, claims that if all information is simultaneously and freely available to everyone in the market, no one can have an edge. In this hypothesis having an edge means that for all intents and purposes you have accurate information that your competitors don't have. It basically means that you can't beat the market, that there is no free lunch.

After the first few weeks, Neil and I began going out to lunch together, to a local Greek place, naturally. The most important thing I taught Neil that summer was that what he learned in the office was not going to determine his success in this business. The only possible way of gaining an edge in the financial industry is by gathering information that others don't have. There are so many smart people in this business that it's impossible to outsmart them, so you simply have to have more and better information than they do. Information on a database that can be purchased is available to everyone; there's no advantage to having it, but the knowledge that one day might make a difference is best obtained from others in simple conversations. It's stuff you can't buy from a database provider; you have to learn it one relationship at a time. In the army we called it human intelligence gathering.

I had established the one-third rule: For every three hours you spend at work you have to spend at least one hour outside the office on professional development. That might mean reading material that might improve your life, but more likely it meant—just as I had learned at Darien Capital—social networking. I encouraged Neil to take advantage of the pub culture in Boston, to go to professional association meetings, and to go to dinners. As I explained to him, that's where the information that one day may make the difference is learned. That's where you find out what other firms are doing to be successful and where they are failing, what their problems are, and how they're dealing with them. For example, in those social conversations you hear about the idiosyncrasies of different traders, so when you see them making a move you know how to properly interpret it. I taught him that it is important to know everything that's going on in your field, in your industry, and in your sector in the industry, and that the only real way to do that is going to lunches and dinners and happy hours and meetings and getting there early and staying late. I taught him that ignorance begins where knowledge ends, so to be successful he needed to be a gatherer and a hoarder of information.

These were the tools we depended on throughout our investigation.

When Neil returned to college in the fall of 1992 to earn credit for his work as an intern, he had to write a paper. This will tell you what you need to know about Neil: The paper he wrote criticized the basic investment strategy we used at Rampart because it violated the efficient markets hypothesis.

Three years later, after working in various jobs at several different types of investment companies, Neil returned to Rampart. Initially he was hired to upgrade our accounting system, with the unspoken hope that eventually it might become something more. For several months Neil ran two accounting systems—our legacy system and the new system—in parallel, and reconciled everything to the penny. If he couldn't get that last penny to balance, he'd work at it until it did. But what he really wanted to do was portfolio management. Eventually our desks were back-to-back; so we sat directly across from each other, separated only by a divider about 18 inches high, for nine hours a day, five days a week. Over several years we got to know each other better than we knew our families. Neil and I were both research geeks who loved the hunt, and we spent considerable time searching for ways to optimally create portfolios that had the highest chance of beating the benchmark with the lowest risk. We pushed each other. So when we first encountered Bernie Madoff it was only logical that we would see it as an academic exercise, as another strategy to be taken apart and analyzed to help us develop a strategy that would benefit our clients, and not as the largest fraud in Wall Street history. We weren't looking for a crime; we simply wanted to see how he made his numbers dance.

It was Frank Casey who first brought Bernie Madoff to my attention. Frank Casey worked on the other side of the ledger; years ago he would have been known as a customer's man, but now he was a marketing representative. Frank is a gregarious Irishman, a man who attacks life and has combined his gift of language with his effervescent personality to become a successful salesman. In addition to selling our financial products, he also would find needs in the market that we might fill. On Wall Street a salesman is an interpreter of numbers. While Frank isn't a quant, being the middleman between the customers and the quants meant that he had to have enough understanding of the market to bring needs and products together.

Frank had been working in the industry doing a great variety of jobs for more than a quarter century when we met. He grew up with a love for the market, using money he earned running a jackhammer on a summer job while still in high school to buy his first stock, Botany 500, a men's clothier. At that time he didn't own a suit, but he had the stock. He doubled his money, and he was hooked. He remembers spending much of his junior and senior years in high school reading the stock market pages and books about investing—and writing poetry. He learned the realities of the market less than a year later; when the 1967 Israeli-Arab War started, he figured American Jews would become patriotic, so he invested in Hebrew National—and watched as the stock sat unmoved. But after that there was no doubt in his mind where he wanted to work. After four years in the military, finishing as an army captain, Airborne Ranger qualified, he started as a trader at Merrill Lynch in 1974 with an interesting strategy: "I figured everybody else who was starting as I was, cold-calling from the Yellow Pages, went from the front to the back. My buddy and I split the book in the middle, he worked middle to the back and I worked middle to the front. We called every business in the Boston Yellow Pages. That was our sophisticated strategy." By 1987 Frank was hedging more than a billion dollars in mortgages for banks. Because during most of his career he has earned his paycheck from commissions rather than from a fixed salary, mostly by creating and executing sales of his own products, he has developed an intuitive feeling about the people working on Wall Street and the products they market. So while at the very beginning he couldn't quite figure out what Bernie Madoff was doing, whatever it was, it just didn't feel right to him.

Frank Casey and Rampart cofounder Dave Fraley had met while both of them were working at Merrill Lynch in the mid-1970s. Like many relationships on Wall Street, their paths had crossed several times through several companies since then. When Frank found out that Rampart was specializing in options, an area in which he had a lot of experience, he approached Fraley, the managing partner in charge of marketing our products, and began working on commission. He was a Wall Street prospector, finding companies that would benefit from Rampart's products. In return, Dave Fraley directed me to execute trades through Frank, for which he earned a small commission. That's how we met. To me, he was an aggressive marketer. As I later found out, to him I was just another geek portfolio manager. It was a typical Wall Street retail versus institutional relationship. We needed each other, so we got along. That began changing in February 1998 when Fraley hired him to market products and develop new business.

It was impossible not to know Frank was there. His office was right next to the trading room and he was salesman-loud. At first we simply shut his door; but his voice boomed right through that closed door, so eventually management had to erect a glass wall so we could concentrate. I got to know him pretty quickly because he would sit down at my desk and ask me to explain our products to him. He understood the marketing aspect, but he wanted to understand exactly how they worked. Frank wanted to know the nuts and bolts of each product, how it worked under various market conditions, and where it fell short. He asked endless questions. What are the trading rules? What are your stop losses? What triggers a trade? What causes you to sit on a position? He wasn't a mathematician, but he wanted us to explain the math to him until it made sense. This was his way of getting that edge over the competition.

There are few things quants like more than explaining their math to an interested listener. And Frank does have that Irishman's way of making you feel comfortable with him. So it was only a matter of time before we were continuing our discussions after work in the better pubs of Boston. Over time we discovered several things we had in common, including the fact that although I was a reserve army officer while he had been regular army, both of us had been commissioned as second lieutenants in the infantry, which allowed us to tell plenty of funny stories about military life; and neither of us had a lot of respect for the corner-cutting ways business was often done in the financial industry.

■ ■ ■

It is surprising that nobody actually knows how many hedge funds or money management firms operating as hedge funds exist in this country. There are no regulations that require funds to register; in fact, there are actually few regulations that they have to follow. But there at least 8,000 hedge funds, and perhaps thousands more. So out of all of those funds, how did I manage to find and identify the single most corrupt operation in the world? (Or at least I certainly hope he was the most corrupt one.) Our investigation of Bernie Madoff started with these conversations between Frank Casey and me.

A properly managed firm invests its clients' money in a variety of financial products. The firm's goal is to create a balanced portfolio that has the potential to earn substantial profits while being protected from any drastic losses. A conservative portfolio, for example, consists of about 60 percent equity—stocks—and 40 percent bonds. Frank would meet regularly with portfolio managers to see what kinds of investments they were looking for and try to fulfill those needs.

Like Neil and me, Frank was always looking to expand the number and quality of Rampart's products. He had been hired because our two primary products, the Rampart Options Management System and a covered call writing program, had lost their sizzle and we needed something new to sell. So almost immediately he began trying to develop innovative ways to market our expertise. Among the products he and Neil worked on were principle-protected notes, which provide the chance of making a profit with the guarantee that you can't lose the principle. Basically they involved using part of the investment to buy zero-coupon Treasury bonds, knowing the return over five or 10 years would equal the entire investment, and using the rest of the money to invest in hedge funds with leverage. The worst-case scenario was that after five or 10 years you'd get the original investment back but without any earnings. Basically, if the investment went south, the most a client could lose was the interest he or she would have made on the principle over five or 10 years. Frank's plan was to have certain banks construct a blended pool of fund managers that could use the investment portion to produce something close to a 1 percent monthly return to the client, with the triple-A-rated bank guaranteeing the return of the original investment. Dave Fraley was supportive, telling Frank to try to build that part of the business. So Frank began prospecting institutions throughout New England, all the way into New York City.

The financial industry is a business of contacts and relationships. No one ever buys a product and says, "That product is the sexiest thing I've ever seen. I don't care who's selling it." Generally people do business with people they trust and like, or people who are recommended by someone they trust. So like any good salesman, Frank was always looking for leads. He was constantly asking us who we knew at what firms. Who could we introduce him to? He used to complain that I never introduced him to my friends, and there was some truth to that. Finally, though, I referred Frank to my old friend Tim Ng, who was then a junior partner at a Madison Avenue fund of funds, Access International Advisors. Basically, Access was a hedge fund of funds whose investments were spread among several other hedge funds. It was what I always referred to as fighting size, meaning it managed more than $1 billion. I only found out later that almost all of its clients were European royalty or high-born old money.

As I told Frank, "I've heard from Tim Ng that his boss found a manager who's putting out one to two percent a month or more net to client. Would that help you in building these principle-protected notes?"

The fact is that I was curious to see how this manager could consistently generate such a high return. Nobody ever beats the market month after month—nobody. The market can go up, remain neutral, or go down. There is no single strategy that provides a consistent return no matter what the market does. So I told Frank, "Why don't you go down there and figure out what their game is?"

Frank wanted to know about this manager, too; if he really was that good, Frank could refer him to the banks that were building portfolios for Rampart. If he actually had discovered the holy grail, we could use him in our products.

They met in Access's Madison Avenue office. Unlike so many of the elaborately decorated financial offices, this one was tastefully but simply decorated. It was an open plan, with steel desks side by side: a working office. Tim explained to Frank that he didn't handle that side of the business and set up an appointment for him with the CEO of Access, a Frenchman named Thierry de la Villehuchet. Like Frank, I would eventually get to know and like Thierry very much. Rene-Thierry Magon de la Villehuchet was a terrific person, a French nobleman who, as it tragically turned out, truly was a noble man, a man of honor. He wasn't an expert in financial math, but he was a great salesman. He and another Frenchman, Patrick Littaye, had founded Access. Both Thierry and Patrick had lived in the United States long enough to consider themselves Americans. They loved the American entrepreneurial spirit and considered themselves Americans in spirit. Thierry believed completely in American values. He took the Statue of Liberty very seriously. As Thierry once explained to me, in a French accent tempered by the years he'd lived here, "The French are socialists; we're not socialists. Americans are capitalists; we're capitalists. We believe in economic freedom; therefore we're Americans."

Thierry had a medium build, and everything about him was impeccable. He was always formal, always dressed in a suit and tie. The product he was marketing was himself, and he sold it well. I never knew precisely how old he was, but I guessed he was in his mid-50s when we met. I never knew how wealthy he was, but clearly he was a quietly rich man. Like Frank, Thierry was passionate about sailing, and one afternoon I took him to a shop that specialized in miniature sailboats and nautical items for home decor. He bought a miniature sailboat for $5,000 for his home in Westchester County, New York. "Maybe I overpaid," he told me, "but I loved that boat."

As it turned out, Thierry had his own motive for meeting Frank Casey. While his firm was called "International," almost all the investments managed by Access came from Europe, and Thierry was trying to raise Wall Street money. So during this first meeting with Frank, Thierry spent considerable time promoting his company. That's probably why he was unusually candid about the business. "At first I was the hedge fund unit of a French bank in the United States," he explained. "I built this business basically to find the best managers early in their careers and lock them up for capacity, so later when people wanted to invest with them I would have access to them. Therefore the name of our firm: Access to the best managers. That's what we provide for our clients."

When Frank asked him specifically about the manager who supposedly was producing a 1 to 2 percent net return each month, Thierry nodded. "It's true. I do have this manager who's producing a good steady one to two percent net, and I found him early in the development here. He's my partner. But I'm sorry—I'm not supposed to tell his name to anyone. If I do he might not give me any capacity."

That was curious. Generally, when someone is consistently able to produce such spectacular returns, they would want their name and success widely circulated. What could possibly be better for business? But this manager was threatening to turn away clients who dared mention his name. Frank asked why this manager wanted his identity kept secret.

"He doesn't hold himself out to be a hedge fund. He has only a few large clients. Actually he's a broker-dealer, but he's using hedge fund strategies in his money management business."

At that moment Frank had no reason to question any of this. And if what Thierry was telling him was true, this manager was a major find.

He told Thierry, "You know, we might be interested in doing business with Access if you could put together a portfolio. If you included managers like him I probably could get the banks to guarantee the return of principle."

Thierry liked that concept. "His name is Bernie Madoff."

Anyone who had worked in the stock market even for a short period of time knew that name, if not his background. The company he'd founded, Madoff Investment Securities LLC, was among the most successful broker-dealers on Wall Street, specializing in over-the-counter stocks. Madoff Securities was a well-known market maker, meaning he both bought and sold stocks, making his profit by selling for a few cents more per share than his purchase price. Madoff Securities was a pioneer in electronic trading, enabling the company to rapidly move large blocks of over-the-counter stocks. But what really set Madoff apart was his willingness to pay for order flow. Normally, the difference between what market makers paid for a stock and what they sold it for was about 12.5 cents. That was their profit. But instead of taking a fee for this service, as was normally done, Bernie actually paid firms as much as two cents per share for their business. Even though he was earning a penny or two less per share, he more than compensated for that with greatly increased volume. In the early 1990s Madoff Securities was reputed to be responsible for almost 10 percent of the daily trading of New York Stock Exchange–listed securities. By the end of the decade the company was the sixth largest market maker on Wall Street. That strategy had made Madoff rich, and had enabled him to become one of the most respected men in the financial industry. He marketed himself as a cofounder of NASDAQ and had served as its chairman; he was a prominent New York philanthropist and a member of numerous industry and private boards and committees. Thierry might have been born with royal blood, but Bernie Madoff was a Wall Street king.

Frank Casey had never heard anything about Bernie Madoff managing money, though. But even more unusual was the arrangement between Access and Madoff. As Thierry explained, "I opened an account with Madoff Securities and he gets to use the money any way he wants. I've given him full discretion to put my client's money with his personal money when it's needed."

"So basically you're loaning him the money, right?" Frank asked.

Thierry agreed, pointing out, "It's secured by his good name." In other words, if you couldn't trust Bernie Madoff with your money, then there was no one who could be trusted. Madoff's investment strategy was a technique known as split-strike conversion, a strategy that Frank knew a lot about—and knew that by design it would produce only limited profits. There was nothing unique or exotic about the split-strike conversion strategy. Option traders often referred to it as a "collar" or "bull spread." Basically, it involved buying a basket of stocks, in Madoff's case 30 to 35 blue-chip stocks that correlated very closely to the Standard & Poor's (S&P) 100-stock index, and then protecting the stocks with put options. By bracketing an investment with puts and calls, you limit your potential profit if the market rises sharply; but in return you've protected yourself against devastating losses should the market drop. The calls created a ceiling on his gains when the market went up; the puts provided a floor to cut his losses when the market went down. As Thierry explained, Madoff had a big advantage: "He determines what stocks to buy or sell based upon his knowledge of the market and his order flow." In other words, he would use the knowledge gained from his role as the middleman in stock trades, which sounded suspiciously like insider trading. Although this was the first time this possibility was raised, we were to hear variations of that claim numerous times in the following years. It was a convenient way of explaining the inexplicable. But however he was doing it, according to Thierry it worked extremely well: "This guy produces about one percent or more every month with almost no downside."

Frank shook his head. Almost a quarter century earlier he'd been working with a young math whiz from MIT named Chuck Werner who was creating new option strategies in his living room. Options were a brand-new business, and Werner was using a PDP 11, a computer about the size of a four-drawer filing cabinet, to figure out what could be done with them. One of those strategies turned out to be the split-strike conversion. Although he'd been in that living room, Frank didn't consider himself an expert on that strategy; but he claimed he knew enough about options to be dangerous. And in all the years since then he'd never heard of anybody consistently producing such substantial returns from a split-strike strategy. The 12 percent annual return was possible in some years; it was the consistent 1 percent a month return—month after month almost without exception, no matter how the market moved— that concerned him. A split-strike strategy certainly wasn't without risk. There were bound to be times when it lost money, much more than was implied by the results he had seen. How could Madoff possibly still be making a profit whether the market went up or down? But Thierry seemed to have an answer for every question. To prove to Frank that Madoff's returns were real, Thierry handed him several sheets of paper listing sales confirmations, explaining, "I get reports every day of which positions are bought, which are sold, and which options are purchased and which are sold." It was all the usual data: On this date he'd bought this many shares of this stock at this price. On that date he'd sold that many shares of that stock at that price. Frank had seen thousands of these confirmations in his career, enough to know that they contained very little real information. It was like opening the hood of a car and looking at the engine. All that confirmed was that there was an engine, but there was no evidence that it ran, or what horsepower it generated, or even if it was powered by seawater. The only thing these papers confirmed was that Madoff was producing paperwork. Frank wondered what Access did with these reports when it received them.

Thierry brought him into another room, where two clerks were busy typing these statements into a computer. "I want to make sure when I get the monthly statement that all of these trades actually show up on that statement," he said. "I'm also trying to reverse engineer what he's doing. I want to see where his edge is."

Frank was incredulous. Access wasn't receiving any electronic con- firmation on execution from Madoff. It was simply getting sheets of paper with numbers on them, typing them into a computer, and logging them on a spreadsheet. "Thierry, basically you told me you give this guy your money. I don't know him from a hole in the wall, but I know he's got full discretion and he's the primary market maker. He writes his own trade tickets. It's not like you have an account at Charles Schwab or Fidelity; this guy is executing his own trades. He produces the trade tickets and the statements. I mean, there aren't even commissions on any of these things, right?"

Thierry agreed that everything was done in-house. Unfortunately, it was Bernie Madoff's house.

Frank may have been the first person to ask Thierry this question about Bernie Madoff: "Let me ask you this, Thierry. What if he's phonying up records? What if he's just printing these tickets?"

"No, no, no," Thierry responded quickly. "It's not possible. Listen, we know this guy. We've been doing business with him for a while and everything has always balanced out. It's got to be real, because I check to see that all the trades match against the monthly statement."

Frank suggested to Thierry that rather than having two men spend their time processing data that Madoff had generated, he should hire one person who should sit down on Friday night and confirm that every stock had actually sold for a price within the day's highs and lows. "If the ticket reports that a stock sold outside the day's highs and lows, you know he isn't doing what he says he's doing. But I don't see the value in what you're doing."

Several months later, we discovered another method Access used to conduct due diligence. When we started to work on another project, Thierry asked Frank and another man to submit handwriting samples, which were then sent to a handwriting analyst in France. This analyst supposedly could determine from an individual's handwriting whether he or she were honest. This pseudo science is called graphology, and in the United States it definitely is not admissible as evidence in the courtroom. In fact, voodoo magic probably has more credibility as a crime-fighting tool than graphology. We were never able to confirm that Madoff had submitted a handwriting sample; but as Access was very serious about it, we assumed that he did. Incredibly, that was the level of Access's due diligence, that and the fact that a check arrived every month, every single month. And money always makes a strong statement.

Frank came away from that meeting believing there was a real opportunity to do business with de la Villehuchet and Access. Madoff was too risky, and Frank didn't want Rampart to get involved with him; but Thierry was different. Although he didn't know precisely how much Access had placed with Madoff—we estimated it at about $300 million but eventually learned it was considerably more, roughly 45 percent of its total investments, about $540 million—Frank believed that if we could create an options strategy that would enable Access to diversify its risk away from Madoff without sacrificing too much profit, Thierry would be able to sell a lot of it to the private banks of Europe.

As Frank has occasionally pointed out, Mother Teresa did not work on Wall Street. The object of the business is to use money to make money; there is no interest in saving souls. Whatever Madoff was doing and precisely how he was actually doing it didn't concern Frank as much as his results. When Frank got back to the office, he handed Dave Fraley copies of Access's revenue stream for at least the last year that Thierry had given him. "Look at this. Access has a guy who's producing one percent, one and a quarter percent a month with a split-strike conversion strategy."

Fraley looked it over. He didn't speak numbers like a quant, but he didn't need that kind of expertise to understand the kind of returns that Madoff was producing. The bottom line was right there. As Fraley stared at it, Frank suggested, "You know, if we can come up with something that'll produce anywhere near those returns, Access can raise a lot of money."

A few minutes later, Frank handed me the copies of the revenue stream. This comes from that manager in New York we were wondering about, he said. He's running a split-strike conversion. And then he added, "Harry, if we do something similar we can make a lot of money."

I glanced at the numbers. I'd spent countless thousands of hours preparing for this moment. And I knew immediately that the numbers made no sense. I just knew it. Numbers exist in relationships, and after you've studied as many of them as I had it was clear something was out of whack. I began shaking my head. I knew what a split-strike strategy was capable of producing, but this particular one was so poorly designed and contained so many glaring errors that I didn't see how it could be functional, much less profitable. At the bottom of the page, a chart of Madoff's return stream rose steadily at a 45-degree angle, which simply doesn't exist in finance. Within five minutes I told Frank, "There's no way this is real. This is bogus."

As I continued examining the numbers, the problems with them began popping out as clearly as a red wagon in a field of snow. There was a stunning lack of financial sophistication. Anyone who understood the math of the market would have seen these problems immediately. A few minutes later I laid the papers down on my desk. "This is a fraud, Frank," I told him. "You're an options guy. You know there's no way in hell this guy's getting these returns from this strategy. He's either got to be front-running or it's a Ponzi scheme. But whatever it is, it's total bullshit."

And that's when we began chasing Bernie Madoff.

Chapter 2

The Slot Machine That Kept Coming Up Cherries

Month after month, year after year, no matter how wildly the market performed, Madoff's returns remained steady. He reported only three down months in more than seven years. His returns were as reliable as the swallows returning to Capistrano. For example, in 1993 when the S&P 500 returned 1.33 percent, Bernie returned 14.55 percent; in 1999 the S&P 500 returned 21.04 percent, and there was Bernie at 16.69 percent. His returns were always good, but rarely spectacular. For limited periods of time, other funds returned as much, or even more, than Madoff's. So it wasn't his returns that bothered me so much—his returns each month were possible—it was that he always returned a profit. There was no existing mathematical model that could explain that consistency. The whole thing made no sense to me. Bernie Madoff was among the most powerful and respected men on Wall Street. He had founded and operated an extremely successful broker-dealer firm. How could he be perpetrating such a blatant fraud? And if it was so obvious, why hadn't other people picked it up? I kept looking at these numbers. I had to be missing something.

I didn't obsess over this, but I was really curious. It was like trying to solve a jigsaw puzzle using pieces that didn't fit. In certain markets a split-strike conversion strategy actually could produce the returns Madoff was delivering, but it can't make money in all types of markets as de la Villehuchet had claimed. You can't take whatever you want from the market; you have to take what it gives you—and sometimes that means a down month. Every product in the entire history of the financial industry has a weakness—except for Bernie Madoff's. He was the slot machine that kept coming up cherries. And I wanted to figure out how he was doing it.

During the next few weeks I began modeling his strategy. He claimed that his basket of about 35 securities correlated to the S&P 100. Right from the beginning that made no sense to me, because it meant he had single stock risk. He couldn't afford for even one of his 35 stocks to go down substantially, because it would kill his returns. So he needed all 35 stocks to go up or at least stay the same. While I knew that in reality it was impossible to successfully pick 35 stocks that would not go down, I accepted the dubious assumption that information from his brokerage dealings allowed him to select the strongest 35 stocks. But because this basket represented about a third of the entire index, there still should have been a strong correlation between his returns and those of the under-lying index. When the whole index went up, his stocks would rise; when the index fell, so would his stocks. But that's not what he was reporting. Whatever the index did, up or down, he returned the same 1 percent per month. In almost seven and one-half years he reported only three down months.

Modeling his strategy was complex. It had a lot of moving parts—at least 35 different securities moving at different rates of change—so it required making some simplifying assumptions. For this exercise I assumed he was front-running, using buy and sell information from his brokerage clients to illegally buy and sell securities based on trades he knew he was going to make. That meant that he knew from his order flow what stocks were going to go up, which obviously would have been extremely beneficial when he was picking stocks for his basket. We found out later that several hedge funds believed he was doing this. I created hypothetical baskets using the best-performing stocks and followed his split-strike strategy, selling the call option to generate income and buying the put option for protection. The following week I'd pick another basket. I expected the correlation coefficient—the relationship between Bernie's returns and the movement of the entire S&P 100—legitimately to be around 50 percent, but it could have been anywhere between 30 percent and 80 percent and I would have accepted it naively. Instead Madoff was coming in at about 6 percent. Six percent! That was impossible. That number was much too low. It meant there was almost no relationship between those stocks and the entire index. I was so startled that the legendary Bernie Madoff was running a hedge fund that supposedly produced these crazy numbers that I didn't trust my math. *Maybe I'm wrong*, I figured. *Maybe I'm missing something.*

I asked Neil to check my numbers. If I'd made an obvious mistake, I was confident he would find it. Neil went through my math with the precision of a forensic accountant. If I'd made any mistakes, he decided, he couldn't find them.

By this time I had been working in the financial industry for 13 years and had built up a reasonably large network of people I knew and respected. In this situation I turned to a man named Dan DiBartolomeo, who had been my advanced quant teacher. Dan is the founder of Northfield Information Services, a collection of math whizzes who provide sophisticated analytical and statistical risk management tools to portfolio managers. He's a super-brilliant mathematician who has probably taught half the quants in Boston and is a lot smarter than Neil or I will ever be.

Neil and I went across the street to see him. Dan is an eccentric, a bow-tie-wearing East Coast surfer with a photographic memory who revels in math. I told him that I thought we'd discovered a fraud, that Bernie Madoff was either front-running or running a Ponzi scheme. I could almost see his brain cells perk up when I said that. Every mathematician loves the hunt for the sour numbers in an equation. After going through my work, Dan told us that whatever Mad*oof*, as he referred to him, was doing, he was not getting his results from the market. Pointing to the 6 percent correlation and the 45-degree return line, he said, "That doesn't look like it came from a finance distribution. We don't have those kinds of charts in finance." I was right, he agreed. Mad*oof*'s strategy description claimed his returns were market-driven, yet his correlation coefficient was only 6 percent to the market and his performance line certainly wasn't coming from the stock market. Volatility is a natural part of the market. It moves up and down—and does it every day. Any graphic representation of the market has to reflect that. Yet Madoff's 45-degree rise represented a market without that volatility. It wasn't possible.

Bernie Madoff was a fraud. And whatever he was actually doing, it was enough to put him in prison.

I knew that was true, but it was just so hard to believe. Several months later I showed another manager's marketing explanation to Leon Gross, at that time the head of equity derivatives research at Citigroup. I don't think I identified Manager B as Madoff to him; I just asked his opinion about the strategy. Leon is way up there on the smart chart, and 30 seconds after looking at the material he said, "No way. This is a loser. If this is what this guy is really doing, he can't beat zero. The way this is designed it's impossible to make money." He shook his head in dismay. "I can't believe people are actually investing in this shit. This guy should be in jail."

That might have been the end of it for me. I might have filed a complaint with the Boston office of the Securities and Exchange Commission (SEC), and it would have made great pub conversation: "I'll bet you didn't know Bernie Madoff—you know, Madoff Securities—is running some kind of scam," and it wouldn't have gone any further. But this was the financial industry, and there was money to be made following Bernie—potentially hundreds of millions of dollars.

■ ■ ■

Frank Casey and Dave Fraley began pushing me hard to reverse engineer Madoff's strategy so Rampart could market a product that would deliver similar returns. Frank didn't believe what Madoff was doing was real; he knew that Madoff was using that split-strike jargon to cover for whatever he actually was doing, but he also didn't believe that it was a Ponzi scheme. "Ponzi's a strong word," he said. "Okay, we know he's a fraud, but maybe he's doing something else and just claiming this to keep it simple." What he did believe was that I could design a financial product that could compete with Madoff. "Just look at the return stream this guy is putting out," he said. "This is what the market wants to buy. Can't you develop something that we could run at Rampart that would compete against Madoff? Believe me, Harry, Thierry de la Villehuchet is looking for something that would net ten, twelve percent to the client. If we can offer him anything even close to that . . ." He didn't need to finish that sentence.

Frank really pushed me to work on the new product. At times we both got a little testy. He was pretty blunt about it. His deal with Rampart guaranteed him a percentage of the business he brought in, and he had a client who could raise hundreds of millions of dollars if he provided the right product. "C'mon, Harry, I need a product to sell. Rampart needs the product. Let's just build the frickin' thing and get it out the door."

But each time he asked me if I was making progress, I explained to him that it was impossible to compete with a man who simply made up his numbers. I couldn't do it. Nobody could. And each time I said that, he would urge me to keep trying. He really wanted to believe Madoff was real, even if he wasn't particularly legal. He suggested a lot of different possibilities, and I'm sure the excuses he offered for Madoff were precisely the same reasons the hedge funds gave for accepting his numbers: He's one of the largest market makers, he's got better execution, he's been doing it for years, these are audited numbers, and, if there was something wrong, didn't I think the SEC would have closed him down years earlier?

I thought this was a complete waste of my time and did my best to avoid working on it. I had a lot of responsibilities at Rampart. But Dave Fraley kept banging on me hard. He saw only the big picture: "Thierry can raise a hell of a lot of money. He's got $300 million invested with this guy. So whether he's real or not, if Thierry's clients want to buy something like this, let's find something we can deliver to them that's pretty close. They want to diversify away from Madoff, and if we're there maybe we can gather in some of these clients."

Finally, one afternoon as he walked past my desk I stopped him. "Hey, Dave, you know what? I think I've got it figured out. I know how we can duplicate it."

"Okay," Fraley said, sitting down at my desk. "How's it work?"

"Well, actually we have a choice. We can either front-run our order flow or just type in our returns every month. It's probably a Ponzi scheme, and that's the only way we can compete with him." Fraley stood up. "What?" I'd done what they had asked. I'd figured out Madoff's magic formula, but they didn't believe me. There were people in management who suspected I just wasn't good enough at the math to figure it out, that Madoff really was superior. They thought I was blowing smoke with my accusations.

I know how frustrated Frank Casey was. He once told someone that working with me required pinning my shoulders down with his knees and then prying out my teeth. He kept challenging me, asking in what I hoped was a joking manner, "How come you can't figure out Madoff?"

I thought I'd already done that. I was really starting to get pissed off. Neil and I had no doubt that Madoff was running some kind of scam, but at least two of the three principals in the firm and maybe Frank Casey weren't so sure. My pride was at stake. I knew my math was better than Bernie's, but even then, even at the very beginning, people just refused to believe me. This was the legendary Bernie Madoff we were talking about. And I was just the slightly eccentric Harry Markopolos.

From the day Frank came back from Access with Bernie's numbers, Neil and I continued talking about it. We spent every day looking across the width of two desks at each other. We became so close that when one of us breathed out the other one breathed in. So unraveling Madoff became the subject of a lot of conversations. We started throwing numbers into the Bloomberg terminals, which allowed us to download a basket of stocks to create models. It wasn't really rocket science, but it required some technical ability. From the beginning we created different scenarios: How do we construct this so we succeed regardless of whether the market goes up, goes sideways, or goes down? We reached the inescapable conclusion that the only possible way to do it was to have perfect market timing ability. You had to be able to forecast the direction of the market, and you had to be right about it almost every time.

At that point I still had no idea how much money Madoff was handling or for how many clients. Nobody did. As we rapidly discovered, that secrecy was key to his success. Because this operation was so secret, everybody thought they were among a select few whose money he had agreed to handle. Madoff had not registered with the SEC as an investment advisory firm or a hedge fund, so he wasn't regulated. He was simply a guy you gave your money to, to do whatever he wanted to do with it, and in return he handed you a nice profit. He was the Wizard of Oz, and he made everybody so happy that they didn't want to look behind the curtain.

Madoff practically swore his investors to secrecy. He threatened to give them back their money if they talked about him, claiming his success depended on keeping his proprietary strategy secret. Obviously, though, his goal was to keep flying below the radar. Madoff's clients believed he was exclusive to only a few investors, and that he carefully picked those few for their discretion. They felt extremely fortunate that he had agreed to accept them as clients. When I started speaking with his investors, I discovered that they felt privileged that he had taken their money.

We began to get some concept of how big he was within a few weeks by looking at the open interest on Bloomberg. The open interest, in this case, was the number of Standard & Poor's 100 index options actually in existence at each moment in time. Like most people in the industry, I had a working knowledge of the hedge fund industry, but I certainly wasn't an expert. Hedge funds were a relatively new concept. The first fund was founded in 1949 by former *Fortune* magazine writer and editor Alfred Winslow Jones, with the concept that he would protect his long stock positions by selling other stocks short, hedging against a big move in the market that could devastate his investment. In 1966, when *Fortune* reported his ability to consistently outperform mutual funds, the hedge fund world exploded. But a lot of those new companies didn't bother to hedge against anything; they became highly leveraged investment firms, and a lot of them went belly-up in down markets. By 1984 there were only 88 known hedge funds.

That began changing again in the 1990s bull market. The hedge fund world exploded once more; by the turn of the new century there were an estimated 4,000 hedge funds investing about half a trillion dollars. Hedge funds long ago had stopped being conservative money management firms; a hedge fund meant simply an investment fund run as a private partnership and limited to wealthy investors and institutions. They were basically unregulated and invested in all types of financial instruments. While Madoff didn't acknowledge that his money management operation was a hedge fund, that's the way he was set up. He accepted money from high-income investors, institutions, and other funds and supposedly invested it. Supposedly.

Madoff's unique structure gave him substantial advantages. As far as we knew at the time, the only entrance to Madoff was through an approved feeder fund. That meant his actual investors couldn't ask him any questions, and they had to rely completely on their funds— who were being well rewarded—to conduct due diligence. I knew about the world's biggest hedge funds: George Soros's Quantum Fund, Julian Robertson's Tiger Fund, Paul Tudor Jones's Tudor Fund, Bruce Kovner's Caxton Associates, and Lewis Bacon's Moore Capital. Everybody did, and we estimated they each managed about $2 billion. Both Neil and I had read Jack Schwager's *Market Wizards*, which profiled the most successful investment managers, and Madoff wasn't even mentioned. So when we started trying to figure out how much money Madoff was running we were stunned. Absolutely stunned. According to what we were able to piece together, Madoff was running at least $6 billion—or three times the size of the largest known hedge funds. He was the largest hedge fund in the world by far—and most market professionals didn't even know he existed!

There was no logical explanation for what we had discovered. It was like going out for a nice stroll and discovering the Grand Canyon. It was just so hard to believe. Neil and I didn't have *faith* in the numbers, we didn't *believe* in the numbers, we knew that numbers can't lie. If our math was correct—the 6 percent correlation to the market, the steady 45-degree return, the number of options Madoff would have to own to carry out his strategy—(and we continually checked our math), the largest hedge fund in history appeared to be a complete fraud.

We never actually initiated an investigation. We never discussed it. Suddenly we were in the middle of it. We had no specific objectives; we just wanted to figure out what was going on. We started by gathering as much information as possible about Madoff's operation. Frank, meanwhile, was continuing to meet with potential clients. Generally in those meetings the portfolio managers would outline their investment strategy and Frank would probe, looking for an opportunity. Among the managers he met with during this period was the Broyhill All-Weather Fund, a hedge fund of funds. In 1980 the Broyhill family had sold its South Carolina furniture manufacturing business and established an investment fund. As the manager of that fund, Paul H. Broyhill, pointed out, "It's a whole lot easier to make money when you're not losing it." Frank met several times with Broyhill representatives in the lobby of a New York hotel. They showed Frank their product, which they explained was steadily producing 1 percent a month, and asked Frank if he could find a bank to guarantee it. As it turned out, the fund depended basically on two managers the Broyhill representatives would identify only as Manager A and Manager B. They handed Frank a promotional pamphlet and a single page showing Manager B's returns.

Frank took one look at it and knew it was Madoff. Either this was an amazing coincidence and Frank had chanced upon two of the few funds investing in Madoff or he was much larger than we had imagined. We began to wonder how far into the industry his tentacles extended.

This material was the first solid evidence we had found. As soon as Frank handed it to me, I began breaking it down. "The manager's investment objective is long term growth on a consistent basis with low volatility," Broyhill's fund description began. It explained that the fund utilized "a strategy often referred to as a 'split-strike conversion,'" which meant purchasing a basket of stocks with a high degree of correlation to the general market. Madoff's subtle—but unspoken— message was that he had access to trade flow information because clients were buying and selling through his brokerage, so he knew what stocks were going up. Well, I had already proven that was false. But then it continued, "To provide the desired hedge the manager then sells out of the money OEX index call options and buys out of the money OEX index put options. The amount of calls that are sold and puts that are bought represent a dollar amount equal to the basket of shares purchased."

Well, that was interesting. Like many people, Neil and I had been actively trading OEX options, but we had stopped and substituted S&P 500 options in the mid-1990s when these options, called the SPX, came to dominate the market and the S&P 100 OEX index options fell by the wayside. We were trading large numbers of option contracts, as much as 30,000 options at one pop. When you do trades like that, it shows up in the market. Bloomberg reports how many contracts are traded and at what price, where the market was when the trade hit the floor, and where it was after the fact. All the details are there. And the market responds. You can't do trades of that size and not be noticed.

If Madoff actually was purchasing these options, we would have seen the footprints of his trades. At the volume he had to be trading to produce the results he claimed, his trades should have been reflected in the market activity. But there was no sign of his presence in the market. He supposedly got in and got out, bought and sold, without leaving a trace. But then I began doing the math. I knew that there was in existence a total of $9 billion of OEX index put options on the Chicago Board Options Exchange (CBOE). Madoff claimed to be hedging his investment with short-term (meaning 30 days or less) options. You can realistically purchase only $1 billion of these, and at various times Madoff needed $3 billion to $65 billion of these options to protect his investments—far more than existed. This was a breathtaking discovery. There simply were not enough options in the entire universe for him to be doing what he claimed he was doing. If that wasn't sufficient proof, then assuming that those options actually existed, the cost of purchasing those puts would eat up the profits he was claiming.

I also knew that he wasn't buying them in the over-the-counter (OTC) market. That would have been prohibitively expensive, and if he had bought them there those dealers would have laid off their risk in the listed markets, and that would have shown up. It hadn't; he wasn't buying them there.

The explanation in Broyhill's marketing literature failed on so many levels. Broyhill's Manager B, Bernie, claimed to be selling call options on individual stocks, which capped his potential profit. That meant that the best-performing stocks in his basket of 35 would be called away; he'd lose the stocks that were going up, leaving him with stocks that didn't rise significantly, stayed at about the same level, or declined. As I pointed out one day to Neil, "You know, this is the only strategy I've ever seen that actually penalizes you for picking great stocks."

Rampart had run similar strategies, although we never took the single stock risks that Madoff claimed to take. We would buy the entire index, all the stocks, and what we had discovered over time was that this strategy gave us about two-thirds of the market's return with one-third the risk. It was a successful strategy—until the market really began rising. If the market went up more than 15 percent, for example, we would miss much or most of all returns above that. In the 1990s, when the market went up as much as 30 percent (or more) in a year, we actually would lose customers, who complained, "The market was up 34 percent this year, and you were up only 22 percent." They didn't want to hear about protection; they wanted everything the market provided. I knew that Madoff would have run into a similar problem, especially if his insider knowledge did allow him to buy the best-performing stocks.

Until this time, which was about two months after we had encountered Madoff, the only people I had discussed him with outside Rampart were Dan DiBartolomeo, Leon Gross, a few other people whose opinions I valued, and my brother Louie, who was an over-the-counter block trader working for a firm in Miami. He knew the hedge fund world and had access to a lot of promotional material. He had agreed with me from the beginning that something was wrong with Madoff, and immediately began contributing marketing literature to our growing pile.

■ ■ ■

The fortunate thing was that at that point we didn't know enough to be scared. It never occurred to us that we were going to be stepping on some potentially very dangerous toes. So at the beginning, at least, I didn't hesitate to ask people I knew throughout the industry about Madoff. After examining the Broyhill materials, for example, I began questioning some of the brokers I worked with on the CBOE. A lot of these guys were longtime phone friends; I did business with them regularly and had gotten to know them on that level. I began bringing up Bernie Madoff in our conversations. It didn't surprise me that almost all of them knew about Bernie's brokerage arm, but knew nothing about his secretive asset management firm. I asked numerous traders if they had ever seen his volume, and they all responded negatively. But a few people who were aware he was running a hedge fund asked us if we could give them his contact information. Everyone wanted to do business with him.

But nobody admitted they were doing business with him. It was as if he had walked through Times Square naked in the middle of a summer afternoon and no one admitted seeing him. He was the ultimate mystery man.

My motive to continue this investigation was basically self-defense. My bosses had continued to pressure me to mirror Madoff so we could pick off some of that business. I knew it was impossible to compete with someone making up his own numbers, and I just wanted to get rid of the pressure. I wanted the intellectual satisfaction of proving to my bosses that they were wrong.

I certainly didn't think of myself as a detective. I didn't own a trench coat like Lieutenant Columbo, I had no physical handicap to overcome like Ironsides, and instead of a talking car to help me like Michael Knight had in *Knight Rider*, I had Neil and Frank. The only weapons we had were our knowledge of the numbers and our Rolodexes.

What I did have in addition, though, was my experience in the purloined fish case and very good military training. I had served 17 years as a commissioned officer in the army's reserve components, seven of those years in a special operations unit as a member of a civil affairs team. I had also served for many years under Major General Boyd Cook as he worked his way up the chain of command from the rank of colonel. In civilian life he was a Maryland dairy farmer, and I learned a lot from him. General Cook did not tolerate fools—and he forced his officers to stretch themselves. He would ask his officers to describe their biggest failure. If you didn't have a big enough failure, he would fire you for not having tried hard enough; his theory was that if you hadn't failed big, then you couldn't achieve bigger. As a result of that philosophy we had a high-performing unit because we were continually trying new things. Not all of them worked, but those that did achieved significant objectives. Oddly, I remember pleasing him one year with a failure, although I can't remember specifically what it was. But he loved the fact that I took a chance, I hadn't backed down, and at least I tried something new.

General Cook had a low tolerance for bullshit. He always wanted to know the bad news, not the good news, and knew that he could determine the quality of his officers not by speaking with them, but rather by questioning the troops they commanded. Among the many things I learned from my military career that would prove invaluable during this investigation were persistence, human-based information-gathering techniques, interviewing skills, and the ability to maintain my composure.

We began by snooping. There are basically three ways to collect information in the financial industry. First, you can collect the publicly available information, including promotional literature, the pitch books firms distribute to create business, and everything on their web sites. I took everything off Madoff's web site, although there wasn't much of value. Second, you can buy data from numerous sources that will provide you with whatever type of esoteric information you want. Everyone has access to this information. And third, as I'd taught Neil, you can get the truly vital information by talking to people, by listening carefully to the rumors and the gossip, the boasting and the complaining. We took all three routes. Once we started working with Access, which was a large feeder fund to Madoff, we got a complete look at all its data. Frank Casey would collect material from his prospects, telling them, "I'm interested in placing money with Madoff," and if we wanted something specific from a fund, my brother Louie would call and explain, "I've got a client who's interested in getting into Madoff. Can you help me?"

Talking to Wall Street people was extremely informative. Most of these people I was talking with during the normal course of Rampart business, but whenever I had an opportunity I would ask a few questions about Madoff. I spoke with the heads of research, traders on derivatives desks, portfolio managers, and investors. Neil was doing the same thing, and both of us were doing it secretly, because if our bosses found out about it they would have demanded that we stop.

Probably what surprised me most was how many people knew Madoff was a fraud. Years later, after his surrender, the question most often asked would be: How could so many smart people not have known? How could he have fooled the brightest people in the business for so long? The answer, as I found out rather quickly, was that he didn't. The fact that there was something strange going on with Bernie Madoff's operation was not a secret on Wall Street. As soon as I started asking questions, I discovered that people had been questioning Madoff's claims for a long time; but even those people who had questioned his strategy had accepted his nonsensical explanations—as long as the returns kept rolling in.

The response I heard most often from people at the funds was that his returns were accurate—but he was generating them illegally from front-running. By paying for order flow for his broker-dealer firm, he had unique access to market information. He knew what stocks were going to move up, and that enabled him to fill his basket with them at a low price and then resell them to his brokerage clients at a higher price. Several people confided in me that they didn't really know what he was doing, then point out that no one else on Wall Street had access to the quality of information he had, and no one generated the consistent returns he did. When those two facts were considered together, it seemed to make a strong argument that he was using his customer order flow to subsidize his hedge fund. Neil, who had done some analysis of payment for order flow when studying for his master's in finance, believed it could truly provide Madoff an edge—but certainly not enough of an edge to generate the types of returns he was delivering.

There were at least some people who told Neil and me, confidentially of course, that Madoff was using the hedge fund as a vehicle for borrowing money from investors. According to these people, Madoff was making substantially more on his trading than the 1 to 2 percent monthly that he was paying in returns, so that payout was simply his cost of obtaining the money. These were sophisticated financial people. When I heard something like this, I just shook my head and wondered if they actually believed what they were saying. There was no reason Madoff would have to pay 12 percent interest—there were many other ways he could have gotten money at a lower cost. The only sensible explanation for this scenario was that he couldn't risk having one of the rating agencies—Moody's Investors Service or Standard & Poor's, for example—come in and look at his operation.

Some of the explanations I heard bordered on the incredible. These were sophisticated guys who knew they had a great thing going and wanted it to keep going. They were smart enough to see the potholes, so they had to invent some preposterous explanation to fill them. They knew, for example, that a split-strike strategy can't produce a profit in all market environments, so they had to explain how Madoff always returned a profit. "Here's what I think it is, Harry," a portfolio manager told me. "He's really smart. It's really important to him that he show his investors low volatility to keep them happy, so what he does when the market is down is he subsidizes them." In other words, in those months when Madoff's fund loses money, he absorbs the loss and continues to return a profit to the investors. "He can afford to eat the losses." This explanation positioned Madoff as the greatest investment manager in the history of Wall Street. He made it impossible for the investor to lose.

Neil admitted to me once that this was not an investment strategy that had ever been discussed at Bentley College. When we heard some of these explanations we would just look at each other and laugh. There was no other sane way of responding. Not only did these people refuse to look behind the curtain, but they granted the wizard even greater powers than he personally claimed.

Apparently Madoff also had the ability to time the market perfectly. He said he invested in the market only six to eight times a year, and even then for only brief periods of time ranging from a few days to maybe three weeks, tops. Fortunately, he had the ability to invest only when the market was going up. I had noticed in his return stream that the market had declined rapidly in July and December 1999. When I asked one of his investors to explain to me how he could have avoided a loss those months, I was told, "He wasn't in the market. He goes one hundred percent cash when he thinks it's going to fall." He had proof of that, this man told me. He had copies of Madoff's trade tickets.

But of all the stories I heard those first few weeks, the one that probably shocked Neil and me the most was told to Frank Casey by the representative of a London-based fund of funds. The majority of people we spoke with actually hadn't invested with Madoff. Those people didn't want to talk about it; they didn't have Madoff, that's all. No explanation. But a trader at one of Wall Street's largest firms told me that Madoff had been up there trying to interest them in investing, but they'd turned him down when he refused to let them conduct the necessary due diligence. They wanted to conduct a standard financial investigation to make certain he was legitimate and had been turned down. That's the brightest warning signal of all.

Due diligence can take many different forms. The object is to make sure the numbers are real. It can include everything from a complete audit of records, which involves matching trading tickets to exchange-reported time, price, and quantity for each trade, to extensive background checks on the fund managers. Conducting a thorough due diligence can take several months and cost more than $100,000. But when you're investing hundreds of millions of dollars, it isn't the time to try to save a few bucks. A London-based hedge fund of funds told Frank a similar story. It was handling a substantial amount of Arab oil money, and before investing with Madoff it had asked his permission to hire one of the Big Six accounting firms to verify his performance. Madoff refused, saying that the only person allowed to see the secret sauce, to audit his books, was his brother-in-law's accounting firm. Actually, we heard this from multiple sources. The fact is that Madoff's accountant for 17 years, beginning in 1992, was David Friehling, who definitely was not his brother-in-law. Friehling operated out of a small storefront office in the upstate New York town of New City. It seems likely that Madoff claimed he was a relative because it was the only plausible reason he could think of to explain why a sophisticated multibillion-dollar hedge fund would use a two-person storefront operation in a small town as its auditor. Brother-in-law or not, this certainly should have been a major stop sign. Even a marginally competent fund manager should have said, "Thank you very much, Mr. Madoff, but no thanks," and run as fast as possible in the other direction. But this fund of funds didn't. Instead, this firm, which had been entrusted by investors with hundreds of millions of dollars, handed Bernie Madoff $200 million. The firm knew enough to ask to see how the machine worked, but after it had been turned down flat *it still handed over $200 million.*

None of us—Frank, Neil, or myself—was naive. We had been in the business long enough to see the corners cut, the dishonesty, and the legal financial scams. But I think even we were surprised at the excuses really smart people made for Bernie. The fact that seemingly sophisticated investors would give Madoff hundreds of millions of dollars after he refused to allow them to conduct ordinary due diligence was a tribute to either greed or stupidity.

The feeder funds—funds that basically raised money for a larger master fund—knew. They knew as much as they wanted to know. They knew they could make money with him; they knew that if they kept their money with him for six years they basically would double their original investment, so they were betting against the clock. And he wasn't that unusual. It wasn't like everybody else in the business was completely honest and he was the only one cheating. They all knew how much of Wall Street's business was done in the shade. This was just another guy cutting some corners. They must have been assuming he was illegally front-running his brokerage arm's order flows, but they accepted it because Bernie was their crook. And he was a crook they knew they could trust. It was a great deal; they were reaping the benefits of this financial theft without having any of the risk. My guess, and this is just a guess, is they assumed that even if Bernie got caught, their ill-gotten profits would end but their money was safe. How could it not be safe? Bernie Madoff was a respected businessman, a respected philanthropist, a respected political donor, a self-proclaimed cofounder of NASDAQ, and a great man.

We were beginning to see him as he really was: a monster preying on others; a master con artist.

Unfortunately, we were only at the beginning of our investigation. We couldn't even imagine how much of that we would encounter in the next eight years.

■ ■ ■

Any lingering doubts any of us had that Bernie Madoff was running a multibillion-dollar scam, maybe even the biggest fraud in history, had long since disappeared, but the question that Neil, Frank, and I continued to debate was: What kind of scheme was it? Was he front-running, was it a Ponzi scheme, or was it maybe even something else? Obviously we weren't shocked to find gambling in Casablanca, or swindlers on Wall Street. The famous 1950s bank robber Willie Sutton was quoted as explaining that he robbed banks "because that's where the money is." It's probably a good thing Willie Sutton didn't know about Wall Street.

Throughout history, where there has been money to be made there have been crooks, con artists, and swindlers ready to sell get-rich-quick (or sometimes slowly but consistently) dreams to willing investors. And with the proliferation of new and extremely complicated financial products, there was more money to be made on Wall Street in the past three decades than probably anyplace else at any time in history. Although Bernie Madoff surrounded himself with all the symbols of success and respectability, in fact he was no different than George Parker, who made a career out of selling the Brooklyn Bridge to tourists, the infamous con man Joseph "Yellow Kid" Weil, or even the legendary Charles Ponzi.

The mechanics of a Ponzi scheme are pretty simple. People are offered an opportunity to invest in a business that seems real and even logical—it's often a business that supposedly exploits some kind of financial loophole—in return for unusually large and rapid profits. These initial investors get every dollar they were promised; they usually earn a profit large enough to make them boast about it to everyone they know. Other people rush to get into this business to receive the same kind of returns, sometimes begging the perpetrators to take their money. In fact, in a true Ponzi scheme there is no underlying business and there are no investments; there is nothing except the cash coming in and the cash going out. The initial investors are paid with seed money used to set up the scam.

From that point until the scheme collapses, investors are paid with funds received from later investors. Generally, a substantial number of these investors reinvest their supposed profits in the business. On paper, they can become wealthy, but only on paper. The scheme can last as long as new investors continue to hand over their money so old investors can be paid.

It didn't originate with Charles Ponzi. A similar scheme is a plot element of Charles Dickens's 1857 novel, *Little Dorrit*. In 1899 a man named William "520 Percent" Miller supposedly stole $1 million by offering investors a return of 10 percent weekly on their money. At one time this type of fraud was known as a "rob Peter to pay Paul" scheme. Ponzi just perfected it. Ponzi's scheme was actually based on a legitimate financial quirk. In 1919 people were able to buy international postal coupons in one country that could be exchanged in another country for stamps that would cover the entire cost of a reply. He realized that if the cost of postage differed in the two countries, it was possible to redeem coupons in one country for a profit. Potential investors who investigated would discover that this actually was true.

Ponzi began promising investors that by investing in postal coupons he could double their investments in three months. And for the initial investors that's what he did. His company, ironically called the Securities Exchange Company, grew so quickly that he had to hire agents to collect the money for him—and he paid them as much as 10 percent of the money they brought in. The scam grew into a regional frenzy. Thousands of people invested their life savings, and other people borrowed money or mortgaged their homes to get in on this get-rich-quick opportunity. It was estimated that more than half the officers of the Boston Police Department were investors.

Even then there were whistleblowers trying to warn people that this was a con game. Ponzi successfully sued a Boston financial writer for libel—winning a $500,000 judgment. There were obvious red flags that everyone ignored; for example, one of his former publicity men wondered why Ponzi had deposited several million dollars in a Boston bank that paid only 5 percent interest when he could easily have doubled it by investing in his own company. Obviously there was no answer to that. That same publicity man later wrote that Ponzi was not very good at math and could hardly add.

Eventually, Clarence Barron, the publisher of *Barron's* financial news-letter, was asked to investigate Ponzi's business. Barron discovered that to cover Ponzi's investors there would have had to be about 160 million postal coupons in existence—and according to the U.S. Postal Service there were only 27,000. That was amazingly similar to our discovery about the number of options on the OEX. But even with all the evidence beginning to pile up, people continued to invest with Ponzi. They refused to believe it was a scam. Supposedly, in a last desperate attempt to stay out of prison, Ponzi went to a racetrack and bet $1 million on a long shot. It's estimated that Ponzi cheated investors out of about $15 million, a fortune at that time, but he served only three and a half years in prison. After being released, he tried several other scams; but none of them were successful, and he died in poverty. His name, though, was attached forever to this get-rich-quick scam.

Rather than investors getting smarter, Ponzi schemes have actually become reasonably common since then. In 1985 it was revealed that a Ponzi scheme run by highly respected San Diego currency trader named David Dominelli had cheated more than a thousand investors out of more than $80 million. Greater Ministries International leader Gerald Payne claimed God was his investment adviser and would double the $500 million that 20,000 people invested in his fake precious metal business. Lou Pearlman, who created the boy bands *N Sync and the Backstreet Boys, swindled investors out of more than $300 million by showing them fake financial statements supposedly produced by non-existent accounting firms to convince them to invest in the fictitious companies he created. In 2003, Reed Slatkin, cofounder of Internet service provider EarthLink, was sentenced to 14 years in prison for a Ponzi scheme that swindled investors out of approximately $250 million. In 2008, a Minnesota businessman named Tom Petters was accused by the government of swindling investors out of as much as $3.5 billion. Neil and his co-workers at Benchmark Plus had determined earlier that Petters was likely to be a fraud.

There were several reasons I believed almost right from the beginning that Madoff's operation was a Ponzi scheme rather than front-running or even something more creative. We found out quickly that Madoff was continually on the prowl for new money—although obviously we had no idea of the full extent of that this early in our investigation—and by definition a Ponzi scheme requires a continuous flow of new money to pay old investors. If you're front-running, you don't need new money. In fact, raising additional cash cuts down on your own profit. Nor did it seem likely that Madoff was using the hedge fund as a vehicle for borrowing money from investors. Just like Charles Ponzi putting money in the bank at only 5 percent interest, why pay investors 1 to 2 percent a month or more for the use of their money when you can borrow it in the overnight markets much more cheaply? That made no sense to me, so I was pretty certain it was a Ponzi scheme.

Frank Casey disagreed completely with me. He felt just as strongly as I did about it, but he was certain Madoff was front-running. It has been my experience that front-running is common in the broker-dealer industry. It's a form of insider trading, and the SEC allows it to go on because they know they can't stop it. They would successfully catch two or three cases a year, and think they actually were accomplishing something. Meanwhile they let thousands of cases continue unmolested.

Front-running is the industry's dirty open secret. Everybody knows it goes on. "Here's what I think is really happening," Frank said to me. "He wants to build the biggest, most powerful independent broker-dealer in the world. He wants to be the biggest market maker, and his biggest problem in doing that is a lack of capital. To take down the block trades, to handle 10 percent of the total volume of the stock market, he needs tremendous amounts of capital. So what he's doing is putting out some fancy-ass story and he's giving his investors some wild explanation of how he's making money for them. What he's really doing is using them to raise dumb equity." That was a phrase Frank used to describe using investors' money as equity on a highly leveraged basis to make a lot of money for himself. "He's treating the equity as a loan. What does he care if he pays them one to two percent a month if he's making one hundred percent or one hundred fifty percent annualized profit?"

What Frank was suggesting was that Madoff used the hedge fund investments over which he had complete discretion to produce profits from his broker-dealer. There were two ways we figured Bernie could have front-run his order flow. If a limit order came in to buy one million shares of IBM at a price of $100 or lower, Madoff could have put in his own order to buy the same number of shares at $100.01. He could then buy a million shares at $100.01 knowing that he had a firm order to buy those same shares at $100, so the most he could lose was a penny per share, or $10,000. However, if IBM went up, he could make unlimited profits. Of course, if a client came in and said, "Buy me one million shares of IBM at the market," then Madoff could have a field day. For market orders all he had to do was buy one million shares of IBM first, which would drive the price of IBM up, and then sell the shares at a guaranteed profit to his trusting client.

Frank knew that as a broker-dealer Madoff printed his own trade tickets. Madoff could print phony tickets and use the cash as his capital base. That way he wouldn't have to raise a lot of attention by continually going to the banks for short-term loans. And he needed the cash to build his broker-dealer. By 1999 most of the independent market makers had been sold to large firms, giving them tremendous cash resources. Madoff was pretty much the last of the large independent market makers. And while there were a lot of people wondering why he refused to sell his operation—he probably could have gotten more than a $100 million and he owned it by himself—he wouldn't sell, so Frank argued that he needed large amounts of cash to continue to pay for the order flow he had to have if he was front-running. If he couldn't get those large orders, he'd lose the inside information he needed to generate profits. As Frank argued, "If you're going to try to take down big positions, if you want to be the guy everybody calls first when they're trying to trade a big block of stock and they don't want to move a market, you have to have a lot of capital."

Neil was ambivalent, but when pressed he leaned toward front-running. For a long time Neil just couldn't get beyond Madoff's reputation. He was a respected public figure who had served on major securities industry boards; he had tremendous credentials. And theoretically he was making so much money from his brokerage there was no need for him to cheat like this. Bernie Madoff was a very wealthy man; if he needed more money, he could easily have raised more than he could possibly spend in his lifetime by selling his broker-dealership and retiring. Neil got caught up in the logic of it. It made no sense. Why would Bernie Madoff risk everything in his life to steal money he didn't need?

We spent a considerable amount of time wondering about it. This was our mystery, and it served as a welcome diversion from the normal work of the day. One theory that seemed to make sense was that Madoff's broker-dealership had been devastated by a technical shift in stock price reporting from fractions to decimals, which had made him desperate for cash. At that time we had no way of knowing precisely how long Madoff's fraud had been in existence. We could trace it back to the beginning of his involvement with Broyhill and Access, which was only a few years earlier. That made us suspect it might have something to do with a fundamental change in the way the market quoted stock prices. Until 1997 the smallest fraction in a stock quote was 1/8, which was 12.5 cents. That meant any change in the value of a stock was a multiple of 12.5 cents. A broker-dealer could easily earn 12.5 cents per share. So if Madoff paid two cents a share to buy the right to market a block, he could still earn more than a dime a share. In 1997, that spread was narrowed to 6.25 cents, substantially cutting profits for the market makers. In 2000, technology allowed the market to begin quoting stock prices in decimals rather than fractions. The good old days of 12.5 cent bid/ask spreads were history. The exchanges began quoting stocks with a five-cent spread; in some instances the spread was only a penny. As Frank pointed out, Madoff's profits were down 92 percent. So we knew that Madoff's broker-dealership was no longer a cash cow for him; it was actually possible that it was losing money, and this sudden and substantial loss of income could have been his motive.

What continued to frustrate me was the insistence of Rampart's management that I create a competitive product. Frustrate me? They were a pain in the ass. How come you can't do it, Harry? Just give us something to sell, Harry. C'mon, Harry, what are we paying you for?

There is no one in the world who can tell you how many different financial products there are. There are literally thousands of really bright people who sit in offices around the world coming up with esoteric ways for people to get around government regulations, income taxes, estate taxes, and other barriers to the creation and preservation of wealth. Mutual funds, for example, were an innovative product in the mid-1920s. One day they didn't exist, and decades later they were worth trillions of dollars. When creating a new product there are very few rules that have to be followed. Frank Casey explains it this way: "I can do anything I want. I could tell a client that I aligned Venus with Mars and when they were in the seventh heaven I bought stock and every time that happened

I bought and I won. And that client might investigate to make sure Venus and Mars actually were aligned and in the seventh heaven when I bought and that I made money! And then that client would willingly invest in my product."

So creating a financial product wasn't the problem; the problem was creating a product that could compete with a Ponzi scheme. In the spring of 2000, less than six months after we had first encountered Bernie Madoff, my anger at being forced into that position became the trigger that made me decide it was time to go to the SEC.

■ ■ ■

I went to the SEC primarily for my own self-interest. After Madoff imploded, people who knew nothing about me would write that I went to the SEC to try to collect a reward, that I did it for personal monetary gain. It is literally impossible to be any more inaccurate than that. I wanted to rid myself of the pressure of having to develop a product that couldn't be created. Bernie Madoff was my competition, and I couldn't compete with him because I had to generate my returns through real trading, while he was creating his returns on a computer. He was playing on my field, in my space, and I knew he was a dirty player. I decided it was time to go to the referee and get him thrown out of the game. The SEC was the referee.

The United States Securities and Exchange Commission was instituted during the Great Depression by President Franklin Delano Roosevelt to restore public trust in the financial markets. Congress established the SEC in 1934 primarily to make sure that the kind of financial abuses that had contributed to the stock market crash of 1929 could never happen again. The SEC, which is supposedly an independent and nonpolitical agency, was created to regulate the entire securities industry. The goal was to level the playing field, to ensure that anyone who wanted to buy or sell securities had access to the same information as everyone else, that they had all the information they needed to make intelligent decisions. As the SEC explains on its web site, its current mission is to "protect investors, [and] maintain fair, orderly, and efficient markets." The efficient markets hypothesis, which Neil even now continues to believe in, theorizes—very basically—that as long as all market information is simultaneously and freely available to everyone, no one can have an edge. And that is completely dependent on the ability of the SEC to do its job. Through the years, though, the SEC had gained a completely undeserved reputation as the agency that effectively policed the financial markets, allowing people to believe that their interests were being protected. That SEC seal of approval was misleading and actually very dangerous.

Actually, the SEC has a lot *less* power than most people assume. While it can take civil action against corporations or individuals in district courts for crimes such as insider trading, accounting fraud, and the failure to divulge information, it has extremely limited investigative authority. The most SEC investigators can do is refer suspected criminal activities to state or federal prosecutors. What most people outside Wall Street don't know is that the SEC doesn't even regulate the over-the-counter markets. The biggest opponent of protecting those OTC markets was Alan Greenspan, who served as chairman of the Federal Reserve for almost two decades and foolishly believed that the markets were self-regulating.

But because the SEC also had the power to revoke licenses and prevent companies or individuals from participating in the market, I figured the least it would be able to do would be to prove publicly that I was right—that Madoff was a fraud—and shut down his hedge fund, eliminating the pressure on me to create a product that mirrored his returns. While I thought he probably deserved to go to jail, I didn't spend much time considering the consequences to him or, in fact, to his investors.

I had very little confidence in the ability of the SEC to investigate Madoff on its own. My experience had proved to me that it was generally a nonfunctional agency, but I figured if I handed him to the SEC with all the evidence it needed carefully laid out, even that organization would be able to take action against him. I didn't think it would be able to resist. It would be an easy case for the agency and would result in a lot of good publicity. The SEC would also be doing precisely what it was originally created to do—protecting investors.

There also was that remote possibility that we could earn a very large reward. Section 21A(e) of the 1934 Act had instituted a bounty program to help the government catch people who violated the insider trading laws. People who provided information that led to the successful civil prosecution of insider trading could theoretically receive as much as 30 percent of the amount actually recovered by the government from a civil penalty. This bounty program was limited to civil cases of insider trading; it didn't cover criminal acts of any kind or any other type of financial crime. If Madoff was a Ponzi scheme, for example, it would not be covered by this program. And even if he was front-running, it would be the decision of the SEC whether that fit under the insider trading regulations. The SEC had the sole legal discretion to determine who would get paid and the amount, and there was no legal recourse. By 2000, when I first went to the SEC, the program had paid just one whistleblower the sum of $3,500. So clearly the chances of us actually receiving a reward for turning in Madoff were only slightly better than me pitching the first game of the World Series for the Red Sox.

I told Neil and Frank what I was going to do, and I explained I would keep their names out of my report. If there were repercussions I would take the hit for the team. If, for example, Rampart's management found out what we were doing, they would not be thrilled. I didn't think they would fire me, but they certainly would put me on notice that the investigation had to end.

Neil was totally supportive, Frank less so. Our relationship at that time was office-friendly but somewhat tense. We still had very different objectives. He wondered if it might not be somewhat premature. "I've got nothing to bring to the SEC. What are you going to tell them?" he asked. "Everything's sort of hypothetical at this point, isn't it?"

Not to me. The numbers were real.

I had established good relationships with two men I respected in the SEC's Boston office, Ed Manion and Joe Mick. Because the SEC considers anything derivatives related to be high-risk and because Rampart managed equity derivatives portfolios, our firm was examined by the SEC every three years—like clockwork. An SEC audit is mostly a paper chase, more to make sure records are up-to-date than any kind of real investigation. In fact, the teams that came in never had any derivatives expertise, so they depended on me to teach them what they should be looking for while they were auditing our books. Because the SEC had no derivatives experts on their staff, on occasion Ed Manion would call on me to answer derivatives questions pertaining to issues the SEC examination teams were encountering in the field. I never knew who the SEC was examining, but I know the Boston SEC office appreciated the fact that I was always willing to help out.

I'd met Joe Mick during our first audit. Joe is a lawyer and pretty senior in that office. I'd kept in touch with him on a professional basis; I trusted him completely, so when people e-mailed me illegal inside information or stock tips I would forward those e-mails directly to him.

Ed Manion had become a trusted friend and role model. We'd met two or three years earlier; I had been serving as vice president of the Boston Security Analysts Society, and he was the cochairman of the ethics committee. I even knew his lovely wife, Mary Ann, from the society social functions we had both attended. Ethics is a big deal for a Chartered Financial Analyst. I knew Ed cared about the ethics of our industry certainly as much as I did. In fact, he offered a course in ethics for our 4,000 members. Like me, Ed is a CFA—but he had about 25 years' experience in the industry. He really knew the numbers; he had been a portfolio manager at Fidelity sitting next to Peter Lynch, who was famous in the industry for turning the $18 million Magellan Fund into a $14 *billion* fund in 13 years. So I had no doubt he would get it instantly—and he would believe me.

There is no prescribed way to tell someone you've discovered one of the largest frauds in history. "Ed, I've got something really serious I need to talk to you about," I began. "I discovered this huge scheme; I'm not sure if this guy is front-running or if it's a Ponzi scheme, but whatever it is, it's bigger than anything you can imagine—unbelievably huge. He's running the largest hedge fund in the world, although no one knows about it because it's run so secretly, and the whole operation is some kind of fraud."

In his typically understated manner, Ed replied, "That sounds rather serious, Harry. When can you bring it in?"

I knew I had to prepare a detailed report, laying out my strongest case in a way even an SEC lawyer could understand. "I might need a few more weeks to prepare," I said.

"Just let me know when you're ready and I'll schedule a meeting."
There. It was done.

I spent quite a few nights over the next few weeks preparing this first written submission, which would reinforce the points I intended to make during my oral presentation. I put a lot of effort into it, knowing

I was about to attack one of the most powerful men on Wall Street. It was pretty obvious that a portfolio manager at a midsize Boston firm shouldn't pick a fight with someone like that unless he had some powerful weapons. This was my weapon. In the end it was only eight pages long, including the Broyhill All-Weather Fund "Manager B" exhibit. It didn't seem like much, considering I was trying to take down a giant, but it was what I had. My expectation was that my detailed explanation of Madoff's operation, accompanied by this presentation, would put the SEC on his trail. It would have to initiate its own investigation, and I was totally confident the SEC would reach the same inescapable conclusion we had. After listening to what I had to say and reading this material, I figured they would have to be complete fools not to realize I was handing them the case of a lifetime.

Who knew?

The report began, "In 25 minutes or less, I will prove one of three scenarios regarding Madoff's hedge fund operation: (1) They are incredibly talented and/or lucky and I'm an idiot for wasting your time; (2) the returns are real, but they are coming from some process other than the one being advertised, in which case an investigation is in order; or (3) the entire case is nothing more than a Ponzi scheme."

As I explained, "My firm's marketing department has asked our investment department to duplicate Madoff's 'split-strike conversion' strategy in hopes of duplicating their return stream. We know from bitter experience that this is impossible. . . . I would like to prove Madoff's a fraud so I don't have to listen to any more nonsense about split-strike conversions being a risk-free absolute return strategy." I added, "If there is a reward for uncovering fraud, I certainly deserve to be compensated. There is no way the SEC would uncover this on their own." I did add that my firm did not know I was making this submission and I did not want anyone to know I was doing it, a reasonable request for a whistleblower to make, and that I had not traded on the information I was presenting.

I assumed this would be the only submission I would have to make to the SEC. I included six red flags, as I described them, taken directly from the Broyhill material, that individually would raise serious questions about the legitimacy of the hedge fund, but taken together made it clear that the whole operation was a fraud. The first red flag explained that if Madoff was using a split-strike strategy, his reported returns could not come from the performance of the market. Second, there were not enough options in existence to provide the hedging he claimed as part of the strategy. Third, the performance chart rising at roughly a 45-degree angle doesn't exist in finance. Fourth, his reported returns couldn't come from the market performance or options hedging, but there was no indication of where they did come from. Fifth, Rampart's returns from products similar to Madoff's had been substantially less than those claimed by Madoff. As I wrote, "In down months, our . . . program experienced losses . . . whereas Madoff reports only 3 losing months out of 87, a claim I believe impossible to obtain using option income strategies. In August 1998, in the midst of the Russian default and the Long Term Capital Management twin crises, the S&P dropped 14.58 percent, yet Madoff earned 0.30 percent. In January 2000, the S&P 500 dropped 5.09 percent, yet Madoff earned 2.72 percent. Our current test portfolios do not support this. . . ." And the sixth red flag specifically noted that while the market had 26 down months in the 87-month period presented, Madoff had only 3, and "the methods given for the return generation are not possible or even plausible. Obviously there are not enough options in existence to delta hedge Madoff's long stock position. . . ."

I also included examples of the many strange explanations I'd heard from experienced people in the industry when I'd asked them how Madoff generated such consistent returns: I had been told he was using the information he gets by paying for order flow to earn profits for his hedge fund, that he was actually borrowing the investors' money to use in his broker-dealer operation and paying them 15.5 percent interest for the use of that money, that he was personally subsidizing the down months to maintain low volatility of returns, and that he had perfect market timing.

And I concluded by pointing out that he did not allow outside performance audits, which no legitimate firm would have any reason to deny.

I was confident that this submission, which I would explain in detail at the meeting and answer any questions it brought up, certainly would arouse the suspicion of the SEC. Given this road map, almost any competent investigative team would easily be able to figure out exactly what Madoff was doing.

I didn't have any idea how long the process would take. Several months, I guessed.

Well, obviously that was a number I got very wrong.

Chapter 3

Falling Down the Rabbit Hole

I f possible, Ed Manion was more determined to expose Bernie Madoff's scheme than I was. After reading my submission, he believed firmly that it was strong enough to convince the Securities and Exchange Commission (SEC) to open an investigation. And bringing down Bernie was going to be a coup for his agency. He had arranged for the two of us to meet with Jim Adelman, a senior enforcement attorney at the agency, whom he respected. Jim's a pretty sharp guy, Ed had told me. He'll get it.

I don't get nervous very often, but truthfully, I was nervous. This was the first time I'd been in the SEC building, and going forward officially with this accusation represented a big step for me. If Rampart found out about this meeting, it would have caused me some serious difficulty. I suspect I would have been asked to drop the investigation, and if I had persisted it might have cost me my job. However, I knew it was the right thing for me to do. My expectation was that the SEC would find that my allegations were credible and would very quickly assign an examination team or an enforcement team to determine if Madoff was simply a financial fraud or a Ponzi scheme. I didn't think they would ignore me; I was handing them the largest case in their history. I was giving them the headlines any government agency craves. This was a tremendous opportunity for them to demonstrate to the nation that the SEC was a bulldog when it came to protecting our financial markets.

In May 2000, Ed and I were waiting in a small conference room when Jim came in and immediately began apologizing. "I'm not going to be attending this meeting, because I've given my notice to the SEC," he explained. "I'm going into private practice, but I just wanted to thank you for coming in today." Then he was gone.

Minutes later Grant Ward, an attorney who was the SEC's New England regional director of enforcement, walked into the room. After introductions I began my formal presentation. As I explained this massive fraud to Ward, it very quickly became clear he didn't understand a single word I said after hello. It wasn't entirely his fault; he never should have been put in that position. He was a securities lawyer who knew little about the financial industry. In preparing my submission I'd specifically left out all the calculus, all the linear algebra. I'd made it as bare-bones as possible so the SEC staff could understand it. But even that wasn't basic enough. I will give Ward credit; he tried to look interested as I explained the numbers. But truthfully, if blank looks were dollar bills I would have walked out of that room a rich man. He was coldly polite, but he didn't ask a single probing question. I never knew if that represented a lack of interest, a lack of comprehension, or simply a desire to go to lunch.

Ed was devastated. He knew how badly it had gone. It seemed clear that his faith in his agency had been shaken. He'd done his job; he'd brought in evidence of a fraud and handed it over to the division charged with investigating it. As we waited for the elevator I asked him, "You think he got it?"

Ed shook his head. "Not one single word of it."

At that moment I still didn't have the slightest idea how truly incompetent the SEC was. On Wall Street the real fear about the SEC was not that it would uncover hidden crimes, but rather that it would bury you beneath an avalanche of paperwork. That's what it was best at. SEC audits consisted primarily of confirming that a checklist of documents existed, not necessarily that these documents were accurate, not even that they reflected real trades—just that you had the proper papers in your files. Firms hated these audits because they were distracting and time-consuming and rarely resulted in anything more than a deficiency notice or even a small fine for some minor compliance issue.

Nobody I knew had a lot respect for the exam teams. Most of these teams consisted of bright young accountants whose primary objective was to learn the industry at the taxpayer's expense, then take that knowledge into the private sector where they could earn a substantial salary. Occasionally there would be a lawyer on the team, but at that level these lawyers wouldn't understand derivatives. In fact, after Madoff was arrested, his secretary revealed that the few times SEC investigators had come to the firm most of them had asked for employment applications. That was typical. If during an exam investigators found a problem, they would report it and issue a deficiency notice or fine, but most of these people weren't looking to derail their careers by bringing big, complicated cases that would take years to resolve against the most powerful people in the industry.

My error was in believing that the SEC actually was capable of protecting investors. The problem was that I knew a few dedicated men like Ed Manion and Joe Mick, and I made the assumption that there were lots of others just like them. And that was a big mistake. As I was to learn over the next few years, the SEC had been created to monitor the stock market and it really had never evolved with the industry. Its investigators had neither the experience nor the training to understand something fairly complicated like fixed income, for example, an array of investments that yields a specific return on a regular basis but is much more complex than it initially appears. Municipal bonds, for example, is an area in which there is well-known and widespread corruption. And if the SEC couldn't do the math for fixed income, it certainly could not do it for complicated derivatives or structured products. Structured products are combinations of underlying assets, like stocks and bonds, combined with various types of derivatives. They are incredibly complex. The SEC certainly doesn't understand them; in fact, a lot of people on Wall Street don't really understand them, so what chance does an individual investor have? All you really need to know about structured products is this—it's the 99 percent of structured products that give the good 1 percent a really bad name.

What should have been obvious to me was that there is a tremendous mismatch in skills between the SEC regulators and the people they are supposed to be regulating. The quants who create these financial products understand differential equations and nonnormal statistics; they program in languages the SEC doesn't speak; they run statistical packages the SEC doesn't even know exist. The quants are busy data mining with supercomputers while the SEC is still panning by hand. I suspect SEC attorneys like Grant Ward are probably well-intentioned. I'm sure they want to do a good job, but they never should have been put in their positions. Sending lawyers to oversee capital markets professionals is like sending chickens to chase foxes; it just doesn't work, because there's an unbridgeable skills gap between the two. It would be akin to asking me to argue a case in front of the Supreme Court.

The only chance the SEC had to even the playing field was the extensive use of whistleblowers. The agency needed people on the inside to expose corruption, but it offered no incentives to encourage those people to come forward. This isn't true only in the SEC; it's pervasive through-out government agencies and private industry. People who come for-ward to expose corruption risk their jobs, their personal relationships, and even their lives. Rather than being celebrated for their honesty and integrity, too often they end up alone and embittered. The sad truth is that in too many cases whistleblowers have gotten badly screwed. In the past few years I've come to know several of them well, and this includes people who have received large rewards for exposing frauds that robbed the government of hundreds of millions of dollars, and the truth is that many of them are sorry they ever got involved. The money they eventually received wasn't worth what they had to go through simply to do the right thing. The SEC whistleblower program was extremely limited in scope—it didn't apply to Ponzi schemes, for example—as well as in the protections it offered.

Like all whistleblowers, I had taken a risk preparing this submission and showing up at the SEC offices. And then to be so easily dismissed by a powerful senior enforcement executive who had absolutely no understanding of the industry he was supposed to be monitoring was really discouraging.

As Ed and I rode down in the elevator we looked for something positive that had come out of that meeting—we rode all the way down to the bottom floor but we couldn't find any positive outcome.

I never received a response of any kind from the Boston office of the SEC after that meeting. Not even a "Thank you, and can we vali-date your parking lot ticket?" Ed really encouraged me to keep going; he kept pushing me. Being smart enough to understand the tremendous damage that Madoff could inflict on the industry, as well as on the SEC, he remained deeply concerned about it. He told me he was going to keep pressing for answers inside the agency, but urged me to continue tracking Madoff and gathering as much additional evidence as possible. At that point I don't believe I had even told Ed about Frank and Neil. I really wanted to keep them out of it for their own safety.

I believe Ed would have tried to move up the SEC food chain, but as he explained to me, he had run into a jurisdictional problem. The SEC's New England region extended south only as far as Greenwich, Connecticut. Even if Ward had wanted to, he would not have been permitted to send an investigative team into New York City. Once you crossed into New York State, you had to deal with the New York regional office. And, Ed admitted, the two offices were extremely competitive; there was not a lot of respect in either office for the other one. Although he was going to forward my submission to New York, he pointed out that the chances of the New York office warmly embracing a case handed to them by the Boston office were somewhat limited. "I really don't have a choice," he told me. "I've got to forward this to New York for action."

Obviously I was disappointed. I had expected that we would hand over this case to the SEC and watch happily from the sidelines as they closed down Madoff. Then I could get back to my real life, which by then included my new wife, Faith. Faith is an amazing woman. She is Chinese; her parents were senior diplomats in the Chinese Foreign Ministry, and for several years they represented the Communist Chinese government in New York. Faith came to the United States as an exchange student and ended up living with a Jewish family who helped her get a scholarship to Wellesley College. When I met her she was working as an analyst at Fidelity.

We got engaged the old-fashioned way. She gave me a deadline and told me if we weren't engaged by that date I was history. Her dream was a two-carat engagement ring and I wanted to fulfill that dream. I found out one carat was $3,000, so I naively assumed that two carats would be $6,000. That assumption was wrong. The price didn't double; it increased geometrically to about $20,000. Maybe Bernie had billions, but I certainly didn't.

I tried to negotiate with her, suggesting, "Maybe we shouldn't do the same old diamond ring thing. Jewelers rip you off. Diamond rings are like new cars—they lose half their value the moment you take them out of the showroom. I think we should get cubic zirconia because diamonds have flaws in them, but cubic zirconias are flawless, just like you."

She didn't buy that one for a second. So I tried to reason logically with her. "I'll tell you what. I have a buddy, Paul, who works at a trading desk down in Westchester, and he thinks the only silicon worth investing in is a set of breast implants. When he got married, instead of giving his wife a diamond ring he gave her a $6,000 set of breast implants." I paused for effect, and added hopefully, "I'm willing to do the same for you. That way it's something we both can enjoy."

We settled for a carat and a half.

After we were married I convinced her to become an American citizen. Truly one of the most memorable days of my life was watching Faith become a citizen. She was part of a large group taking the oath of allegiance together. I cried, literally. When you're watching this ceremony, when you're listening to a cacophony of accents reciting the pledge of allegiance, it is absolutely impossible not to think about this country and the American values. I'm not going to claim I thought about Bernie Madoff at that moment, but I did think of my Greek family who came here to earn an honest living and taught their children the difference between right and wrong.

I have been asked many times why I continued to pursue Bernie Madoff when no one except the members of my team showed any interest and, if I was right and this was a Ponzi scheme, there was no chance of receiving a bounty. The answer is because what he was doing was wrong and he needed to be stopped. I didn't put any human face on it. I didn't do it for any potential reward or to save corporate investments. At that time I didn't even know about affinity schemes. I did it because my parents had taught me the difference between right and wrong.

That was the reason that even after Ward showed no interest in my submission it never even occurred to me to drop our investigation. Frank, Neil, and I never even discussed that possibility. We were intellectually and emotionally engaged in the pursuit of a master criminal, disguised in plain sight as a highly respected member of the community. In some ways it was like playing a real-life game of Clue: Bernie's in the parlor with $5 billion!

We were living with the constant feeling that we were just about there, that if we could get just a little more evidence the SEC would be forced to listen to us. And when that happened, it would be bye-bye Bernie.

For Frank, of course, there actually was the potential of a pot of gold at the end of this particular rainbow. Frank continued to believe that Bernie was front-running. If Madoff's fund was closed down, Access alone had at least $300 million to invest, and Frank was confident that I could create a legitimate product whose returns mimicked Bernie closely enough to grab a chunk of that business—and perhaps a lot more.

■ ■ ■

What our investigation lacked up to that point was any inside information. We had Bernie Madoff's numbers, but we knew nothing about him or the way he operated. He existed only through his reports and charts and beautiful returns. I had seen photographs of his brother, Peter, and his two sons, but I had no idea what he looked like. The word most often used to describe him was *distinguished*, which on Wall Street generally means rich and powerful. Later, as our investigation intensified, I would try to find a disgruntled employee or a former employee who was willing to talk about the company. I've done several investigations since this first one and I've always been able to recruit one or two insiders who would talk to me. But in this case we were never able to find anyone like that. If there were unhappy employees who knew anything about Madoff and his hedge fund operation, we never found them. He kept his employees. He paid them very well and apparently provided great benefits. And those few people who had left for other opportunities either had no inside information or felt they had been treated fairly.

But in the winter of 2001 we got very lucky, and added an investigative journalist to our team. Frank Casey had been invited by the hedge fund industry magazine *MARHedge* to speak to potential investors at a conference in Barcelona, Spain. *MARHedge* had been founded in 1994 to provide information for the rapidly growing hedge fund industry. It was the first monthly magazine aimed specifically at fund managers and investors, and had become a must-read for everybody in that industry. *MARHedge* conferences brought together the heavy hitters from both the United States and Europe, so this was an important sales opportunity for Frank. He had been invited to speak to fund managers on the potential value of structured financial notes to hedge funds. He was trying to convince managers to let Rampart run a portfolio of those notes for their funds.

As Frank and his wife climbed into the backseat of a cab that would take them from the Barcelona airport to the hotel, a somewhat harried younger man asked, "Do you mind if I share the cab? I'm also on my way to the conference."

After settling in the front seat, Michael Ocrant introduced himself. "I'm from *Managed Accounts Reports*," he said, reaching across the seatback and shaking hands.

"I'm with Rampart," Frank responded. "We're an options management house," he continued, explaining his product. Frank and Mike Ocrant were doing the industry dance, learning as much about each other as quickly as possible, calculating to see if there was a common ground on which they might meet for some mutual benefit. Frank Casey assumed that Ocrant knew a lot of the fund managers and might well be able to make some valuable introductions. Ocrant was a reporter, continually building a deep reservoir of sources and information, always searching for his next big story—although it's doubtful he realized his next big story was sitting in the backseat of this cab. Finally Frank asked, "And what do you do for *MAR*?"

"I'm the editor-in-chief, but I also do some investigative reporting on a selective basis," Ocrant said, in a way that Frank remembered was self-assured but not overbearing. As they began talking, Ocrant explained that he had been the reporter who uncovered the Hillary Clinton cattle-trading scam. He said, smiling, "I'll bet you didn't know that Hillary was the world's best cattle trader."

In 1994, as Ocrant explained to Frank and his wife, the *New York Times* had revealed that in 1978 Hillary Clinton, at that time the wife of the governor of Arkansas, had successfully turned a $1,000 investment in cattle futures into $100,000 in only a year. In 1978 $100,000 was a substantial sum of money. Just after the story was published, Ocrant had been at a cocktail party at the Futures Industry Association conference in Boca Raton, Florida. A well-known futures industry executive had whispered in his ear, "Look at the broker," then walked off. Ocrant did his homework, discovering through research and sources that a corrupt broker had been allocating his trades, giving the successful trades to his friends and most important clients, while giving the bad trades, the losers, to people who never realized what he was doing. In response to the initial reports Hillary had claimed she made that money by reading the *Wall Street Journal*. Unlikely, Ocrant thought, and had spoken to the chairman of a commodities exchange, an older, completely bald man. "I said to him," Ocrant told Frank Casey, " 'What are the chances that she's telling the truth—that it really happened that way?'

"And he responded, 'About the same as me waking up tomorrow with a full head of hair.' " Mike Ocrant's story was carried around the world, and he later received the National Press Club's annual award for breaking news.

It was sometime during this long drive to the hotel that it occurred to Frank that Ocrant could be a very valuable ally in the pursuit of Madoff.

He heard the opening he was looking for when Ocrant began discussing the hedge fund industry, claiming that he knew most of the major players in the business. *MARHedge* maintained a database that tracked about three-quarters of the fund managers. There weren't that many of them. At that time you could count on your fingers the number of funds running even $2 billion in assets.

Frank listened politely, then said, "Tell you what, Mike. I'll bet you dinner in Barcelona for my wife and myself that I can name a hedge fund manager that you don't know anything about, and he's running more money than anyone you've got in your database."

"That's impossible," Ocrant responded. "I know about everybody in that world on that level. Most of them I know personally."

Frank held up his hands. "There's an out for you because technically he's not a hedge fund, but there are funds that have been formed for the sole purpose of giving him money. He might be running upwards of seven billion dollars."

Ocrant nodded. "Okay, it's a bet. Who is it?"

Frank said quietly, "Bernie Madoff."

Ocrant whipped his head around in surprise. "Bernard Madoff Securities? The market maker?"

"Yep."

"No, that's not possible. He's not running hedge funds."

"I told you that was your out. But we know that he's running seven billion worth of hedge fund money given to him basically as a loan to his broker-dealer. He's got full discretion; he can do anything he wants with it."

Frank and his wife had a lovely dinner in Barcelona with Mike Ocrant. By that time they shared an objective: Frank wanted Ocrant to write about Madoff, hoping the publicity would expose the scam. And Ocrant didn't need much convincing; the fact that a well-known market maker was quietly running the biggest hedge-fund-like operation in the world was major news for that industry.

It was during their dinner that Frank revealed the details of the investigation. His whole operation was a scam, he said. Madoff was either front-running or it was the biggest Ponzi scheme in history. Like a good reporter, Ocrant casually absorbed the information. He didn't really respond, but in fact his reaction was typical; he had a tough time believing that Bernard Madoff was running a Ponzi scheme. His professional experience had shown him how difficult it is to sustain a Ponzi scheme for even a couple of years, so it was hard for him to accept the claim that this had been going on for at least a decade. But more than that, he got hung up on the lack of a motive. Once again, it made no sense. If Madoff was going to take a risk, he thought, it would be the type of crime that might cost him a million-dollar fine and might hurt his reputation—but why would he take a risk that if discovered would put him in jail for money he seemingly didn't need?

Ocrant said he'd like to pursue the story, but admitted it would be difficult for him to investigate Madoff, because he knew very little about the options business.

"That's okay," Frank said quickly. "We'll educate you." Mike Ocrant turned out to be the perfect person to become the fourth member of our team. Unlike the rest of us, he had grown up with a con man and had already exposed a major Ponzi scheme.

Mike Ocrant had been born in Chicago but had moved with his parents to a suburb of Denver, where they had decided to open what was probably the city's first Jewish deli. Mike's parents knew absolutely nothing about the restaurant business and their concept of Judaism was eating lox and bagels on Sunday, so naturally they opened a Jewish deli. It closed in less than a year and his parents lost everything.

Also living in Denver at that time was his father's half-brother, a man who had one great similarity to Madoff—neither one of them had a conscience. "He was so smooth," Mike remembered. "He had so much confidence. He was only five feet two but he insisted he was five feet ten. That was his skill; he had the ability to deny the undeniable."

His uncle, while brilliant, was also ambitious and craved financial success to prove his own worth. On several occasions he was accused of unauthorized trading in customer accounts to generate commissions. In one instance he went into the account of a relative and lost her entire nest egg—and never showed the slightest remorse.

It was at the University of Colorado at Denver that Mike decided to become a business journalist. He had a professor, a Marine veteran named Greg Pearson, who taught him that whatever story he was working on, it would eventually come back to the money. Money linked everything together. Follow the money.

After working at several trade publications, among them *Mass Market Retailers*, he became a reporter at McGraw-Hill's *Securities Week*—eventually rising to managing editor—covering the commodities markets. As he learned quickly, commodities is the contact sport of finance. "These are the elbow-in-the-face sort of guys, who came from the streets of New York and Chicago," he explained. "A lot of them are without college educations. They're very smart, most of them, just not book smart, and they know how to make trades. And nothing stands in their way, or if it does, it doesn't remain standing. It's a great place to learn about the ruthlessness of the financial industry."

When he moved to *MARHedge* in 2000, he knew almost nothing about the hedge fund industry, but he learned quickly. In fact, at one point he got a tip about New Jersey currency traders who were regularly returning as much as 20 percent a month. It had all the hallmarks of a classic Ponzi scheme. After gathering evidence that this was indeed a scam, he phoned the company and requested an interview with either or both of the two principles running the firm. "I could tell immediately from the secretary's reaction that something was very wrong,"

Michael remembered. "There was a lot of nervousness in her voice, a lot of anxiety. At first she said they would call me back, but later they started making excuses, telling me they were going to be out of town for a while."

Ocrant reported this company to the Commodity Futures Trading Commission, the regulator for the futures market, which almost immediately began an investigation and shut down the company. This company had cheated investors out of several hundred million dollars, making it one of the largest frauds in New Jersey history.

After this scheme had collapsed, several of the victims had contacted Ocrant to tell him their stories. An older woman who had been using the returns to care for her retarded brother had lost everything; she didn't know where the two of them would live. A CPA on Long Island had lost both his and his wife's retirement funds as well as their children's college funds. "I just got those redemptions and kept investing more. After a while I never took anything out," he said, casually defining the horror of a Ponzi scheme. There was nothing Ocrant could do but listen and sympathize.

So while I talked about Madoff's Ponzi scheme in the abstract, Mike Ocrant knew what a real Ponzi scheme smelled like, and he knew the human damage it did.

To Ocrant, this just didn't smell like a Ponzi scheme. He didn't know exactly what it was, possibly front-running, but he just couldn't believe the evidence. When he returned to New York he began his education, spending several hours on the phone with Frank, learning the language of options, and like any good reporter, trying to punch holes in our theory. But he also quietly initiated his own investigation of Madoff. If we were right and he could prove it, this was potentially a career-changing story.

He began by asking the managing editor, who reported to him, as well as the president of the company, if they'd ever heard any rumors about Bernie Madoff managing money. Madoff, the market maker? No, neither of them knew anything about it. They had been working in the industry for years, but had never heard a word about Bernie Madoff's money management operation.

That's sort of strange, he thought. Then he expanded his investigation, casually questioning several knowledgeable contacts in the business. And all the evidence he compiled seemed to confirm that Casey was right. One contact, a serious quant who had managed a billion-dollar portfolio for the Tiger Fund, explained to Ocrant that when he made a small trade, for example half a million dollars in a stock or option, that trade would cause the market to change. The pros would see it and react; you literally could see the fluctuations. "With the amount of trading Madoff would have to do," he told Ocrant, "you'd see those fluctuations—and they aren't there."

Point by point Ocrant confirmed Frank's claims about Madoff. And just as had happened to us, the more he learned the more intrigued he became. Madoff's name began slipping into most of his conversations. He was on the phone one afternoon with Hunt Taylor, the former chairman of the Cotton Exchange who was then managing the family office for the Stern family, owners of Hartz Mountain. Whatever the original purpose of the call, eventually Ocrant found himself asking the now-familiar question: "Have you ever heard about Bernie Madoff managing money?"

"God," Taylor responded. "It's funny you should mention that, because I just came back from a conference, and me and a bunch of guys were sitting around the table talking about that. One of them told me he knew someone who had three hundred million dollars with Madoff. Somebody else said he knew someone who had more than that. Before we knew it we were up to six or seven billion dollars."

Ocrant was careful to hide his surprise. If this group could account for at least six billion, how much money was Madoff managing? More and more it seemed like Casey was right, that this was potentially the largest fraud in history.

While Mike Ocrant was working on the story, we continued to compile as much evidence as possible. This investigation wasn't our primary objective, because we all had paying day jobs to do, but whenever possible we asked the right questions and collected the documents. In March 2001, one member of the team (truthfully, I have no record of the source—it could have been Frank or my brother or someone we'd spoken with) faxed me the "Use of Proceeds and Investment Program Offered by Fairfield Sentry," and managed by Bernie Madoff. Obviously, I don't know where the source got it, but it was easily available. From that time forward we continually tracked this fund. Why not? Fairfield had an amazing product to sell. The document included Fairfield's pitch to potential investors as well as charts of the fund's return stream. It was typical Bernie. Everybody is a winner!

Inside the SEC Boston district office (or BDO, as it was referred to officially back then), Ed Manion was growing increasingly frustrated. As we later discovered, my report had not been forwarded to the SEC's Northeast Regional Office (NERO) in New York. Grant Ward hadn't understood it and just dropped it. Almost a year had passed since our meeting, and Manion urged me to resubmit my report. I added some of the new information we had gathered from the feeder funds and pre- pared an analysis comparing Madoff's returns to the market. During the period for which I had returns, the market had 26 down months, whereas Bernie had three. In his worst month he was down 0.55 percent, whereas in its worst month the market was down 14.58 percent. As I wrote, "His numbers really are too good to be true."

Included in this March 2001 submission was an offer. If the SEC couldn't prove Madoff was a fraud, I would do it for them. "I can provide you with detailed questions for your audit team," I wrote. "In fact, I would be willing to accompany a team undercover under certain condi- tions (new identity, disguise, proper compensation) . . . and serve under the command & control of the SEC. In return, I would take a leave of absence from my firm. . . ."

It was a no-cost offer with 100 percent upside and no downside. I was confident I could walk into Madoff's office and within a few minutes prove he was a complete fraud. I didn't think it would take me more than five or six of the right questions and one hour of my time. If SEC investigators weren't capable of figuring out this operation, than I would do it for them. Now, I don't know if I ever seriously believed they might actually take me up on this offer, but I did walk myself through my plan if I ever did get inside. I was going to ask Madoff's people to take me directly to his derivatives trading desk. That was all I needed to do. Chances were they would have looked at me as if I was the crazy one. Madoff wasn't making any trades, so there was no reason for him to maintain an equity derivatives trading desk. But assuming he had prepared for this investigation and had set up a Potemkin trading desk, meaning a phony front, I would have asked for copies of trading tickets. These fake tickets were the center of gravity. They were the hard evidence that would prove his operation was nothing more than a house of cards. Once I had those, he would be toast.

I knew the trading tickets existed, because he supplied copies of them to his clients. Somebody somewhere was sitting in a back room making them up and printing them out. Once I had them, I would go to a Bloomberg terminal or some other data vendor and get copies of the Option Price Reporting Authority (OPRA) tape. The OPRA tapes are the permanent record of every trade. Madoff's trading tickets would not match up with the OPRA tapes. Once I proved to the SEC that he had falsified those trading tickets, it would be game over, case closed, *sayonara*.

This was in early 2001, when we estimated he was running less than $20 billion. When he surrendered in 2008, it was estimated he was running roughly $65 billion. You do the sad math.

About three years later Neil confirmed this to be a viable scenario. By that time he was working at Benchmark Plus in Tacoma, Washington. His employer was friendly with an extraordinarily successful investor named Edward Thorp, who had conducted due diligence on behalf of another institution many years earlier. As he told Neil's boss, he'd gotten ahold of some of Madoff's trade tickets and compared them to OPRA tapes. He was nice about it, but said he found some *discrepancies*— meaning he was unable to match all the reported trades against the OPRA data. Thorp promptly advised his clients and anyone in his network to stay away from Madoff, but didn't take it any further. And this is why self-regulation doesn't work. If industry practitioners don't report suspected fraud, nor have any meaningful incentive to do so, and if government agencies don't have systems set up to take in, evaluate, and investigate whistleblower tips—then self-regulation can never work.

I never got a response from the SEC for this second submission, either. It wasn't until September 2009 that I finally found out what had happened to it. David Kotz, the SEC inspector general, who was charged with trying to figure out why the agency had proved to be completely dysfunctional, reported, "Although this time the BDO did refer Markopolos' complaint, NERO decided not to investigate the complaint one day after receiving it. The matter was assigned to an Assistant Regional Director in Enforcement for the initial inquiry, who reviewed the complaint, determined that Madoff was not registered as an investment advisor and the next day sent an e-mail stating, 'I don't think we should pursue this matter further.' The OIG could find no explanation for why Markopolos' complaint, which the Enforcement Attorney and the former head of NERO acknowledged was 'more detailed than the average complaint' was disregarded so quickly."

Of course, I didn't know any of that. I was still suffering under the delusion that the SEC was a reasonably competent agency that actually served some purpose. So we just kept going.

■ ■ ■

Like Ocrant, we were beginning to believe that our original estimates of the size of Madoff's fraud were low, maybe very low. He was voracious, sucking up hundreds of millions of dollars from feeder funds around the world—many of whom did not even know about the others. Every couple of months we were identifying another fund that was feeding cash to him. Madoff just kept growing. Originally we had him at $3 billion; then it was $7 billion. It was getting beyond absurd. I'd get a phone call from Frank, who'd tell me, "You're not going to believe this, but it's $8 billion and guess who has him?"

Before receiving that fax in early March identifying Fairfield Greenwich's Sentry Fund, for example, I had never heard of it. So I had no way of knowing that this fund, which basically did nothing more than hand over its then $3.3 billion portfolio to Madoff, charging a fee to investors of 1 percent of the assets it was managing and 20 percent of the profits it reported, was Madoff's biggest American client. Biggest *American* client. It's doubtful anyone will know how much the European and Asian funds had invested with him, as we were to learn there were some pretty important reasons many Europeans never admitted they had money with Madoff. But in the material I received, Fairfield boasted that the fund had lost money in only four of 139 consecutive months. This was arguably the most extraordinary winning streak in Wall Street history: In almost 12 years of running a market-sensitive strategy, Fairfield claimed to have suffered losses in only four months. And somehow investors believed that!

By now Neil and I were used to reading these astonishing claims. Whenever we got another one in, Neil would look at it and shake his head. "Wow," he'd say, the sarcasm dripping from his words. "Bernie is amazing. Bernie is the best."

The few pages I got basically duplicated what we'd seen previously— "We're handing your money to a manager who will use a 'split-strike strategy' and make whatever investment decisions he chooses"—although they were very careful never to specifically identify Bernie Madoff. When I went to the Fairfield Greenwich web site I was immediately struck by its extensive claims about how the firm protected its investors' money: "The nature of FGG's manager transparency model employs a significantly higher level of due diligence work than that typically performed by most fund of funds and consulting firms. This model requires a thorough understanding of a manager's business, staff, operational practices, and infrastructure."

When Mike Ocrant got this material as part of his investigation, he decided to have his experts crunch the numbers. The *MARHedge* database included historical hedge fund returns that could be analyzed using proprietary software that could compare the Fairfield returns to the returns of all other hedge funds in the database, as well as to those of hedge funds using the same or different strategies. It could slice and dice the Fairfield numbers to provide a great amount of information. This historical comparison concluded that not only was Madoff the largest hedge fund in existence, but on a risk-adjusted basis it was one of the best-performing hedge funds in history. What it didn't tell Ocrant—what it wasn't programmed to find—was that the numbers were fictitious.

Mike called Frank when he got the analysis with the results. "It's amazing," he told him. "This guy has got beyond astounding returns for a guy we've never heard of."

Ocrant went further. At an Association of Financial Engineers conference he had heard a lecture by Andrew Weisman, who was then the chief investment officer and a board member at Nikko Securities, where he oversaw that firm's hedge fund of funds operation, and was generally considered one of the real experts in hedge funds. He called Weisman and asked him to take a look at a return stream to see if it made sense. He sent him only the raw data, removing any references that would have allowed anyone to identify Fairfield or Madoff.

Weisman called him about a week later. He'd asked his team to do some reverse engineering, he explained, then said, "This could be done. You could get this kind of return stream if you were a market maker."

Then he added, "But to get this kind of smooth return you probably have to have some front-running involved."

"Okay. Now what if I told you that this is a fund managing as much as eight billion dollars."

Weisman didn't hesitate. "It's impossible," he said flatly. "In that case, I'd have to think it might be a Ponzi scheme."

Ocrant took a long, deep breath. His journalism professor had nailed it: It always comes back to the money.

We were an extremely loosely knit team. Ocrant never officially signed on; we just began including him in our communications. Neither Neil nor I had ever met Mike Ocrant; in fact, we wouldn't meet face-to-face for many years, and we spoke only a few times. But we were connected through the Internet and the telephone. We shared documents, information, and rumors; we taught Mike the basics of the business, and at some point, we finally understood that the four of us had fallen down the rabbit hole together. The four of us had evidence that certainly would change the financial world. It would create havoc in the markets world-wide—and nobody cared. Maybe even more than a commitment to do the right thing, we became bound together by our frustration.

I continued speaking regularly with Ed Manion. Nothing's happening, he told me. "I'm not getting any feedback at all." Having failed to interest the government, I figured my best shot was to publicly expose Madoff's operation. Once the existence of this fraud was known, even if he didn't go to jail he'd be out of business. I figured that if people found out this whole thing was a scam, the investors would take their money out and nobody in their right mind would put in new money.

I knew Ocrant was working on an article, but I had no idea how far along it was or when and if it might be published. That *if* was actually a major consideration. Bernie Madoff was a very powerful man. I didn't have the slightest idea how long his reach was, and I wondered if a subscription-dependent trade magazine would risk its relationship with Madoff and everyone he knew in the industry by printing an exposé. So in early March I sent a copy of my May 2000 SEC submission to a senior reporter at *Forbes*, a man I'd been casually introduced to by a friend who was my former finance professor at Boston College. I explained that I was enclosing evidence of what I believed to be the largest Ponzi scheme in history. I like to believe that if someone put a potentially Pulitzer Prize–winning story in my hands and said, take it, I'd be smart enough to at least investigate. But boy, the lack of serious interest was astonishing. I think the editors at *Forbes*, like so many others we were to encounter, were victims of their own hubris. These were people who took pride in knowing that they were the experts on the financial industry. They *knew* that the largest hedge funds were running $2 billion, give or take a few hundred million. So when this editor received a several-page letter from some guy in Boston he'd never heard of claiming that he had discovered a hedge fund six to 10 times larger than anything the experts knew about and it's a complete fraud, it was pretty doubtful that he was going to take it very seriously. In fact, I suspect that the only way he would have taken it less seriously was if it had been written in crayon. He was just too smart to recognize the truth.

This is an important point. Madoff's operation was too big to be believed. Once I stated how many billions he purportedly was managing, people stopped listening. In a world in which a $2 billion hedge fund was considered huge, the fact that I was claiming Madoff was running between $12 and $20 billion made me about as believable as those people claiming NASA had staged the moon landing in a warehouse. Journalists, SEC staff, and others just didn't have enough professional skepticism to at least conduct an initial investigation to see if any of my claims just might be valid.

As it turned out, it didn't make any difference. When Mike Ocrant finally accepted the fact that Madoff was doing something illegal— whatever he was doing—and that he had enough evidence to support his story, he picked up the phone and called Bernie Madoff. That's just good journalism; any fair investigative reporter gives the subject of a story a chance to answer all the questions before writing the story. And when the subject refuses to be interviewed, as often happens, it adds just a bit of spice to the story.

But to everyone's tremendous surprise, Bernie Madoff didn't refuse. In fact, he welcomed the opportunity. Ocrant placed a cold call to his secretary, introducing himself as a reporter for *MARHedge* and explaining that he was working on a story about Madoff's money management company and had some serious questions he wanted to ask him. Rather than the secretary making the expected excuses, as had happened when he investigated the New Jersey currency scam, she was calm, polite, and professional. "Can we call you back, please?"

Ocrant figured that was the easiest way to avoid him, that the call would never be returned; but within minutes his phone rang. Madoff was returning his call. Ocrant believes in being direct with his sources. "I understand that you manage quite a bit of money as part of a separate operation within your securities firm," he said. "I've been talking to a lot of people in the hedge fund industry and they've raised some serious questions about this fund, and I'd like to ask you several questions about it."

People who have something to hide find ways not to talk about it. That's a big clue to an investigative reporter. Honest people most often will talk until the tape recorder batteries wear out. Mike expected to hear Madoff explain why he couldn't meet with him at that time, which would be followed almost immediately by a phone call from an officious senior executive at the firm's public relations agency, asking what specifically Ocrant wanted to talk about and then putting off the meeting for as close to never as they could get.

But none of that happened. Madoff was gracious, if not friendly. He said he was surprised that anyone would be interested in doing a story about his company. He may even have said it was a pretty standard operation. And then he suggested, "Why don't you come down and we can talk about it?"

"Great," Ocrant responded. "Let me look at my schedule. When's a good time for you?"

Madoff didn't hesitate. If he was hiding, Ocrant thought, he was doing it in plain sight. "Why don't you come down today?"

Ocrant was incredulous. It had been his experience that CEOs did not often agree to spontaneous meetings, that their days were usually carefully scheduled. But Madoff acted like he had nothing else to do. "Now?" Madoff couldn't possibly mean right at that moment.

"Does this afternoon work for you?"

It happened so fast that Ocrant only had time to make a quick call to Frank. "Good luck," Frank told him. "Ask him if he's running $10 billion."

Ocrant actually had met Madoff a couple of times and spoken with him to get comments while covering other market stories. In Ocrant's experience, he had always been accessible and he always responded to questions with colorful answers. That history, his reputation, and the fact that he had immediately agreed to the interview caused Ocrant to wonder if there might be more to the numbers than he had seen.

By the time he got to Madoff's office in the Lipstick Building, on Third Avenue between 53rd and 54th Streets in Manhattan, the trading day was over and the office was quiet. Most of the traders and Madoff's secretary were gone. Madoff invited him into his office, offered him something to drink, and sat down at his desk. The office was surprisingly nondescript. A large window allowed Madoff to watch the activity on the trading floor. He leaned back comfortably, his body language certainly not indicating he was hiding a great secret, and invited Ocrant to ask his questions.

"He was very generous with his time," Ocrant remembered. "It was obvious he intended to sit there until I ran out of questions. One by one I went through all the questions that people had raised about his strategy, the lack of volatility in his returns, and the fact that his trading activity didn't show up in the listed market.

"He had an answer for everything. He said he did a lot of his trading over-the-counter, so it wouldn't necessarily show up on the exchange. He just dismissed the idea that somehow the volume was missing. He responded directly to every one of my questions, not always with an answer that made perfect sense, but in many instances they had a degree of plausibility. When he claimed, for example, that he was using a 'black box' strategy—meaning some sort of proprietary computer program—developed over a long period of time, based on his knowledge of the market and his experience, it made sense; it was well known that Madoff Securities had tremendous market knowledge, and it also had a reputation for developing and using proprietory technology. So what he was saying wasn't completely unreasonable.

"When I asked for more details about this 'black box,' he smiled and refused to answer. 'I'm not going to give information that can help my competitors. Why should I do that?' Within the hedge fund industry that is quite a plausible answer. A lot of hedge funds would respond the same way.

"It wasn't just the signals from the 'black box,' he emphasized. The system he had set up relied on the input from his professional traders.

He wanted them to use their gut feelings. 'I don't want to get on an airplane without a pilot in the seat,' he said. 'I only trust the autopilot so much.'

"It didn't matter what question I asked him—there was at least an element of plausibility to every answer. Several times when I wasn't completely satisfied with his answer I asked the same question a different way. He never complained, and he was responsive to every question. When I said that it appeared that he was managing as much as $8 billion, he admitted that he had at least $7 billion and then shrugged, meaning maybe it was a little more. And he did it without hesitation.

"He confirmed that Fairfield Sentry was a feeder fund, he confirmed that he was using a split-strike conversion strategy, and he confirmed that he often placed his assets in Treasury bills while he waited for specific market opportunities. He denied that he subsidized the down months by using profits from the market-making operation, and when I pressed him he explained, as if there was nothing else to say, 'The strategy is the strategy and the returns are the returns.'

"It wasn't so much his answers that impressed me, but rather it was his entire demeanor. It was almost impossible to sit there with him and believe he was a complete fraud. I remember thinking to myself, *If Frank is right and he's running a Ponzi scheme, he's either the best actor I've ever seen or a total sociopath.* There wasn't even a hint of guilt or shame or remorse. He was very low-key, almost as if he found the interview amusing. His attitude was sort of 'Who in their right mind could doubt me? I can't believe people care about this.'

"Overall he seemed like a very personable, nice, straightforward guy."

The only question that Ocrant had decided not to ask directly was: 'Are you running a massive Ponzi scheme?' He was afraid those words might end the interview. Instead he danced around it, asking him about front-running—which Madoff denied, naturally.

Years later, after Madoff had surrendered and his Ponzi scheme had collapsed, people would wonder how Madoff could have fooled so many people for so long. This interview provides a good answer to that question. Mike Ocrant is a very good investigative reporter. He has uncovered other Ponzi schemes, he has broken numerous other important stories, and he has won prestigious awards; in his career he has conducted a thousand interviews with powerful executives trying desperately and forcefully to convince him to accept their positions. And Bernie Madoff snowed him. There is a reason Madoff was able pull off the largest financial crime in history. Madoff was so smooth, so convincing, that even an experienced journalist like Mike Ocrant came away from that interview doubting what he had believed to be true.

As soon as he got back to his office he called Frank. "Are you guys really sure about this?" he asked. "Because I gotta tell you, Frank, this guy was as cool as can be. I mean, I didn't see the slightest indication that anything was wrong. In fact, rather than worrying about the story I was writing, he acted like he was inviting me over for Sunday tea.

"He doesn't act like he's got something to hide. He spent more than two hours with me. He showed me around the whole operation. He even offered to answer any other questions. Guilty people usually don't act this way."

The numbers don't lie, Frank emphasized.

Ocrant wasn't so sure of that. "Is it possible we're missing something?" he wondered aloud. While writing his story, Ocrant reviewed the facts countless times. Madoff had been firm in his explanations: "Listen, we've got great market intelligence," he'd pointed out. "We've got an incredible infrastructure. We're well known as being on the leading edge of technology, and we've got 40 years of experience in the market."

It made sense. All of it made sense. All of it except those numbers.

In addition to his face-to-face interview with Madoff, while working on the story Ocrant had spoken with him several times on the telephone to clarify certain points. Madoff was always friendly and forthcoming, and if he was nervous about this forthcoming article, Ocrant never heard a hint of it in his voice.

Mike Ocrant's story was published in *MARHedge* on May 1, 2001. It was a very low-key story, extremely well written, simply laying out the facts and offering Madoff's explanations. He wrote that Madoff's $6 billion to $7 billion in assets "would put it in the number one or two spot in the Zurich (formerly MAR) database of more than 1,100 hedge funds, and would place it at or near the top of any well-known database in existence defined by assets.

"More important, perhaps, most of those who are aware of Madoff's status in the hedge fund world are baffled by the way the firm has obtained such consistent, non-volatile returns month after month and year after year."

Point by point Ocrant laid out the arguments we'd made. "Skeptics who express a mixture of amazement, fascination, and curiosity about the program wonder, first, about the relative complete lack of volatility in the reported monthly returns.

"But among other things, they also marvel at the seemingly astonishing ability to time the market and move to cash in the underlying securities before market conditions turn negative; and the related ability to buy and sell the underlying stocks without noticeably affecting the market.

"In addition, experts ask why no one has been able to duplicate similar returns using the strategy and why other firms on Wall Street haven't become aware of the fund and its strategy and traded against it, as has happened so often in other cases; why Madoff Securities is willing to earn commissions on the trades but not set up a separate asset management division to offer hedge funds directly to investors and keep all the incentive fees for itself, or conversely, why it doesn't borrow money from creditors . . . and manage the funds on a proprietary basis."

And then he presented Madoff's responses, describing him as appearing "genuinely amused by the interest and attention aimed at an asset management strategy designed to generate conservative, low-risk returns that he notes are nowhere near the top results of well-known fund managers on an absolute return basis.

"The apparent lack of volatility in the performance of the fund, Madoff says, is an illusion based on a review of monthly and annual returns. On an intraday, intraweek, and intramonth basis, he says, 'the volatility is all over the place, with the fund down by as much as 1 percent.''

An illusion? Only magicians do illusions. Maybe that was right— magic was as good an explanation for his returns as anything he said. As Ocrant wrote, "Market timing and stock pricing are both important for the strategy to work, and to those who express astonishment at the firm's ability in those areas, Madoff points to long experience, excellent technology that provides superb and low-cost execution capabilities, good proprietary stock and options pricing models, well-established infrastructure, market making ability, and market intelligence derived from the massive amount of order flow it handles each day."

And how does he make his massive stock and options moving invisible so that no one ever sees it? "Avoiding market impact by trading the underlying securities, he says, is one of the strategy's primary goals. This is done by creating a variety of stock baskets, sometimes as many as a dozen, with different weightings that allow positions to be taken or unwound slowly over a two-week period.

"Madoff says the baskets comprise the most highly capitalized liquid securities in the market, making entry and exit strategies easier to manage."

And why doesn't he simply open a hedge fund, which would enable him to make even bigger profits? He even had an answer for that one: "Setting up a division to offer funds directly, says Madoff, is not an attractive proposition simply because he and the firm have no desire to get involved with the administration and marketing required for the effort, nor to deal with investors."

"Many parts of the firms' operations could be similarly leveraged, he notes, but the firm generally believes in concentrating on its core strengths and not overextending itself."

Finally, as for all the rumors in the industry about the way he conducts his business, he dismissed them completely: "[T]hose who believe there is something more to it and are seeking an answer beyond that are wasting their time."

■ ■ ■

As Frank, Neil, and I read Ocrant's article, we started high-fiving each other. We'd gotten him! We were certain there was no way SEC investigators could read it without opening an investigation. I was ecstatic, but Frank was exuberant because once Madoff was gone he had a clear path to Thierry's $300 million. "This is it," Frank said. "The SEC's gonna ride into town with a posse and they're gonna shut him down!"

Hidden within the story was even more evidence of Madoff's deception. He had admitted for the first time that he was running as much as $7 billion, which meant he had to have an established line of credit from some bank, and there wasn't a bank in the world that was going to give a multibillion-dollar line of credit to a single broker-dealer without equity and without completely revealing the nuts and bolts of the entire operation.

We waited expectantly for the response. It never came. Mike received more than a dozen phone calls from industry people who confirmed that their investigation of Madoff had shown that something strange was going on, and they were glad Mike had made it public, but he didn't get a single phone call from any regulatory group interested in pursuing this story or from any investors who were dissuaded from giving Madoff their money because of it.

The silence from the SEC was particularly discouraging. It was difficult to believe that they could read this story and not open an investigation. As I later learned, the answer was that they didn't read the story. Apparently the SEC does not have a publication budget, meaning staff members have to pay out of their own pockets for any industry material. They even have to pay for their own subscriptions to the *Wall Street Journal*, so obviously very few of them would be reading *MARHedge*, which cost more than a thousand dollars annually.

One phone call Ocrant did get the day after his story appeared was from a reporter at *Barron's* magazine, Erin Arvedlund, who told him she had been working on a similar story about Madoff. To our surprise, amazement, and delight, her story was published six days after the *MARHedge* piece. Although Arvedlund later claimed she had been working on the story for months and had done her own research, in essence the story was little more than a summation of Mike's. She did have a conversation with Madoff, though, presumably on the phone, in which he called claims that he was front-running, "ridiculous," and she did interview at least one investment manager who refused to be identified. Arvedlund reported, "Madoff's investors rave about his performance—even though they don't understand how he does it. 'Even knowledgeable people can't really tell you what he's doing,' one very satisfied investor told *Barron's*. 'People who have all the trade confirmations and statements still can't define it very well. The only thing I know is he's often in cash' when volatility levels get extreme.

"This investor declined to be quoted by name. Why? Because Madoff politely requests that his investors not reveal that he runs their money. 'What Madoff told us was, if you invest with me, you must never tell anyone that you're invested with me. It's no one's business what goes on here,' says an investment manager who took over a pool of assets that included an investment in a Madoff fund. 'When he couldn't explain how they were up or down in a particular month,' he added, 'I pulled the money out.'"

Although Ocrant was justifiably upset by what appeared to be basically a rewrite of his reporting, we were elated. We knew there was no way Madoff could remain standing after two articles this devastating were published within a week of each other. While *MARHedge* had a limited and exclusive readership, *Barron's* was a business magazine for the consumer. It had a large circulation. This was a double-barreled shotgun. We had reached the Wall Street insiders and the general public. We didn't think there was any way he could survive it.

I remember speaking with Ed Manion's wife, Mary Ann; we were both confident it was finally over. The SEC would have to take action. In fact, just to make sure that the SEC could connect the dots, the day *Barron's* published Arvedlund's article someone from the BDO, presumably Ed Manion, called the New York office and spoke to the director. The caller told him about the *Barron's* article, reminded him that they had my second submission in their office, and volunteered to send the director a copy of the article. This was no longer just a road map; it wasn't even a GPS. This was a guide dog leading a blind man to the Promised Land.

I believe that the director wasn't interested, that he wouldn't even reconsider initiating an investigation, and I know of no evidence that he ever read either Ocrant's piece or the *Barron's* article.

The two magazine stories together made as much impact as a single snowflake. We were astonished, shocked. It was like watching the monster march into the city and seeing the bullets bounce harmlessly off him. That's when we first began to wonder exactly what we were dealing with. How powerful was Bernie Madoff? How could he have remained standing after these attacks? Who did he know? What strings was he pulling? It was a chilling thought.

■ ■ ■

Mike Ocrant spoke with Madoff once more. After the *Barron's* article was published, he called Madoff's office. This time Madoff was unavailable, out of town. But a few hours later Madoff returned the call. He was on a golf course in Europe, he said. Ocrant wanted Madoff to know that he had nothing to do with the *Barron's* piece, that he wasn't trying to attack him. He also acknowledged that there was a minor factual error in that article. This was Ocrant's way of keeping the door open in case he needed to do a follow-up.

Madoff was extremely gracious about it. No problem, don't worry about it, everybody's just doing their job, and thanks for the call.

We had shot our biggest guns, and our target hadn't even been wounded. In the movies good always triumphs over evil, and sometimes there's a tendency to believe that's also true in real life. As we were being taught, that isn't true. Not only didn't we slay the monster, but it was growing. And it would soon become more dangerous than ever.

Chapter 4

Finding More Peters (to Pay Paul)

A t the height of my frustration I sent this e-mail to Neil, outlining my new plan to expose Madoff: "You know, maybe we should launch a fund just like Bernie's only we'll offer slightly higher returns with a 4 percent annual volatility. We raise $2 billion in maybe a year or 18 months, divide it equally and flee to a country without extradition. We then sell our story to Larry King and point out that we only did it to alert investors to the much larger Bernie Madoff Ponzi scheme and that Bernie is our hero for teaching us how to run a really good Ponzi. Bernie then goes down, we look like heroes, and we live happily ever after in Switzerland."

Ah, that Neil. He thought I was kidding.

But I didn't know what else to do. Nobody was listening. Even at Rampart the only thing management cared about was finding a product that could compete with Madoff. When I explained once again that it was impossible, they agreed with me, and then asked when I was going to have it ready.

After it became clear to them that I didn't want to do it, they began looking outside. Finally, through a web site Frank found an options trader on the Pacific Exchange who appeared to have created a very interesting product. It looked like he had found that elusive inefficiency in the market structure. Basically, until the turn of the century the major options exchanges in Chicago, New York, Philadelphia, and San Francisco really didn't compete with each other. They would each trade options on specific stocks and the other exchanges would honor that exclusivity. But as the big institutions began to move into the options market that tacit arrangement broke down. When the volume increased, the competition got a lot tougher—and so did the risks traders were forced to take. To protect themselves they had to lay off some of their risk. The whole business was changing, and this trader Frank found believed there was the opportunity to make a lot of money by taking some of that risk in exchange for a piece of the profits—but he needed a lot of seed capital to build his business.

It was an interesting concept. This trader came into the office to explain it to Neil and me. We weren't impressed. But when Neil and I offered to examine this strategy and determine if it was any good, management blocked us. For a reason we've never discovered, they did not want us digging into it. It was very strange. We spent all day, every day, researching and trading options; they found someone with an options product and they never even asked our opinion about it. Neil kept pushing them to let us rip it apart to see if it made sense, but they wouldn't allow us to do it. One afternoon we sat down with the three founders of the firm and asked them, "Explain a trade to me. Just one." They would explain loosely how they believed the strategy worked. But no one could actually answer any of our questions about it. The fact that they couldn't didn't seem to bother anyone; they had dollar signs in their eyes.

Frank thought it could work and brought Thierry de la Villehuchet of Access into the deal. He'd found an options trader, he explained. "He's got a theory that sounds like it might have some traction. I'm going to need capital to fund him. We want to bring him in-house and form a fifty–fifty joint venture with Access."

Thierry also needed a new product. He had all his nest eggs in the Madoff basket and wanted to spread them out. Rampart Managing Director Dave Fraley, Frank, and Thierry heavily recruited this trader, eventually convincing him to give up his seat on the exchange and move to Boston. The Rampart office was too small for these big plans, so they rented an office for him—and gave him the $75,000 he demanded up front. Frank had done some background research. He had spoken with people this guy worked with on the floor, and they'd said that this trader showed up every day, did his trades, and appeared to be making money. Frank wanted to do a little more investigating before the deal was finalized, but the trader gave Rampart a deadline to make a decision.

Frank, however, couldn't get rid of his uneasy feeling that something was wrong. The guy just grated against him. Once Frank had connected him to the traders the guy turned around and tried to push Frank out of the deal. So when it was done, Frank took him aside and said firmly, "If you're screwing us, I promise you, we're gonna go after you like a pack of wild dogs." That's not typically the way Frank talks.

While these negotiations were in progress, Frank spent considerable time with Thierry. They bonded over their love of ocean sailing. At some point Frank sat down at dinner with him and told him flatly that Madoff was a fraud. Thierry just couldn't accept that. "He can't be," Thierry insisted.

Frank was trying to save him. "But listen, what if you're wrong about him?"

"If I'm wrong, Frank," he said, "then I'm a dead man."

Frank forced a smile. "You don't mean that literally?"

Thierry didn't answer directly. "I'm totally committed to him. I've done my own form of due diligence. I'm comfortable with it. He comes with an impeccable reputation. I mean, my God, he's one of the biggest market makers in the U.S." He paused and then said softly, "I've got all my money in it. I've got most of my family's money in it. I've got all my friends—the wealthy families of Europe—they're all with Madoff. I've got every private banker that I've ever dealt with in this damn thing."

As Frank remembered this conversation later, he couldn't be certain that Thierry mentioned royalty. But several months later we would confirm that among Madoff's European investors were the rich, the royal, and the noble. We did know that Prince Charles had been approached by his distant cousin, Prince Michel of Yugoslavia.

When Thierry insisted, "You just don't have all the facts," Frank backed off. He never mentioned it to Thierry again.

Thierry remained excited about the potential of the new coventure. The agreement was that Rampart would run the trading operation and Access would raise the capital. To get it started, the two companies each put up $125,000. Then we began seeking other investors. Several risk managers from a major international bank flew into Boston for a presentation. They were intrigued by the trader's explanation—although they weren't sure it actually could be done the way he described it. They wanted to see several trades done, and if it worked as well in practice as it did in the presentation, they offered to leverage it at 7:1 the first day and after two to three months they would go up to 10:1. They wanted in.

While less than a complete vote of confidence, it was a strong indication of enthusiasm. That's a tremendous leverage potential. What made the deal so appealing was that the risk was controlled and the potential profit was tremendous. Frank was hoping for a return in the high teens. I was thrilled, of course, because it took the pressure off me. This was a product that would give funds an alternative to Madoff.

Rampart and Access moved the trader to Boston. But the more time Frank spent with him, the less he liked him. I think his precise words were: "This guy is an arrogant son of a bitch with an ugly personality." And Rampart was about to place a sizable aspect of its business in his hands—without giving Neil and myself a legitimate chance to review the nuts and bolts of the strategy.

Nobody on Wall Street has ever let a poor personality stand in the way of profit, but Frank just didn't trust this guy. So he decided to conduct his own investigation. This trader had shown up at a dinner one night wearing an Olympic team jacket. When Frank asked him about it, the trader revealed that he had sailed with legendary star class yachtsman Paul Cayard on the Olympic squad. Well, to a man who loves sailing like Frank does, that was impressive—even if he didn't quite believe it. When he began his investigation he contacted the Olympic sailing committee. They had never heard of the trader, although they suggested he might have been a volunteer worker. But he was never a member of any Olympic team.

Frank remembered a conversation they'd had about bike racing. Hanging in the trader's office was an impressive photograph of him racing around a track wearing an aerodynamic helmet. When Frank asked about it, the trader claimed that he'd won a Masters race—a racing division for competitors over 30 years old. So Frank called the Bicycling Hall of Fame in Newport, Rhode Island. After some research they reported that the trader had indeed competed in a Masters race— but he hadn't placed.

Now Frank had caught him in two lies. He reported that to two principals at Rampart. Remember, this is the financial industry; they didn't care if his nose grew every time he opened his mouth, as long as his product could generate profits.

In fact, the management at Rampart basically considered Frank, Neil, and me the wet blankets, pessimists always trying to stomp on their best ideas.

To Frank's credit, he continued to try to stop them from making this deal. He told Thierry about his discoveries. Thierry then had his own compliance manager investigate—and when he found nothing negative about the trader on the Internet he reported that he was clean. Thierry then asked the trader and Frank to submit handwriting samples for Access's graphologist in France to examine. Both men did, and both men passed.

But Thierry also hired a well-known private detective to conduct an in-depth investigation. And he discovered that this trader had been convicted of interstate wire fraud, had worn a wire in an FBI sting operation, and was still on probation and not supposed to be traveling outside the state of California to places like Boston, for example.

Thierry, Rampart management, and Frank confronted the trader. He admitted that he had been convicted, but claimed he had fallen on his sword to protect his employees. In fact, what he was doing was taking licensed software, duplicating it, and selling it retail. He was fired before he walked out of the room—but he challenged Access and Rampart to sue him. Both companies decided the negative publicity wouldn't be worth the potential recovery, so the trader walked away with more than $100,000.

Neil and I remained curious about his strategy, though. We continued talking about it, trying to find the fallacy in it. We explained it roughly to a lot of brokers, each of whom had an opinion about it. Some of them did think it would work. But a broker whom I consider one of the best options traders in the world, Jeff Fritz at Oxford Trading Associates, finally put it in perspective, telling us, "Yeah, maybe he can do that once or twice, but after you screw the market maker a few times he's not gonna bend over and take it again. People learn pretty quickly when they lose money." That made sense to us.

You can't continually fleece someone and expect them to continue picking up the other side of the trade. And when you've got no trading partner, you're done.

Several months later, though, when Frank learned that a Chicago options firm was about to make the same mistake, he called and told them to contact the private eye. They purchased a copy of the original report—and ended negotiations with the trader.

But for Frank, the damage to his relationship with Rampart's management was irreparable. Who knows if they were more upset that he had brought in this trader or that he had discovered the fraud. It didn't matter; it was pretty obvious that Frank was on his way out. Frank's anger was directed almost exclusively at the trader. He decided to leave Rampart before management had a chance to make that decision. It wasn't a big deal, as few people in the financial industry stay at one firm for their career. It's a very fluid industry, with tremendous movement, and for Frank it was just time to make his next move.

It was also obvious that I needed to give them a product to replace the trader's scheme. Rampart and Access were now working together, and both companies needed something to sell. Financial products aren't like big-screen TVs; you can't just pull a big one off the shelf and deliver it. Every new financial product has to be tailored specifically to accomplish certain goals to fit a narrow set of market realities. What Rampart needed was a low-risk product that delivered high returns with low volatility.

Who didn't?

■ ■ ■

Finally, I accepted the challenge. They wanted me to create an option-based product that returned 1 or 2 percent a month. I'd had a lot of experience running these types of option-sensitive products. It took several months of playing with numbers to fulfill those parameters. Neil, of course, was a major contributor, and I got a lot of data from various major firms. From Citigroup for example, I got the complete S&P 500 price return histories from 1926 to the day I received it. Then I began putting things in, taking things out, testing and retesting and back-testing to see how each package would perform in various market environments.

I did this knowing full well that Bernie hadn't bothered to do any of this. He just sat down and made it up. It's considerably easier that way—and you always get the results you want!

Eventually I developed a product we named the Rampart Options Statistical Arbitrage. It was a product that would do extremely well in a market environment with low to moderately high volatility. As long as the market didn't move more than 8 to 10 percent over a 10- to 15-day trading period, it would perform very well.

Of course, if there was extremely high volatility or if the market did make a substantial move in either direction over that period, it was possible to lose about 50 percent of its value.

To mitigate the risk, we had to be able to transition quickly from short volatility to long volatility to stem our losses, and doing that successfully required having a strategy in place. Whatever the market did, we had to have a prepackaged plan thought out well in advance. For every action the market took we had to have a counteraction already in place, because there would be no time to think when the inevitable occurred.

Obviously, that was impossible because there is an infinite number of things the market can do. So I prepared several basic strategies that would cover as many different scenarios as we could imagine. I tested these scenarios against historical markets going back to 1926. The worst-case scenario for this product was a period from 1929 through the early 1930s, but that was also the worst period for almost everything else in the market. Almost all of the trading plans I developed for these positions were based on market moves in the 1930s, because there was tremendous volatility during that decade. So for several months I was living in the past trying to figure out how to prevent losses in the future.

Admittedly, it wasn't the greatest financial product ever created on Wall Street. In October 2001, Frank finally left Rampart and moved to New Jersey, where he began selling a fund called Benchmark Plus. By this time we had become good friends and stayed in close contact. In his new job he continued digging up Madoff material. When I created this product he thought he might be able to find some investors, so I went down to see him. He read the prospectus and said correctly, "Harry, this is horseshit. Basically, what you're saying is you have to wake up on the right side of the bed and make every right move to protect your ass because you could lose everything. Who's gonna buy this?"

"They wanted something, and I had to give it to them," I said, not at all defensively. I knew what it was.

What I did not know was that I had made one slight mistake in my math. Unfortunately, I discovered that mistake at the worst possible time.

Rampart and Access initially raised about $6 million. Firms were sort of testing the product, to see how it would perform in actual market conditions before making any substantial investment. For several months it did quite well, but then volatility started getting very low so options lost value. It got kind of rocky. Then we had one month where there was some extremely high volatility. I had a plan in place for that situation, and I successfully traded out of the market. Neil and I were feeling pretty good about it—it was working even better than we had anticipated. I began thinking, *Well, maybe this is a product we really can push.* We'd gone through one of my bad scenarios and come out profitably.

Then we ran into a problem. One morning the market opened way down and our positions started working against us. The markets were getting crushed right before our options were expiring, and our positions were moving against us fast. I had a strategy for this type of situation. It meant taking a loss, but certainly it was survivable. As the day progressed, though, the market got a little worse than I had anticipated. Suddenly a manager of one of the funds who had about $500,000 in it called. He was in a complete panic. "Where am I? What's my loss?" His potential loss was capped at $250,000, but he was still far from that figure, I thought. As the market plunged he called back several times, and finally he told me (actually he ordered me), "Close me out right now."

I hung up the phone and told Neil, who pointed out, "Taking an order from a client in a situation like this is probably never a good thing. We should get him to fax us his instructions."

I sold his position and he took a substantial loss. The way I had modeled this strategy allowed me to close out the position that was going against me while the position going for me continued to run. That cut my losses substantially. So I went into the market and started trading. As I made each trade I told it to Neil, who logged the trade ticket and updated the portfolio. I finished the trade that basically closed me out of my losing position and hung up the phone. I figured we were okay. But I could see that Neil was confused, almost in a panic, about something. He was looking over the models and the portfolios as they updated rapidly with each market change. "What's the matter?" I asked.

"Harry, there's something wrong here," he said, looking at the numbers. "This isn't adding up."

He showed me his calculations. "Either we're doing something wrong, or we didn't think about this scenario."

That's when I discovered my mistake. As I looked at his calculations I realized I'd made a math error. As a result, instead of being down the maximum 50 percent, I was actually down more than 100 percent. Potentially, I was looking at a financial disaster. The only hope I had was that the market would move in favor of the positions I'd kept. Typically when you make a mistake the market goes against you, but this time it was moving to our benefit. Neil was running spreadsheets trying to find that point at which we would come out whole. I was on the phone, placing orders, trying to ride this wave out of danger. I placed my orders and hung up. Neil and I sat there silently, staring at the screen, holding our breaths and twiddling our thumbs as we watched the market proceed to save my ass. We had traded out of the position perfectly. In fact, every one of our clients, except the fund manager who bailed, ended up with a slight gain. We'd been breathtakingly close to losing several million dollars.

So we had successfully proved that this product had some potentially serious problems. But Thierry and Tim Ng were sold on it. They believed it could be a viable alternative for those clients too deeply invested with Madoff. I thought I had done my part by creating it; I wasn't a salesman. But in early December 2001, Rampart's senior investment officer, George Devoe, who normally would have sold it, was diagnosed with a fatal form of brain cancer. That was stunning, devastating. George sat a few feet away from Neil and me. George was a runner and a biker and a hiker; he was a mountain climber; he was the epitome of good health. At lunch he would sit there making fun of Neil, who was devouring a sauce-dripping sub sandwich for lunch and eight or nine sodas and never gaining one ounce, while he was eating a healthy salad and taking his vitamins and washing it all down with mineral water. But one day he told us he wasn't feeling too great and went to his doctor. He had an MRI and was told he had inoperable brain cancer. Three months later he was dead. It was really an awful situation, and it left me as the senior investment manager. So when Thierry wanted to market my product to European hedge funds in June 2002, I was really the only person who could go with him.

I had been to Europe briefly several times in my life. I had done a three-week art tour in France while I was in college, I'd vacationed in Greece with my family, and the army had sent me to Germany and Belgium a few times. But this trip was different. During this trip I met the rich and the royals of Europe. But also during this trip I got to really know Thierry de la Villehuchet. His founding partner at Access, Patrick Littaye, went with me to several meetings, and I also spent time with Prince Michel of Yugoslavia, who was marketing for Access; but mostly I was with Thierry. Thierry de la Villehuchet was a nice person, a French nobleman who was a noble man. He lived his life, and he died, by a very strict code of honor and obligation.

I think I began to understand the burden he was carrying the day we drove past the Arc de Triomphe. "Look up there, Harry," he said. "Look at those names under Napoleon." As I read those names, I recognized several of them. These were the people we were going to be meeting with on this trip. Several lines down was the name Flaghac. François de Flaghac was also selling my product, and Thierry explained, "His father was only a general. Everybody else was a field marshall or an admiral."

Thierry had been born into royalty. His clients were people of his social class. These people didn't have a particularly good understanding of finance, or even math, but they believed completely in the strength of their relationships. In some cases their families had been doing business for two hundred years. There was a firmly rooted trust between them that went far beyond any type of due diligence. On this level a man's word was paramount. Men like Thierry had started these funds to raise money from the nobles and well-connected and invest it, and these people invested with him because they knew his family could be trusted. Thierry understood that; that was the way he conducted his life, and he believed in it all. He was a fascinating man. In the United States he had been warm and personable, but in Europe he played his role of a nobleman. He returned to his roots there. It was good business.

That became clear to me on the first day of this trip, June 20, 2002. We spent the day in London. I was jet-lagged and went to my room for a nap. Later that day I met Prince Michel and learned that he had taken Thierry out to the polo fields to introduce him to Prince Charles and his sons, Harry and William. I was told that Prince Michel was somehow related to Prince Charles. It seems to me that the only logical reason for this meeting was to interest Prince Charles in either Madoff or, if he was already invested, our product. That's certainly a guess and I never found out anything more, although after Madoff surrendered, Prince Charles's spokesman did say he was not an investor (although if he had invested in Madoff through an offshore fund, it's unlikely he would have admitted it).

Thierry and Michel told me that they hadn't invited me to this meeting because I didn't know how to curtsy. Obviously that was their joke, and so I responded, "Of course I do. But by tradition Americans don't curtsy to British royalty because they never defeated us on the battlefield. That's why Americans don't bow when meeting the Queen."

I don't think they liked my joke. I was scheduled to have dinner with the two of them that night but it never happened. In fact, throughout the entire trip, after the last meeting of the day I got kicked to the curb. We didn't eat a single dinner together. Obviously I was good enough to have breakfast and lunch with them, but I didn't make the dinner cut. I wasn't particularly pleased with that, but I was polite enough not to remind them who won the Revolutionary War. We were there to conduct business, as much business as was possible, and if they believed that this was the most effective way to get it done I didn't care if I had dinner with them.

We had 20 meetings in three countries in 10 days. It was a whirlwind tour of Europe. We met with various hedge funds and funds of funds. The meetings eventually ran together in my memory, but it seemed like each office or conference room was more luxurious than the previous one. The floors were covered with plush Persian carpets; the walls were done in rich walnut and cherry woods, and hung on many of them were oil paintings; we were served only with sterling silver, and the fixtures were gold. These rooms had been decorated to impress clients, to show them that money didn't matter—which they apparently believed was an effective means of convincing clients to give them their money.

We met with many of the leading investment banks and private banks of Europe. The system there is quite different than here, as wealthy investors use private banks to conduct their business. I went with Patrick Littaye to a meeting with members of the L'Oreal family. At JPMorgan I met with a member of the Givenchy family, who spent considerable time complaining about the Hermès family, who apparently were suing his family over an investment that had soured. At lunch one day with Prince Michel we sat at a table near Mark Rich, the disgraced financier whom Bill Clinton had so controversially pardoned. All these people knew each other. These were the kind of people we were with every day. In Geneva, we were supposed to meet with Philippe Junot, the playboy who had been married to Princess Caroline of Monaco, but he canceled, I was told, because he thought my strategy was too risky, and he preferred to stay with Madoff.

Thierry began every one of our 20 meetings the same way: "Harry is just like Madoff. It's an option-based derivative strategy, only he offers a higher risk and a higher return. But it's different enough from Madoff that you should have him in your portfolio. If you have Madoff and you want some diversification, this will do it."

And every time he said it I got furious. What I wanted to shout out loud was that I was offering higher returns than Madoff because my returns were real and his were not. And now that I had corrected my math error, I was a lot lower risk, because at most I was going to lose only 50 percent of their money while with Bernie they were going down a full load.

But I didn't. Instead I smiled and explained how this strategy worked. After that we would drill down to the details. I'd go through my pitch book. Then they would ask the usual range of questions: What are your risk controls? What are your trading rules? What is the frequency of the bad events that can hurt you?

It was the potential risk that scared them. I told them that way less than 1 percent of events could hurt the product, although admittedly should it happen it could be catastrophic. I was honest: "You could lose half your money very quickly." I didn't bother to describe the near meltdown Neil and I had survived—and learned from.

The only fund that asked what I thought were the right questions about my due diligence was Société Générale. The people I met with there knew their derivative math. They told me, "We like your risk controls. You're the only guy who's ever come in here and specified what we can lose. But that risk is too high for us." Ironically, we found out in January 2008 that they actually weren't such good risk managers, as an employee named Jérôme Kerviel defrauded them of more than $7 billion by executing a series of "elaborate, off-the-books transactions that circumvented the bank's internal controls."

These meetings generally lasted about 90 minutes, and Thierry would end each one the same way: "When can I have your answer? When shall I call you to find out how much you'd like to invest?" It was never "if you want to invest," always "how much." He was a master salesman.

While the objective of this trip was to introduce my product to these fund managers, it also turned out to be an extremely educational trip for me. I came back with a lot more knowledge about Bernie Madoff than I had expected—and what I learned changed my life.

My team had absolutely no concept of how big Madoff was in Europe. We assumed several European funds and funds of funds had invested with him, but we never appreciated the number of funds or the size of their investments. It became clear to me during this trip for the first time that Madoff presented a clear and present danger to the American capital markets—and to the reputation of the Securities and Exchange Commission (SEC). While obviously I had lost confidence in the SEC, I also knew that investors around the world believed that it offered them a great level of protection and that their money was safe. That was one reason they invested here. When they discovered that wasn't true, that confidence in the integrity of the American markets that led people to invest in them was going to be badly shaken. When Madoff went down, and that was inevitable, the American financial system was going to take a worldwide beating to its reputation. A primary reason to invest in the United States would have disappeared.

Of the 20 meetings we had, the managers from 14 of those funds told me they believed in Bernie. Listening to them, I got the feeling it wasn't so much an investment as it was some sort of financial cult. What was almost frightening was the fact that every one of those 14 funds thought that they had a special relationship with him and theirs was the only fund from which he was continuing to take new money. At first I thought the only reason they would admit to me, someone they didn't know at all, that Madoff was managing their money was because they trusted Thierry, but then I began to understand that they were telling me this to impress me. The message was practically the same in every one of those 14 meetings: "We have a special relationship with Mr. Madoff. He's closed to new investors and he takes money only from us."

When I heard that said the first time I accepted it. When I heard it the second time I began to get suspicious. And when I heard it 14 times in less than two weeks, I knew it was a Ponzi scheme. I didn't say anything about the fact that I heard the same claim of exclusivity from several other funds. If I had, or if I had tried to warn anyone, they would have responded by dumping on me. Who was I to attack their god?

What I did wonder about was what was going on in Thierry's mind. He heard these 14 fund managers bragging, literally bragging about this special access, just like I did, and he knew it was a lie just like I did. But we never discussed it. Like Frank, I had previously tried to warn him. Before we'd left for Europe I'd told him, in these precise words, "You know Madoff is a fraud, don't you?"

And just as he had done when Frank told him, Thierry became extremely defensive. "Oh no, that's not possible," he'd replied. "He's one of the most respected financiers in the world. We check every trade ticket. We have them faxed. We put them in a journal. He's not a fraud."

I had considered asking to see those trade tickets, knowing I could use them to prove to Thierry I was right, but I didn't. I was afraid that if I asked to see them he would think I was using them to reverse engineer Madoff, and I knew he wouldn't let me kill his golden goose.

I cared about Thierry and I wanted to save him. After it had become clear that Thierry wouldn't listen to me, I called Access's director of research, who was a bright guy and understood derivative math, and told him that I had compiled a substantial amount of evidence proving Madoff was a fraud. "I get into the office at 6:30 in the morning," I'd told him. "If you'll come over half an hour early before tomorrow's scheduled meeting, I can prove to you mathematically that Madoff is a fraud."

He never showed up. And then I got it. He didn't want to know. Thierry didn't want to know. They were committed to Madoff; without him they didn't exist. It was their access to Bernie Madoff that allowed Access International to prosper. So when Thierry heard each of these funds claim an exclusive relationship, there was nothing he could do about it. It changed nothing. I also felt absolutely no obligation to tell any of the 14 asset managers that Madoff was a fraud. I had no personal relationship with any of them, and I certainly didn't want Bernie Madoff to know we were tracking him. Like Access, these funds needed Bernie to survive; they didn't need me. Where would their loyalty be? And what would happen to me when Madoff found out I had warned them?

I did appreciate the fact that they were trapped. They had to have Madoff to compete. No one had a risk-return ratio like Bernie. If you didn't have him in your portfolio, your returns paled in comparison to those competitors who did. If you were a private banker and a client told you someone he knew had invested with Madoff and was getting 12 percent annually with ultralow volatility, what choice do you have? You're going to either get Madoff for that client or lose the client to a banker who has him. And Madoff not only made it easy; he made it lucrative. He allowed the feeder funds to earn higher fees than anyone else and always returned a profit.

That was the reason so many European funds gave their millions to him. It was after these meetings that I strongly suspected Madoff was even bigger in Europe than he was in the United States. I estimated the minimum amount of money Bernie had taken out of Europe was $10 billion and in retrospect even that probably was low.

Once I realized how much money he had taken out of Europe—and was continuing to take—there was no longer any doubt in my mind that he wasn't front-running. This was a Ponzi scheme. If he was front-running he wouldn't want new money, because it would lower his return on invested capital. The money to pay the investors in his hedge fund would have had to come from investors in his broker-dealership. The more money invested in the fund, the more money he would have been forced to drain from the broker-dealership. Eventually it would have been spotted by some of his more sophisticated customers. And once those investors figured out they were getting bad price fills—which eventually they would have—that business would have declined rapidly, making it impossible for Bernie to continue paying such huge hedge fund fees and returns.

So he wasn't front-running. For a Ponzi scheme to continue to survive you have to bring in new money faster than it is flowing out, because you're robbing Peter to pay Paul. The more Pauls you have to pay, the more Peters you need to find. It's a ravenous monster that needs to be continuously fed. It never stops devouring cash. To me, the amount of money invested with Bernie, and the secrecy he required, were vital pieces of information.

But it became clear to me that the Europeans believed he was front-running—and they took great comfort in it. They thought it was phenomenal because it meant the returns were real and high and consistent and that they were the beneficiaries of it. They certainly didn't object to it; there was a real sense of entitlement on this level. To them, the fact that he had a seemingly successful broker-dealer arm was tremendously reassuring, because it gave him plenty of opportunity to steal from his brokerage clients and pass the returns on to them. They never bothered to look a little deeper to see if he was cheating other clients—like them, for example. What they didn't understand was that a great crook cheats everybody. They thought they were too respectable, too important to be cheated. Madoff was useful to them, so they used him.

They were attracted to Bernie like moths to a flame.

Just like the Americans, they knew. *They knew.* Several people admitted to me, "Well, of course we don't believe he is really using split-strike conversions. We think he has access to order flow." It was said with a proverbial wink and a nod—we know what he's doing. And if the American Madoff got caught, well, *c'est la vie.* They believed that the worst that could happen was that he could get caught and go to prison for a long, long time; but they would get to keep their ill-gotten returns and would get their principals back because they were offshore investors and the U.S. courts have no legal hold on them.

But for me, the most chilling discovery of this trip was the fact that many of these funds were operating offshore. It was not something that was spoken about; it was just something I picked up in conversation. Offshore funds are known as tax havens, places for people to quietly hide money so governments won't know about it. It's a means of avoiding law-enforcement and tax authorities. They're particularly popular in nations with high tax brackets, like France. While offshore funds certainly can be completely legitimate, to me it indicated that at least some of these funds were handling dirty money, untaxed money.

An offshore fund allows investors from a high-tax jurisdiction to pretend their income is coming from a low- or no-tax jurisdiction. While I have no direct knowledge, I definitely don't believe that all income from offshore tax havens is eventually declared to the proper government. But what was a lot more frightening to me was the fact that offshore investments are used by some very dangerous people to launder a lot of money. It is common knowledge that offshore funds are used by members of organized crime and the drug cartels that have billions of dollars and no legitimate place to invest them.

For me, that suddenly added a frightening new perspective. It wasn't just the people in these luxurious offices who were going to be destroyed when Madoff went down; it also was some of the worst people in the world. I was pretty certain the Russian mafia had to be investing through one of those funds. I didn't know about the Latin American drug cartels, but I knew they went offshore and were probably into Madoff in a big way. Obviously Bernie had to be worried about a lot more than going to jail. These were men who had their own way of dealing with people who zero out their accounts. Maybe Bernie was close to being a billionaire—we had no idea how much of the money he was keeping for himself—but we knew that even he couldn't afford that.

■ ■ ■

The knowledge that offshore funds were so heavily invested in Madoff staggered me, absolutely staggered me. It wasn't until this trip that I realized that my life was in danger. People kill to protect their money, and if my team was successful, a lot of people were going to lose a lot of money. And while I didn't know the names of these investors, I felt quite certain that if these people discovered what I was doing they would have to try to take me out. I was the most active threat to them. Even Bernie Madoff, the respected Mr. Madoff, was potentially a threat to my life. He was playing a dangerous game of unimaginable complexity. How was he going to respond if he found out that I was trying to bring him down? Was it better for Bernie to get rid of me or let these offshore investors get rid of him?

This wasn't paranoia. Everybody in the money business has heard stories and rumors about what happened to people who made bad decisions and created problems. Some of them may be apocryphal—but a lot of them aren't. I remembered the story Frank Casey had told me about a problem he'd had early in his career. In 1980 he had devised a strategy that fell into that gray area of legality. Its legality depended completely on an interpretation of the tax law. It was called a commodities straddle, a very complicated, highly leveraged strategy that allowed him to move money from one tax year to the next for individuals who needed that done, and then convert it to long-term capital gains. Basically it involved buying a commodity in December and taking all the tax benefits, then selling it the following year. These were riskless trades designed solely to create short-term losses for one tax year while providing long-term capital gains for the following year. Wall Street firms were doing it for their wealthy clients with a variety of commodities, ranging from silver to soybeans. And like the product I created, it could go south quickly. If it worked it was beautiful—it would save clients about 30 percent of their taxable dollars. The product Frank designed was slightly different. While his product had the same benefits—it would save clients about 30 percent—it also included some risk, which made it ethical and completely legal. And even if it blew up, the way Frank hedged it the most his clients could lose was 10 percent. So it had a 3:1 reward-to-risk ratio, a very nice ratio.

In late November 1980 a Merrill Lynch broker who specialized in private wealth management asked Frank to meet several of his clients in Carteret, New Jersey. The clients wanted to do a commodity tax straddle; for tax purposes they wanted to move income into the following year. Because Frank's strategy depended on some market volatility for success, he normally started by early September, which gave the market plenty of time to move. Beginning too late in the year was risky, because if the market stayed flat the strategy wouldn't work.

As Frank described this meeting, "Four guys with no necks were sitting there and one of them is a lawyer. It seemed obvious to me that the other three men were not exactly legitimate businessmen. I didn't care. This investment was legal and ethical and was going to be reported as required. The lawyer explained that they had flipped some property and ended up with a one-and-a-half-million-dollar short-term capital gains liability that they wanted stretched into the following year. I told them the risks—that if the market flatlined there was nothing I could do about it. They agreed to pay me a fifty-thousand-dollar commission, which I would split with the broker.

"I set up the strategy and the market went flat. Nothing happened, no movement. The lawyer with no neck began calling me every day. 'How much did we save today?' he'd ask. When I'd tell him, 'Nothing,' I could hear the silence.

"Finally, the second week in December he called me and said pretty clearly, 'Frank, you gotta make something happen. I don't think you understand the situation. There are extenuating circumstances. We can't be caught flat-footed like this. This money cannot be on the books. You need to create a million-two in losses.'

"I reminded him that I'd warned his clients about this possibility. That there was nothing . . .

" 'Frank, that is not an answer. And if I don't get the right answer I'm gonna put a bullet in you.'

"I didn't think I heard that correctly, or maybe I was just hoping I hadn't heard it right. 'Excuse me?' I said.

" 'I said you either do this thing right or we're gonna put a bullet in you.'

"But the market didn't move and I was trapped. Late one afternoon they showed up at my office. 'Do something now,' the lawyer said. The whole scenario was out of a bad movie. These were just dumpy-looking guys, wearing brown suits. They looked like anybody out of the neighborhood, except they seemed serious about shooting me. I went to my boss and I told him I had to lever up my position about five to one over what I had already leveraged, knowing I could get at least some movement out of that. I told the people from Carteret that I needed another twenty-five grand, which they handed over, and I put this monster position on. I warned them that they easily could lose thirty percent of their money on this deal.

"It did occur to me they had no intention of losing any money."

Frank had been through military Ranger training; he was capable and experienced with a weapon. So he began carrying a .357 with hollow-point bullets. This was a pretty tough time in his life. He was going through a difficult divorce, he had started drinking heavily, and four mob guys from New Jersey were threatening his life. It wasn't precisely what he had envisioned when he decided to work on Wall Street.

It got very scary. As he explains, "I was scared. I'll bet I rotted out a dozen shirts from sweat. I was drinking heavily. One night in Boston, I remember, I'd been drinking and I was driving home late at night. I looked in my rearview mirror and realized a car was following me, tailgating me. Whoever was driving made no attempt to hide the fact he was trailing me. I took back roads I knew and he stayed right on my ass. Finally I got to my house. I raced into the driveway and slammed on my brakes, rolled down my window, and leaped out of the car. As the other stopped by my driveway I scrambled to get behind my door for protection. As I did I pulled out my .357, and as soon as I got behind the door I pointed it through the open window at the driver. He just sat there, staring at me, then pulled away. I never saw his face. I do believe they were sending me a message: They knew where I lived. I got the message; believe me, I got it."

Gradually, Frank's strategy began working. He took his gains in small pieces—$10,000, $15,000, occasionally $100,000. It was painfully slow, but it was working. Finally the lawyer called again. As Frank remembers, "He said, 'This isn't fast enough. You got one week or we're gonna have to do something about it.'

"That was it for me. I called the broker who brought me into the deal and told him, 'You call that lawyer in Carteret and you tell him if I receive one more call I'm coming down to get them. Trust me—they won't even know what hit them.' I never got that call. I successfully moved $1.1 million of the one and a half million dollars before the end of the year. I wanted to get out then, but these people loved the profits and insisted we stay in. I had positions that were worth millions of dollars and I did not have discretion over the account so there was nothing I could do about that. They wouldn't let me out. They thought it was a money-making machine; they didn't understand it simply deferred taxes. I told them this was designed for one purpose, to move $1.2 million in two weeks. 'I just built you the atom bomb,'

I said. 'Trust me—you don't want to use it.' But all they saw were the profits.

"Of course they eventually lost most of it and left me with a debt of a hundred twenty thousand dollars. I actually wanted to sue them for the money, but Merrill Lynch was beginning to understand that this was potentially a bigger problem than it was worth to them and pushed me into arbitration. I got most of that money back. Merrill Lynch eventually absorbed the remaining losses.

"But there was no question in my mind that my life was at risk if this strategy had failed."

Professionally, the European trip was a failure. For my product to be profitable we had to raise at least $10 million, and we came home with commitments of slightly more than $6 million. It wasn't going to be profitable enough to pursue. And the truth was that these funds didn't need me; they had Madoff. There was no reason for them to invest in riskier products. At no time during the trip did I even consider revealing what we knew to any of these asset managers. There was no reason for them to believe me, and they were already addicted to his returns. Just like the American funds, they needed him to survive—and they needed him a lot more than they needed me. Who knows what they might do if they knew I was trying to expose him? So it was just too risky, and in retrospect that probably was one of the most intelligent decisions I made during this whole investigation.

■ ■ ■

When I got home from Europe, I did two things: First, I told my team, "You wouldn't believe it. He's bigger in Europe than he is here. Fourteen of the twenty funds we met with there have him, and obviously there are a lot more." And second, I began seriously upgrading my home security.

From that moment on there wasn't a day I didn't consider the security of my family and my team before taking any action. It wasn't just money—I believed that lives were at stake. I had been careful to keep the names of my team secret. Mine was the only name on my submissions. If someone in the SEC was revealing information to Madoff (and considering how close he was to the SEC in New York that certainly was a possibility), Markopolos was the only name they could give him.

I'd learned in the army that a leader leads. I'd gotten Frank and Neil into this, so it was my responsibility to protect their identities. And personally, I began carrying a gun.

I really didn't know what to do next. My two submissions to the SEC had been ignored, the two articles that should have prompted an investigation of his operation were long forgotten, and *Forbes* had ignored me. The only thing I knew for sure was that until my information was made public my life would be in jeopardy. Once it was published or the SEC took action, I would be safe. So I had to find some means of exposing Madoff to the public. I was just beginning to feel the first tinges of desperation.

Only three people have impressed me with their efforts to regulate the worst practices of Wall Street: William Galvin, who was elected Massachusetts secretary of the commonwealth in 1994, which put him in charge of the state Securities Division, and New York State's attorney generals: Andrew Cuomo and Eliot Spitzer. These are the only people who have brought big cases against the sacred cows of Wall Street. They were doing the job the SEC should have been doing but wasn't. So in late 2002 when I learned from Chuck Hill, who would succeed me as president of the Boston Security Analysts Society, that Spitzer was going to be speaking at the J.F.K. Library in Boston in its Profiles in Courage lecture series, I decided to personally deliver my material to him. Obviously this was years before his personal scandal erupted. Kitty Kennedy, the Analysts Society's executive director, secured an invitation for me.

Admittedly, I had some reservations. While I admired Spitzer for what he'd accomplished as the attorney general, I was also aware from my own research that his family had invested heavily in hedge funds and that he was a trust fund baby. It was quite possible that he was a Madoff investor and even more probable that he knew Madoff. In fact, I thought that was likely, as they were both members of the wealthy Jewish community in New York City. For all I knew they might even attend the same prestigious synagogue. So I knew it was a big risk for me. But I had to do something, and Spitzer appeared to me to be honest and ambitious. He was in the perfect position to initiate an investigation of Madoff. And the headlines he would earn by exposing him could make his political career.

The safest thing to do, I decided, was to get this information to him anonymously. I had identical twin sons due to be born in just a few months, and those boys were going to need a father. It wasn't just my wife and me; now I had a family to think about.

I took a lot of precautions. In retrospect, I suppose, it may seem like I was overly cautious, but that's only in retrospect. At the time all I knew for certain was that when our investigation was made public, many thousands of lives were going to be changed—and not one of them for the better. I certainly wasn't looking for personal credit. I was hoping for justice.

I started by printing out my entire submission on clean sheets of paper, taking out my name or any information that could identify me. I made certain I didn't leave any fingerprints on those pages. I put on a pair of gloves and slipped the submission into a 9 × 12 manila envelope and wrote Spitzer's name on it. Then I slipped that inside a larger 10 × 13 envelope. I was ready to hand it off.

It was cold that December night. I put on extra-heavy clothing and the biggest coat I owned. I was careful to dress down; I didn't want anyone to notice me. I sat quietly for Spitzer's speech. When he was done, as he stood near the podium speaking personally to members of the audience, I put on my coat and my gloves as if I was ready to go out into the cold, then walked to the front of the room. A library staff member was standing a few feet away from Spitzer. I took the 9 × 12 envelope out of the larger envelope and handed it to her. "Would you do me a favor, please?" I asked. "Could you please make sure Mr. Spitzer gets this?"

"Of course," she said.

"It's important," I added. Then I turned around and walked out into the blackness of a cold wintry night.

There is no evidence that Eliot Spitzer ever read my submission. I don't even know for sure that he got it. But he never acted on it. Maybe this was a tactical error on my part. I should have realized that few people take anonymous submissions seriously. Perhaps if I had walked up to him and looked him in the eyes and said, "Mr. Attorney General, my name is Harry Markopolos. I'm president of the four-thousand-member Boston Security Analysts Society, and I have evidence here of the largest fraud in history," and handed the envelope to him, he might have taken it seriously. But I did what seemed safest at that time.

Slightly more than three years had passed since we had discovered Madoff. We had compiled a strong case against him. Our original reason for trying to bring him down—that he was competition we couldn't compete against—had ended with the failure of the Rampart Options Statistical Arbitrage strategy. But we were so deeply into this thing that it became impossible to put it down. We had actually developed into a pretty good team. We had two investigators in the field, Frank and Mike, and two quants in Neil and me able to find the defects in the materials they collected.

And they did continue to add to our growing pile of evidence. Frank's new job at Benchmark Plus caused him to spend most of his time with hedge fund and risk managers, and at some point in each conversation he never failed to ask them, "What do you know about Bernie?" As he remembers, "I was in their office talking about other things but eventually we'd start talking about the industry in general and the rates of return in the marketplace, and I would ask them what they knew about Bernie. I wouldn't even have to use his last name. They knew Bernie. Most of them told me, 'I got money with Bernie,' or 'I know somebody who has money with him,' or 'This fund is raising a lot of money for Bernie.'"

At least several of those funds had ceased operating as traditional hedge funds and had become nothing more than Madoff's sales force. They did nothing for their clients except shovel the money directly to Madoff. They didn't do any due diligence, they didn't make any other investments, and they certainly did not diversify to protect their clients' money. Instead, they thought they had the deal of the century. They raised money and handed it to Bernie, and in return he paid them substantially higher management fees than they could possibility have gotten anywhere else, which, combined with the percentage of the profits they were taking from their investors, meant they were making huge profits. Notice I said "making," not "earning," because they earned nothing. But Bernie was paying 16 percent gross returns and keeping way, way less than 1 percent per year for himself to keep his clients satisfied—and trapped. These feeder funds were earning almost 4 percent per year in fees while passing along 12 percent to their investors. It was a merry-go-round that stopped only to let new people get on, because nobody wanted to get off. Everybody was happy—the investors who were getting a regular return, the fund managers who were making a fortune without having to do any work at all, and Bernie. Who really knows what was going on in his head? Or how truly insane he was?

Let me explain how brilliant Madoff was in letting the feeder funds earn well over 90 percent of the available fees to lure in new victims. By being the top bid for new money, Madoff was every feeder fund's best relationship. Bernie had great returns with low volatility, and he effectively paid the most for new investors. And Madoff didn't need a lot of money for himself personally. For example, if I challenged you to spend a billion dollars, could you do it? Probably not unless you got a divorce is my guess. By offering unbelievably steady returns with almost no volatility he was providing the holy grail of investment products, and he was paying the feeder funds more than anybody else to sign up new investors. That's what kept the scheme going for so long, and that's why it was able to get so big.

What continued to amaze us was his size. He was already significantly larger than any other fund in existence, yet he just kept growing. We calculated that the minimum amount of money he was handling had to be at least $15 billion, possibly $20 billion. The numbers kept ratcheting up. They had long passed from unbelievable into fantasyland. At times Neil and I would just sit there and speculate about what would happen when Madoff blew up. There were no historical references to look at, as nothing like this had ever existed before. Compared to Madoff, the most infamous crimes in the world were small potatoes. I was certain that his arrest would put a lot of hedge funds of funds out of business. We assumed that most of the funds had 5 to 20 percent of their assets invested with him. It never even occurred to us that some of these funds would be almost all Madoff. We didn't believe that any responsible asset manager would have 100 percent of its funds with one man with one strategy. Even investing 20 percent of a fund in one manager is extreme; 25 percent is insanely extreme, and anything beyond that is just plain crazy. But even those funds with a limited investment would be in trouble because their investors would panic and immediately withdraw the rest of their funds. That would cause the market to go down, which subsequently would force the innocent hedge funds to sell assets. My best guess was that the impact was going to cause the U.S. markets to fall between 7 percent and 10 percent in a relatively short period of time. It would be a category 2 or 3 hurricane. It would cause some damage, but most industry people would recover.

After I returned from Europe we knew it would have a worldwide effect. The French, who loved him, would be slaughtered, while places like Turkey, which stayed away from him, would not be hurt as badly. I also knew that we would never know the full extent of European losses. As I had learned, a great percentage of the European investments were made through offshore funds, funds that traditionally are used to hide pretax income. People who had put their money in those funds to avoid being taxed by their countries would not be able to acknowledge their losses; they couldn't admit to having the untaxed money, so they certainly couldn't admit to losing it. That group, I believe, includes everyone from European royalty to drug lords. And I still believe we'll never know the full extent of the European losses, but they're substantially more than losses in the United States.

We knew a lot of investors would be devastated, and many of them wiped out, but what we didn't realize was how many people that included. We had assumed that most people invested in Madoff through the funds, and as we later found out we had assumed wrong. Although Mike Ocrant had told us that Madoff was so well known in the New York Jewish community that he was referred to as "the Jewish T-bill," we really had no concept of the size of the affinity scheme. That was my fault for not realizing it. An affinity scheme targets people with similar affiliations; Bernie was Jewish, so he targeted the New York metropolitan area and Florida Jewish communities. Historically, almost by definition Ponzi schemes start within a well-defined community, often an ethnic or religious community. If I were trying to start a Ponzi scheme, for example, I would do it inside the Greek community. The reason for that is trust; nobody thinks one of their own is going to cheat them, not when they can cheat so many others. We were focused on the institutional accounts, so we didn't have the slightest concept that Madoff was using separately managed accounts to ransack the synagogues for every cent he could pull out of them. I should have guessed that.

We also knew that the SEC would be roasted for not doing its job, although again at that time we still hadn't realized how nonfunctional it was. My mistake was assuming that the problem was mostly with New York, when in fact it was systemic. While there was nothing we could have done to save investors beyond alerting this agency and trying to go public, the SEC could have shut Madoff down as far back as 1992, when it first investigated him and let him off the hook. This was certainly one of the most expensive mistakes in history. Had the SEC stopped him then, depending on the way you choose to calculate the total losses, it could have saved investors more than $60 billion.

So Neil and I believed that Madoff's fall would cause a temporary disruption in the markets but that was all. There was no way we could have anticipated that Madoff's fall would be caused by a worldwide recession that resulted in stock markets collapsing and led to investors desperately trying to pull their money from hedge funds to meet other demands. The moment a Ponzi scheme has to pay out more money than it is taking in, it's done. But Madoff still had a few more years before we began to see signs of that.

■ ■ ■

While our investigation continued, all of our lives were changing. Over the next few years my wife and I had three children, which completely changed my perspective on the world. And Neil, who had started as my intern and become a trusted friend and collaborator, had decided to leave Rampart.

There were several reasons for his decision. After George Devoe's death the dynamic had changed. Without him to act as a buffer for Neil and me, we really lost our voice within Rampart. Any input we'd had into the decision-making process disappeared, which at times caused some resentment. We also were forced into dealing with a trading group we didn't particularly like, rather than the people we'd been working with for a while. But probably more than that, it was time.

Although Neil had been named a vice president and had a wide range of responsibilities, as long as he stayed at Rampart he was going to be my assistant and he had outgrown that role. At least partially because of our investigation, he'd become fascinated with hedge funds and hedge fund strategies. So when Frank Casey heard that the company he was raising money for, Benchmark Plus, was looking for a senior analyst, he tossed Neil's hat into the ring. He thought it would be a perfect fit.

It was. In October 2003, Neil accepted the job and moved to Tacoma, Washington. A super-smart guy named Stu Rosenthal took his seat across the desks from me. In his new position Neil was responsible for interviewing potential hedge fund managers to be included in the Benchmark Plus portfolios and doling out funds for them to manage. It put him a position to meet even more people. So rather than our investigation being sidetracked, as we physically moved further apart, the pursuit of Bernie Madoff became the glue that held the team together.

Chapter 5

The Goddess of Justice Wears a Blindfold

If I needed a reminder of how potentially dangerous an investigation of the financial industry can be to a whistleblower, I got it in February 2003. An honest man named Peter Scannell was working in Putnam Investments' Quincy, Massachusetts, call center, basically taking customer buy and sell orders. Eventually he realized that some of his customers were market-timing; at the end of the trading day, if the American stock market had gone up they bought mutual funds loaded with foreign stocks, figuring those stocks would rise when trading began in the foreign markets the next day. Many of those trades were being done by members of the Boilermakers Union. Although technically it's not illegal, it's a violation of the National Association of Securities Dealers regulations because it penalizes long-term investors, and most funds won't accept trades from market timers. But when Scannell informed Putnam's management, they reportedly ignored him. Although he was not supported by management, Scannell finally began refusing orders from the Boilermakers.

On a cold, snowy February night a few days later he was sitting in his car drinking a cup of coffee. He was parked in a dark church parking lot less than a dozen miles from my home. According to Scannell, a heavyset man dressed in a gray sweatshirt with "Boilermakers Local 5" emblazoned on it suddenly attacked him, hitting him in the head over and over with a brick, screaming that he'd better "shut the fuck up." Scannell was left to die in that parking lot. Fortunately, a police officer found him lying there. At first he thought Scannell was drunk—it was only when he went to wake him that he saw the blood and rushed him to the hospital. Scannell barely survived. But I got the message: If a member of a local union had tried to kill Scannell over millions, it was not hard for me to imagine what organized crime would do for billions.

Ironically, this assault on Scannell changed my life, too. Scannell eventually brought his complaint about the market timers to the Boston office of the Securities and Exchange Commission (SEC). After waiting five months without any response, he finally went to Massachusetts Secretary of the Commonwealth William Galvin, who initiated an investigation that led to fraud charges being filed against Putnam, the resignation of its CEO, and the withdrawal of tens of billions of dollars by its clients. It also caused the head of the SEC's Boston office, Juan Marcelino, to resign in November, several days after it was reported that the SEC had paid no attention to Scannell's complaint. On September 9, 2003, New York State Attorney General Eliot Spitzer and Secretary of the Commonwealth of Massachusetts Galvin announced indictments against a number of hedge funds in New York and Putnam Investments in Boston for allowing market timers to steal returns from long-term fund shareholders.

The SEC's Boston office was publicly humiliated and set out to rectify that by finding and prosecuting market-timing cases. And the SEC was willing to pay a reward for information. Ed Manion called me to ask if I knew about people market-timing in Boston, telling me, "If you have any cases for us, we do have this bounty program. We can pay you up to 10 percent and triple damages."

I had known a little about the bounty program. I knew, for example, that Madoff wasn't front-running, so it didn't apply to him; but Ed described it in detail. "This definitely applies," he said. "There's money in this one. Bring us a big case and you can make millions of dollars."

Over the next few days I started thinking about that. Millions of dollars? I now had a wife and two children, and I was bogged down in a job that was no longer very interesting to me. Millions of dollars? *Maybe this is something I'd really enjoy doing*, I thought. I began learning a lot more about the world of whistleblowers. I ordered several books about whistleblowers and fraud investigation from Amazon and quickly read through them. I was right—I was fascinated by these stories. Then I ordered several more books and raced through them. *I can do this,* I thought, *and it would be a hell of a lot more interesting than what I'm doing right now.*

Market timing is not at all unusual. The world markets are open 24 hours a day. The trading day begins in Asia, moves through Europe, and ends in the United States at the close of business. The European and Asian markets generally follow the U.S. markets; if we go up in the afternoon, then generally those markets will rise the next day. But the prices of stocks on those markets do not reflect the results of the U.S. trading day, which leaves four hours to arbitrage. Market timers buy international mutual funds, take out their gains right away and leave long-term mutual fund holders saddled with all the trading costs. Basically, market timers are picking the pockets of long-term investors. What was illegal about it was that the mutual funds claimed they did not allow it, when in fact they did allow certain large, favored customers to market-time their funds at will. They allowed their high-dollar clients to participate while they were telling their smaller investors it wasn't going on. They were committing fraud against their fund shareholders.

As past president of the Boston Security Analysts Society, I knew people in the industry throughout the country who would be in a position to know about market timing. I'd met most of them at Chartered Financial Analyst conferences. I began making phone calls at night, just dipping my toes in the investigative waters. I told those people that the SEC was desperate for market-timing cases and had a bounty program that would pay up to 30 percent of the ill-gotten gains or losses avoided. "It's a ticket out of the industry," I said flatly, offering, "If we do a case together I'll split it with you." Over months I began building an investigative organization. I found a legal team that would handle the cases on a contingency basis and I learned how to protect the identity of anyone working with me. Investigating market-timing cases became my second job. I'd come home at night and practically rush up to my attic office to go to work. Doing this work excited the hell out of me. These companies were cheating their clients, and I was helping to catch them—and maybe I was going to make a few million bucks doing it. I worked endless hours, nights and through the weekends, completely erasing any boundaries between my work and my personal life. I had to find cases of fraud, recruit my whistleblowers, and document those cases so my legal team could prepare a submission. I had to teach my whistleblowers what to look for and what the legal boundaries were, as well as continually providing the emotional reinforcement they required.

Being a whistleblower is an extraordinarily lonely existence. You're putting your livelihood at risk, maybe your life, and you can't tell anyone about it. You have to go through every workday as if everything is normal, when in fact you've made a conscious decision to expose illegal actions your company is taking, and you're doing it with the knowledge that the people you work with are going to suffer because of that, and some of them may even go to jail. It's incredibly tough. So I became an adviser and a confessor to many of my people.

And the only person who knew I was doing this was my wife, Faith.

I had to teach myself an entirely new business. After I had found several strong cases, I called the smartest securities lawyer I knew and told him what I had. His firm couldn't handle those cases, he explained. It was a defense firm; it represented the companies the SEC would be suing, large corporations that paid his firm by the hour. I needed a plaintiffs' firm, which are generally smaller firms that file these cases and work on a contingency basis, meaning they take their fees from the proceeds—if they win. "It's in our interest that plaintiffs' firms file these cases—so we can defend them," he explained, just before giving me the phone numbers of several good plaintiffs' firms.

Which is how I found a legal firm to work with me.

Over an extended period I was able to identify 20 cases of market timing in which investors had been defrauded out of at least $20 billion. The companies participating in this included some very large mutual funds and foundations. Twenty billion dollars. Finding them was not especially difficult, although obviously you never see a CEO admit in his annual report to investors, "Fraud was up 25 percent this year. We had a great year in fraud; it's our highest-margin product. My expectation for fraud is that we intend to grow it 25 percent a year to infinity. I have a really good fraud team; we believe we have the best crooks in the business." In fact, most of my cases began when I examined companies' publicly reported numbers. The clues were always in their annual reports, income statements, balance sheets, and footnotes—if you knew what to look for. And knowing that required having experience in the financial industry and great math skills. To me, some of these numbers popped out like a glowing neon sign flashing in red letters, "We are a fraud. Our numbers are too good to be true." I found these cases by analyzing the numbers, convincing some employees to speak to me, and getting information from them that gave me insight into the way their company did business. Recruiting those employees proved to be the most difficult task. Eventually I would file all 20 of those cases with the SEC, confident that in every one of those cases I had established beyond any doubt that these companies were defrauding their investors by market timing.

On paper, I was a rich man.

Early in 2004 I began to consider leaving Rampart. Not because I was rich on paper, but rather because when I woke up in the morning the thought of another day in the industry depressed me. On some level I had never felt like I belonged in the finance industry. I knew there were at least 100 people in equity derivatives who were better than me. Everybody in finance was smart, but the only way to get that edge was to be superbrilliant. I knew some of those superbrilliant people quite well, and I knew I wasn't one of them. I wasn't in the top 1 percent. It had been at least five years since I'd seen any exciting new math. It was just the same old repackaged stuff in a different form. I just didn't feel the industry was providing products that people should be buying. Basically, I was getting really bored.

Investigating Bernie Madoff, as well as the work I had started doing on the market-timing cases, convinced me I could be successful at fraud investigation. And I was enjoying it. When I had started looking at Wall Street through my fraud lens, I realized how much of the business was based on deception and outright fraud. Those people who work in the industry know it is not pretty. There were times I would watch the television commercials for some of the large funds and just sit there shaking my head in disbelief. The fantasy they were selling had absolutely nothing to do with reality as I knew it to be. It isn't every person or every firm, but the dishonesty is widespread and there is little the honest majority in the industry can do about the corrupt minority without the assistance of local, state, and federal agencies. And that support just doesn't exist.

I was confident I knew how to weed out those frauds. My derivatives background gave me the math skills to look closely at pitch books, annual reports, and other public documents and pick them out. And I also knew there was enough fraud ingrained in the business practices of the finance industry that I wanted to be on the other side.

I discussed this at length with Faith. While the thought of losing the security of my paycheck made her very nervous, she told me simply and directly, "If you're not happy doing what you're doing, you shouldn't be doing it." We both knew that if I did this we would have to live on the money I'd managed to save, but we'd be depending mostly on her paycheck until I was able to settle some cases. I was confident that would happen pretty quickly, but there were no guarantees. Fortunately, Faith was doing very well in her career, working as a senior analyst at a very large Boston-based mutual fund company. Leaving Rampart meant we would have to survive for at least a little while on one Wall Street salary, but we finally decided it was time. Fortunately for us, we had always lived well below our means, had bought an affordable home with only a small mortgage payment, owned both of our cars, and had no debt otherwise to worry about. Thanks to our years of living frugally and wise investing, financially we could afford for me to start a new career.

When I had first casually examined Madoff's split-strike strategy five years earlier, there was no way I could have imagined the twists it would take—or that it would lead directly to the end of my career as a derivatives portfolio manager.

In May 2004, I gave notice at Rampart and offered to stay until the end of October, giving the firm ample time to find and train a suitable replacement. I felt great loyalty to that company. I'd been there almost 13 years, and I appreciated everything my employer had done for me. I explained that I had been investigating fraud cases for some time, although I certainly never mentioned Madoff. I'd discovered there were a lot of frauds being perpetrated on investors, and thanks to my years at Rampart I had the tools, the experience, and the knowledge to stop them. At least some of them. They were gracious about it. I recommended my successor, a really smart guy named Nick Penna, and in mid-August they hired him. And two weeks later, on the last day of August, they surprised me by informing me that it was my last day.

But I'd prepared for that months earlier, gradually taking home anything personal that I would need. What was left was already stored and ready to be moved. Truthfully, like any good geek I am a little germ phobic. I'm not obsessive, just aware. At Rampart I always kept a bottle of rubbing alcohol and cotton swabs in my desk, and occasionally I'd wipe down my keyboard, mouse, and phone. George Devoe, our late senior investment officer, used to get colds, and he'd sneeze or cough without covering his mouth or nose. The last thing I did on my last day was take out my rubbing alcohol and carefully swab down my keyboard, mouse, and phone. Then I walked out the door into my new life.

■ ■ ■

I wasn't the only member of our team looking for new challenges in 2004. Frank Casey's job with Parkway Capital had prevented him from sailing, the passion that had been the bond between him and Thierry de la Villehuchet. During the week, he and his wife Judy lived in Freehold, New Jersey, returning to Boston each weekend. So when a close friend, Kevin Leary, invited him to sail from Boston to Bermuda on the 38-foot *Sennen*, he happily accepted. The third member of the crew was a bulky Russian woman who had responded to Kevin's Internet ad for a cook/crew member, claiming to be a medical doctor with considerable ocean sailing experience.

The *Sennen* sailed out of Boston Harbor on July 31. As they left, for the first time in their 24 years together, Frank's wife Judy cried—and asked where the insurance policies were kept. That seemed odd. Kevin and Frank had responsibly checked all the weather patterns before departing and saw nothing to raise any concern. But as they sailed through calm waters the first few days, Frank began having doubts about the cook, who didn't seem to know how to correctly set the sails and wasn't familiar with certain medical terms. It didn't seem to matter too much, though; for a six-day sail it shouldn't cause any problems.

On the third day out, a weather fax reported that a tropical storm had formed off the coast of Florida and was moving northeast up the coast. They decided to continue toward Bermuda, sailing across the Gulf

Stream and using it as a warm-water shield to shelter them from the storm. But it was vital to get across it before the storm hit. As Frank knew, "Strong winds blowing against this vast current of water produce tremendous waves with flat sides like a barn wall. . . . Picture a bowling alley with the storm being the ball; you do not want to be the pins. Sailors know they might survive a hurricane in open ocean, but would likely die if caught by one in the Gulf Stream."

Late in the afternoon of the third day, they learned that the tropical storm had grown into the first hurricane of the season, Hurricane Alex, and was moving northeast much faster than initial estimates. It was moving directly toward their position. To survive, they were going to have to race through the night, away from Bermuda, toward Africa.

By this point it was obvious the Russian cook had little sailing experience. She was told to stay below and secure the cabin to prevent projectiles from flying if they were hit by a wave. Frank and Kevin spent the night in the cockpit, handing off the tiller every 15 minutes, "being beaten to death in a wild mouse ride in storm-tossed seas. . . . Any slip of concentration could mean disaster." By the afternoon they had put 200 miles between their position and Hurricane Alex's track. They were going to be three or four days late to Bermuda, but they had successfully skirted the hurricane. For the first time in two days, they breathed easily.

As the captain's log reads: "Later that evening, around 9 P.M. Boston, *Sennen* was knocked over by one enormous rogue wave. . . . Seawater gushed past the closed but submerged companionway hatch. This seawater immediately ruined much of the boat's electrical system, including all three radios, navigational computer, electrical monitor and inverter, and the GPS. The rogue wave also crushed the fiberglass dingy and disabled both the monitor and auto-helm steering devices. In addition, the wave forced seawater into the fuel tanks . . . making the engine inoperative."

Frank had been resting in the cabin when the wave hit. Later he estimated it to be 60 feet high or higher. He went flying through the air as water rushed around the gangway hatch boards. *My God*, he thought, *we're under water.* As he eventually told me, "We snapped back as the keel righted the boat, and I flew back across the cabin into the starboard cabinetry. All I could hear was the cook screaming."

The wave had picked up the boat, then smashed it down vertically through the water like a falling knife. The electronics and engine were dead. The fuel and drinking water had been polluted by sea water. For Frank, the threat was real and immediate. In this life-and-death struggle, Bernie didn't exist.

The *Sennen* was still seaworthy, so they set sail and decided to try to reach Bermuda. But they were not going to make it. "I was on watch late in the evening," Frank recalled. "Suddenly the wind died and I whispered a curse to myself. . . . I heard a freight train bearing down as I moved to face the onslaught: a white squall? Even in the dark I knew I was hearing a vertical wind-driven wall of rain; it hit, [and] *Sennen* took off like a spooked horse."

Again, they survived; somehow the *Sennen* had remained afloat. But a day later they were hit again, this time by a monster wave. "We slid sideways down this monster's front," and again, somehow, the *Sennen* remained seaworthy. There was little more they could do. They were exhausted, running out of supplies, and having to deal with the hysterical cook, who screamed in fear through the nights. Their options were very limited; with no ability to get weather information, they had to decide whether to risk the long sail to Bermuda on a badly wounded boat or trigger the emergency position-indicating radio beacons (EPIRBs). Although they were reluctant to risk the lives of others, they decided they had no other options. They turned on the emergency beacon, reaching into the night for help.

It was about 10 hours later that the Coast Guard C130 cargo plane found them. The pilot dropped a radio, and arrangements were made for the crew to be rescued by the tanker *Golar Freeze*, then about a half hour away. Climbing aboard that massive ship from a small sailboat in high rolling seas without being crushed between the two ships proved as dangerous as the storms. Kevin and the cook had to be hauled the 90 feet to the tanker's deck by a cargo net held by the crew. But eventually they all made it.

As Frank concluded, "Three months after we abandoned *Sennen* she was located in the Sargasso Sea . . . still attached to a drogue to slow her movement and drifting one-half mile per hour toward Europe. After being battered by the seas and *Golar Freeze*, her value was dubious and no one would bother salvaging her. She was left to her fate, bobbing in an area of the ocean where few would ever go. I cried when I saw pictures of her. I felt like I had left a great wounded friend out in a storm. *Sennen* had kept us alive, and now she would die alone."

■ ■ ■

While Frank was battling nature, I had begun my career fighting a much more subtle enemy. I had become a full-time fraud investigator—a financial detective. Faith and I were taking a big gamble on my ability to find massive cases of fraud, collect evidence, and prove to the government that a financial crime had taken place. I wasn't interested in going after any particular person or group. I was living with the fear generated by the Madoff case, and I wasn't interested in putting my whistleblowers in a similar situation.

Eventually I took all my documents proving 20 cases of market timing and submitted them to the SEC under its bounty program. I was fully aware that the SEC has the option of either accepting a case for further investigation or rejecting it. It receives hundreds of thousands of submissions annually, and it doesn't even have a system in place to process whistleblower tips. It was a beauty contest to see who uncovers the most evil schemes. My cases were competing against all the other submissions that the SEC received. But I had a great deal of confidence in the quality of the cases that I presented.

Essentially, the SEC turned down all of my cases the same day that I submitted them. I was appalled. I had handed over evidence proving that companies had stolen billions of dollars from investors, and the SEC had responded that it was okay—the companies were not going to do it again. In one instance, one of the nation's five largest mutual fund companies had monthly turnover percentages in its international equity funds in the 1,100 to 1,300 percent range per month! Now, there is absolutely no way on earth that those were legitimate trades done by honest buy-and-hold long-term investors. But these SEC enforcement attorneys couldn't have cared less. I was told by a high-ranking enforcement official at the SEC in Washington, D.C., in these words: "We're done with market timing. The industry has gotten the message."

Even worse, one of my cases involved a midlevel whistleblower at a bank-owned mutual fund subsidiary that was allowing a few hedge funds to trade its mutual funds after hours, a felony known as late trading.

When I told one of the SEC's top enforcement attorneys about that, he told me that in a few weeks this bank was going to be purchased by a much larger bank, and the Federal Reserve wouldn't appreciate our starting this case now, because it could gum up the merger. "It doesn't serve any purpose to go after them now," he said.

On paper, as well as in reality, I was no longer a rich man.

I was truly incredulous. I asked him, "What about the billions of dollars taken out of mutual fund shareholders' pockets?" The SEC had no answer for that. While I would have loved to pursue these cases, there was nothing I could do. I had to drop them. Without the support of the SEC it was simply too dangerous for my whistleblowers to blow any whistles. They might very well have lost their jobs and been placed on the industry's blacklist. It just wasn't fair to these brave men and women or their families that they would have to suffer severe financial hardship just because the government agency charged with being the industry's watchdog was deaf, blind, and mute.

It was then that I began to understand that the SEC is a government agency that had been captured by the private industry it was created to regulate. The mission of the agency supposedly was to protect investors from the financial predators in the industry; instead it was protecting those financial predators in the industry from the investors. The people charged with regulating the industry were primarily concerned with their own paychecks. They didn't care a rat's ass about protecting investors. And it was then that I realized that I had two opponents, Bernie Madoff and this nonfunctioning agency that seemed to me to be doing everything possible to insulate him.

I have a temper; I just don't let it out very often. It's not productive to do so. I had learned years earlier that I got more results with honey than I did with vinegar. I also didn't get hurt as much. As a kid growing up in a relatively rough area, I used to fight all the time. I've never been very big, so I lost some of those fights. I didn't mind that—you can knock me down and you can beat the hell out of me, but I'm going to be ready to fight you again tomorrow. In this instance I contained my anger; there was nothing to gain by losing my temper. So I took this intellectual beating and I got up the next day to fight again.

I was left with a box of evidence piled up in the middle of my office. This small mountain of cardboard and paper documented a theft of $20 billion that the SEC was going to allow these companies to get away with. I decided to see if the Massachusetts Securities Division would be interested in pursuing these cases. For me, this was also sort of a test. If the state would aggressively pursue these cases, I would hand them Madoff. My local state representative at that time, a wonderful woman named Kathleen Teahan, lived only a few blocks from me. I often saw her on the streets of our small town, and one day I happened to run into her, ironically in front of the bank. I have a problem, I told her. I've uncovered several cases of securities fraud. A lot of people were being victimized, and I thought it might be something William Galvin would be interested in.

No elected official has ever done a better job for a constituent than Kathleen. Without knowing all the details, she arranged a meeting for me with two senior members of Galvin's staff, picked me up in front of my house and drove me to the statehouse, accompanied me into the meeting room, and introduced me to the people I was scheduled to meet with. Unfortunately, that was all she could do. I explained to them that I had several cases in which mutual funds were making millions by market timing and that the SEC was not interested in enforcing any of its investor protection statutes. I pointed out to them that my cases didn't involve fraud against the government—these companies had defrauded citizens of the state. Then I asked, "Does the state have a bounty program?" It did not. "Would you be willing to enact one?" Nope.

While these were nice people, and maybe they even wanted to do the proper thing, I was not impressed with their knowledge of the securities laws. I had considered trusting them with my biggest case, Bernie, but the market timing meeting went so poorly that I never said a word about it.

For me, of course, it meant that I wasn't going to earn any money for more than a year's work. The bounty that I had expected was never going to be paid, but by far the most difficult task I had was telling my whistleblowers that the government had not accepted their case. These were heroes, people who had risked their careers, as it turned out, for nothing. It was very difficult for some of those people to ease back into their regular routines. Now they understood why the goddess of justice was wearing a blindfold.

My Madoff team was now split up and living in four different places. I was in Boston; Neil was in Tacoma, Washington; Frank was in

Manalapan, New Jersey; and Mike remained in New York. But our investigation never stopped; it never even slowed down. The investigation of Bernie Madoff simply had become a part of our lives—it no longer had any specific objective or end in sight. We kept doing it because we had been doing it, and I think the surreal aspect of it amazed us. We had discovered the largest financial crime in history. Many people knew about it, and apparently there was no mechanism available to stop it. I had considered approaching law enforcement—the Federal Bureau of Investigation (FBI), for example—but it seemed obvious to me that if the federal agency charged with stopping this type of criminal activity couldn't find the crime, the people at the FBI certainly wouldn't take my charges seriously. And even if they did, it was very doubtful they would understand it. By 2004 the FBI's focus was on catching terrorists, and it had been busy transferring agents from white-collar fraud to counterterrorism units.

During the years we continued working on this case, several huge Wall Street crimes had been uncovered. Among them, Tyco's CEO Dennis Kozlowski supposedly had taken more than $400 million in unauthorized bonuses from his company and used some of that money to buy $700 office garbage pails and throw a multimillion-dollar Roman-orgy-themed birthday party in Sardinia for his wife's 40th birthday; Enron's Ken Lay and Jeff Skilling had bankrupted that company and defrauded millions of energy consumers of billions of dollars; and WorldCom's Bernie Ebbers had been convicted of using phony accounting to defraud investors of as much as $11 billion. As each of these crimes made headlines, law enforcement and other people on Wall Street made somber statements about how they were taking steps to make sure that kind of fraud couldn't happen again, and what they were doing to protect investors. There was nothing we could do but laugh at them. I had told them about an ongoing crime that dwarfed the rest of them, a fraud that would directly affect more lives than any of the others, and they just didn't care. So we just kept going. The situation was crazy and we knew it, and we made a lot of jokes about it because there was simply nothing else we could do.

We were actively tracking 20 feeder funds that we knew had Bernie. We spoke on the phone from time to time, but communicated mostly by e-mail. I still hadn't even met Mike Ocrant. Neil, in particular, was in a much better position at Benchmark Plus to gather information than he had been at Rampart. Shortly after Frank had been hired by Benchmark, we had lunch in Manalapan with Scott Franzblau, a Benchmark partner and the head of marketing. I assumed that Manalapan was an Indian word for cornfields and cows, because that's all that surrounded Benchmark's office. The nearest place to eat was a golf club more than a mile down the road, and we had lunch there.

It's probable that Frank had already warned Scott about Madoff, because Scott already knew that he was a fraud. I remember him shaking his head in disbelief as we went through some of our evidence. He got it. After that he continued to be supportive of Frank's—and later Neil's—efforts to gather additional evidence against Madoff. He knew Bernie was polluting his pool, and he wanted him out. I like to think Scott was typical of managers in the industry in this regard, but I'm not certain that's so. Unfortunately, there were too few bosses like Scott encouraging their employees to do the right thing. Too many others discovered that Madoff was a fraud and kept that information to themselves.

In his position at Benchmark, Neil met and spoke to literally thousands of managers working at hundreds of different funds, among them Fairfield Greenwich and Oppenheimer's mutual fund, Tremont, which we later learned had invested $3.3 billion with Madoff. Because Neil had hundreds of millions of dollars to distribute, these funds were happy to open their kimonos for him, giving him more access to information than we had ever gotten before. He was collecting year-end financial statements and copies of model portfolios; these managers were thrilled to answer every question he asked. Because Neil had the mathematical background that Frank lacked, he was able to gather far more detailed information than we'd ever gotten before.

Because I had left the industry, I was no longer able to gather information. Instead I would regularly collect all the new material sent to me by Frank, Neil, and Mike, then spend hours in my office integrating it with what we already had. I was analyzing everything, writing the reports, and, finally, contacting the government. By choice, I was the point man, the only one visible to the enemy—or enemies. I'd long ago given up any hope of ever earning any money from this work—we all had—but it had to be done and we were doing it. If we didn't do it, who would? Way back in 2000, I'd thought we had more than enough to nail Madoff, but since that time we had uncovered so much more information.

As a result of hundreds of conversations, pouring through thousands of pages of documents, and even my trip to Europe, we had identified more than 17 new red flags since that first submission. Probably the most glaring was the fact that Madoff was voluntarily giving up huge profits. Nobody any of us ever knew in the industry voluntarily left money on the table—except for Bernie. Had Madoff been operating as a hedge fund, he would have been charging 1 percent management fees and 20 percent of the profit, which in his case would have been about 4 percent annually on the amount of assets he managed. Instead he was supposedly happy receiving only commissions for the trading he claimed he had conducted. He was earning less than the funds that were doing nothing but handing him money. That made no sense. Who knew Bernie was such a giving soul? But it turned out that was the core of his scheme. By giving the funds the lion's share of the fees, he got them to continue raising money for him. The nice way of describing it is that he was overcompensating them; the less nice way is that he bought their souls.

Although, this being Wall Street, you have to question the assumption that they had souls.

In fact, when we examined the financial structure of his operation, there seemed to be no logical reason for him to be in business. Running his fund actually was costing him a fortune, in addition to the immense time and effort it required to keep it going. Bernie needed money to invest. Assuming the profits he returned to his investors were his cost of getting that money, it would have been substantially less expensive for him simply to borrow the money from short-term credit markets.

This red flag would have been waving in the face of anyone with a financial background or enough fingers and toes to figure out the difference between the average 12 percent annual return investors received and the smaller interest rate at which Bernie could have borrowed the money. Why would a sane person go to all the trouble of running a complicated business that actually cost him money? Particularly considering the fact that he was already running a major business, his broker-dealer arm.

Then there was the super-duper secret oath that he supposedly made all his clients adhere to. This was perhaps the only successful business in history that not only rejected all publicity, but in fact warned clients that if they revealed any information about their investment with Madoff they risked having their money returned. They would be thrown out of the money club! In an industry where the huge funds boasted about their size as a way of attracting new clients, this was not only unusual; it was absurd. It made no sense at all.

I also had kept a list of the various explanations for these and other generally inexplicable problems that we had gotten from the feeder fund managers. This included the claim that he subsidized the down months from his broker-dealer arm to keep his investors satisfied and that he had perfect market timing ability. Conversely, it was obvious, at least in my opinion, that the largest investment firms either knew or suspected that Madoff was a fraud. None of them—Merrill Lynch, Citigroup, Morgan Stanley—had invested with him. In fact, a managing director at Goldman Sachs's brokerage operation admitted to me that they didn't believe Madoff's returns were legitimate, so they had decided not to do business with him.

■ ■ ■

The only person at the SEC that I had continued to speak with regularly was Ed Manion. Ed was embarrassed about the agency. He knew what I had and he also knew there was very little he could do to help me, although he continually asked for updates and urged me to keep going. Early in 2005 he began pushing me to put all the material together and make another submission. Grant Ward had been replaced as director of enforcement by David Bergers. A new branch chief, a man named Mike Garrity, had come on board. "You'll like him," Ed said. "He's really smart and he's trying to change things around here." After all we'd been through with the SEC, I wasn't as confident. But after a while Ed began to wear me down. "Try it one more time," he said. "C'mon, Harry, one more time. It'll be different this time. Garrity'll listen to you."

One more time. Putting in all the work that would be required didn't concern me, but the possibility—no, the probability—that the SEC would ignore us once again was really holding me back. The thought of gearing all the way up only to be shot all the way down was just too depressing for me.

It was in June that we got the very first hint that Madoff was in trouble. Frank was having lunch with a Benchmark Plus client, an Italian who ran an F3, a fund of funds of hedge funds. An F-cubed meant that investors were paying three levels of fees, but a lot of them believed it gave them increased stability. At some point during this lunch, Frank asked the same question that by now he'd asked five hundred times: "What do you know about Bernie?"

This time he got a very different answer. "Oh, Bernie," the client said, waving his hands in disgust. "They're saying in Europe that he's been looking to take loans from banks." He mentioned one bank that had actually refused to give him a credit line.

"That's strange," Frank responded. "Why would he need money? He's got $30 billion from his clients. What does he need the banks for?"

The Italian had more news. "The banks have pulled him from their approved list." He explained that two major international banks, the Royal Bank of Canada and Société Générale, were no longer lending money to their clients to invest with Madoff. "So he's out looking for money."

"I don't get it," Frank said, getting it. "I thought he was closed. Supposedly he isn't taking any new money."

"I don't know," the Italian said, clearly knowing. "But he's getting aggressive. He needs money." The Italian also mentioned that Bernie's returns had decreased. When we had first looked at Broyhill's numbers (discussed in Chapter 2), he was producing 19 percent net returns, but those had dropped steadily over the years.

"Who knows?"

Frank knew. And when he sent me an e-mail relating this conversation, I knew. Bernie was in trouble. He was having difficulty raising new money to feed the beast. The worldwide economy was slowing down, and he was beginning to feel it. I knew it was only a matter of time now before he collapsed completely. To me, that meant that like any cornered animal he was more dangerous than ever. He would do anything necessary to survive. So it made sense for me to do whatever I could to bring him down as quickly as possible—even if it meant going back to the SEC.

Finally, and reluctantly, I told Ed to set up a meeting with Garrity. It was scheduled for late October 2005. In preparation I began working on the submission that would accompany my presentation. I remembered that in August 2001 the Bush administration had successfully avoided paying any attention to an intelligence briefing entitled "Bin Laden Determined to Strike in U.S." I hoped that the government had learned at least some lesson from that failure, so to make sure anyone reading my submission would know exactly what it contained, I titled it subtly "The World's Largest Hedge Fund Is a Fraud."

"The World's Largest Hedge Fund Is a Fraud." That was a pretty brash statement. I hoped it would make *someone* at the SEC besides Ed Manion pay attention.

For my protection, my name appeared nowhere in the report. So I had to establish my credentials. "I am the original source for the information presented herein . . ." my submission began. After outlining the way I gathered the information, I outlined my qualifications: "I am a derivatives expert and have traded or assisted in the trading of several billion $US in option strategies for hedge funds and institutional clients. I have experience managing split-strike conversion products both using index options and using individual stock options, both with and without index puts. Very few people in the world have the mathematical background needed to manage these types of products but I am one of them. . . ."

And then I explained my fears. "As a result of this case, several careers on Wall Street and in Europe will be ruined. Therefore, I have not signed or put my name on this report. I request that my name not be released to anyone outside this SEC region without my express written permission. The fewer people who know who wrote this report the better. I am worried about the personal safety of myself and my family. . . ."

And then over the next 15 pages, plus several attachments, I made my case. I described Madoff as "effectively the world's largest hedge fund" but admitted no one knew how much money he was managing. I estimated it as somewhere between $20 billion to $50 billion, adding that "we don't even know the size of the hedge fund industry so none of this should be surprising." Then, I described 30 red flags, any one of which should have raised suspicion, but taken together they made it clear Madoff was a fraud. While I had no doubt it was a Ponzi scheme,

Frank and Mike still were not entirely convinced he wasn't front-running, so I did mention both possibilities, although I pointed out, "If BM was front-running, a highly profitable activity, then he wouldn't need to borrow funds from investors at 12 percent implied interest. Therefore it is far more likely that BM is a Ponzi scheme. . . . The elaborateness of BM's fund-raising, his need for secrecy, his high 12 percent average cost of funds, and reliance on a derivatives investment scheme that few investors (or regulators) would be capable of comprehending lead to a weight of the evidence conclusion that this is a Ponzi scheme."

I went through a lot of mathematical data, trying to simplify it wherever possible, but understanding did require at least a basic comprehension of the way the market functions. Red Flag #5, for example, read as follows: "Assuming BM bought 3 month out-of-the-money OEX put options that are 3% out-of-the-money, and that he paid 3% for them, then the market would have to drop 6% in order for his investors to recoup their cost on the puts. More importantly, the individual stock call options sold against each stock holding would not earn enough of a return to offset losses in the stocks during periods of significant market decline. Yet BM had only ONE MONTHLY LOSS OF 6 BASIS POINTS during 1997's Asian Currency Crises, the 1998 Russian and LTCM Crises and the market blood bath of 2000–2002. According to Fairfield Sentry Limited's return data (attachment 1) BM posted a −0.06% loss in August 2002. These return numbers are too good to be true! And, in my experience, whenever a hedge fund has posted returns that are too good to be true they've turned out not to be true."

I finished this report with a series of predictions about what would happen *if* Madoff was a Ponzi scheme. "Congress will be up in arms," I wrote, "and there will be Senate and House hearings. . . ."

And then I outlined the financial version of *A Christmas Carol*, pointing out to them the good things that might happen for the SEC if it took action: "The SEC will gain political strength in Washington from this episode but only if the SEC is proactive and launches an immediate, full-scale investigation into all of the Red Flags surrounding Madoff Investment Securities, L.L.C.," but also warning what could happen if it didn't: "Otherwise it is almost certain that NYAG Eliot Spitzer will launch his investigation first and once again beat the SEC to the punch, causing the SEC further public embarrassment."

Boston SEC Branch Chief Mike Garrity didn't understand the numbers, but unlike so many of the other people I'd met at that agency, he knew it and was willing to admit it. Most important, he wanted to learn. That was surprising. I met with Garrity and several other people in an SEC office on October 25. Garrity was a former journalist and an attorney, so he knew how to ask questions and the legal consequences of the answers. He'd read my report, he said, and thought it was very credible. He had hours' worth of questions to ask. There was a whiteboard in the front of the meeting room, and when there was something he didn't understand he had me outline it on the board until he got it. I spent hours drawing charts and diagrams and guiding him through the mathematics. A lot of it was high school algebra and trigonometry, basic math. I worked from an x-axis and y-axis, explaining complex calculations in simple layman's terms. When we know the market goes both up and down, it wasn't that difficult for him to look at a performance line rising at a 45-degree angle and understand that something was very wrong. He wouldn't let me sit down until he was confident he understood the point I was making. He asked endless questions: What are the stocks doing? What should the stocks be doing? What can't they be doing? What are the options doing? How are they affecting the portfolio's returns? At one point he and I discussed the possibility that I was totally wrong. "You've got two fraud theories," he asked. "What if his returns are real? Is there any possible explanation for that?"

Actually there was one conceivable explanation, I said, and unfortunately I'd left it out of my submission. "The only way these returns are real is that Bernie Madoff is an alien from outer space who has perfect foreknowledge of what the capital markets are about to do."

Mike Garrity considered that in the spirit in which I'd proposed it. If I was right, he suggested, and Madoff is an alien, it would destabilize the U.S. financial industry. "Investors don't want to have to trade against aliens," he pointed out.

"No, that wouldn't be fair," I agreed, laughing, pleased with the knowledge that Garrity was deeply suspicious about Madoff's reported returns.

By the time we finished that meeting, Garrity not only understood the math, he understood the threat that Madoff posed to the world economy. He explained that he would immediately begin an investigation and would respond to me as quickly as possible. I left that meeting more excited than I had ever thought possible. I thought Garrity was smart, tenacious, and talented. And he got it. He called me less than a week later. "Harry, I've investigated," he said. "I've found some serious irregularities that are very disturbing. I'm not at liberty to share them with you, but I think it's so serious that I need to put you in touch with our New York regional office.

"If this was taking place in our jurisdiction I'd have teams in there tomorrow tearing the place apart. Unfortunately, it's not. It's in New York, and I have to tell you we don't have a great relationship with that office."

He promised me he would do as much as he could before passing it along to New York. He gave me the names of the two people he would be contacting. The only thing that I asked for in return was that my identity be protected. I said, "I want only two people in New York to know who I am, the branch chief and the investigation's team leader. Just forward the submission to them and tell them it came from the Boston whistleblower. I'll call one of them and identify myself as the Boston whistleblower and reveal my identity to them. But really, I want only those two people to know my name." I assumed that based on Garrity's recommendation New York would finally send in investigators, and I wanted the people on the ground to be able to ask me questions. If possible, I would have liked to prep the team before they went in to make sure they asked the right questions and demanded the right documents. Garrity gave me his word he would do the best he could to make that happen.

As I learned later, the regional administrator of the Boston office, Walter Ricciardi, wanted to keep this case for himself. He knew what it was; he knew it was potentially a career maker. He wrestled with the decision to turn it over to New York. He felt it was the strongest case he'd seen in his entire career. But as he told the SEC's inspector general, he had spent his career preaching cooperation between the different regions, and it was up to him to take a leadership role in making that happen. He knew that if he turned over to New York a case that would generate headlines and promotions, everyone would know how serious he was about regional cooperation. I knew that if Boston had kept the case they would have investigated thoroughly and I would have been right there to advise them.

The last thing any of us expected was that the New York office would take the evidence and basically bury it. In retrospect, I don't know why I was surprised. Expecting the New York office to respond any differently than it had in the past was sort of like handing the Three Stooges a rubber mallet and expecting them not to hit each other over the head with it.

Ironically, two days after my initial presentation, Ricciardi was appointed a deputy director of the SEC's Division of Enforcement in Washington. In that position, his job was to "assist in planning and directing the Commission's investigations and other enforcement efforts." He was the right guy in the perfect position. I'm not certain I ever told Neil or Frank that we finally had Bernie, but that's what I was thinking. His empire was tottering financially and I was confident the SEC was about to launch an investigation. There was no way he could remain standing after this barrage.

Ah, that was just me being an optimist again.

The two names Garrity gave me were New York Branch Chief Meaghan Cheung and Assistant Director Doria Bachenheimer. I had never heard either name before. Meaghan Cheung was the New York equivalent of Mike Garrity, but as it turned out that was in title only. As Garrity had suggested, in early November I called Meaghan Cheung and identified myself as the Boston whistleblower. I guess I expected some kind of reaction from her, even something as obvious as "I read your report and I have a couple of questions."

Instead, the most she would acknowledge was that she had read the report. She didn't ask me a single question about it. Not one. The strongest impression that I got from her was that I was bothering her. There was no excitement, no enthusiasm, no recognition that I had just put in her hands the biggest case she would ever have in her career. I had to draw every sentence out of her. When I asked her if she had any questions about my report or if there was anything in it she didn't understand, she acted as if I were insulting her intelligence. I remember asking her, "Well, do you understand derivatives?"

She responded, as if answering my question, "I did the Adelphia case."

When I pointed out that the Adelphia case was basically a $3 billion accounting fraud case, a case in which executives cooked the books to loot the company for their personal use, and that this was many times bigger and substantially more complicated, she seemed offended. I told her that a derivatives fraud required a much higher level of financial sophistication than an accounting fraud. It wasn't necessary for her to understand derivatives, she said, telling me that the SEC's Office of Economic Analysis in Washington, D.C., was staffed with PhD's who were capable of understanding derivatives.

When this conversation began I was hoping we would have a collaborative relationship; instead it was turning confrontational. I explained to her that the formulas used by PhD's in academia were completely different from those used in the industry. I wasn't trying to be insulting; I was just trying to explain to her that the math was different and the way it was used in practice was very different than in academic institutions. I spent the previous decade of my career taking these financial instruments apart backward and forward. I'd done it so often I could do it in my sleep. Those people working in her Office of Economic Analysis just wouldn't have that experience.

The point I was trying to make was that I could help her; the point she was trying to make was that she didn't want my help. That was the way our relationship progressed. Over the next few months I would call her or e-mail her from time to time. She would always take my call, but she never initiated a conversation or followed up a discussion. She seemed totally disinterested in speaking with me. No matter what questions I asked, she remained noncommittal. "What's the status of the investigation?"

"I can't tell you."

"Has it gone to a formal investigation yet?"—meaning that the SEC has decided to issue subpoenas to get the information it needs.

"No."

"Can you tell me anything about what's going on?"

"No."

"Is there anything you need from me?"

"If we do, we'll call you."

I tried everything I could think of to convince her to investigate Madoff. I told her that I had a list of 47 respected professionals in the industry who would speak with her if she called and every one of them could confirm everything I said. Among the people on that list were

Citibank's head of global equity derivatives research, Leon Gross; Bud Haslet, who was the chief option strategist at Miller Tabak Securities; and Mike Ocrant. As far as I know, she never called anyone.

Poor Ed Manion. He was the really good guy through all of this. At least once a week I'd call him and let all my frustration out on him. "Your agency sucks!" I told him. "Your people are beyond incompetent. I don't think they're capable of catching a cold in the winter. I can't even believe some of these people get dressed by themselves in the morning. I mean, most of your staff barely respond to heat and light.

"Believe me, Ed, this Meaghan Cheung is no Mike Garrity. I'm handing her the biggest case of her life and she treats me like I'm bothering her. There's no way she's the slightest bit interested in this case. I'm telling you, the next question she asks'll be the first one. What kind of agency are you people running?"

Ed felt as terrible about it as I did, but there was nothing he could do about it. He reminded me that Boston and New York had a competitive relationship. If a referral came to New York from Boston, the New Yorkers were more likely to think Boston was trying to dump a crap case on them rather than respecting policy. Probably the last thing they believed was that Boston had a career-making case and was handing it over because it was the right thing to do. It was like the Red Sox trading Babe Ruth to the Yankees.

I was furious with Meaghan Cheung, but I understood that none of this was really her fault. She was simply a product of the system. She had all the training that the SEC required; she had all the resources that were available to someone on her level; and it wasn't nearly enough. The SEC's capital markets work experience requirements were way too low, the exam quality standards were abysmally low, and that started at a level much higher than Meaghan Cheung. As an employee she was no better and no worse than most employees of the agency. In fact, we later found out that none of these people, Cheung, Bachenheimer, or their assistant, enforcement attorney Simona Suh, had ever investigated a Ponzi scheme. They wouldn't have known what to look for, and as part of the bureaucracy they didn't want to look unqualified or unprepared by asking someone like me for assistance. It's the Ed Manions and Mike Garritys who are the exceptions, whereas she was typical.

While this was going on, Cheung and the other executives in her office spent their time investigating minor frauds and getting an occasional conviction and headline. They were going after the fleas instead of the elephant, which is what they had been trained to do, and there was no incentive for them to do anything beyond that. In the world of the SEC, a case is a case, and going after a hard target like Madoff counts the same as going after some tiny retail broker. There are no bonuses for doing the big cases that require a tremendous amount of work; in fact, that may create problems because those big guys, the sacred cows, are often major political donors. I was told by a government agency, for example, that at some point New York Senator Chuck Schumer called the SEC to inquire about the Madoff investigation. There is absolutely no evidence of any wrongdoing on Schumer's part at all, zero, and no suggestion that there was any intent on his part to interfere. Senator Schumer apparently made the call on behalf of his constituents. The problem is that the SEC is funded by Congress, so its employees are particularly sensitive to congressional inquiries. So for a middle-level SEC employee with ambitions, any case in which an important politician is involved is a case he or she wants to stay far away from. It's a lot safer to go after small potatoes.

As the weeks passed, it became obvious to me not only that Cheung wasn't going to do anything to stop Madoff, but that she didn't seem to appreciate the danger I was in. What was really frightening to me was the fact that she knew my identity. It was clear to me that she was incompetent for this type of case. It was possible she was corrupt—although I had no evidence of that, but it would not have surprised me if she was also careless enough to allow my name to get out. The more I considered the potential danger, the more anxious I got. I began wondering if I had raised my head too much. It seemed like every time we peeled another layer of the onion it became a little more frightening because we found another layer. From the large but local fraud we originally discovered this had grown paper by paper into a massive international scheme spread across several continents and involving the rich, European royalty, and probably some of the most dangerous men in the world.

I was boxed in: I was trying to alert the government about how big this thing was, but because it was so big the government refused to take me seriously. Basically, their attitude was nothing could be that big without being discovered, so they wouldn't take the actions necessary to discover it. To the SEC, I suspect, I was simply crying wolf, and it seemed like every time they ignored me that wolf got bigger, which made it less likely there actually was a wolf.

The fear was growing inside me. I'd experienced something like it before. In September 1985 the army had sent my National Guard infantry brigade's command group to Germany for training and we had been targeted by the Red Army Faction terrorist group then waging a bombing campaign in Frankfurt. We'd been put through a pretty good training course that taught us how to protect ourselves, which included checking vehicles for bombs and what to do if we were taken hostage. The enemy then had been a well-organized terrorist cell that had prepared a hit list; they were gunning for us. But this was different. This time the enemy was a grandfatherly philanthropist, the most respected man in his community, perhaps the very last person anyone would suspect of violence. But we already knew that his reputation was his disguise, and that in fact he was a world-class criminal. What nobody could predict was how far he would go to protect himself—and what the consequences would be to anyone in his path. If it did reach that point, I was nothing more than an inconvenience to him.

■ ■ ■

Looking over my shoulder when I walked down the street or checking underneath the chassis and in the wheel wells of my car before I turned the key no longer seemed like enough protection. I had started carrying an airweight Model 642 Smith and Wesson everywhere I went. Finally I decided it was time to get some outside help.

I knew the only people I could depend on to be there for me and my family 24 hours a day were the officers of the Whitman, Massachusetts, police department. I trusted my local police department far more than any federal agency. I'd spent years being disappointed by the federal government. To the Massachusetts state police, or even the Plymouth County sheriff's department, I was simply another citizen living in their jurisdiction. That left the local cops, whose station was only a few blocks from my house.

Whitman is a typical New England small town, with a population under 15,000. We have a long history and a small town center, which has always been a good place for neighbors to meet. Some of our houses date to before the Revolution, and it's possible to determine on which side of that fight the residents were by looking at their chimneys— loyalists to the crown had a black stripe around the top, which in some cases is still there. Later Whitman became the home of Toll House cookies. Faith and I had lived there happily for almost seven years, but suddenly I began to see the most familiar places in a different kind of way. Would that corner be a good place for an ambush? Or who was that person sitting across from us having a slice of pizza in the Venus? It was odd; Bernie Madoff had become a central figure in my life—and my fervent hope was that he didn't even know I existed.

Whitman measures only 6.97 square miles, meaning it would take a police car about a minute to get to my house from anywhere in the town. And no one cares about the citizens of the town of Whitman more than our local police department.

When Faith and I had moved to Whitman, I had gone to the local precinct to apply for a firearms permit. I had met Sergeant Harry Bates that day and since then I had often seen him around our town center. It was always pleasant, always calm, so when I came barging into his office one afternoon pale as a ghost, sweating profusely, he knew that whatever was bothering me was serious. "I need to talk to you," I told him, "in your office."

Truthfully I don't remember exactly what it was that had set off my panic button. It might have been something as simple as a hang-up call or a car that stopped in front of my house and sat there too long. Maybe it was something I read, a seemingly innocent comment somebody made, or two pieces of information that didn't fit together easily. But whatever it was, it pushed all my buttons. I realized suddenly that I had to make sure somebody was going to come running when I yelled for help. Somebody with firepower.

Harry Bates settled comfortably into his chair. "What's going on, Harry?"

I laid out the broad strokes for him. Basically, I told him I had uncovered a multibillion-dollar Ponzi scheme that was global and the biggest fraud in history and I was afraid people might try to kill me to shut me up. While he didn't know what a Ponzi scheme was, he certainly understood billions of dollars.

"What do you want us to do?" he asked. "Where do you want me to take this?"

"You have to keep this very quiet," I explained. "If you put this in the precinct log and the newspapers pick it up, my life is going to be in jeopardy. If you talk about it and the word gets out, my life is going to be in jeopardy." It took a little while for Sergeant Bates to understand I was deadly serious about this, but to his credit he began working with me to set up the safest possible situation. We agreed on a simple plan. He knew if I called for help he had to come running with the whole cavalry. He knew if my home alarm went off it wasn't a going to be a false alarm.

Then he asked me, "You carrying?" We talked about guns for a while. Obviously he knew I had a license; he'd filled out the forms. I told him that I was now carrying a weapon with me wherever I went. I'd opted for a lightweight gun, I said. I felt it was better to have a weapon I could fire rapidly than something with massive stopping power. He reviewed the state gun control laws, particularly what was permitted in public. Massachusetts has tough regulations and he didn't want me to have any problems.

Then he asked me if I wanted to wear body armor. I had thought about it. The army had taught me there were three things you had to be able to do to protect yourself: shoot, move, and communicate. I certainly was trying to communicate; I had been trained pretty well to handle the shooting part; that left mobility—which was why I decided not to wear a bullet-proof vest. I actually tried on several different types, but all of them restricted my movement. If Madoff wanted to kill me he was going to use professionals, and that meant a double-tap with two bullets to the back of my head. In that situation a bullet-proof vest wasn't going to be any help. I knew that my only hope in that situation was to survive the initial attempt, fire as many shots as quickly as I could, and either get out of there or get help. There were no good options.

By the time I walked out of Sergeant Bates's office I had calmed down. His confidence had been somewhat reassuring. I knew that if anything happened to me, my family would be protected.

But in addition to meeting with him, I took several additional precautions to make sure I was never put in that situation. I upgraded the alarm system in and around my home, including pick-proof locks. I began altering the routes I traveled to get home at night. I never drove more than a couple of blocks without checking continually in my rearview mirror. In addition, Faith got her handgun license and took lessons in properly handling a weapon—and firing it to hit the target. Eventually she became an excellent shot. We kept guns safely locked up in the house, but always within quick and easy reach.

By nature I'm a cautious person. I am actually one of those strange people who will stand on a street corner waiting for the walk sign, even if I don't see a car coming. In this situation I was taking every possible precaution to stay alive. There was no way of knowing if, or when, Madoff would figure me out. And finally I made a decision. If he contacted me and threatened me, I was going to drive down to New York and take him out. At that point it would have come down to him or me; it was as simple as that. The government would have forced me into it by failing to do its job, and failing to protect me. In that situation I felt I had no other options. I was going to kill him.

Chapter 6

Didn't Anyone Want a Pulitzer?

My father was a tough man. For a while he owned two diners and two bar-lounges in Erie, Pennsylvania. He also owned the storefront next to the New York Lunch, as one of the diners was named. He had rented that space to a motorcycle repair shop, which, naturally, became the hangout for the local chapter of the Hell's Angels. I was in that restaurant one afternoon when my father threw a biker out of the place for causing some kind of problem. A few minutes later the biker came back, tearing through the front door on his Harley, and started doing circles in the middle of the restaurant.

I remember people scrambling to get out of the way, but my father didn't hesitate. He came running out from behind the counter and knocked him off his bike, then started fighting him. He didn't care that this guy had a gang backing him up. He was just protecting his livelihood, protecting his family. The fight ended when the short-order cook, Rusty, called the police, ran into the back room and came out pointing a double-barreled shotgun at the biker. A 12-gauge ends a lot of arguments.

I never saw my father back down. I saw him challenge customers who tried to walk out of his place with silverware. I remember him coming home from one of the bars some nights with his face swollen and his knuckles bloody because he'd had to throw a drunk out. I had learned right and wrong from him and that whatever the cost I was supposed to fight the bad guys. So for as long as possible I would continue to fight Madoff with documents, but now I was aware it could get much more dangerous.

■ ■ ■

In my head, I had worked out my plan to go to New York and kill him if he threatened me. I didn't tell anyone about it; I certainly didn't tell Faith or Frank or Neil. I didn't want to make any of them an accessory to murder. I knew how they would respond if I told them. At first they wouldn't believe me: Harry? Kill someone? Forget it, it isn't going to happen. But when they realized I was serious, they would try desperately to talk me out of it.

I wasn't interested in those conversations. I knew how crazy my plan sounded, but I also knew it was my life and my family's lives that were in jeopardy.

We had been pursuing Bernie Madoff for almost five years, and the cost of this fight was continuing to rise. Five years earlier I had been in comfortable control of my life. I was earning a reasonable salary working on the equity derivatives desk of a respectable firm, and if it wasn't particularly exciting most of the time, at least it was interesting. Then Frank Casey dropped Bernie Madoff into my life. I'd ended up leaving that company, in fact leaving the entire industry, because of that, and here I was working in an attic office, never leaving my house without being armed, and always being careful to avoid shady areas. I hadn't earned a paycheck in more than a year, and I was forced to watch helplessly as Madoff continued to steal billions more dollars and the people who could stop him instead treated me as their enemy.

Only the fact that I was part of a team made it tolerable. Frank Casey, Neil Chelo, and Mike Ocrant continued to gather information and feed it to me, and whenever we heard something new or got hold of a Madoff document, a flurry of angry, funny, sarcastic, ironic, and occasionally bitter e-mails would circulate among us. Early in 2006, for example, Neil finally found a former employee of Madoff who was willing to talk. This man had worked for Madoff for three years in the mid-1990s and was currently at a hedge fund. Neil certainly gave him no indication he was investigating; it was normal business chitchat. This man was pretty open with Neil about Bernie. He had no reason not to be—he believed Bernie's operation was honest. But he had worked on the 19th floor as a proprietary trader in the brokerage, and had little knowledge about the hedge fund. He'd left on very good terms, convinced that Bernie was "the real deal," although he admitted that having knowledge of the order book was a big moneymaker. He never saw any of the options transactions, he told Neil, but that didn't bother him. Bernie and his sons were "brilliant and hardworking," he told Neil. As Neil concluded his e-mail to me, "He believes in Bernie."

This type of communication between us was very common and because of that, I never felt like I was in it alone. In addition to the three of them, I also had come to rely on a man named Pat Burns for advice. Pat Burns was the director of communications for Taxpayers Against Fraud, a whistleblower organization in Washington, D.C., and had seen this kind of insanity up close several times before.

Being a whistleblower is extraordinarily lonely, and eventually I had begun searching for other people in a similar circumstance, people who understood what I was going through and who shared my fears. I had found Pat Burns's organization through an Internet search. I called him and introduced myself, explaining that I had several good cases and I was interested in learning more about the bounty programs.

I was exploring a new world, a world in which people took great risks to expose corruption, and Pat Burns became my guide. We spoke on the phone often and traded e-mails, but it was actually more than a year before we met in person. Pat is tall and balding and, like me, has a broad sense of humor and a visceral dislike for bad guys. He hates to see them win as much as I do. And in the sometimes chaotic world of whistleblowers he was the steady hand. I think it's accurate to say that he knows more about white-collar fraud in the United States than any man in history. He knows how lawyers and lobbyists work to protect their clients and what can happen to whistleblowers, both the bad and the good. He told me right from the beginning that there was considerably more bad than good, that few whistleblowers ever win and go on to live happily ever after. He's seen lives destroyed. But beyond answering my questions and helping me navigate through these unfamiliar waters, his presence served as a constant reminder that I wasn't hanging out there alone.

Eventually I had told Pat everything about our Madoff investigation. I sent him the 2005 submission with the instructions, "If anything should happen to me you've got a green light to go to the media immediately. Give the story to anybody who'll print it."

He told me that there was an annual conference of whistleblower attorneys and fraud investigators—like me—who met to exchange information and receive updates on new case law. Eventually I went to my first conference and I began learning about the False Claims Act, the law that hopefully would allow me to eventually earn a living. The False Claims Act is the statute that allows anyone to bring legal action against contractors who are cheating the federal government. If the government agrees to prosecute, under the *qui tam* provision the person filing the case is entitled to a reward that is usually between 15 and 25 percent. *Qui tam* is a Latin phrase meaning that person "who brings forth a case on behalf of our lord the King, and for himself." There are "relators," as the person who finds the case and brings it to the government is known, who have earned many millions of dollars.

The False Claims Act was originally passed by Congress in 1863 to reward people for warning the Union government about dishonest suppliers who were selling them sick horses and mules, spoiled food, and faulty weapons. It became known as the False Claims Act because it was intended to stop people from submitting false claims for government payment, but it also covered several other areas of fraud against the government. It has been strengthened several times since its original passage and is the primary tool used by whistleblowers. The federal government has recovered more than $25 billion in the past two decades. The government accepts only between 15 and 20 percent of the best cases submitted for intervention and, hopefully, a reward. Through Pat Burns I was to become very familiar with all the provisions of this act. I had to; my future depended on it.

Obviously Madoff didn't fit under this provision (he was cheating everybody *except* the government), but Pat Burns certainly took an interest in the case. He understood immediately the risks that I was taking. I had seen enough movies in which people are in jeopardy because they have some information that someone wants to keep private, and I would sit there in the audience wondering why the person in jeopardy didn't simply tell a reporter and get the story published. Once it was published, theoretically at least his life would be saved because the secret would be out and the spotlight would be on the bad guy. That strategy had always made sense to me, but in May 2001 two stories had been published by respected magazines within the span of six days, and it hadn't done any good at all. For some reason I just couldn't figure out, journalists didn't seem to understand the magnitude of this story. Through the years Mike Ocrant had been approached several times by journalists from various publications who were interested in pursuing the story. But mostly they wanted him to hand it to them. Mike, who had left journalism in 2003, had continued to urge other reporters to pursue the story. Any diligent financial reporter should have been able to use the information already made public as a foundation for their own investigation. But finding a news peg, something new that would excite editors, remained elusive.

In late 2005 a reporter from the hedge fund magazine *Absolute Return*, another publication owned by the company that would later acquire the parent company of *MARHedge*, got hold of a copy of my 2005 Securities and Exchange Commission (SEC) submission. Ironically, Mike had gone to work at the company, Institutional Investor, after leaving *MARHedge*. Mike hadn't given it to him, and he was reluctant to ask this reporter about his source. We had all agreed that we would keep the identities of everyone—except mine—secret. There is no reason to believe that reporter knew that Mike and I were working together, and Mike didn't even want to hint at it.

The reporter had come to Mike because he had written the original Madoff piece and was wondering if there was a new way to approach it. "He's looking for a new angle," Mike told me. "He wants to do another piece, but he needs something to make it newsworthy. He says that a lot of the stuff in the submission has already been reported, and what's new isn't a game changer. Is there anything else we should give them?" It was not news that Madoff was managing a lot of money, the reporter had told Mike, and the new red flags in the submission were certainly more detailed than Ocrant had written almost five years earlier, but mostly these things had already been reported.

Sometimes I wondered what world these people were living in. Didn't anyone want to win a Pulitzer Prize?

The team batted around some ideas that might convince them to do the story. We had heard a rumor, literally nothing more than a rumor and I don't remember the source, that based on my submission the SEC had opened an informal inquiry. That was considerably less than a formal investigation, but it was more than twiddling their thumbs and singing "Home on the Range." Mike finally told the reporter, "I've been told, but I can't tell you my source, that the SEC has opened up an informal inquiry. If you can get somebody to confirm that, that's probably a pretty good angle."

Apparently the SEC refused to confirm that information. Without this new peg, the reporter went to look for a story that would be more pertinent for the magazine's hedge fund readership.

By this time I don't think I was capable of being surprised or disappointed by anything that happened in this investigation. Ocrant and *Barron's* reporter Erin Arvedlund had done their job in 2001—they'd exposed Madoff. So I understood the way journalists were thinking now; if nobody had been outraged by those stories, they needed much stronger ammunition before going after Madoff. What was so obvious to me and my team was obviously confusing to the media.

It was Pat Burns who convinced me not to give up on the media. "Go public and finish this guy," he said. "If investors read the story, he's going to collapse and he's going to end up behind bars. Once he's behind bars you're safe."

Pat is an arranger; he has tremendous contacts throughout the entire financial industry and enjoys bringing people together for their common benefit. So not only did he urge me to go public, but he also introduced me to John Wilke, an investigative reporter at the *Wall Street Journal* whom he greatly respected. "This is the guy," he told me. "This is the guy."

Pat Burns made the initial contact with Wilke. In preparation for that I sent him a one-page memo suggesting a three-part package for the *Journal*, which that paper could promote as "the largest hedge fund blowup since that of Long-Term Capital Management in August–October 1998. And, in reality, since it will likely involve hundreds of billions in selling pressure, the losses to investors will be akin to the largest company in the S&P 500, General Electric (with a market capitalization of $373 billion) suddenly collapsing." I sat in my office late into the night, and as I wrote this I could almost feel the hope igniting inside me again. I included everything I could think of to make this reporter understand how important this story would be. "Therefore," I wrote, believing completely that this was true, "this is a much bigger story than the falls of Enron and WorldCom, and truly is the biggest finance story since LTCM's demise that almost led to a systemic collapse of the world's financial system."

What reporter could resist that pitch?

There were actually three stories in this package, I pointed out to Pat. The first one would require "calling the senior equity derivatives folks on Wall Street for their opinion on BM's strategy. . . . An earthquake will soon follow."

The second story would be tracking the complete destruction of Madoff's empire that would inevitably follow the first story. And the third story would highlight the complete ineptitude of the SEC, which would include "the fact that the SEC's Section 21A(e) bounty program has paid bounties to whistleblowers only twice in its 71-year history and that the bounty only pays rewards for information related to insider-trading cases. General securities fraud is not rewarded. . . . The lack of a meaningful bounty program allows and encourages small frauds into becoming large frauds."

Pat e-mailed me the day he met with Wilke: "This reporter is a repeat player and he understands we are elephant hunting. If he can get a clear shot at the target he will bag this trophy story . . . [but] the *Wall Street Journal* is always cautious. . . ."

Wilke was interested, Pat reported after their meeting. He'd like to talk to me.

"I'm a senior investigative reporter," John Wilke explained when we spoke for the first time. His tone was courteous and professional, and maybe a little bit dubious. "I don't pump out stories on a daily basis like a lot of guys. I do in-depth reporting and sometimes a story'll take me several months. So if you're in a hurry, I'm probably not the right person for you to be talking to.

"On the other hand, when I do land a story it usually ends up on the front page." As I found out, John Wilke was one of the best investigative reporters in the newspaper business. He wrote about antitrust cases, crooks in Congress malfeasance, the Chinese vitamin industry, and corruption in the financial industry. He had put people in jail. After our first conversation I began following his stories, and he turned up on the *Journal*'s front page so often that I nicknamed him Front Page Wilke, which he loved.

It was clear to me that Pat Burns was right: Wilke was obviously the right reporter for this story. He had reliable sources inside the financial industry, so he could do the necessary background investigation; he knew the difference between puts and calls and had law enforcement connections who would act on his reporting; and he was based in Washington, D.C., rather than New York. That made me feel a lot safer. I had been taught in the army to camouflage the direction of the main attack, so if a Washington-based reporter broke the story, hopefully Madoff would be looking south and never suspect that the article had originated northward from Boston. Finally I sent him all my material.

We spoke on the phone often, and finally he decided to pursue the story. John never made a commitment that the story would run, but certainly he gave me every indication he was going to investigate and see where the facts took him. Eventually I went to a Taxpayers Against Fraud conference in Washington and snuck out to meet secretly with him at a local bar—naturally.

We sat in a corner for several hours. Wilke asked all the right questions, the questions the SEC had failed to ask: Who is involved? How do you know? Where did you go to find out? Who did you speak to? Who, what, when, where, and how much? (Especially how much?) Finally, as I wrote to the team, "Right now he's jammed with a front page story exposing fraud by a major mutual fund family which involves an aerobics instructor (sounds like it'll be sex with financial fraud so it'll be juicy). Once that story hits, Bernie is next."

Based on the discussions I'd had with Wilke, I continued, "The current thinking is that this story can't just be a rehash of the Ocrant article in *MARHedge* and the *Barron's* article which Madoff somehow survived. They're going to want to dig deep, real deep, and it looks like they're going to investigate BM's entire 40-year career looking for dirt. This could take several weeks."

Bernie is next; that's what Wilke had told me. And if Charlie Brown's Lucy had been standing there holding the football right in front of me I couldn't have been more confident we finally were going to take down Bernie Madoff.

■ ■ ■

What I did not know for sure at that time was that the SEC had finally decided to investigate Madoff. As I'd told Ocrant, I'd heard rumors that something was happening, but no one—and that includes Ed Manion and Mike Garrity—would provide any details. The report issued in September 2009 by the SEC's inspector general, David Kotz, confirmed many of my suspicions—as well as my worst fears—about what was going on inside the SEC. Whereas Garrity had sent my report forward and stated that it was about the most complete filing he'd ever seen, and in the Boston office I was regarded as a "credible" person, the New York office treated me and my submission with disdain. Basically, according to this 477-page report, Meaghan Cheung's team was incapable of winning a game of Clue if they were given all the answers, which is pretty much what happened in this situation. For example, the only thing about my red flags that concerned Doria Bachenheimer, the assistant director of enforcement, was the fact that Madoff's earnings were so consistent. As she told Kotz, "I was trying to come up with a theory of what he was doing, so I was thinking was this like an accounting case, is this like cookie-cutter reserves, does he have money somewhere else? When he said he had these other accounts, I just thought let's get the records and see if there is some way he's smoothing earnings. I don't even know if you can do that. I was wondering."

Once again, your tax dollars at work.

Bachenheimer sent my submission to Simona Suh, an attorney on the enforcement staff. Suh had even less experience in this area than Bachenheimer; in fact, this was the first time she had led an investigation. She had never been involved in a Ponzi scheme and had no idea how to proceed. So I guess this was on-the-job training to prepare her if a really big case came in.

Bachenheimer told the inspector general that she didn't really think I was credible because I didn't work for Madoff and hadn't invested with him. As she said, Markopolos "was not an employee and, as far as I knew, received no information from Madoff." In other words, Madoff didn't tell me he was running a Ponzi scheme. As for all the red flags in my report, she thought they were only "theories" and that "it wasn't something we could take and bring a lawsuit with. . . . We had to test it and substantiate it."

This was from the assistant director of enforcement. What did she think enforcement meant?

As Bachenheimer explained, "It's very challenging to develop evidence that something is going wrong until the thing actually falls apart."

In case you're wondering, I am quoting word for word from the inspector general's report.

Cheung claimed she was skeptical about my claims because "I remember thinking after I spoke to him that he wasn't technically a whistleblower because it wasn't inside information so that was, I think, a distinction that I'm sure I made."

The inspector general did confirm that at least part of Cheung's reluctance to accept my offer to help may have come from the fact that she simply didn't like me. Simona Suh told David Kotz that she didn't know why Cheung disliked me. Asked why Meaghan Cheung refused to meet with me, she said, "I don't know what her reasons were. I knew her general impression of him was she was skeptical of him, but I don't know what her reasons for not meeting with him were." Later she added, "I remember hearing that she thought he was kind of condescending to the SEC."

Certainly one reason that office paid so little attention to my submission is that they believed my motive for pursuing Madoff was to collect a big reward. Bachenheimer described me to SEC Inspector General David Kotz as "a competitor of Madoff's who had been criticized for not being able to meet Madoff's returns, and that he was looking for a bounty"—information she probably got from my previous public testimony. She added, "If the first thing I hear from someone is what's in it for me, then it raises my antenna a little bit."

As it should—although she didn't bother to add that I wrote in the submission that I believed Madoff was running a Ponzi scheme, and therefore I would not be able to collect any reward. But probably because these people weren't smart enough to understand my message, they decided the problem had to be with the messenger. The fourth member of the SEC's investigation unit was Peter Lamoure, who agreed with Cheung. "In short," he wrote in an e-mail, "these are basically the same allegations we have heard before. The author's motives are to make money by uncovering the alleged fraud. I think he is on a fishing expedition and doesn't have the detailed understanding of Madoff's operations that we do, which refutes most of his allegations."

Simona Suh also admitted later that the staff had been skeptical of my claims because Madoff "didn't fit the profile of a Ponzi schemer, at least as we—in the world that we knew then." The prime requisite for someone to successfully run a Ponzi scheme is to not look like they are running a Ponzi scheme. I can't even imagine what a profile of a Ponzi schemer would look like.

The real problem was that too many of the SEC's investigators were lawyers, so they were expecting me to provide legal proof, which basically is the lowest standard beyond which you go to jail. Certainly a math proof is a much higher level of proof than a legal proof. In a legal case, two juries hearing precisely the same evidence can easily reach two different verdicts; but with a math problem there is only one correct answer. Two people or two hundred thousand people can do that math problem, and there still is only one correct answer. It's an absolute answer, and even the greatest lawyers who have ever lived couldn't change it; it isn't trying to determine if the glove fits or find the legal definition of *is*. There is only one answer to an equation. For example, a man claims he is trading $30 billion in options and there is only $1 billion of these options in existence. There is an answer for that: It's impossible. The math doesn't work. This one red flag should have been sufficient evidence for the SEC to launch a full investigation of Madoff. But there were so many others. A split-strike strategy by definition couldn't produce the returns Madoff was delivering. His basket of stocks had to have a reasonable mathematical correlation to the exchange on which the stocks were traded, and they did not. It shouldn't have mattered whether the SEC liked me. Meaghan Cheung and her team just weren't smart enough to understand that.

I never learned very much about the actual investigation, except for the fact that according to the FBI, Madoff operated his hedge fund on the 17th floor and his broker-dealer on the 18th and 19th floors of the same building, and the SEC team went to the wrong floors. As the agent told me, "They were conducting an investigation for two years and never even figured out there was a seventeenth floor; that's how dumb they were. You really shouldn't give them any more of your cases. Your quality of work is way beyond the SEC's capabilities. From now on when you have a case, just give us a call." After reading my entire submission the SEC officially opened a Matter Under Inquiry (MUI) of Madoff's broker-dealer business to determine if he was in violation of government regulations by operating as an investment advisory service, a hedge fund.

Apparently Cheung's team informed Madoff that the SEC had opened this investigation and intended to question him as well as some of the fund managers whose assets he was handling. It turned out that Bernie thought even less about the capabilities of the SEC than I did. During a December 2005 telephone conversation with Amit Vijayvergiya, the chief risk officer of the Fairfield Greenwich Group, and General Counsel Mark McKeefrey, Madoff warned, "Obviously, first of all, this call never took place." Then he urged Vijayvergiya not to show any anxiety: "You don't want them to think you're concerned about anything. You're best off, [if] you just be casual."

According to transcripts, Madoff told Vijayvergiya that this was simply a "fishing expedition," and the best way to handle the SEC's questions was to avoid them. "You don't have to be exact on this stuff because . . . no one pays attention to these types of things." Later in the conversation he gave them some advice about how to handle the investigators: "These guys ask a zillion different questions and we look at them sometimes and we laugh and we say, 'Are you guys writing a book?' "

Madoff told him how to answer the questions he anticipated they would be asked, primarily how the relationship between Fairfield Greenwich and Madoff theoretically was structured. "Your position is to say, listen, Madoff has been in business for 45 years, you know, he executes, you know, a huge percentage of the industry's orders, he's a well-known broker. You know, 'We make the assumption that he's doing everything properly.' " It appears from this conversation that Vijayvergiya had very little knowledge of what Madoff was actually doing, that he was little more than a middleman; he simply handed over his clients' money to Madoff and distributed Madoff's returns to those clients. So he needed to be told how their relationship would have worked if it was legitimate. For example, when Vijayvergiya asked Madoff how he would have been certain that his clients were receiving a pro rata allocation of profits based on their allocation if this was a real fund, Madoff replied that he should simply tell them that he knew it was correct because Bernie told him it was, but then Madoff reassured him: "You know, you don't have to be too brilliant with these guys because you don't have to be; you're not supposed to have that knowledge and, you know, you wind up saying something which is either wrong, or, you know, it's just not something you have to do."

Madoff continually reassured Vijayvergiya that there was nothing to be concerned about, that the SEC basically was incompetent. "Fifty percent of the marketplace and the hedge funds operate in totally different ways than they used to. You know, you have all these funds; you know, it's just, it's just changed the landscape and the Commission has no idea what the hell is going on and of course they always think the worst, which is what they're supposed to do."

He concluded, accurately and derisively, "These guys, they work for five years at the Commission, then they become a compliance manager at a hedge fund." And, he added, he knew that was true because every time an SEC investigator came up to his office he or she would ask for an employment application.

■ ■ ■

Remember, I didn't know that my submission had led to an investigation. So I also didn't know that Madoff testified voluntarily, without being represented by an attorney, on May 19, 2006. That was typical Madoff bravado; the natural assumption is that a man who is trying to conceal something certainly would bring his lawyer with him. There are many people who believe that in order to successfully manage this scam as long as he did without being discovered, Bernie Madoff had to be a genius. That reminds me of the story of the two hunters who were trapped by a bear. The first hunter said to the second hunter, "Don't move. You can't outrun a bear. Stand perfectly still and maybe he'll go away."

The second hunter looked at him, then took off running as fast as he could. "Don't!" the first hunter yelled. "You can't outrun a bear."

As the second hunter picked up speed, he turned and yelled back, "I only have to outrun you!"

That was Bernie Madoff's challenge. He didn't have to be a genius; he just had to be smarter than the SEC. And as the inspector general summed up Madoff's interview, "During Madoff's testimony, he provided evasive answers to important questions, provided some answers that contradicted his previous representations, and provided some information that could have been used to discover that he was operating a Ponzi scheme. However, the Enforcement staff did not follow up with respect to any of the information that was relevant to Madoff's Ponzi scheme."

Madoff was smart enough to know that the lies he told could easily be checked by anyone with even moderate intelligence, and when they did check he would be finished. He made several statements that could have been confirmed or proven to be lies with just a single phone call. But there was no attempt to verify his claims. As he later admitted, "I thought this was the end game, over." Fortunately for him, and unfortunately for the investors over the next two and a half years, he was dealing with the SEC. "I was astonished," he said about not being arrested. "After all this, I got lucky."

The SEC Division of Enforcement officially closed this investigation more than a year later, in November 2007. Their report acknowledged that Madoff had lied, or as they described it, "did not fully disclose" to the examiners "the nature of the trading conducted in the hedge fund accounts or the number of such accounts." But even then they concluded, "The staff found no evidence of fraud. The staff did find, however, that BLM acted as an investment advisor to certain hedge funds, institutions and high net worth individuals in violation of the registration requirements of the Advisors Act. The staff also found that Fairfield Greenwich Group disclosures to its investors did not adequately describe BLM's advisory role and described BLM as merely an executing broker to FFG's accounts. As a result of discussions with the staff, BLM registered with the Commission as an investment advisor and FFG revised its disclosures to investors to reflect BLM's advisory role.

"We recommend closing this investigation because both BLM and FFG voluntarily remedied the uncovered violations, and because those violations were not so serious as to warrant an enforcement action."

In her 2007 performance review, Meaghan Cheung specifically cited her work in this investigation, writing, "In Madoff, we investigated the asset management services provided by a broker-dealer specializing in hedge funds who was not registered as an investment advisor. After our investigation, we conducted discussions among the staff, the Division of Investment Management, and Madoff's counsel. We also held separate discussions with Madoff's largest hedge fund client. As a result of those discussions, Madoff's firm registered with the Commission as an investment advisor, and its hedge fund corrected its disclosure."

What really bugs me is that the SEC caught Madoff lying to its investigators repeatedly, and making false statements to a federal official is supposed to carry a five-year (rarely imposed) maximum sentence; yet they never referred him to the Department of Justice for criminal prosecution. It seems that there is a double standard at the SEC where the big firms don't get prosecuted for anything other than misdemeanors, but the small firms get shut down for anything more than minor infractions. Trained fraud examiners know to immediately expand the scope of their exam as soon as someone lies to them. That's the signal to dig in and redouble your efforts, because once you catch them in a lie you know you have them back on their heels. One would think that SEC enforcement lawyers would at least comprehend that making false statements is a criminal offense and have the courage to stand up to a powerful Wall Street figure and send a deterrent message to industry that this sort of behavior will not be tolerated.

I like to tell a joke about the SEC that sometimes gets me into trouble. The difference between a male and female SEC employee, I explain, is that a male employee can count to 21—but only if he takes off his pants. That usually irritates the women, until I add, "But that assumes that he can find it, and unfortunately at the SEC none of them can actually find it. That's how clueless they are."

These were the people who knew my identity. And as I also learned later, they hadn't hesitated to identify me by name in internal e-mails, e-mails that were seen by several people, which was precisely what I had tried so hard to avoid.

While this dubious investigation was taking place, I was regularly in contact with John Wilke at the *Wall Street Journal*. On December 27 the *Journal* ran his front-page investigative piece reporting that legendary mutual fund billionaire Mario Gabelli had set up phony small companies, fronts, to enable him to bid for Federal Communications Commission (FCC) cellular band wave licenses potentially worth hundreds of millions of dollars. This was a False Claims Act case brought by a whistleblower, and Gabelli and his associates eventually agreed to pay a fine of $130 million.

But as soon as I read the story I knew Wilke was about to start working on our story. I even sent an e-mail to the team, alerting them to Wilke's Gabelli story and informing them, "He's going to be writing the Madoff story starting in January, but I don't know how long it will take. The Gabelli story took time and I'm sure this one will too."

In late January John and I agreed that he would meet me in Boston in mid-February. I made copies of all our material in preparation for this meeting. In addition I made suggestions about how he could bring himself up to date on Madoff. I suggested he speak with five people—Frank, Neil, Mike, Erin Arvedlund, and Matt Moran, the vice president of marketing at the Chicago Board Options Exchange (CBOE). I then provided him with my list of 47 derivatives experts in the financial industry, including Northfield Information Services founder Dan DiBartolomeo, my friend who had first checked my math and agreed that Madoff's returns couldn't be derived from the market; Meaghan Cheung; and Goldman Sachs (Boston) Managing Director Daniel E. Holland III. I wanted them to speak with him because "Goldman Sachs is one of the largest traders of equity derivates and if they don't handle Madoff's flow or see it in the markets then something's rotten," and Citibank's Leon Gross, whom "I met with in September 2005 when he came right out and said to me, 'I can't believe that Madoff hasn't been shut down by the SEC yet.

How can anyone invest in that stupid strategy? It shouldn't even be able to earn a positive return.' "

While I knew most of these people, with the exception of Dan DiBartolomeo, only a few of them knew about my investigation. In fact, I'd guess that about half the people on the list probably didn't even know that Madoff was running a hedge fund. They were all derivatives experts, and if they were asked the proper questions they would have told Wilke that Madoff could not have achieved his returns with this strategy. The big negative was that many of the people on the list worked for large firms with compliance lawyers on staff who would squash any attempt by an employee to report out to either the SEC or the press without first reporting up through the company and obtaining permission. And naturally these compliance lawyers would never grant permission for fear of rocking the boat, for fear the information might be wrong or that a nasty lawsuit might result from it.

But there were several derivatives experts on this list who knew that Madoff was a fraud, and if the SEC had called their firms and requested interviews with them, they would have been very happy to cooperate—and what they would have said would have toppled Madoff. It wouldn't have required any legal action to get them to speak. Unfortunately, the SEC didn't train its investigators to reach out to independent third witnesses for assistance. The SEC staff never picked up the phone to contact even one of my witnesses, nor did they ever express interest in obtaining my comprehensive master list of 47 witnesses even after I offered it to them. The SEC's employees are not trained as fraud examiners, nor are they trained to call witnesses.

I also suggested two sets of questions for John Wilke to ask everyone he interviewed. If those people he interviewed responded that they were not aware of the strategy used by Madoff, after explaining the strategy he should ask questions such as: Could $20 billion plus be run by a single hedge fund manager using the strategy I just described without you having heard about it? Could this split-strike option conversion strategy be capable of earning average annual gross returns of 16 percent with only seven monthly losses during the past 14 years? But if this person had heard of Bernie Madoff, among the questions I suggested were: Do you know who Bernie Madoff trades his over-the-counter OEX index options through? Have you ever seen the footprints of Bernie Madoff's trades in the markets that you trade? How realistic do you consider Bernie Madoff's performance numbers to be? Have you heard any stories about Bernie Madoff going to cash ahead of major market sell-offs? If so, how do you think he manages to sell ahead of the market?

In the world of numbers, it should take only a few pointed questions to figure out what's real. If Wilke had asked these questions to several people on the list, any doubts he had about our Madoff claims would have been settled right there. As I had told the SEC, give me Madoff for five minutes and three questions and I could have put him away. Ironically, this was the same month that the Integral Investment Management hedge fund fraud went to trial five years after being discovered. That one hadn't surprised me at all. Several years earlier Frank Casey had pitched the Rampart product I'd created to the Chicago Art Institute, and its directors had shown a lot of interest. At that time, they told Frank, they were heavily invested in a very successful Integral derivatives fund, so Frank had borrowed Integral's PowerPoint presentation and asked me to take a look at it. After looking at it, I couldn't figure out what the hell they were doing. Like Madoff, their strategy made no sense. Frank and I called a manager at Integral and claimed we were interested in investing. We asked him seven questions and he responded with seven totally wrong answers, making it obvious the whole thing was a fraud. Integral didn't know the first thing about options. Integral was basically a much smaller Ponzi scheme than Madoff, but we were too deeply entrenched in Bernie to take on another fight. Its founder, Conrad Seghers, was convicted of violating the antifraud provisions of the securities laws and was barred from the investment industry.

But all it took to find out was asking seven questions on the telephone.

Wilke couldn't make it to Boston in February because he was working on a major political story, as well as a report on alleged price fixing by Chinese vitamin supplement suppliers. In April he broke the story about Congressman Alan Mollohan, who, according to the *Journal*, set up several nonprofits in his West Virginia district and then helped those organizations obtain millions of dollars in congressional earmarks, while at the same time increasing his own personal wealth from about

$500,000 to more than $6 million in four years. When it ran I sent a copy to the team, explaining, "John Wilke, the senior investigative reporter for the *Wall Street Journal*, published this cover story on Friday, which is why he is so late in getting to Boston. He said he's coming up either late this week or late next week and that his next big cover story will be Madoff.

"John's working on a drug scandal that likely gets into the *WSJ* next week but then he's going to work on Madoff. John's been covering the Lipitor scandal pretty heavily lately but he's just doing maintenance follows as that investigation continues."

When I spoke with John Wilke I still could hear his enthusiasm in his voice. Admittedly I was starting to get a little anxious, knowing that once this story was published I would no longer be in jeopardy, but when the finest investigative reporter in the business tells you he's doing your story, there is no reason to doubt him.

He was still coming in May and June, but by this time I had started worrying. Was Madoff so big he had a line into the editors of the *Journal*? If Wilke had turned down this story six months earlier I would have accepted it, but he hadn't. He'd actively pursued it, and he had continued to assure me that he intended to pursue this story.

While this was being played out, whenever possible Mike Ocrant would urge a reporter he knew at the *New York Times* to pursue this and several other possible stories. Ocrant was no longer reporting at *MARHedge*, instead having joined Institutional Investor, a global publisher and conference operator, as director of alternative investment conferences. When Mike told this *Times* reporter about Madoff, she had responded with some mild interest. She'd read his story and asked a few pertinent questions. But every time he brought it up to her she replied that, just like Wilke, she was under pressure to finish another piece or was in the middle of another assignment or any one of the many other reasons she just didn't have time to conduct an investigation.

In June, Ben Stein, the *Barron's* financial writer and TV comedian, was the featured speaker at the Boston Security Analysts Society's annual dinner. I had always admired him. I felt he was a lot smarter than the reporters in the finance world, and when he showed up at this dinner wearing a nice suit and yellow sneakers, my respect for him grew even more. I introduced myself to him at the cocktail party before the dinner, explaining I was investigating securities fraud cases and I had discovered several billion-dollar frauds. He seemed interested and we exchanged e-mail addresses. While I didn't mention Madoff to him, I thought he'd be the perfect person to go to if the *Journal* didn't work out. He already had his own soapbox and he was funny enough to be taken seriously.

The next day I sent him an e-mail. He responded. I followed up one more time, but still not mentioning Madoff. This time he didn't respond, and I never heard from him again. I'm sure he has no idea how close he came to being able to break the Madoff story and save people billions of dollars.

Even though he obviously wasn't interested, I was not above turning our brief conversation into something just short of a death-bed promise. I e-mailed John Wilke and explained, "If you guys don't want it, Ben Stein over at *Barron's* said he'd take it."

I got an immediate response. Of course the *Journal* wants it, Wilke wrote. And we set up another date to get together. He was going to come to Boston and get started on the story.

John Wilke and I continued dancing together. He was always just about ready to start working on the story, and then something always came up. In November, I sent an update to the team, and I can still read my hope and my optimism in my e-mail: "Because the reporter, John Wilke, did all of those front-page *WSJ* articles on Congressional corruption, he wasn't able to get to Madoff. The 3 Congressmen (2 Republicans and 1 Democrat) he exposed are all being investigated by the FBI. He and I just talked on a different front-page story he's doing in December that I gave him. John told me that his editor has read my Madoff analysis and is very, very excited to start their investigation in January. . . .

"He said that his editor thinks that hedge fund scrutiny will increase now that the Democrats are in power and greenlighted John's investigation starting in January. I guess we'll wait and see what transpires. I'll keep you posted. This guy does top shelf corruption stories, but everything he investigates is on a schedule."

I continued to speak with John regularly. That other story I referred to was about one of my investigations, which we finally agreed to postpone until there was an indictment. But in those conversations I suddenly began to hear his interest in the Madoff investigation waning. Something was going on, but I couldn't figure out what it was. For the first time he began talking about needing "a new angle, something different from what's been already written." In February 2007, I sent the team an e-mail admitting, "The *Wall Street Journal's* John Wilke has been a big disappointment. Obviously they were the wrong choice. Eventually Bernie will blow up and everybody will say, 'I told you so.' Feel free to buy 45-day maturity, 5% out-of-the-money puts once the first news of the Madoff blowup comes out. I suspect he'll be considered the Enron of hedge funds."

I don't know if I was more disappointed or confused, but more than either one, I was scared. There was never a moment I doubted John Wilke's honesty or commitment. We spoke too often for me to ever believe he was just stringing me along, but clearly something (or someone) had happened at the *Journal* to prevent him from doing this story. If he wasn't interested in this story, all he had to do was tell me he'd decided not to pursue it for whatever reasons. But he never did that. Until he began peppering our conversations with the need for a new angle, he had never even indicated there was any problem at all. It was always next week or next month. The only assumption I could make was that one of his editors—or perhaps the Dow Jones lawyers—had stopped him. In my mind, at least, I was convinced that someone high up at the *Journal* had decided it was too dangerous to go after Bernie Madoff.

The question I wrestled with for a long time was: Why? When the newspaper that existed only to cover the financial world was handed a detailed explanation of the biggest fraud in Wall Street history, why wouldn't someone at least conduct a cursory investigation? Three phone calls, two phone calls, that's all it would have taken to verify that I wasn't some kind of nut, that the accusations I was making were based on fact. A half hour, that's all. Instead, Wilke spent more than a year making commitments that he never fulfilled. Of course it occurred to me that Madoff might have a good contact at the paper and was able to convince them there was nothing to this story. And more frightening, considering that I was already worried that the SEC had revealed my identity, was the possibility that whoever had killed the story at the *Journal* had leaked my name to Madoff.

I never blamed John Wilke. John was phenomenal; he was aces. I didn't even blame the *Journal*; in fact, after Madoff went down I again handed the *Journal* the story it could have published three years and tens of billions of dollars earlier. I never found out why the *Journal* had not done the story.

While I spoke with John regularly about my other cases, we carefully avoided talking about Madoff. I was very busy with my other cases; I knew that John could be of great importance to me, and he knew that I was a credible source of important stories. We talked about the other cases I was working on, with Madoff silently between us. Pat Burns trusted him completely, so I did, too. Unfortunately, terribly, in October 2008 John was diagnosed with a very aggressive form of pancreatic cancer. He died in May 2009.

After it was clear the *Journal* was not going to investigate Madoff, I didn't know where else to turn. The government had proven to be willfully blind to Madoff, and now my attempt to bring the case to the attention of the public had failed. I had been working on this for too many years, and I was finally beginning to consider the possibility that Bernie Madoff was untouchable—that he was simply too powerful to be brought down. Not only because he had billions of dollars and knew the most important people in the industry and could make or break careers, but because he was a pillar of the financial industry. If he was a fraud, it brought into question everything these people believed in. Bernie Madoff was the ultimate insider; I was the bothersome outsider. I was some quant from Boston nobody had ever heard of. For those insiders, the people who knew Bernie personally, who took pride when he acknowledged them at restaurants and openings, the people who invested their own money or their clients' money with him, for those people to admit that Bernie was a fraud meant admitting that everything they believed in was questionable. Maybe even worse, if some skinny guy who wasn't even from New York could look at a few documents and figure out in five minutes that Madoff was a fraud, how could they have missed it for so many years? Or just as likely, how could they have known about it and never tried to stop it while thousands of people lost billions of dollars? So it was easier just to hope I went away. I mean, what could happen?

■ ■ ■

The team kept me going through this endless series of disappointments. In our conversations we'd make jokes about the incompetence of the SEC, about Bernie's ability to continue to bring in new money, about the fact that we could see that the emperor was stark naked.

But as a result of this latest failure, as well as the fact that I was also working on as many as a dozen other cases of fraud, each of them involving more than a billion dollars, I increased my electronic security. Actually, only a few of those cases were financial frauds; most of them were medical frauds. It was very exciting work and I loved the challenge, but I had encountered a problem in my new career as a fraud investigator that I hadn't anticipated and didn't know how to solve. It was pretty basic: How was I going to earn a living? I wasn't going to earn any money from my investigative work until one of my False Claims Act cases settled. And based on history, it could take several more years before that happened. Faith was amazingly supportive; she never complained, but it really bothered me that we had become so dependent on her salary. I just couldn't figure out how to make this business profitable.

There was no one I could turn to for advice. As I had learned, while there were other fraud investigators, there was no precedent for what I was doing. The law firms that routinely did False Claims Act cases would work directly with the whistleblower, and the statute provides for the whistleblower to get compensated from the bounty; the legal advisers would receive a percentage of that payment. But I wasn't a whistleblower.

Law firms are also permitted to hire consultants and pay them a fee, but I didn't have a law degree, so I couldn't be a legal consultant, and generally the law firm approached and hired consultants rather than consultants approaching the firm. But I was initiating the contact with law firms.

And law firms are not permitted to pay referral fees or share revenue from cases with nonlawyers. So we couldn't simply make a deal to share whatever monies we received.

The statute simply hadn't anticipated someone like me. I was preparing the entire case; I was discovering the fraud, researching it, recruiting whistleblowers, conducting my own investigation, and compiling the evidence needed for conviction. And finally I would hand it over to an attorney to guide it through the legal system and collect the bounty.

I had spoken with several lawyers, and none of them could figure out how to make that fit in the existing structure of the False Claims Act.

I began to solve that problem one evening in August, when I attended the Cambridge Chamber of Commerce's Summer Bash. It was held at Millennium Pharmaceuticals, which was located not too far from MIT. So for $50 you got drinks, a world-class dinner, and the opportunity to meet some of the smartest people in the world. For me, meetings like this one were very good places to network; I particularly wanted to meet people from the pharmaceutical world, which I had discovered was ripe with fraud. As I had learned in my investigations, the health care industry makes Wall Street look honest. It's a $2-trillion-a-year business with no controls and with limited auditing. On Wall Street the crooks at least have the decency to try to hide their frauds, but those people cheating Medicare don't even bother doing that. Wall Street is only taking your life savings, but in health care they may be stealing your life. I was surprised to discover how little "care" there is in health care. It's obviously no surprise that the pharmaceutical industry is a completely profit-driven business, but the methods companies devised to earn some of those profits were surprising—and in the case I discovered, illegal.

I've been working on several cases that remain under investigation or under seal, meaning in both cases I can't discuss them. Truthfully, my career aspiration is to prove that a drug with more than a billion dollars in annual sales is actually killing Americans and citizens across the globe, that in the clinical trials the dangers of this drug were revealed, and that the executives knew about the dangers and went ahead and marketed it anyway. I've been working on this case for a few years now without much success, but I hope someday I'll be able to find a key witness and get this case filed with the Department of Justice.

There was a large crowd at the Summer Bash, but I noticed a small, attractive woman involved in a very intense conversation with several people I knew. Eventually we were standing in the same group. I introduced myself to her, and she told me her name was Gaytri Kachroo.

I wasn't sure I'd heard that correctly. She smiled and repeated it: "Gaytri Kachroo."

"What does that mean?" I asked.

She replied, "I'm Gaytri, the Hindu goddess of wisdom and knowledge."

Well. Now that was an unusual introduction, I thought. Actually, Gaytri Kachroo explained, she was an attorney—with five law degrees, including a master's and a doctorate in law from the Harvard Law School. She had been born in Srinagar, Kashmir India, had grown up in the middle of a war, and had moved with her family to Montreal in 1971. At the time we met she was serving as general counsel to a number of small firms both in the United States and abroad. I told her, "I have to be honest. I don't like lawyers."

"Neither do I," she agreed.

During this conversation I told her that I had a unique problem. I was a full-time financial fraud investigator but I couldn't figure out how to earn any money doing it. I could find cases, and I could investigate them and hand over my evidence to law firms that could bring them to the government under the False Claims Act and earn many millions of dollars from the settlements—but I had been told by several attorneys that law firms were legally not permitted to pay what was basically a finder's fee or a referral fee to people who brought cases to them. In other words, they couldn't pay me for my work.

Somehow, I needed to create a new business model that would enable me to earn a living uncovering fraud.

Gaytri didn't equivocate. "Whoever's telling you that doesn't know what they're talking about," she said. "Most lawyers believe that because they're trained in old case law and don't think in the future. I know what you're doing is amazing. You're making the cases that count from the ground up and possibly new case law." She thought about it, then nodded. "I'm sure with a little thought we can figure this out. What you're doing is a good thing. And since the outcome is legal, I can't imagine there isn't a legal solution. I'm sure I can figure out a way to make that structure work and I can make it legal."

We sat down in her office the next day to try to create a business model that would work. I explained to her that at the behest of the Boston office of the SEC I had filed several market-timing cases. I specifically did not mention Madoff to her. In fact, she knew nothing about it until December 11, 2008; when Madoff's arrest was announced I called and told her that I was the Madoff whistleblower they were talking about on television. So when we began working together, there was no way for me to predict that she would become the fifth member of the team.

As I eventually discovered, Gaytri was as unusual as her name. She was raised in war as India and Pakistan fought over Kashmir. As a child she remembered hiding in the bomb shelter in her back-yard as bombs dropped around her "like thunder and lightning." She had faced terror early in her life, so standing up to the SEC was not going to scare her. Her father was a mathematician recruited by Montreal's McGill University in 1965; the rest of her family—her mother, herself, and two brothers—had moved to Montreal almost six years later.

Her father was extremely controlling. Because he was afraid that his children would fall prey to western culture, he tried hard to shield them. As she told me one night, "It was important to him that we kept our roots, although he also stressed that we should experience the best of both cultures." Growing up, though, Gaytri was not allowed to have friends outside of school, and when she went to Wellesley College, a women's school, she actually was chaperoned by her brother, who was at MIT. Although she had been trained in mathematics at home, she rebelled, and rather than math or science, got her initial degree in studio arts and fine arts. After graduating, she ran away with a man she had been seeing secretly, whom she would later marry. During this dramatic escape from home she climbed out of a first-floor window as her boyfriend waited below, got on a bus, and tried to get away. Her brother, who was chaperoning her, jumped on the bus while her mother followed in her car. When the bus finally stopped at a café, the police were called and permitted Gaytri to leave.

Eventually the couple married and had two children, while Gaytri was getting her legal degrees from the University of Ottawa and McGill University. Eventually, she left the security of her marriage and returned to the United States with her young children. Enrolling at Harvard Law School, she became the first single parent to get a master's and doctorate in law.

By the time I met her, she had worked as a civil prosecutor in Canada and for several of the most prestigious law firms in Canada and the United States, and was busy establishing her own international practice. It was not until we started working on my congressional testimony together that she told me that as a child of 15 she had tied the World Chess Champion, Anatoly Karpov, in a chess game.

After what she had been through, absolutely nothing fazed her, although when we first started talking it's doubtful she envisioned sitting next to me in front of Congress as we attacked the SEC.

Initially Gaytri had only the vaguest knowledge about the False Claims Act, so she began by reading it, as well as the case law that had developed from it. We discussed numerous different possibilities— one of them even included me going to law school so I would qualify for a bounty. That one I rejected immediately. Truthfully, it had not even occurred to me that it was possible to earn an income from my work other than the reward money. But eventually we worked out a novel approach to my problem: After I had gathered enough evidence to believe a fraud was being committed, I would approach a law firm—there are firms around the country that specialize in this type of work—and if the lawyers were interested in pursuing it they would hire me as a consultant for a negotiated hourly rate. This hourly billing would be my salary while I continued developing the case. I had already recruited the relators, as the whistleblowers are referred to legally, and in return for developing the case and guiding the whistleblower team through the entire process, I would receive a previously negotiated percentage of whatever reward the whistleblowers received.

It was logical and legal. A private citizen, a whistleblower, can share fees with anybody he or she wants to. They can give a piece to a law firm, which is the way most contingency law firms work, or they can also give a share to the team leader, which was me.

Gaytri Kachroo became my lawyer. She began negotiating with different firms, trying to find lawyers who would agree to those conditions. And eventually we found firms in several states. Those market-timing cases were Gaytri's introduction to the SEC, and she got a good dose of its incompetence early in our relationship. When the SEC dropped all of my cases, I was livid. I was furious. I tend to be restrained; I like to be in emotional control, but this time my frustration was too much to hold inside. "These guys are good for nothing!" I screamed into the phone. "They're never gonna get it. I can't believe I keep giving them chances and they never get it!"

Because I had told Gaytri absolutely nothing about Madoff, she probably thought I was overreacting. But as she listened to me yelling about the SEC's incompetence, about their stupidity, about their refusal to do their job, as she listened to me letting all my anger and frustration come out, she finally realized that I'd had previous encounters with that agency. And she began wondering about that.

Chapter 7

More Red Flags Than the Soviet Union

I n August 2007 Frank Casey sent me an e-mail about a new financial product he'd found on the Internet site NakedShorts: "Investment dealers are excited to announce the newest structured finance product—*Constant Obligation Leveraged Originated Structured Oscillating Money Bridged Asset Guarantees*, or Colostomy Bags. Designed to accommodate the most sophisticated investment strategies, Colostomy Bags contain the equity tranches of Structured High Interest Taxable derivatives, or Shit, and are leveraged an infinite amount of times through the innovative use of derivatives."

I probably smiled sadly as I read it, knowing that it was no less real than Madoff, and that if it actually existed and somebody could make money from it, they would sell it. I wrote back, "That's an awesome-sounding product! Who do I call to get an allocation? I want to take down a small piece first, say $100 million, then pitch them to the French HFOF's as a higher return, slightly higher volume product than Madoff."

■ ■ ■

When Neil was sitting across the desk from me at Rampart and things got a little hairy, he would remind me that his mother, who never invested in anything more risky than a certificate of deposit, had tried to talk him out of going into the financial industry. "My Dad was in favor of it, telling me Wall Street people are smart. They make a lot of money. Get in the trenches and do a good job. But my Mom thought investment people were scam artists, and wanted me to become something respectable: 'Be a doctor or a lawyer.' "

Then he would add, "And we aren't even Jewish!" We'd laugh and manage to somehow get through the current crisis. But as the years went by, it occurred to me that maybe she knew what she was talking about. After spending so many years trying to convince government officials, reporters, and fund managers that Madoff was a fraud and being rejected or ignored by every one of them, it's human nature to at least wonder if maybe everybody else was right and I was wrong. But the truth is that I never doubted myself. There is a single irrefutable fact that I relied on: Numbers can't lie. That's the basis of my career. First examine the numbers, then investigate how those numbers were generated.

The question I've struggled with, which all of us on the team have struggled with, is why did so many people permit this fraud to continue for so long? The industry knew, there's no question about that. After Madoff collapsed, I was told so many stories about people who knew he was a fraud and warned others. For example, I've been told about an e-mail a manager at one of the largest investment houses sent to a Madoff client in 2005, warning him that "everybody here knows Madoff is a fraud" and urging him to get his funds out.

Another very smart guy Neil and I knew ran a fixed income arbitrage strategy for one of the major feeder funds that was heavily invested in Madoff. This manager joined the firm long after it had made its initial investments in Bernie, and I believe he eventually became a partner. This person is very outspoken, but he knows what he's talking about. He speaks numbers. For example, when Rampart was marketing the product I'd created, he'd looked at it and figured out almost immediately that "This is a trade; it's not a strategy."

I explained to him that I was delivering a product that fulfilled certain demands, but he just crushed it. Neil and I wondered how somebody that smart could have gotten involved with this fund. He looked at my numbers and knew what I was doing, so he must have known what Madoff was doing.

Finally, Neil told him right to his face that Madoff was a fraud. When the man started to defend his fund's investments, Neil challenged him: "Check the trade tickets. There are no trades."

We have good reason to believe that he did exactly that, and that he discovered that the volume never happened at the prices Madoff quoted at the time Madoff said they did. It wouldn't have been hard for him to do that; in fact, had the SEC investigators done it they would have discovered that the trades didn't exist and Madoff would not have been able to explain it. But this manager quietly left this hedge fund and opened his own fund with a unique strategy he had developed. He was immediately successful and, as part of Neil's job recruiting managers for Benchmark Plus, Neil visited him in his new East Coast office. "I spoke to him for a few hours," Neil told me. "His desk was covered with papers and I saw the logo from [his former employer] on his desk and I was trying to read them without being caught as he explained his strategy to me. I couldn't do it, though.

"Finally I just asked him straight out, 'You were at [the fund] for a long time. I just gotta ask you, what did you really think about Madoff?'"

"And?" I asked.

"He hesitated, like he was trying to find the right way of answering. I can't really explain it, Harry, but you should have seen how uncomfortable he was with this question. His whole body sort of sat up and I could hear the strain in his voice. 'Basically,' he said, 'I did my own thing while I was there. The Madoff thing was [he named another partner]; he took care of all that.' I pressed him, and the closest he got to admitting anything was telling me that there was enough going on where he thought it was a good time to exit. He said, 'I was running my own strategy anyway, so it seemed like the right thing to do.'"

Neil and I both believed very strongly that he knew. He was much too smart to believe in either the tooth fairy or Bernie Madoff. But his attitude was very typical of the attitude on Wall Street. Those people who knew something was wrong and had not invested with him went along with the unspoken industry code: If it's not my business and it doesn't affect my business, I'm not going to get involved. And those people who were invested with him and knew something was wrong kept silent because his returns were too good. Bernie Madoff could not possibly have gotten away with it for so long without the silence of so many people. Madoff wasn't an aberration; he was a creation of the profit-at-all-costs culture of Wall Street. And maybe the scariest thing about Bernie Madoff?

He isn't the only one. Like unvanquished monsters, there are more of them out there in the dark.

When we had discovered Madoff in 1999, Frank, Neil, and I had been working at Rampart. In the eight years since then, each of our lives had changed drastically. Neil had moved to Tacoma and had become the director of research—meaning he hired hedge fund managers—for Benchmark Plus; Frank had survived a catastrophe at sea and was living in New Jersey, working for a marketing firm dedicated to raising pension assets for hedge funds and funds of funds called Parkway Capital; I had started my own business, and Faith and I now had three little children. About the only thing that hadn't changed was our pursuit of Madoff. Month and month, year after year, we continued compiling a growing mountain of damning evidence that nobody seemed to care about.

In 1999 Madoff had easily been the largest hedge fund in the world, and he had continued to grow bigger and bigger. It was no longer possible to estimate accurately how large he had become; we guessed $35 billion to $40 billion, but certainly it could have been substantially more. After he collapsed, investigators found evidence that he was taking money from well over 339 funds of funds in over 40 countries, and estimates of the total amounts investors thought they had invested with Madoff as of their November 2008 monthly statements were as high as $65 billion.

And no matter how many red flags we discovered, there were always more. Early in 2007, Neil was speaking to a third party marketer (someone who sells for various hedge funds), who started telling him about an incredible fund he had discovered. As soon as he said "phenomenal returns" and "split-strike conversion," Neil knew who he was talking about.

"Are you talking about Bernie Madoff?" It was the Fairfield Greenwich Sentry Fund. Neil laughed. He liked this guy, and told him that he had heard—not that he had spent almost eight years investigat-

My family owned several Arthur Treacher's Fish & Chips restaurants, where I got my start in the numbers game. It was also there that I made my first foray into fraud investigation when I caught a chef stealing fish.

Frank Casey on Wall Street. Casey first brought the Bernard Madoff case to my attention in 1999.

Casey (*left*) worked with me at Rampart Investment Management from 1998 to 2001. Here he shares a table with me at a Rampart executive's birthday party in April 2000.

PHOTO CREDIT: © David Woo.

Neil Chelo, who worked with me to uncover the Madoff fraud, was interviewed for a news story by CNBC's Mary Thompson in February 2009.

PHOTO CREDIT: © February 2009 Jeremy Gollehon with credit to Steve Bargelt.

Michael Ocrant became a member of our team after learning about Madoff from Frank Casey and beginning his investigation that led to first published expose of the fraud in *MARHedge*.
PHOTO CREDIT: Michael Ocrant.

The only hero in the whole mess in my opinion is Boston Securities and Exchange Commission investigator Ed Manion, who desperately tried to convince the SEC to seriously consider my submissions.
PHOTO CREDIT: Edward Manion.

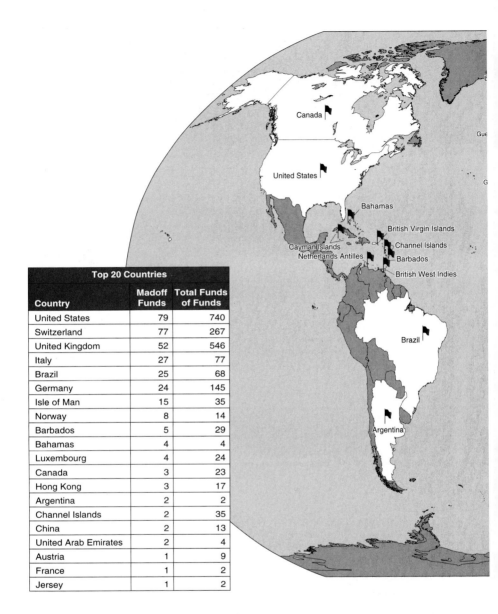

Top 20 Countries		
Country	Madoff Funds	Total Funds of Funds
United States	79	740
Switzerland	77	267
United Kingdom	52	546
Italy	27	77
Brazil	25	68
Germany	24	145
Isle of Man	15	35
Norway	8	14
Barbados	5	29
Bahamas	4	4
Luxembourg	4	24
Canada	3	23
Hong Kong	3	17
Argentina	2	2
Channel Islands	2	35
China	2	13
United Arab Emirates	2	4
Austria	1	9
France	1	2
Jersey	1	2

Madoff's Global Reach: Over 40 countries, 339 funds of funds, and 59 asset management companies were invested with Madoff. An estimated $65 billion was lost by investors around the world, the largest fraud ever committed. If the SEC had reacted proactively to information my team supplied, an estimated $50 billion might have been saved.

DATA SOURCE: Publicly available information and Symplectic Partners databases. Data restricted to funds of funds with at least two years' worth of return data through March 2008. For more information, see George A. Martin's article "Who Invested with Madoff? A Flash Analysis of Funds of Funds" (*Journal of Alternative Investments*, Summer 2009).

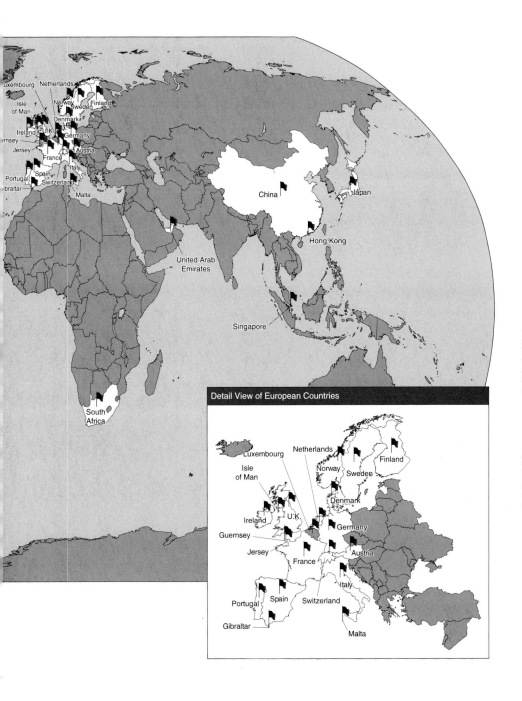

Luxembourg Netherlands

Isle
of Man
Norway Finland
Sweden
Denmark
Ireland U.K. Germany
rnsey
Jersey Austria
France
Italy
Portugal Spain
Switzerland
ibraltar

Malta

China

Japan

Hong Kong

United Arab
Emirates

Singapore

South
Africa

Detail View of European Countries

Luxembourg Netherlands

Isle
of Man
Norway Finland
Sweden

Denmark
Ireland U.K.

Guernsey Germany

Jersey Austria
France

Italy
Portugal Spain Switzerland

Gibraltar

Malta

Bernie Madoff (*left*), wife Ruth, and son Mark in November 2001,
Long Island, New York.

Photo credit: GI/BM/Getty Images.

Bernie Madoff, brother Peter Madoff, and sons Andrew and Mark (*from left to right*) in July 1995, Montauk, New York.

Photo credit: GI/BM/Getty Images.

Access International CEO Rene-Thierry Magon de la Villehuchet on November 30, 2007. De la Villehuchet lost more than $1 billion of his own, his family's, and his clients' money to Madoff. Two weeks after Madoff surrendered, de la Villehuchet committed suicide at his Manhattan office.

PHOTO CREDIT: Guy Gurney/Sipa Press/0812241922 (Sipa via AP Images).

The names of French noble families are inscribed on the inside of the Arc de Triomphe in Paris. During the 2002 European sales trip, de la Villehuchet told me that many of his investors belonged to those families.

PHOTO CREDITS: Hisham Ibrahim/Photodisc/Getty Images (inscribed names); © 2009 by Sam Lin (Arc de Triomphe).

During my February 4, 2009, House testimony, I demonstrate that Madoff's returns showed a steady 45-degree increase—a financially impossible feat.

PHOTO CREDIT: AP Images/Susan Walsh.

SEC Inspector General David Kotz testifies at the Senate hearing.

PHOTO CREDIT: Chip Somodevilla/ Getty Images North America.

I make a second appearance before Congress on September 10, 2009, this time to the Senate Banking Committee. I am pictured here (left) next to my lawyer, Gaytri Kachroo.

PHOTO CREDIT: Chip Somodevilla/Getty Images North America.

"Markopolos, do you have any more metaphors for us?" Senate Banking Committee Chairman Chuck Schumer asked during the September 2009 testimony.

PHOTO CREDIT: © February 5, 2006, Lauren Victoria Burke/WDCPIX.COM.

ing Madoff—that there was something wrong with Madoff, that he might be a fraud.

"I've heard that, too," this man responded, "but there's nothing to it." Madoff had been around forever. He couldn't be a fraud, the marketer explained to Neil. How could he have pulled off a fraud for 20 years? And besides, the SEC had investigated him and didn't find any problems.

Neil had become a pretty good investigator. So rather than simply dismissing the concept, he asked if it was possible to see Madoff's audits. At that point we didn't realize how much Bernie needed every million dollars he could get his hands on, so this investment adviser was delighted to provide to Neil copies of Madoff's audited financial statements from 2004 to 2006. As he wrote to Neil in two e-mails, "I have attached the last three audits for the Fairfield Sentry Fund, which is the domestic Madoff strategy. . . .

"The year-end audits show only the snapshot of what the fund is holding on December 31 of that year. . . . Madoff is always in T-bills at year-end, so that is all you see. . . . He has closed out his trades and put the money into Treasuries for year-end, which is typical for him.

"I know it is odd. I am still working on getting the actual trade examples for you, and again, I am happy to put you in touch with someone at the Sentry Fund to walk you through how the trade works and the process."

As soon as Neil got them he forwarded them to me. And after even a brief examination we were amazed.

Each of those three statements was done by a different accounting firm. In 2004 Madoff had used a regional firm based in Stamford, Connecticut. In 2005 he had used PricewaterhouseCoopers in Rotterdam, the Netherlands; and a year later he had used PricewaterhouseCoopers in Toronto. Obviously he was auditor shopping. It meant he didn't want to have an ongoing relationship with an auditor because the auditor knew too much from the previous year's audit. Using PricewaterhouseCoopers in different countries was pretty clever. Many people looking at these statements would see the PricewaterhouseCoopers name and assume it was PricewaterhouseCoopers U.S., a respected firm. And they'd see that name at least two years in a row, probably more. What many people don't realize is that PricewaterhouseCoopers is actually a different corporation in different countries. The corporations have the same brand name, but basically they're franchises. They operate independently under the same name. Very few people know the accounting system or the standards for licensing an accountant in those countries. While it's the same brand, it may not be the same quality as in the United States. That's an obvious red flag.

And at least I have to wonder if anyone at these auditing firms ever questioned why a large American hedge fund had picked them out, above all the thousands of qualified accounting firms in the United States, to conduct its year-end audit.

Even more surprising was what we found when we examined these audits. Supposedly Madoff had gone to all cash at the end of each of these three audited years, and was holding Treasury bills. While Madoff had boasted he was invested in the market only six to eight times a year, the fact that he had nothing to audit at the end of the year—no stocks, no options—was much too convenient, and especially because he was in T-bills. In more than two decades of looking at audits, none of us had ever seen this before. It made the audit useless because there was nothing for the auditors to inspect.

The bigger problem was that he claimed to be holding T-bills worth roughly $160 million at those year-ends and had no trading positions. The obvious question that should have been asked was: What happened to the rest of those billions? But the auditors had no way of knowing what wasn't there. If Madoff claimed all his money was in T-bills, there was nothing else for them to look at. I wrote to Neil that "the audits that show only T-bills worth $160 million or so on a $1.47 billion portfolio have me wondering where did the missing $1.31 billion go? There's more holes in the Madoff portfolio than all the golf courses in Florida. Why is he in T-bills at year-end? Name a broker that he trades thru?"

If the auditors had only bothered to conduct a simple examination, they, too, would have discovered that this was a fraud. Instead it appears that they just assumed that one of the most powerful men on Wall Street could be trusted to actually own the $160 million in T-bills he claimed. It would have been simple to check. When you buy a T-bill, there has to be a counterparty selling it to you. There are a limited number of places from which you can buy them. Madoff could have bought them from the Federal Reserve Bank of New York directly or from a primary dealer. He even could have bought them in a secondary market, although most people don't do that. What the accountants could have done was ask him, "Say, Bernie, who'd you buy these things from?" Bernie would have told them something, and then they could have gone to that party and asked, "Did you sell Bernie Madoff a hundred sixty million dollars' worth of T-bills? Mind if I take a look at the trade confirmations?"

My guess is that the party's answer would have been "No," because I doubt that those T-bills ever existed, except on Bernie's fantasy audits. This raises the question: What good are Big Four accounting firm audits if these accounting firms aren't checking for fraud? Why pay for an audit if the auditors are not also trained as fraud examiners? What good is a clean audit opinion on a crooked company, anyway? Enron, WorldCom, Global Crossing, Adelphia, HealthSouth, and all the other corporate felons all had clean audit opinions from the most respected accounting firms. Believe me, a lot of the hedge funds of funds had clean audit opinions, and these audits didn't detect that Madoff was a fraud.

There is one other noninnocent explanation for why Fairfield Greenwich Sentry Fund had three different auditors in three different countries for three consecutive year-ends. Accountants have something called accountant-client privilege, and some states recognize it but usually in a much more limited sense than attorney–client privilege. Shockingly, especially in a profession like accounting where you would at least hope that they held fast to some sort of code of conduct, you'd think that once external auditors discovered accounting fraud they'd immediately go to law enforcement and report it. But you'd be wrong. Instead what most accounting firms do in these situations is "make a noisy withdrawal" by resigning the account but telling nobody why they resigned and, in effect, firing their client. Board members, law enforcement, and investors are supposed to be able to immediately know that whenever accountants resign, the reasons for it are serious and should be delved into. This may or may not be the case with Fairfield Greenwich Sentry's use of three different auditors, but if it was the case, that says all you need to know about accounting firms and professional ethics. One would hope that this profession would require its members to report criminal activity upon discovery.

Lots of large banks, particularly European banks, ended up in bed with Bernie Madoff—which should give all investors pause when trusting any financial institution with their hard-earned money. In finance, 90 percent of the skullduggery takes place beneath the surface.

One thing that galls me about the hedge fund of fund business is how many of these charlatans claimed to be using large, prestigious banks as their custodians to keep control of the securities in investors' accounts. Yet, somehow, Madoff and these HFOFs were able to subvert even this commonsense safeguard. Investors may have wired their money to prestigious Custody Bank A but unbeknownst to them, this bank then wired the money straight to Bernie Madoff who, acting as sub-custodian, "self-custodied" the assets himself and then stole every dime. Obviously these large custody banks "rented" their "good names" to these HFOF charlatans but unfortunately investors didn't realize they were being hoodwinked.

Third party plan administrators who are charged with record keeping and performance accounting were also fooled by Bernie Madoff—or were they? HFOFs like to brag about their use of these so-called third party plan administrators as an additional investor safeguard, but do they really offer investors an impervious shield against fraud? Definitely not! If a third party plan administrator does come across fraud, he'll likely just resign the account and remain silent.

The other thing you should know about these third party plan administrators is that they are supposed to be providing independent valuations of the securities held in your account, but all too often they don't have a clue how to value complex securities. Instead, the hedge fund manager ends up telling the plan administrator how to value the securities. In other words, these plan administrators aren't nearly as independent as they would have you believe.

Personally, I wouldn't want any third party plan administrator hired on my behalf *unless* they had a policy of mandatory fraud reporting to the authorities as soon as they spotted something amiss. Otherwise, I don't see how a Big Four accounting firm, custody bank, or third party plan administrator offers me any value whatsoever. My view is that if you hold yourself up as a professional you have to uphold a sense of ethical duty to your clients.

Another glaring shortfall is in the sad state of HFOF due diligence. For the most part, these fund of funds are nothing more than marketing machines that pretend to conduct exhaustive due diligence. If you don't believe me, ask what their budget for due diligence is this year in both dollar terms and as a percent of revenue. If they can't give you an immediate answer, then they aren't even taking the time to measure what is supposed to be their most important function—preserving your capital! My observation is that most fund of funds spend a lot more effort on their marketing than on their due diligence which, of course, doesn't help their investors very much.

A well run HFOF can provide a diversified portfolio and generate attractive returns for their investors. While too many HFOFs got caught up in the Madoff Ponzi scheme, I applaud those organizations that did their homework and helped their investors avoid this disaster. In the United States, almost 11 percent of the HFOFs had Madoff—so 89 percent avoided him. But in Europe, particularly Switzerland, the HFOFs got hit hard. Switzerland had Madoff exposure in almost 29 percent of its HFOFs. On the plus side, most of those HFOFs are no longer operating. The key for investors is to conduct their own due diligence of their HFOF to determine that the people behind it really do know what they're doing and actually do what they say they're doing.

But as usual where Madoff was concerned, the numbers didn't work. If he returned 1 percent net a month to his investors and in addition effectively paid the funds 4 percent, he had to gross 16 percent annually. He claimed that six to eight times a year, when his magical black box told him that the moon was in the seventh sun or the bones had fallen in a promising way, or whatever way he supposedly was getting the word, he would sell his T-bills and buy 35 stocks from the S&P 100 and protect them with options. Weeks later when the genie awakened again to tell him the market was going to tank, he would get out with large profits. So he wasn't continually in the market. And when he wasn't in the market, his money was in T-bills. That was where his math made no sense: How is he earning those returns when he isn't in the market? He needed to be buying 16 percent T-bills in a world in which Treasury bills haven't yielded 16 percent since the early 1980s.

Sometimes it seemed like there were more red flags in Madoff's claims than in the former Soviet Union.

But Neil had opened a potentially very valuable link. Neil had given no reasons for this adviser to suspect his interest in Madoff was anything but responsible due diligence. This adviser still believed Neil was seriously interested in investing millions of dollars in Fairfield Greenwich Group (FGG), so he was willing to do whatever was necessary to nail it down. He even offered to set up a conversation for Neil with Amit Vijayvergiya, FGG's chief risk officer. Neil couldn't believe it. He immediately sent me an e-mail, wondering what questions he should ask. Even though I was busy with a dozen active cases, I dropped everything and started writing just a few thoughts. And then a few more. Eventually I had three pages of questions, more than 80 of them, although, as I wrote, "Gee, I could write questions all night. Somehow I think they're not going to answer many of these questions in great detail in order to protect their proprietary trading methodology."

The questions covered all of the red flags we'd been waving for so long: If two stocks with a total portfolio weight of 4 percent drop 50 percent due to company-specific risk (say subprime exposure), how are you protected against a 2 percent portfolio loss? What are your total assets under management? I'm hearing numbers in the $30 billion to $50 billion range.

Who are your leading brokers for stocks? How do you guard against front-running? How do you explain your lack of a down month?

Who are your traders? Where did they learn how to trade your strategy? Can I sit on your trading desk for a day to get a feel of how you run your operation?

What scenario keeps you up at night? What are your strategies' worst-case scenarios?

I was having fun writing them, and I continued writing them even though I knew there was absolutely no hope he would be able to answer many of them. If he was to be honest, his answers would all have to be nothing, zero, we don't, I don't know, and (most often) never. How large is your compliance staff? We don't have one. Who does your trades? We don't make trades. How do you explain your lack of a down month? We just make up the numbers. What scenarios keep you up at night? Getting exposed. What is the maximum size that your strategy can handle without watering down returns? As much money as you're willing to hand over to a Ponzi scheme.

I was actually very excited about this conversation. In all the years we'd been investigating, other than Mike's 2001 interview and the few questions we'd asked the former employee of his broker-dealer operation, we'd had very few opportunities to get a really good look inside Madoff. As we later verified, the Fairfield Sentry Fund was his single largest feeder fund. When we'd started our investigation, it had about $3 billion in assets; by this time that had increased to more than $7 billion—and every penny of it had been channeled to him. The fund charged its clients 20 percent of profits and a 1 percent management fee, so on a 16 percent gross return, which is roughly what Madoff supplied, it earned close to $40 million for every billion invested. Considering that Fairfield Sentry had $7 billion with Madoff they were earning approximately $280 million per year in fees to look the other way and not ask the tough questions.

So Fairfield Sentry had several million reasons to protect Bernie.

As Neil told me later, Vijayvergiya was pleasant but officious. He certainly wasn't prepared for the barrage of questions Neil asked, and wasn't able to answer many of them. He began by explaining the relationship between Madoff and Fairfield Sentry. Madoff was registered with the SEC—he didn't mention he had been forced to register after the 2005 SEC so-called investigation—and his broker-dealer had $640 million in capital. FGG had been investing in Madoff since 1990 and at that point, according to Vijayvergiya, had slightly more than $7 billion with him. "So about how much is he managing overall?" Neil asked.

Vijayvergiya admitted he didn't know, but estimated Madoff had a total of $14 billion under management with a dozen people. The head of risk management didn't know how much money the man who was handling $7 billion for them was managing? Neil took a deep breath—that was astonishing. Within five minutes, he told me, "I was thinking this whole thing was a joke, an absolute joke. He couldn't have been serious."

It wasn't a joke; it was a tragedy. When Neil started asking specific questions, it got worse. Neil asked who took the other side of all the trades Bernie was making. Amit replied that for large trades Bernie got quotes from three or four big brokers and took the best one, then instantly got filled on the option side.

Neil was sitting at his desk in Tacoma shaking his head in disbelief. One of the first things I'd taught him was to be very careful about approaching multiple buyers for a quote on the same trade, because there was nothing to prevent a buyer who didn't get the trade from front-running—buying or selling before I could make my deal, knowing that my deal was going to move the market. It's illegal, but it's absurd to believe that someone with this information isn't going to take advantage of it. It's part of the reality of the marketplace.

Neil pushed Amit on this, asking repeatedly who was taking the other side of these deals, because these large deals Madoff supposedly was making didn't seem to be showing up anywhere. "If they're off-loading it," Neil said, "the easiest way of doing it would be to go into the S&P or the OEX pit, and how come no one's ever been able to find a trace of any of these trades in the market?"

Amit told Neil that it was an interesting question, then claimed he'd never really thought about it. In other words, he just plain didn't know.

Neil eventually focused on Madoff's split-strike conversion strategy. It had become obvious to him that Vijayvergiya didn't understand that this strategy couldn't produce the rates of return Madoff claimed. "What am I missing here?" Neil asked. "You basically need to have some directional bias, whether the market's up or down or flat. Is there some kind of arbitrage I don't know about? I have to tell you, Amit, I don't understand how he does it."

This was a question Amit had been prepared to answer. He told Neil that Madoff was market-timing the entry and exit of all his trades. "Bernie's got a proprietary model that helps him decide when to put trades on and when to take them off," he said. "It's got three core factors—momentum, volatility, and liquidity. That allows him to be long when the markets go up and out of the market when it is not favorable."

"Let me be clear," Neil pressed. "When you put a trade on, you have to put it on with some kind of bias, right? What I want to know is how is he doing that?"

"Well, he's got a market-timing model."

Neil asked him why, if this strategy had been so incredibly success-ful, other people had not been able to duplicate it. Amit attempted to answer that question, pointing out that no one else had Madoff's proprietary model, which told him when to enter and exit split-strike trades.

The conversation grew increasingly more absurd. Given that Madoff had this perfect knowledge of the market, Neil asked, why does he need all these other funds? According to the model, Madoff was actually earning considerably less than those funds. So why didn't he just eliminate the middlemen, set up his own hedge fund, and charge 1 percent or 2 percent fees and 20 percent of the profit? Neil told me that when Vijayvergiya said seriously that "Madoff doesn't have the operational capability to set up a hedge fund structure," he had to con-sciously stop himself from laughing out loud.

This guy actually expected Neil to believe that Bernie Madoff, who had helped found NASDAQ and who had built his own mar-ket-making operation, couldn't set up his own hedge fund. It probably takes about $50,000, a computer, and some office furniture to open a hedge fund. There are no barriers to entry into the hedge fund world. All you have to do is copy someone else's documents and file a few papers, and you're in business.

Neil finally replied, "Well, I can't believe Bernie couldn't just open a hedge fund and hire all the people he needs around the world for less than $20 million a year and keep all the rest for himself. He wouldn't have to deal with all the headaches that come with these other funds and he would keep most of the money himself. It makes sense. Why wouldn't he do that?"

Vijayvergiya literally did not answer. Instead, he continued pitch-ing the same nonsense we'd been reading about for almost eight years. Neil had to wonder how many people had listened to it and accepted it without questioning it, instead being seduced by the returns. Well, at least $7 billion worth. Obviously, there had been many other people who had heard it and walked away from the table; for example, none of the major New York investment houses had bought it. But this time Vijayvergiya was talking to someone who intended to call him on it. "Would you explain that to me? I've got to tell you, I've never heard anything like that before. Are you telling me that Madoff literally knows when the market's going to go up and when it's going to go down?" And basically, Vijayvergiya claimed that was true. Neil wondered, do you actually believe that? It's been proven over and over and over by academic studies that no one can time the market, let alone time the market consistently for 17 consecutive years. It made no sense, so Neil asked, "Are you telling me Bernie basically has had perfect market timing every month for the last 17 years?"

Vijayvergiya didn't respond directly to that.

"I just don't get it," Neil continued. "If you had perfect market timing like Madoff says he does, a split-strike conversion is the last strategy you'd use. I mean, if you really knew which way the market was going, you'd be buying leveraged futures or options. You could make a killing with a lot of other strategies, but this one actually limits you."

Vijayvergiya basically had no answer for that.

Neil then asked him why Madoff traded over the counter (OTC) rather than doing listed trades. Again, he didn't have an answer.

Neil asked him the cost of trading OTC against listed stocks. He had no answer.

Later, when Neil was telling me about this, he just kept repeating, "It was comical. This guy didn't know anything. I kept asking him about how the trades actually get executed, and I was drilling him every which way. Are they instantaneous, does he do the options all at once, does he package trade, does he toss in a third market?—every possible question you could ask about how a trade is implemented. I was firing away at him and eventually he says, 'There might be a three- or four-hour time lag from the time he actually does the stock trade verses the options.' He estimated that about 20 percent of Madoff's trades were done that way."

Neil told me, "Immediately I was like, 'Well, when you leg into a trade, when you only do one side and not the other side instantaneously, there's always the risk of it going against you before you get the other side of the trade off. I've done that, and I know you can get burnt really hard, really fast. So how does he protect himself?' "

Vijayvergiya basically had no answer for that question, either.

Neil spent about 45 minutes on the phone with him. In hindsight, he was sorry he hadn't stayed on the phone for hours and run through all our questions. But 45 minutes was all Neil could take. When he hung up, he was frustrated and angry. After all these years, Neil still thought there was a small possibility it was front running rather than a Ponzi, but this call settled that for him once and for all. He e-mailed me, "I can't believe they have kept this Ponzi scheme going on for this long."

Probably the only thing about this conversation that surprised us was the reality that Fairfield had so little respect for the people with whom it was dealing that they hadn't even bothered to make up some sort of plausible answers to these questions. The attitude was, you want these returns? Then you accept what I'm telling you—or rather what I'm not telling you.

All you have to do to get rich is believe in Bernie.

Even after that disastrous phone conversation, the third party marketer called Neil and asked if he was still interested in giving several million dollars to FGG to handle. Neil made him an offer. "Tell you what," he said. "I'll give him fifty million dollars right now. I'll cut you a check for fifty million bucks. I can get it done next week—but it's gotta be done in my separate account with my prime broker and only with listed OEX options. He can charge me his two and twenty, whatever he wants to charge me, but my fifty million has to go in my separate account in Goldman Sachs." Neil said this knowing it was an offer they had to refuse.

Maintaining a separate account meant that Neil would be able to see the execution of all the stock trades with the prime broker. And since no trades were being made and there would be nothing for him to see, there was no way Madoff could allow this. The marketer said, "Honestly, I don't know if he's done that before. I have to check."

He called back the next day and as expected told Neil it wasn't possible. Neil responded, "No shit. He can't do it because his whole operation is a fraud." Neil didn't mention my name or tell him that he had been investigating Madoff for years. Instead he pointed out that no legitimate manager would refuse a $50 million separate account. The fees would more than offset the hassle. But this marketer refused to believe him. Like so many other people, he just had too much at stake to accept it.

When Neil e-mailed me with this response, I wrote back, "My belief is that the HFOFs [hedge funds of funds] like Fairfield are either in on the scheme or willfully blind. Willful blindness is not a defense."

And when Neil offered, "Feel free to pass my notes on to SEC. Just remove my name," I pointed out it would do no good. "I'm not sure sending the SEC anything would help those morons solve the case. They're so lame, I'll bet they don't even catch colds in winter."

I'd finally given up on the SEC. A month earlier I'd sent it my final submission—and as usual I'd gotten no response. I'd sent a prospectus from Prospect Capital's Wickford Fund, another fund that channeled money to Madoff through Fairfield Sentry. But what made this one different was the fact that Madoff had started accepting leveraged money, a strong sign that he was running out of cash.

Frank Casey had found it in early June. He had been searching an Internet database for stable managers, trying to keep up to date with what Benchmark's competitors were doing. As he remembers, "Eventually the Wickford Fund popped up as a fund of funds. I got on their web site and discovered that it was offering a three-to-one swap written with a counterparty bank that was willing to lend two dollars for every dollar invested in a manager strategy."

Frank called me right away and said, "Madoff's got to be running short of cash. He's doing a three-to-one triple leveraged product with [and he named the bank]."

"My God," I said. "He's in trouble. He's gotta be getting close because he's willing to take in leveraged money. That means he's running out of money. He's getting desperate." Equally interesting was the fact that one of the two Wickford Funds was offshore, registered in the Cayman Islands, which made it attractive to American citizens who wanted to hide money from the IRS.

The 3:1 offer was a big red flag that Madoff was in trouble. This was a win-win-win-win situation—everybody wins except the investor. Normally, the investor would put up one dollar, Fairfield would get one dollar, and Madoff would get one dollar as well. But they were able to find a bank stupid enough to lend the investor two additional dollars for every dollar invested, so the investor was then on the hook for three dollars. Prospect Capital would give three dollars to Fairfield and take triple its management fees. That's one win. Prospect Capital is happy. Fairfield would invest three dollars in Madoff, so it is making three times its fees and profits. That's two wins. Bernie would get the same three dollars instead of one dollar. That's three wins. And the bank gets the interest rate spread, so it wins. If this were a legitimate investment, the victim would get three times the return minus the interest and fees that he or she is paying to borrow the money and invest. In a legitimate investment that would be a big win, but because this is a fraud, in addition to the initial investment the victim could possibly lose double that investment that he or she borrowed from the bank. In fact, I doubt the victim would ever have to repay the bank. The investor probably would have a strong lawsuit against the bank, but the best thing that would happen is a substantial loss and years of lawsuits.

"This is so odd," I wrote to Neil. "If you're a Ponzi scheme, why would you allow leverage? You end up paying well over double for each new dollar 'invested.' Is this a signal that Bernie is at the end of his rope and needs to offer juicier returns in order to keep the Ponzi scheme going? Is he this desperate for cash? My bet is Bernie is nearing the end of his run if he's allowing triple leverage."

With the possible collapse of his scam now somewhere just beyond the horizon, I began to wonder what the fallout might be—and if it was possible for him to ever get out of this without going to prison. I continued writing to Neil, "Let's see now, if BM is a fraud and I am your typical dumb (bank) client and purchase the total return swap, when the underlying returns are found to be bogus, does that mean I receive nothing back or do I get my principle back and nothing else? What if BM is waiting for a systemic market crisis to occur and then says, 'Oops, sorry, I bet wrong and lost 90 percent of your money, so, sorry, here's the 10 percent that's left. We're closing down and we want you to have it back.' That would be a great way out for him."

I also wrote to Citigroup's Leon Gross to see if he agreed with my prediction: "If Madoff is allowing a third party marketer to pitch this sort of product, my guess is that he's running low on new investors' cash inflows and needs to feed the Ponzi scheme or face ruin. Any insight on your part on what you might be hearing? Is Madoff running short of new cash?

"We all know how Ponzi schemes turn out."

While I don't remember his response, he certainly said nothing to change my opinion.

We found out after Madoff's collapse that we were right; he was desperate for cash. He was running out of big fish, so he had started casting a much wider net. Banks in Europe and Asia had begun offering certificates that allowed small investors to buy into Bernie for as little as $150. To promote sales, some of these banks actually offered a 3:1 leverage; for example, the Fairfield Sigma 3X Leveraged Certificates sold by Japan's largest brokerage for 10,000 included a loan that boosted the investment to 30,000, contributing to that bank's $300 million loss.

In late June I made my final submission to the SEC. The fact that I did that is probably a reasonably good definition of optimism. Actually, I wasn't naive enough to believe the SEC would do anything, but I wanted to make sure they had a complete record. Hope dies hard. "Hello Meaghan," I began an e-mail to Meaghan Cheung. I went on to say: "1. Attached are some very troubling documents that show the Madoff scheme is getting even more brazen. 2. Wickford is showing a monthly estimated pro forma set of returns of an investment in Madoff that is leveraged by a factor of 3.0 to 3.25 times and earns annual returns ranging between a low of 11.75 percent (2005) to a high of 33.42 percent (1997). 3. Madoff couldn't possibly be managing billions in this strategy unlevered, much less levered. I thought you would want to see these Wickford documents. And 4. When Madoff finally does blow up, it's going to be spectacular and lead to massive selling by hedge funds and funds of funds as they face investor redemptions. Regards. . . ."

The SEC's inspector general found out that as far as Cheung was concerned, by the time she received this e-mail she considered the Madoff case "for all intents and purposes closed without the formalities." She did claim that she forwarded it to Suh, the attorney, but Suh has no memory of ever receiving it.

The possibility that Madoff was in trouble was obviously very good news for me. I didn't care how he collapsed as long as he was no longer a threat to me. The day he was arrested or went out of business or died would be the first day I could take a deep and very safe breath.

Maybe other people might have wondered what was going on in Bernie's mind at this time. Was he panicking? Was he looking for an escape route? I knew that once he was exposed there would be no place in this world that was safe for him; if the legal system didn't put him away, then his offshore investors who had lost millions certainly would. But throughout this entire investigation I never took the time to put myself in his position. I never wondered what he was thinking or when he started this Ponzi scheme or why he did it or whether his family was involved. All I had to know was that Bernie Madoff was the enemy of everything in which I believed and his continued existence was an insult to all the people in this industry who tried to do it right.

Besides, I didn't have time to think about Bernie. I was much too busy investigating other crooks. By the summer of 2007 I had been working full-time on my fraud investigations for almost three years—without settling a single case. I was working with 20, 30, 40 whistle-blowers on more than a dozen cases. What depressed me was how easy it was to find my cases. Fraud in the United States was a growth industry. Maybe I should figure out a good fraud and franchise it, I thought. There really wasn't much risk of getting caught. I'd discovered that among government regulatory agencies the SEC wasn't unusually inept. It was simply as bad as all the rest of them. It required an unusual level of stupidity or tremendous bad luck to get caught by any government agencies other than the IRS, the FBI, and the Department of Justice, which are highly competent but vastly underresourced.

Bernie wasn't a genius, but he certainly wasn't stupid—and his luck had held for decades. For my team, pursuing Madoff had probably become more of a hobby than a live investigation, something that came into our lives on occasion like an old friend showing up unexpectedly. He remained the link that held my team together, and whenever anything happened in the industry, we immediately related it back to him. For example, CNN reported in February that "The SEC confirmed that it was investigating whether the major brokerage houses were tipping off hedge funds to the trades the brokers handle for big clients like mutual funds. . . . The SEC is also likely to scour trading records to see if the brokers are using info about clients' moves to invest their own capital." Frank wrote to ask if that meant "Bernie is tipping himself off."

As always, we tried to find the humor in everything Bernie. In April an article in *Absolute Return* entitled "To Catch a Thief" featured Fairfield

Greenwich managing director Douglas Reid—but not the way any of us anticipated. "In the 1955 Alfred Hitchcock movie *To Catch a Thief* it takes reformed cat burglar Cary Grant to capture the thief responsible for a series of jewelry heists across the French Riviera. Douglas Reid, managing director and investment committee member for $12 billion alternative management firm Fairfield Greenwich Group, believes the same approach holds true in creating and operating hedge funds.

"'Who better than a hedge fund manager to understand the business of another hedge fund manager?' asks Reid. . . . FGG, which added $2 billion in capital last year, is keen to expand its global reach."

Frank had sent it to me with the suggestion, "Maybe you should send him an e-mail on Bernie?"

"To Catch a Thief"? I wondered if Doug Reid had the slightest concept of how ironic that title was. I suspected he did. I responded to Frank, "If Doug Reid doesn't know about Bernie I'd be surprised, since his fund is 2/3rds Bernie and 1/3rd other managers. Besides, what are the odds that Fairfield could pull $8 billion out from Madoff and see any of the money? My bet is BM would fold like a cheap tent if someone made a large cash call."

I hadn't given up completely on exposing him, but as I don't believe in miracles I was realistic about the chances of that ever happening. I'd gone to the SEC in Boston—and gotten no satisfaction. I'd gone to the SEC in New York—and gotten no satisfaction. I'd gone to the SEC in Washington, D.C.—and gotten no satisfaction. I had no place else to go. If Madoff was going to be exposed, his luck was going to have to change. Nothing else seemed capable of stopping him. No matter what was going on in the market, he just kept rolling and rolling. In August 2007, for example, when the market declined, most hedge funds took a beating. Goldman Sachs's largest hedge fund lost 22.5 percent, JPMorgan's statistical hedge fund dropped 18 percent, and the $3 billion computer-driven statistical Tewksbury Investment Fund lost 8 percent. Overall, it was the worst month for hedge funds in almost a decade—except for Bernie. Fairfield Sentry still returned a profit! "Bernie's the best ever!" I wrote Frank. "And to think I thought he'd show a loss just to prove he's not an alien from outer space with perfect market-timing ability. Geez, the Sci-Fi channel should feature him."

And then, just as I was about ready to finally give up, the SEC's new director of risk management, Jonathan Sokobin, contacted me to see what I knew about emerging risks for the capital market. Emerging risks? That's like worrying if Godzilla had fleas. I had been recommended to Sokobin by Rudi Schadt, the director of risk management at Oppenheimer Funds. Rudi was a friend, and although he did not know about the Madoff investigation, he did know that I had a broad knowledge of risky schemes in the derivatives world. I couldn't warn him, because Oppenheimer Funds owned Tremont, which was the second largest investor in Madoff.

I had a long conversation with Sokobin in which we discussed several areas of possible concern. Although he had his PhD in finance from the University of Chicago, apparently he didn't have a lot of industry experience. He didn't seem to fully grasp the concepts that I was presenting to him. For example, I remember I told him there was a serious potential risk to the stock exchanges with investment banks owning too many seats. (If an investment bank filed for bankruptcy, it could put the entire exchange at risk.) He certainly seemed interested, but I got the feeling this was not what he was looking for.

I don't remember whether I told him specifically about Madoff during that conversation. When we hung up, though, I knew I had his attention. On April 2, 2008, I sent him an e-mail, attaching to it "a submission I've made to the SEC three times in Boston. Each time Boston sent this to New York. Meaghan Cheung, branch chief, in New York actually investigated this but with no result that I am aware of. In my conversations with her, I did not believe that she had the derivatives or mathematical background to understand the violations.

"Interestingly, a former derivatives PM who I know is now Director of Research at an HFOF [this was Neil, but I didn't identify him] tells me a counterpart at another HFOF pulled his money out of Madoff after asking Madoff to see his trade tickets. He then went to the OPRA [Option Price Reporting Authority] time and sales price feed and discovered that none of the Madoff trade tickets matched any time & sales reports on OPRA. He quickly concluded that Madoff was a fraud and pulled significant assets out of the fund."

I attached the 2005 submission to the SEC and wrote in the subject line, "$30 Billion Equity Derivative Hedge Fund Fraud in New York."

It literally would have been impossible to provide any more evidence of risk to the director of risk management than I did in this e-mail. I was also handing him a set of directions—try to match Madoff's trade tickets to the OPRA record of transactions. If he followed these instructions, he would discover they didn't match. For the detectives at the SEC, that would have been considered a clue!

I also gave him a list of people in the media he might contact to confirm my accusations, finishing my e-mail "Best of luck in your new position."

While I wasn't optimistic, I did believe it was at least possible that he was too new to have become part of that entrenched system. Imagine what might have happened if he had followed up, and the first investigation of his career had exposed the biggest crime in financial history? You'll have to imagine it because it never happened. I never received a response from him. I guess the director of risk management had managed not to take a risk. That was my final contact with the SEC.

There just wasn't much more we could do to stop Madoff. All we could do was watch and wait for his inevitable downfall. And wait. And continue waiting. I never lost interest; whenever I had the opportunity I'd take a look at his returns—and always shake my head in disbelief. As I finally had to admit to Neil, "I hate to say it, but Bernie's pulled off the perfect crime. He finds HFOFs that need his return stream to sell their stupid (high net worth) clients. He's got to be managing at least $30 billion." And as long as he was able to raise more money each month than he had to pay out, he could keep going indefinitely; by offering such a high and steady return, presumably he had attracted many clients who were using their investment with him as a savings account. Bernie was their bank; they invested their money with him and left it there, and it grew 10 percent a year, every year, far more than they possibly could earn anywhere else. As long as they didn't need it to pay the mortgage or pay for college tuition or buy a new Porsche, there was no reason to take it out.

That's exactly what Bernie was banking on, too.

■ ■ ■

We never stopped speculating on what would happen when he went down, how substantially the industry would be damaged; but we never considered the impact on individual investors. Oddly enough, after years of investigation we didn't know that Madoff had opened up direct accounts, that individuals were involved other than through feeder funds. For example, while Mike Ocrant told me that in the Jewish community Bernie was referred to respectfully as "the Jewish T-bill," none of us had any idea how deeply he had penetrated into the synagogues of New York and Florida.

When we got the opportunity, we did try to warn people. In 2003, just after Neil had started working at Benchmark Plus, he attended the annual Bank of America hedge fund conference at the Ritz in San Francisco. It was an opportunity for funds of funds to find fund managers. Each hedge fund had precisely 10 minutes to make a pitch. At this conference Neil met a man who had inherited several hundred million dollars and was a hedge fund investor. With his inheritance as the foundation, this investor had opened his own hedge fund of funds. Neil had heard that about half of the money in it was his own, and he had been successful enough to win several important awards. Neil met him at subsequent conferences and gradually the two men had become friendly. Neil had heard rumors that somewhere between 40 percent and 80 percent of his personal assets were invested with Madoff.

At almost every conference Neil ended up talking investments with him — and sometimes talking Madoff. Neil can't directly recall telling him that Madoff was a fraud. Rather, he tried to find ways to warn him without revealing that he'd been investigating Madoff for several years and without handing him a long list of red flags. "You know, something about Madoff doesn't look right," Neil would tell him. "It doesn't smell right. Look at his strategy; it doesn't make sense. Look at the open interest. I think maybe it's a fraud."

But like the many thousands of other investors, no one wanted to hear it. People who had invested in Madoff through Tremont believed it must be safe, because Tremont had done substantial due diligence.

Neil tried with him and many others he'd met in the hedge fund industry. I tried with Thierry. Mike Ocrant made it clear to people in the industry that Madoff wasn't kosher. But just like the SEC and the media, nobody listened.

The reality that a lot of individual investors were going to be devastated when Madoff collapsed was brought home to us in the fall of 2008. Frank Casey had left Benchmark and had started repping a British money management firm that built customized portfolios for investors. He had been pitching this company to an executive who approves new products to be sold by a major insurance company. As Frank remembers, the man listened carefully for almost an hour, then told him thank you very much but it wasn't a good fit for his brokers. It was too complicated for them, he said; they didn't know how to sell customized products.

Frank packed his briefcase as he had done countless times before and got up to leave. The two men shook hands, and as Frank turned to leave the man asked suddenly, "Frank, what do you know about Bernie Madoff?"

Frank was stunned. That question had come out of nowhere. His first thought was that he had been set up. He turned around and said sharply, "Who are you and why are you asking?"

"You know who I am."

"No, I don't," Frank snapped. "I know your name and I know your position in this firm, but who are you and why are you asking me about Madoff?"

The man explained calmly, "I don't want to tell you why I'm asking yet, because it may affect your answer; but I've been sitting here for 40 minutes listening to you talking about hedge funds and mitigation of risk and customization of portfolios, and what I was thinking the whole time was that you've got gray hair, and you told me you've been around the industry in derivatives for 34 years; so I figured you had to know something about Madoff."

Frank sat down. "Okay, you're right. I know a lot about him. What do you want to know?"

"Everything."

As Frank later explained to me, he felt somewhat reassured by the fact that this man wasn't in the financial industry; he worked for an insurance company. And Frank was very curious; why Bernie? "Okay, you want to know about Bernie Madoff. I'll tell you," he decided. And for the next half hour he related in detail the whole story of our investigation. It was the first time he'd told the complete story from beginning to end, and after holding it inside for seven years it just seemed to flow out of him—although he was careful not to mention any of our names or where we worked. When he'd finished, he looked this man right in the eyes and said, "Now. You tell me: What's this all about?"

"Two years ago I married into a very wealthy Jewish family," the executive began. "My wife is the sole heir to her father's estate. At our wedding Bernie Madoff came up to me and introduced himself; then he put his arm around my shoulders and told me, 'I've known [my wife] since she was just a little girl. Now that you're family, I'm gonna let you in. Come in and talk to me when you have a little time and we'll get you set up.'

"I knew all about Bernie from her father. He'd had most of his money with Bernie forever and he couldn't stop talking about it. Bernie this, Bernie that. Bernie'll give you the best returns with no risk. He wanted me to get in right away. But before I did anything I took a look at his strategy. Frank, believe me, I don't know that much about derivatives, but I couldn't figure out how his returns could be so steady if he was doing what he said he was doing. I decided not to give him any of our money until I could get some answers. So I declined.

"You can imagine what that's done to my relationship with my father-in-law. Every time I see him it's 'Why haven't you called Bernie?' He's like 'It's your job now as my son-in-law to take care of my daughter, and you should be putting your money with Bernie. He'll take care of you.' It's really causing a problem in the family. My father-in-law's making a real issue about this."

Frank smiled at that. "Boy, did you nail it," he said. "What we can't understand is why nobody else seems to be able to figure it out. We think he's going to blow soon."

The executive took a long, deep breath. "What I really want to do is convince him to get his money out as soon as possible. I'm sick and tired of listening to him, and I'm really afraid my wife is going to lose her inheritance. Can you help me? Can you put any of what you just told me in writing?"

Frank laughed at that suggestion. "Oh sure," he said. "I don't think so—I don't want a bullet in my head. Sorry."

The executive practically begged him. "Frank, I'm afraid my wife's gonna lose everything if you don't help me," he said. "Her father isn't going to listen to me unless I have some proof." Frank thought about it. And then he sat down and wrote a long e-mail, using as his foundation the red flags from my 2005 submission to the SEC. He knew it was risky, that it could put him in jeopardy, but he felt he had a moral obligation to help. He also knew, when he paused to think about it, that it was really a stupid thing to do.

Knowing that there was a real chance this person might confront Bernie with this information, he did as much as possible to protect himself. Rather than just scanning in the submission, he created a completely new document, eliminating several of the most technical points as well as anything that might lead back to me. He changed the order, renumbered the flags, and substituted the phrase *unknown scheme* for Ponzi scheme because he didn't want to be out in public with that accusation. At the top of the e-mail he wrote a disclaimer, stating that this was not his opinion and certainly not his firm's opinion, but that he had run into an unnamed analyst extremely knowledgeable about derivatives, who had shown him these red flags. "I'm not stating that the analyst has it nailed," he wrote. "I haven't done my due diligence on this analyst. I present this information solely for your own use and you have to do your own due diligence."

Then he moved the cursor to the upper lefthand corner of his screen and hit send. And then forgot all about it. It would be more than a month before he received a response, and by that time the whole world had changed.

■ ■ ■

It's impossible to pinpoint the moment at which Bernie Madoff realized it was over for him. It wasn't beauty that killed this beast; it was the cold numbers. As it turned out, the market that Madoff had dominated for decades finally destroyed him.

Beginning sometime in 2007 the world financial system was staggered when the American housing bubble burst. Millions of people who had been living on the rising equity in their homes saw that cushion disappear. Within several months trillions of dollars in real estate value was lost. People with low-interest adjustable-rate mortgages saw their payments rise and could no longer afford those mortgages, causing banks to foreclose. Banks had issued millions of those mortgages to people who were not financially qualified and whose only viable exit strategy was to sell their homes at a higher price, but these homeowners now saw that option collapse. Investment firms had wrapped those mortgages into financial products called mortgage-backed securities. Those securities had been sold as high-quality assets, but in fact were low-quality realty. They were also very illiquid, and when people realized there was little or no underlying value to them and saw no new buyers coming into the markets, their value plunged.

It was like a big game of musical chairs, but in this game when the music stopped those institutions holding these securities were out hundreds of billions of dollars. Within two years the American housing market had lost about 20 percent of its value. As the market collapsed, banks stopped lending and the years of easily obtainable credit ended. Even people and businesses with really good credit couldn't get loans. At the same time commodity prices, especially oil, rose rapidly. By September 2008, this had become a global financial crisis. Banks began closing. There was a real sense of panic as the media wondered if we were on the edge of a second Great Depression.

The stock market, which had been in a somewhat orderly decline for about a year, suddenly began dropping fast. In October, the head of the International Monetary Fund warned that the international financial system potentially could collapse. The week of October 5 the S&P 500 lost 20 percent of its value and the Dow Jones Industrial Average lost 18 percent. The deputy governor of the Bank of England called it "possibly the largest financial crisis of its kind in human history." By November the markets had fallen almost 40 percent. While hundreds of other hedge funds had been forced to close or had stopped allowing redemptions, Madoff was still claiming to be profitable. Incredibly, there were numerous people who still believed in Bernie, and rushed to get out of money-losing investments and into the safer Madoff funds. Bernie told Fairfield he was open and would take whatever FGG could raise for him. Maybe he still had some hope that he could survive. Who knows?

But too many of Madoff's investors were desperate for cash to protect their investments and meet their growing client redemptions, and attempted to withdraw their money—apparently these requests totaled more than $7 billion. There was no possible way Madoff could cover all these requests, but he wouldn't give up. He started scrambling, desperately trying to raise cash. In late November Fairfield announced the creation of a new fund, Fairfield Emerald. But it was too late; it was over for him.

Finally, on December 10, 2008, he supposedly told his two sons that his investment business was a fraud, "Basically, a giant Ponzi scheme." Early the following morning, December 11, 2008, two FBI agents knocked on his front door and asked him if there was an innocent explanation.

He shook his head. "There is no innocent explanation." The two agents immediately placed him under arrest. The largest Ponzi scheme in history had finally collapsed.

Chapter 8

Closing the Biggest Barn Door in Wall Street History

The moment they put the handcuffs on Madoff, my life was changed forever. I just didn't find out about it for several hours. That morning Frank and I had been to a partnership breakfast of an organization called World Boston. World Boston is part of the 60-year-old World Affairs Council that brought politicians and dignitaries from around the world to Boston to speak to local leaders of the business community. We were there to support Gaytri Kachroo, who was on its board. Among the other people there were bank chairs, investment officers, and fund managers. It was a terrific event; even the food was good. We couldn't have known it, but we were sitting in a sea of Madoff victims.

I'd gotten home from that meeting just in time to take my twin boys for their karate lesson. It was while I was waiting for them at the dojo that my life changed. Madoff had admitted he was running a Ponzi scheme. Madoff had been arrested. Billions of dollars were gone. The whole financial industry was shaken. People were panicking.

After dealing with the initial shock, I didn't really know how to react. I wanted to do a hundred things first, and my brain sorted through them rapidly, trying to put them into some kind of sensible order. But I was in new territory. I needed information. I needed to know what had happened, when, and how. I needed to have all the details. I called Dave Henry back. "It's finally over," he said, bringing me up to the minute. "There could be a bloodbath on Wall Street." We tried to guess the ramifications, who was going down, but we had no real idea. I returned Andre Mehta's call, but he was being overwhelmed by clients. Wall Street was in an uproar; everybody was trying to find out who and what was affected. People were desperate for information.

The energy generated by my excitement was surging through my body and I couldn't stand still; as we spoke I kept walking in tight circles. I began thinking, *One enemy down*; but there still was one battle to fight. The one that might have gotten me killed was finished, but the Securities and Exchange Commission (SEC) was still potentially very dangerous to me. The papers I had in my possession would expose the incompetence of the SEC to the world. Unless it could prevent me from getting my documents published, the reputation of that agency was going down in flames, and careers were going to end that day. Those papers were sitting in folders in my house. I realized I had to get them out of the house right away, before anyone could get a court order to stop me. And I had to get them published. I'll call Wilke, I thought. I'll bet he's gonna want 'em now.

Finding John Wilke was going to be a problem. I knew that on Thursdays he was at Johns Hopkins University receiving radiation or chemo, or both, to fight his aggressive cancer. Medical facilities did not permit cell phones to be used around that equipment. I called anyway, three different times, and left a brief and nervous message each time.

I knew I needed to get my kids home as quickly as possible and start getting organized. I began running through checklists in my head, trying to prioritize. Minutes later my boys finished their lesson and we walked outside into a driving rainstorm. After the mandatory check for bombs underneath my vehicle I loaded the twins into the car. Five minutes later I was up in my office, digging out papers, making piles. The phone hadn't stopped ringing, but I didn't want to answer it. When it rang again I checked the caller ID and recognized a New York area code and figured it was one of my Wall Street derivatives buddies calling with the Madoff news. But when I answered, a voice I didn't recognize asked, "Are you the Madoff whistleblower?"

My first reaction to that call was anger. "Who is this?"

"This is Greg Zuckerman of the *Wall Street Journal*," the caller said. "CNBC is reporting the existence of a Madoff whistleblower. Is that you?"

"You fucking damn well know it is," I snapped. "You people have had this story for three fucking years and you didn't do shit with it."

"Well, I don't know anything about that," Zuckerman said. "But whatever happened before I'd really like to talk to you now." I had never spoken to Greg Zuckerman, but with John Wilke unavailable I had no choice but to work with him. I needed to get my documents published, and whatever had happened in the past, the *Journal* was still the best place for that. So I needed Zuckerman almost as much as he needed me. I found out later that he'd learned my identity—and gotten my phone number—from Mike Ocrant, who considered him a reliable and ethical journalist.

■ ■ ■

Frank Casey, Neil Chelo, and Mike Ocrant were each going through similar experiences. I called Frank as soon as I could. He had just left his apartment in a high-rise on the Boston waterfront and was riding down in the elevator when I found him. "You're not gonna believe this," I said. I was calling from my office as I gathered my papers. "Bernie just blew up. He admitted the whole thing was a Ponzi scheme."

"I'll call you right back," he said. Frank got out of the elevator and went right back up to his apartment. "He just crumbled," I continued, and began filling him in on the few details I had learned. As we were talking, Frank's other cell phone rang. It was Mike Ocrant, calling from New York. "Oh my God," he said. "Did you hear the news?"

Frank was balancing two phones when his house phone rang. His wife answered it and indicated it sounded important. "I'll call you back," he told me and Ocrant. The insurance executive he'd met only weeks earlier and warned about Bernie was calling. "First of all," the man said, "I want to say thank you. Thank you for everything you tried to do for me."

Frank could tell from the sadness in his voice that the outcome hadn't been good. "What happened?"

"I took your e-mail to my father-in-law and I read it to him word for word," he said, his voice choking. "He said, 'This is incredulous. I don't believe it. Bernie would never do this to me; he wouldn't do it.' He wouldn't do anything about it. We lost everything, absolutely every penny."

"I'm really sorry," Frank said.

"No, I really want to thank you for your effort," the executive said, and after another few awkward words they hung up. Frank turned on the television to try to find out what was going on.

Mike Ocrant had been in a team meeting to discuss an upcoming conference. As he walked into his office his phone was ringing. It was a close friend, Hal Lux, a former top financial journalist who had joined the hedge fund industry and most recently had become a senior fellow at Harvard's Kennedy School of Government, where he focuses on financial market research. "Did you hear?"

"Hear what?"

"You were right," he said. "Your story was totally right. Madoff just got arrested for running a Ponzi scheme. You're the man!"

Seven years too late, Mike thought, *seven years too late*. A few minutes later he called Frank, who was talking to me. "Harry was right the whole time," Mike told him. "It wasn't front-running; it was a Ponzi."

"I know. I'm on the other phone with him right now."

Neil had been having a very difficult day. Personal problems were hitting him hard and he was trying to escape into work. When he checked his e-mail, he found a message from a hedge fund manager with whom he'd been friendly for years. It was a cryptic message: "No Madoff, right?" Without knowing Madoff had collapsed, that message made no sense. Neil wondered if he had told this manager about our investigation. Maybe, but he wasn't sure. So what did that mean—"No Madoff, right?"

He called the fund manager, who told him, "Check out Bloomberg. It's the headline. Madoff turned himself in." Neil turned and looked at the Bloomberg terminal. The headline confirmed it. Bernie Madoff had been arrested for running a $50 billion Ponzi scheme.

Neil took a deep breath, then turned away from the monitor and went back to work. The day was too hard for him to get any satisfaction from this. Later in the West Coast afternoon he began trading e-mails with me and the rest of the team.

When I told my attorney for my other fraud cases, Gaytri Kachroo, that Madoff had surrendered, she asked curiously, "Who's Madoff?" I had never told her about this case, and at first she didn't comprehend how big or serious it was. "This was my first case," I explained. "I've been working on it for a long, long time."

Her primary concerns were how it would affect me and how it would impact the cases on which we were working. "Just calm down," she told me. "You have a responsibility to the whistleblowers on your other cases, so we need to go slow with this."

As the story unfolded over the next few days, she began to grasp its significance. But it wasn't until she was on an Air India flight to Delhi with her children that she finally got it. As she told me, she was stunned to hear the people sitting near her on the plane talking about me—in French. *They're talking about Harry*, she thought. *That's my client!* And when the plane landed in Paris for a stopover she bought a copy of the newspaper *Le Monde*—and found a story about me on the front page. That was also the first time she realized that her life was about to change, too.

In Whitman, it would be almost a full day before Sergeant Harry Bates of the Whitman police department saw my picture pop up on the TV screen. He stood there with his mouth open, thinking, *I don't believe this. I do not believe this. This is the biggest thing to happen around here since ice cream!* And he shook his head and smiled, knowing that nobody in the station was going to believe what he was about to tell them.

I knew I wasn't in any personal danger from the SEC. But the only way that agency could emerge intact from this debacle was to prevent my submissions from being published. I was afraid they would raid my house under some security pretext and confiscate my computers and my documents and then find some flimsy excuse to get rid of them. I knew they had no criminal powers to stage that raid, but I also knew how desperate they must have been feeling.

I loaded a 12-gauge pump shotgun with double-ought buckshot, attached six more rounds to the stock, and draped a bandolier of 20 more rounds on top of my locked gun cabinet. Next I got out my old army gas mask in case they came in using tear gas. If an SEC raid team showed up, I only had to scare them or slow them down long enough for Sergeant Harry Bates and the Whitman police department to show up and take possession of my documents and computers. SEC staff aren't armed, so while I didn't think they'd try anything illegal, my military training kicked in and I prepared countermeasures for the worst possible course of action on the SEC's part.

The *Wall Street Journal* was my way out. This time they were practically begging me for copies of my documents. I knew Greg Zuckerman by his byline. I'd read some of the stories he'd done. If I couldn't get hold of John Wilke, Zuckerman would serve my purpose.

My safety lay in providing the *Journal* with copies of the same documents they'd had for three years. I was fighting an information war with the SEC; the army had taught me that in that kind of warfare it was vital to get out in front, to shape the battlefield for your own benefit. I decided to work with the *Journal* because I wanted the story to get out my way and by working with only one newspaper I maintained some control. I gave my story to the *Journal* because it fit my needs. I told Zuckerman that John Wilke had copies of all my documents and speculated that they were still on his computer or on the *Journal's* server in Washington. Zuckerman explained that he was in New York and had no access to that material. "I need you to send it to me again," he said. "Can you do it today?"

I wanted to laugh at him. Today? "You've had this material for three years," I snapped. "I handed you a Pulitzer and you didn't want it."

Zuckerman paused. "That wasn't me," he said. I accepted that. I didn't know anything about the internal workings at the *Journal*. As I had learned through my own work as an investigator, secrecy is absolutely vital. So it made sense that Wilke would not have mentioned the story he was working on to Zuckerman. Greg must have guessed what I was thinking—that the fact that John had dropped the story wasn't going to look good for him—and he added, somewhat cryptically, "We gotta protect Wilke."

"Don't worry about it," I responded. "I never thought it was him."

I'd stored my Madoff documents in my dead cases filing cabinet so they wouldn't get mixed up with more active cases. I spent the early evening hours digging them out and trying to put them into some kind of sensible order. I'd known that Madoff was going to blow someday, but I'd decided by the time that happened I would no longer be involved. I was never so happy to be wrong.

The only fax I had in my house wasn't working. I wasn't really comfortable using it, anyway. A lot of the documents I received and sent were intended to be secret, and at that time I didn't have a secure phone line. I'd used the fax machines from different Staples and Kinko's locations, but by the time I was ready to transmit they were all closed. I decided to go over to my local pizza restaurant, the Venus Cafe, figuring every restaurant must have a fax to receive lunch orders.

It was a miserable New England night. We were in the middle of a rain and ice storm, and power lines were going down in the western part of Massachusetts. *That figures*, I thought as I trudged through the storm carrying all my papers. I loved the Venus. My family and I spent so much time there that it was almost like our second kitchen. It's owned and run by the Drosos family, and they knew me well enough to consider me the local eccentric. I was the guy who had been coming in for years telling bad Greek jokes and sitting at a table reading forensic accounting books.

I rushed into the restaurant disheveled, dripping wet, and admittedly very agitated. There was a television set hanging above the bar, and a photo of Bernie Madoff was on the screen. "Elaine," I said, "Elaine, that's my case. That's what I've been working on. I'm the whistleblower. Do you have a fax machine? I have to get this to the *Wall Street Journal* and I don't want the wrong people to find out about it."

"Now calm down, Harry," Elaine Drosos said. "What's going on?" I blurted out the whole story as quickly as I could. All I wanted to do was get to that fax machine. She listened intently, nodding from time to time, and when I was done she asked, "What's a Ponzi scheme?"

She had no idea what I was talking about. It didn't matter; the restaurant didn't have a working fax machine. Fortunately, sitting at the bar was the owner of a trucking company whose office was about three miles down the highway. "You're the whistleblower on that thing?" he asked, indicating the television set.

"Yes sir, the SEC screwed it up totally and these papers prove it. I've got to send them to the *Wall Street Journal*."

"Count me in," he said. "I got a fax machine at my place. Let's go." He left his beer and pizza on the bar, proving that he was a dedicated American citizen, and we drove to his office in his SUV. It turned out he was pretty angry with the government because of the Wall Street bailouts, so he was thrilled to participate in anything that would embarrass the SEC. I got on my cell phone with Zuckerman as we started sending documents from a fax machine on the first floor of the trucking company office. *Finally*, I thought, *finally*.

The fax machine stopped. We tried it again. It started, then cut out again. The owner shook his head and sighed. "I got another one upstairs that's not so modern, but it tends to work better whenever we have a problem." As we later learned, the problem wasn't the fax machine; the ice storm was knocking out phone lines all over the state. But the second machine worked as long as we fed it continuously. It took more than an hour to get all the documents faxed successfully. While that was going on Zuckerman asked me, "Do you want to help me write this story?"

I'd been waiting for that opportunity for nine years. "You bet I do," I said.

When we got back to the restaurant, I put whatever cash I had in my pocket on the bar and told Elaine, "This man eats and drinks as long as this holds out!"

So much was happening so fast. In addition to Gaytri, who was my personal lawyer, I called Phil Michael, an attorney who was representing several of my False Claims Act cases. He was in Mexico. He called me back but we had a poor connection. He told me I could talk about Madoff as much as I wanted to, but I couldn't mention any of the other cases. Then I thought he said, "Cooperate with the press and milk the publicity." In fact, that was exactly the opposite of what he'd said.

That night I never slept. I was too busy copying computer files containing Madoff case documents, e-mails, and SEC submissions to CD-ROMs in order to preserve evidence in case the SEC raided my home in a last-ditch attempt to destroy evidence. I also e-mailed files to my legal teams in Boston and New York and also to Taxpayers

Against Fraud in Washington. Getting those e-mails out during the ice storm was quite a challenge and took hours longer than it would have if the weather had been cooperating.

The next morning I sent my wife, Faith, into Boston on the commuter rail carrying a set of very incriminating documents burned onto a CD. She carried it on her person all morning; then at lunchtime she surreptitiously made her way through the narrow, crowded streets of Boston's Chinatown, where she clandestinely passed the CD to one of her trusted girlfriends. They met in a restaurant frequented almost solely by Chinese patrons. Unless the SEC somehow managed to trail her with Chinese Mandarin–speaking agency employees, they'd never be able to track that CD. I now had case documents spread safely up and down the East Coast between Boston, New York, and Washington. If the SEC tried anything illegal, it would only backfire on the agency once those documents started surfacing.

My brother hadn't heard that Madoff had surrendered. His phone starting ringing at 6 A.M. the next morning with calls from media outlets who wanted to know if he was the Madoff whistleblower featured in the *Wall Street Journal*. After a half dozen calls he realized that the *Journal* was lying on his front porch and figured he'd better get up and find out exactly what I'd done this time.

I was barraged by phone calls, most of which I didn't answer. But when I saw the phone number of the Boston office of the SEC, I figured I'd better pick it up. The caller was a person in that office other than Ed Manion, a person I knew well from the caller's former job, and probably the last person I expected to make this particular phone call. This individual was risking their career, which was not something I would have believed was part of the person's character. Obviously I can't identify this individual, who warned me, "Harry, Operation Cover-Up has started here. They're telling us we don't know you, we never heard of you. I got a call from the senior staff five minutes ago telling me not to have any contact with you. Watch your back, buddy."

Now my precautions of the previous night preparing my shotgun seemed vindicated. I was holed up in my office preparing documents all morning. Vans and cars were showing up in front of the house. Reporters were getting out and ringing the front doorbell (at least we hoped they were journalists and not SEC employees). I left my mother-in-law to answer the door and shoo reporters away. It was frightening each time she opened that front door. If they came in a TV news van and had TV cameras, that was actually a relief since we knew the SEC couldn't carry out that elaborate a ruse. From our vantage point we could plainly see strange folks walking up and down the neighborhood knocking on my neighbors' doors and asking questions. We live in the town center, so these folks were also canvassing the local merchants, no doubt asking questions about me. We hoped they were journalists and nothing more. It was a scary time for us, particularly when the school bus dropped the boys off that afternoon.

I also got several calls from a reporter at the *Washington Post* telling me that the SEC was denying the existence of a whistleblower. "They're saying they get hundreds of thousands of whistleblower tips every year and they can't investigate all of them and they don't know anything about you."

"Thank you," I said, but I was thinking, *Wait, just wait.* My informer inside the SEC had been absolutely correct: The agency was trying to cover up its malfeasance. I had to wonder how far the SEC would go to protect itself.

■ ■ ■

Within a day of Madoff's surrender, my house was under media siege. Cameras were set up on my front lawn and it seemed like every TV producer in the business had my phone numbers on speed dial. My phone never stopped ringing. I had to come up with a plan, so I decided I'd speak to the *Journal* for print, make one big TV appearance, and do one radio show.

Meanwhile, Zuckerman and I were working 16 to 20 hours a day, desperately trying to get the story published as quickly as possible. I was living on adrenaline; I couldn't sleep. I knew I wasn't going to be vindicated until the story was published. I'd sleep then. I kept feeding him more and more documents, whatever he said he needed. Finally, he asked me, "Are you for real? I mean, are you making this stuff up?" Later I found out that he actually called Frank and Neil to confirm my story.

"You're kidding me, right, Greg?" I said. "How could anybody write all this stuff on short notice and in such great detail?"

"I know that," he admitted. "No one could. But this stuff you're sending me—it's too good to be true. It's amazing. You knew all of this was going on?"

"Yes, I did."

"Jeez," he said, impressed. I could hear the astonishment in his voice as the full impact of this information hit him. This was proof that the SEC had been warned about Madoff eight years earlier and had done nothing to stop him. They were $50 billion too late. "Jeez," he said again.

Later that evening John Wilke finally called me. I knew he was excited about the story, but from the sound of his voice it was obvious that the chemo was draining all his energy. There was an overwhelming sadness in this conversation; this should have been another scoop for Front Page Wilke, but physically he couldn't write it. He did call Zuckerman, though, and gave me great reviews. "He's totally legit," he told Zuckerman, and then admitted, "We've had all this information for a couple of years."

What continued to astonish me was the SEC's denial that I existed. It was obvious they were desperately trying to contain the damage and were hoping that somehow I wouldn't surface. I was the smoking gun that could destroy that agency. And as long as they were able to maintain the fiction that there was no whistle-blower and they knew nothing about Madoff, I believed I was still in jeopardy.

Finally, five days after Madoff's surrender, Zuckerman called the SEC's Washington office and asked specifically, "On April 2, 2008, did your director of risk management, Jonathan Sokobin, get the following e-mail with the subject line, '$30 Billion Equity Derivative Hedge Fund Fraud in New York'?"

That was the first time the SEC knew that the *Wall Street Journal* had copies of my submissions. They were finished. That night SEC Chairman Christopher Cox issued a long statement in which he reviewed the progress the agency was making in closing the biggest barn door in Wall Street history. Basically, he began with several excuses, claiming that Madoff took "complicated steps . . . to deceive investors, the public and *regulators*," and that he "kept several sets of books and false documents, and provided false information."

It was only in the third paragraph that he finally admitted, "The Commission has learned that credible and specific allegations regarding Mr. Madoff's financial wrongdoing, going back to at least 1999, were repeatedly brought to the attention of the SEC staff, but were never recommended to the Commission for action. I am gravely concerned by the apparent multiple failures over at least a decade to thoroughly investigate these allegations. . . .

"In response . . . I have directed a full and immediate review of the past allegations regarding Mr. Madoff and his firm and the reasons they were not found credible, to be led by the SEC's Inspector General. The review will also cover the internal policies at the SEC . . . and whether improvements to those policies are necessary."

Basically, he threw his staff under the bus. I'd won.

Once the SEC issued its mea culpa acknowledging my existence, the editors at the *Wall Street Journal* told Greg Zuckerman that his story was not going to be published as scheduled. They had decided to double the size of the article, add pictures, and move it to the top slot as the page one cover story for the following day's edition. Greg called me excitedly and asked me if I minded the delay in order to appear on the front cover. I said, "No, but only if you agree to post my 2005 SEC submission on your web site so that the world knows exactly what information the SEC had and failed to act on." He readily agreed, and we started working overtime to get the story written.

I think we were both too excited to sleep well that night. I knew that this story was going to rock the SEC's world with earthquake-like force. Once that story was out and my SEC submissions, along with a few e-mails, were posted online, my family and I would have nothing to fear from the SEC ever again.

Greg and I worked feverishly through the next day. Late the follo-wing afternoon the *Journal* posted the one-star edition onto its online edition, which we both read. He kept writing, adding more and more detail until finally late that evening the five-star late edition made its way onto the web site and out to printing presses. My wife came up to my office and accused me of being Greg Zuckerman's unpaid love slave, to which I replied, "Well, I am Greek and I bet he's probably very cute in person." She laughed and went to bed.

On Thursday, December 18, the *Journal* published Greg Zuckerman's story, "Madoff Misled SEC in '06, Got Off." The second paragraph began, "Harry Markopolos—who once worked for a Madoff rival—sparked the probe with his nearly decade-long campaign to persuade the SEC that Mr. Madoff's returns were too good to be true. In recent days, the *Wall Street Journal* reviewed e-mails, letters, and other documents that Mr. Markopolos shared with the SEC over the years.

"When he first began studying Mr. Madoff's investment performance a decade ago, Mr. Markopolos told a colleague at the time, 'It doesn't make any damn sense,' he and the colleague recall. 'This has to be a Ponzi scheme.'"

We had decided at this point not to name the other members of the team, although Zuckerman had spoken to both Neil and Frank.

The article continued, "The SEC's documents indicate the agency had Mr. Madoff in its sights amid multiple violations that, if pursued, could have blown open his alleged multibillion-dollar scam. Instead his firm registered as an investment advisor, at the agency's request, and the public got no word of the violations.

"For Mr. Markopolos, the arrest a few days ago of Mr. Madoff was something of a vindication after his long campaign. At a certain point, he says, 'I was just the boy who cried wolf.'"

Zuckerman's lengthy story covered the entire eight-year-long investigation, from the day I got Madoff's returns through all my dealings with the SEC. He quoted me as saying, "Some people play fantasy sports; that was how it was with us—Madoff was our fantasy sport. We wanted him nailed."

As for the response from the SEC, Zuckerman wrote, "An SEC spokesman wouldn't comment on the agency's communication with Mr. Markopolos." And later in the story, after describing my final submission to the director of risk management, he added, "Mr. Sokobin, through an SEC spokesman, declined to comment."

Well before dawn the next morning, I quietly left my home and took the first train into Boston. I didn't want to be at my house, because I knew the media would have it surrounded shortly after daybreak. It was an emotional day for me. I'd just lifted the world off my shoulders, and I spent the day moving around the city simply thanking all the people who had contributed to the investigation—my lawyers; friends like Dan DiBartolomeo; Andre Mehta at Cambridge Associates, the most prestigious consulting firm in the world; and the staff at the Boston Security Analysts Society. It was a victory for all of us.

The one person whose hand I really wanted to shake was Ed Manion's, but I figured I probably wouldn't be welcome at that particular office.

We'd won the biggest battle, but we hadn't won the war. I believed the SEC remained a serious danger to the American people. It was obvious that it was no longer capable of regulating the financial industry, and unless it was completely transformed it would never be able to do that. It wasn't just a few cosmetic changes that were necessary. It wasn't just a few scapegoats who needed to be replaced. The SEC had to be fundamentally changed if investors were ever going to be able to rely on it again.

■ ■ ■

The damage done by Madoff was reverberating throughout the financial markets of the world, as well as in millions of homes. In an instant, thousands of people had been financially devastated. Their investments were wiped out. Within days stories began appearing in the media about elderly people who had been living on their regular returns from Bernie who were left with nothing. Houses were going up for sale in an already distressed real estate market. The entire hedge fund industry was shaken.

The media coverage was insatiable. They were reporting how many people had been wiped out, which we had totally missed. We had never realized that Madoff was accepting individual accounts. I didn't know he was taking Jewish charities and Jewish endowments to the cleaners, just wiping them out. We were tracking the feeder funds, and as finance professionals, Neil, Mike, Frank, and I couldn't conceive of anybody putting 100 percent in a single investment. That's just not in our vocabulary. We thought by tracking the feeder funds we were tracking Madoff. We weren't dealing with individuals; we were focused on large funds. And maybe that was the luckiest break in our investigation, because if we had found out it might have gotten us killed.

The problem for reporters was that there were few people other than the victims to speak to. They couldn't get to Bernie Madoff or any members of his family. That pretty much left me. I was getting what seemed like hundreds of requests every day. I turned down every offer; in fact, a Hollywood-based agent called and told me a producer had offered me $1 million to appear on *Oprah*. I don't have the slightest idea if that was a real offer or what other rights it might have included. It certainly seemed like too big a number to be real but I never pursued it. "I'm not interested," I said. "It's not appropriate." I didn't want to be seen as profiting from my work; and *Oprah* certainly was not the right forum. I made the decision that I would tell my story on only one TV program; and if I was going to do only one show, I wanted it to be a serious investigative program with the most extensive coverage possible. So I accepted an invitation to appear on *60 Minutes*.

But because I wanted to keep control of the story, I asked the members of my team, as well as friends like Dave Henry and Dan DiBartolomeo, to do the interviews. Frank Casey, in particular, was deluged with requests. He did numerous interviews; and as he quickly discovered, many of the reporters covering this story had no background in finance; they didn't know the difference between a split-strike conversion and a two-point conversion. But he patiently answered their questions.

In addition to all the invitations from the media, I was also contacted by several government agencies, including the House of Representatives Financial Services Committee. This committee, which is chaired by Massachusetts Congressman Barney Frank, had already scheduled hearings into the incompetence of the SEC and invited me to appear. To me, this seemed a little like a Frank Capra movie, *Harry Goes to Washington*, but there was no humor in this story. Somebody needed to warn the public that the SEC was an out-of-control agency that served no obvious purpose other than to fool people into believing it was actually offering investors protection. The hearing was scheduled for early January, and I'd agreed to meet with a senior committee staffer on December 24 to discuss my appearance.

The day before that meeting, I was in my office catching up on some of my other cases when Frank Casey called. He didn't even say hello. "Hey Harry," he said in a weary voice. "I just heard Thierry committed suicide."

"Oh my God, no," I said. "Thierry?" At that moment all the emotions I'd been holding inside for the past 11 days erupted. I started crying and I couldn't stop. I was devastated. Why didn't I call him? I kept asking myself. Why didn't I call him?

Thierry de la Villehuchet was a man of honor, truly a noble man, and apparently he felt that this was the only way he could really show his contrition to his family and friends and clients whose money he had lost. Thierry was also my friend, and I believed Bernie Madoff killed him.

Access International had lost about $1.4 billion, including investments from the royal families across Europe, Thierry's own $55 million personal fortune, and the fortune of his partner, Patrick Littaye. As I later learned, for several days after Madoff's Ponzi scheme had collapsed Thierry believed he would be able to get at least some of that money back. But when he realized that wasn't possible, he sat down in his office, wrote notes to his wife, his brother Bertrand, Littaye, and one other person, swallowed some pills, then rested his feet on his desk and slit both of his wrists with a box cutter. His life bled out into trash cans, no doubt placed there by Thierry so he would not inconvenience others with a mess.

As Patrick Littaye revealed, the letter that Thierry left for him "assured me of his friendship and asked me to look out for his wife." While so many other people were running away from their own responsibility, desperately looking for someone, anyone else, to blame, Thierry accepted responsibility and acknowledged what he had done. His family was once so wealthy and respected it had lent money to the Sun King, Louis XIV, but Bernie Madoff had wiped out that fortune. Thierry had trusted Madoff completely. He'd led his friends and clients into a catastrophic situation. For him, committing suicide was a positive act of honor.

His widow, Claudine, put it simply, telling reporters that Madoff was "a murderer. . . . He killed my husband."

I hadn't been sleeping much before this, and after everything else that had happened Thierry's suicide was almost too much to bear. Frank, too, was crushed. Investigating Madoff had been an intellectual pursuit. We had kept our emotional distance, and none of us had been touched personally by him. No more. Thierry de la Villehuchet was a man we liked and respected. I considered him a friend.

I cried on and off for three days. Once I'd let loose my emotions I just couldn't stop. I had a terrible time sleeping for many nights after that. And truthfully, I've never stopped wondering if I could have saved his life. What if I had called him, if I had offered him some encouragement—would it have made a difference? Maybe Bernie Madoff was the reason he was dead, but the SEC had a role in it. Apparently Access International had about 30 percent invested in Madoff when Rampart first got involved with them, but that increased gradually until by early 2008 as much as 75 percent of its assets were committed to him. If the SEC had done its job and stopped Madoff years earlier, Thierry might have been able to survive that loss. That certainly wasn't my only reason for wanting to bring down the SEC, but I knew that the lives of many, many thousands of other investors had been changed drastically because these arrogant people failed to do their jobs. I admit it: I wanted them to pay.

■ ■ ■

I was exhausted and depressed when I met with the special counsel of the House Financial Services Committee, Jim Segel, on December 24. Diane Schulman, a False Claims Act fraud investigator similar to myself, was very close friends with Jim and she had set up this meeting. We met at my favorite pub in the West Roxbury neighborhood of Boston, and Jim Segel explained that the committee wanted me to appear before them as a friendly witness. I sort of laughed at that, pointing out to him that I might be friendly to Congress, but when the executive branch heard what I had to say they certainly wouldn't consider me very friendly.

"That's fine," Segel said. "We just want to hear the truth."

"I'm only going to tell the truth." The committee asked me to appear the first week in January. Too soon, I told them. I intended to take on the SEC at this hearing, so I wanted plenty of time to prepare. I wanted to be strong and healthy for this battle. I'd been waiting years for this opportunity—years—and I intended to take advantage of it.

I had one favor I asked in return. I asked Segel if Congressman Frank could make sure that Ed Manion wouldn't be fired for helping me press this case within the SEC's ranks for the past eight and a half years. I was very worried that the SEC would extract retribution from him for assisting me with the case. Ed was ill and needed to retain his government health insurance for three more years until he reached retirement age. Segel assured me that nothing would happen to Manion. He and Ed had been friends for a long, long time, he told me, and Barney Frank also knew and respected Ed. That made me feel a lot better. The last thing I wanted was to see a man I considered a hero retaliated against for doing his job, for standing up for investors.

I also explained that I did not feel comfortable testifying before President-elect Obama took office in just a few weeks. I knew that what I was going to say would reflect very badly on the Bush administration, and an administration in its dying days was prone to do anything to avoid being embarrassed on its way out the door.

Then I made one additional request. I told Jim Segel that I had several *quitam* cases under court-ordered seal against major financial institutions for stealing from the government. As such, I needed to have two attorneys at the witness table with me, not the one attorney that House rules allow. One attorney, Phil Michael, would be there to represent the government's interests in those cases. Gaytri Kachroo would be on my other side and she would be representing me personally. That wouldn't be a problem, Jim replied.

Two days after that meeting, the day after Christmas, the SEC's inspector general, David Kotz, called to introduce himself. Kotz had joined the SEC almost exactly a year earlier, after leaving his private law practice to become the inspector general of the Peace Corps. I didn't know much about him, although people I respected told me he'd done a good job in a short time. Kotz then asked if I would be willing to cooperate with his investigation. He had been given a mandate to investigate the SEC's failures in the Madoff case, he explained, and make the appropriate recommendations to fix what was broken. He told me he intended to make sure that the culture inside the agency that had allowed Madoff to survive would be changed.

Kotz sounded sincere, but it would be a stretch to say that I trusted anyone or anything inside the SEC (except Ed Manion and Mike Garrity, of course). I didn't know Kotz, and I didn't particularly like the concept of a government agency investigating itself. That's not exactly a recipe for good government. I didn't say no, though; instead I suggested he contact my attorney to see what we could work out.

Gaytri Kachroo was still in India, and Kotz reached her while she was at a dinner at the old British Turf Club. She walked outside into a gorgeous night and stood on a beautiful moonlit green while they spoke. The whole situation was surreal; two weeks earlier she had never even heard of Bernie Madoff, and now she was in India, representing a key player in what was being described as the greatest financial crime in history. Although she had traveled to India to attend a conference focusing on business opportunities emanating from the new nuclear agreement between the United States and India, she immediately decided to cut short her trip to return to Boston and help me prepare my testimony for the congressional hearing.

Gaytri, who was representing me personally on my False Claims Act cases, quickly got permission from the law firm she had recently joined, the Boston office of McCarter & English, to also represent me—pro bono—for these government hearings. It was very gracious of that firm, and I would estimate that over the next few months McCarter & English would absorb over $100,000 in legal fees. Burt Winnick, the managing partner of McCarter's Boston office, told me he personally knew dozens of victims, so he felt obligated to help out. During our first meeting, several partners made a point of coming into the conference room to shake my hand, and each of them promised to do everything in their power to assist me in getting ready to testify.

Gaytri's concern, beginning with this phone call from Kotz, was to protect me and to protect the other cases I was working on. All my other cases were under seal, meaning I could not talk about them publicly, and she wanted to ensure that those cases were not jeopardized. At that time we weren't certain what kind of investigation Kotz intended to conduct. If it was going to be a whitewash or a cover-up, if low-level employees were going to get blamed, if Kotz was going to try to describe this as an anomaly rather than a systematic failure, I didn't want anything to do with him. But if he was serious, I wanted in.

Kotz wanted to meet with me while I was in Washington to testify. Gaytri gave him a firm lawyerly nonanswer, telling him we would absolutely consider it. But almost immediately she ended her trip and returned to Boston.

During one of her subsequent conversations with Kotz, he asked for copies of all the documents I had previously provided to the SEC. That set Gaytri's antenna straight up. "Why do you need all that material?" she asked. "Didn't you already get them from the SEC? They have everything Harry's submitted."

Kotz's answer to that was our first hint that he might be serious about going after his agency. They do have the documents, he agreed, "But to tell you the truth, I have no idea what the SEC is going to give me." That was the moment that Gaytri and I began to believe he was earnest about investigating his own agency.

That was a stunning admission. The SEC's own inspector general did not trust his agency to provide him with a complete set of my documents. It meant that Kotz was suspicious that there was a cover-up taking place inside the agency. If that was true, my papers would help him expose it. So we agreed to provide him with copies of all my submissions and supporting materials—but we did so only 36 hours in advance of our scheduled congressional testimony, just in case. I gave him everything I had except a couple of documents that were criminal in nature and more appropriately should be shared only with law enforcement agencies. Publishing those documents in the *Congressional Record* might adversely affect active criminal investigations in progress, and I didn't want Madoff's aiders and abettors to have any advance notice of what was headed their way.

While I've had many dreams in my life, testifying in front of a congressional committee was not one of them. It was not something I would have chosen to do. Given the choice, I would have picked fortune over fame; but suddenly I was famous. Fame, or maybe recognition, is a fascinating tool, as I was discovering. People were intrigued by Madoff, and they wanted to hear what I had to say about his scheme. I intended to use that tool first to focus attention on the SEC and then, if it still remained sharp enough, to celebrate the importance of whistleblowers to expose corruption in our system. But achieving those objectives meant being well-prepared; I had to use my few minutes in the spotlight to make my points. I spent more than 100 hours preparing for my two- or three-hour testimony. As I found out, it takes a lot of preparation and rehearsal to appear spontaneous.

Unfortunately, the lack of sleep and the stress of having my home surrounded by the press caught up with me. The trigger that sent my health in a downward spiral was a letter from Congress requesting my testimony on January 5, 2009. I received a letter on December 30 asking me to submit my documents before the deadline—which had passed a week before I received the letter! I'd never felt so low. I requested a postponement. I spent the next two weeks trying to recover from the worst cold of my life and devoting every waking hour to preparing my testimony.

On January 5, 2009, David Kotz testified in front of Barney Frank's subcommittee. In preparation for my own appearance—which had been rescheduled for early February—Gaytri and I watched the five-hour hearing, then watched the tape all over again. I took notes. I got a feel for each member of the committee, what type of questions each asked, how detailed they were, and whether each committee member listened to witnesses' answers and asked intelligent follow-up questions. The representatives from New York were the most irate, obviously because New York was hit pretty hard by Madoff, but everybody seemed to be pretty angry with the SEC. Good.

I was finally scheduled to testify on February 4. I'd written a 12-minute opening statement in which I just ripped into the SEC. The military had taught me that you open an attack with massive fire. You deliver the most devastating volume of fire possible to destroy and demoralize your enemy. And I wanted to put down the SEC quick and hard. Oh, writing that statement felt so good. I was able to let loose and I did. In fact, my attorneys felt it was too aggressive and edited it for me. Their version was politically correct; if there is one thing about myself in which I do take pride, it is the fact that I am not politically correct. I'm Greek, so by nature I'm going to be blunt and tell people exactly how I feel. I'm not going to be gentle. I read their version and said, "I'll never give that."

"You should," they advised.

I was pretty insistent. "I'll always regret it if I'm not brutally honest. These people deserve it."

Witnesses are required to give Congress an advance copy of their written testimony for review. Gaytri warned me that as soon as we handed it in it would be leaked to the media. Being naive, I didn't think the government of the United States would hand over documents to the media that casually. But we waited until the last possible minute, until Monday night, February 2, at 10 P.M., before submitting it. And rather than submitting my opening 12 minutes of blistering oral testimony, I submitted my attorneys' politically correct version. I kept the testimony I intended to give in my hip pocket.

By 7 A.M. the following morning my written testimony was on the Internet. By 9 A.M. I was getting phone calls from reporters asking for a statement. The hearing was scheduled to be carried on CSPAN3, which is about as low down the dial as it is possible to go and still have a picture. Congress leaked it, Gaytri suggested, because the members wanted more people to watch CSPAN3. I felt I was going to speak to four audiences: The most important audience was going to be the victims around the world. They deserved an explanation of what had gone so terribly wrong, and I was going to give it to them. Someone owed them the truth, and I knew that the SEC wasn't going to tell it. I was also speaking to both domestic and international investors, because I wanted them to know that no one was protecting them. They were on their own. The SEC is useless, and it was my opinion that the Financial Industry Regulatory Authority (FINRA) was equally incompetent, if not corrupt. The third audience was the American public, especially people who might one day intend to invest in our markets. And finally, my fourth audience was the government, both this subcommittee and the SEC itself.

Officially, I was going to appear before the House Subcommittee on Capital Markets, Insurance, and Government-Sponsored Enterprises for a hearing entitled "Assessing the Madoff Ponzi Scheme and Regulatory Failures"—which was the polite way of saying "How the SEC Screwed Millions of People." My only concern was that I would be asked about those cases I had under seal; to prevent that, Phil Michael was going to be there with me to represent the interests of the government in those cases as well as members of my whistleblower teams. Gaytri was going to be sitting on my other side. And right in front of me *60 Minutes* was going to be shooting my testimony in high definition.

The night before I was to appear, we got a copy of the SEC's testimony. It was ridiculous, nothing more than a smokescreen. The SEC admitted it had no defense, but also refused to admit culpability and didn't have the courtesy to offer an apology to the victims. Reading it made me very confident that they had no idea what was about to hit them. Clearly they were not prepared for this battle. They hadn't had weeks of nights with little or no sleep; they hadn't spent 100 hours preparing. Basically, they had copied their web site. Their entire defense appeared to be, we don't have to defend ourselves because we're the good guys.

At dinner that night I sat with my lawyers, along with Jeb White and Pat Burns of Taxpayers Against Fraud, as they read the SEC's testimony. I knew we were in good shape when they started laughing at it. "I can't believe they're going to go with this," Phil Michael said. "This is like no-testimony testimony or the no-defense defense."

When Gaytri added, "It looks like they're going to rely on their reputation," everybody laughed again. When we returned to the hotel, Gaytri and I had a final discussion about the statement I would make the next morning. Until that time she had strongly advocated giving the milder presentation, but reading the SEC's arrogant nontestimony had completely changed her mind. "You should go with your original," she said. "Get 'em, Harry."

■ ■ ■

On the morning of the 4th I woke up early and excited. I ironed my suit to make sure the creases were sharp. When we got to the Capitol building we found a long line of people waiting to get in. We actually got held up briefly at security because Phil Michael's knee replacement set off the alarms. I felt like an athlete in the locker room before the biggest game of his career. I went into the men's room and called my cousin, Pam, and gave myself my own pep talk. "I'm really going to let them have it," I told her. "I've spent eight and a half years being treated like the SEC's doormat. These people have put me through hell and now it's my turn and I'm going to let them have it with both barrels. I'm going to put them down in my opening statement and I'm never going to let them get back up. I've got lots of ammo and I'm going to keep shooting until the chairman tells me to stop. I'm going to kick ass and name names."

My goal was to make this the worst day in the entire history of the SEC, not just because it had earned it, but because the only way it was ever going to improve was to hit rock bottom. I really did want it to be better; I wanted it to rebuild. But that wouldn't happen if it continued to believe it was a functioning agency with only minor problems.

The hearing room was considerably smaller than it appears on television, and when I walked in, it was almost completely full. A group of SEC staff members was sitting together, and right next to them was a large number of reporters. I'd brought with me hand-outs about whistleblowers from the Certified Fraud Examiners' 2008 Report to the Nation that I wanted to distribute to the media so that they would learn about the tremendous value that whistleblowers bring to law enforcement. I walked across the room, right past the SEC employees, and started chatting with those journalists. As I handed out the Certified Fraud Examiners report, I told them, just loudly enough to make sure the SEC staffers heard me, "You should read this. It's not in my written testimony but I'm going to refer to it. There are a lot of important statistics about whistleblowers in here."

Bill Zucker, another McCarter & English attorney, was sitting with Pat Burns and Jeb White of Taxpayers Against Fraud near the SEC staff section. I stopped in front of them and told a few bad jokes, hoping to send a message to the SEC that I wasn't the slightest bit nervous and that they were about to have a very bad day. I remember asking Pat Burns, "Do I have any blood on my lips? I had raw meat for breakfast. I'm in a bloodthirsty mood." The SEC staffers were listening intently, and several of them started texting—but none of them were laughing.

Just before we began the session, the ranking Republican member, Scott Garrett from New Jersey, walked up to the witness table and introduced himself to me and then said the most astonishing thing: "I just wanted to shake your hand and thank you for appearing before this subcommittee. I realize that no one would listen to you, but I want to assure you that we're here to listen and learn. Maybe the Democrats are right; maybe we do need to change the regulations."

Maybe the Democrats were right? Who knew that Bernie Madoff was so awful he could even bring the Democrats and Republicans together?

In Chairman Paul Kanjorski's opening statement, he explained, "We are using the largest known instance of securities fraud as a case study to guide the work of the Financial Services Committee in reshaping and reforming our nation's financial services regulatory system. We preside in a crucial moment in our history, and our work . . . will influence the securities industry for generations to come.

"Congress last undertook a wholesale rewrite of these laws in the wake of the Great Depression. . . . The world, however, has now changed and the motor is broken beyond repair. We therefore need to invent a new engine. . . ."

I began my opening statement by offering my sympathy to Bernie Madoff's victims. For the first time I acknowledged Neil, Frank, and Mike, identifying them as "my eyes and ears out in the hedge fund world," and Ed Manion, who "kept getting ignored because he was not a securities lawyer, only a Chartered Financial Analyst with 25 years of trading and portfolio management experience in the industry. . . . The SEC to this day holds against him the fact that he kept bringing this case to their attention, and I believe he would be fired if he ever went public."

I was really pleased to be able to make sure Ed Manion got the credit he had earned—and the public protection he probably needed. I made sure Mike Garrity, the Boston office branch chief who had given his best efforts to convince the New York office to investigate Madoff, also received credit for his support.

And then I went big agency hunting. "The SEC is also captive to the industry it regulates, and it is afraid of bringing big cases against the largest, most powerful firms." In their previous testimony, top SEC officials had complained that a lack of staff and resources meant they could respond to only the highest-priority matters—which of course was their attempt to excuse their failures. "If a $50 billion Ponzi scheme doesn't make the SEC's priority list," I responded, "then I want to know who sets their priorities."

I was just getting started, and while my voice was controlled, my anger was real. "You have no excuses," I said, speaking for the victims.

"But you darn well have a lot of explaining to do to the American taxpayers. . . .

"The incoming SEC chairwoman needs to come in and clean house with a wide broom. The SEC needs a new senior staff because the current staff has led our nation's financial system to the brink of collapse. . . . They haven't earned their paychecks and they need to be replaced."

As I was speaking I could actually hear the SEC staff behind me sucking in their breaths when I landed a body blow. I think they were very surprised I went after their senior leadership so strongly. They weren't used to hearing these people attacked.

I was thoroughly enjoying every single minute of my testimony. I loved it. Anytime I had the slightest thought of holding back, I thought about the victims. What I did not know was that the interest in my testimony was so high that several cable stations broadcast it live. In addition to my family and team members, just about everybody on Wall Street and in the extended financial industry was watching. I suspect it wasn't a popular program inside the SEC's building, though. It also wasn't very popular with my kids. Faith explained to them, "Mr. Madoff was trying to steal money from people, and Daddy caught him." They misunderstood—they thought I had physically apprehended him. But the fact that Daddy was on TV didn't really interest them. They watched for about 10 minutes, then wanted to play with their toys.

I had been well prepared to respond to the committee members' questions. I certainly was no kinder to the SEC in my answers. "The SEC was never capable of catching Mr. Madoff," I said flatly. "He could have easily gone to $100 billion if we hadn't had the financial crisis last year and he hadn't run out of money to pay off existing investors."

When asked whether I felt the SEC had failed to catch Madoff because it didn't understand my red flags or it just had a lack of desire, I replied that it probably was a mix of the two: "They were totally incapable of doing that math. They have no one on their staff probably systemwide that could do the math. . . . And they just looked at his size and said, 'He is big firm and we don't attack big firms.'"

I didn't limit my criticism to the SEC. When asked by California Democratic Congressman Brad Sherman, who was a CPA, if the

National Association of Securities Dealers (NASD), which had become FINRA, might have investigated Madoff, I replied that I would never have taken this case to those industry-created organizations. "I had a lot of bad experiences as an over-the-counter trader in the late 1980s with the NASD," I said. "What I found them to be was a very corrupt self-regulatory organization, that if you took a fraud to them they would ignore it as soon as they received it. They were there to assist industry in avoiding stricter regulation from the SEC."

Representative Sherman got it. "You have basically said that our two main securities regulatory agencies see their role as protecting the major institutions on Wall Street rather than protecting investors."

That wasn't precisely accurate. I never said, "basically." And then I added, "I would say that FINRA is even less competent than the SEC."

I had long ago burned any bridges that might one day lead me back to the financial industry, and I felt it was my duty to report to the American people what I had learned in my career—not just about the government, but also about Wall Street. And it wasn't pretty. For example, Indiana Democrat Joe Donnelly wondered why all those people on Wall Street who knew something was wrong with Madoff kept silent, pointing out that these were the same people Americans trusted with their retirement savings. I agreed: "It is misplaced trust in fraudsters, especially the white-collar variety. These people are much more dangerous than any bank robber or armed robber, because these people, the white-collar fraudsters, are the most prestigious citizens. They live in the biggest and best houses and have the most impressive resumes. So when they commit a fraud scheme, they destroy companies and throw thousands of people out of work, and they destroy confidence in the American system such that capital becomes unavailable at any price."

At times as I was responding to these questions I would glance down in front of me at the *60 Minutes* cameraman. He was looking directly at the people behind me, and when I struck a particularly telling blow he'd smile and give me a thumbs-up.

Although my testimony was serious, there certainly were a few humorous moments. When I told West Virginia Republican Congress-woman Shelly Capito about some of the firms that my team had warned, she asked me, "Could you explain to me what the theater funds, what that entails?"

I began, "A feeder fund . . ."

"Oh feeder fund," she interrupted. "I thought you were saying 'theater fund.'"

During this hearing several members took time to compliment me, using terms that would have made me blush if I hadn't been so focused. But I did appreciate the fact that a number of those people also acknowledged the real danger my whole team faced. As Texas Democrat Al Green said, "I and many others can understand why you were in fear for your life. And I believe that fear to have been well-founded because you were dealing with a ruthless person who was in bed with other ruthless people. And when you deal with the kind of characters that you were trying to bring to the bar of justice, you have to be concerned not only about yourself but about other family members that are near and dear to you."

And as I had told the reporters before the hearing began, I used this opportunity to emphasize the importance of whistleblowers. Among the changes that I said had to be made if the SEC was to become an effective organization was the creation of a program that rewarded whistleblowers for reporting illegal or unethical practices. The government has to make it worthwhile for people who are risking their careers, and sometimes their personal safety, by putting the public good before their employers. Good wishes and congratulatory letters aren't enough. I got the opportunity to make that point when my own Congressman, Massachusetts Democrat Stephen Lynch, related a conversation he'd had recently about a hotline the SEC had set up—for industry use. As he said, "I was told that senior management had actually gone to an industry—a financial services industry conference and basically said to the firms out there, 'If you feel that you are being too aggressively investigated, then I want you to call this office.' And that was a senior person, two senior people at the SEC."

Imagine that. The SEC actually had set up a whistleblowers' hotline—so companies being investigated could stop or slow down that investigation! That was incredible—although not really surprising. We already knew that the SEC was a captive of the industry. The point that I wanted to make was that whistleblowers in this country generally have a very difficult time, but they perform a tremendous service. As I told Congressman Lynch, "I brought with me the Association of Certified Fraud Examiners' 2008 Report to the Nation, and it lists in here the best way to find fraud. Fifty-four percent of the frauds get discovered by tips, whistleblower tips; only 4 percent by external auditors, which—the SEC is an external auditor. Therefore, whistleblower tips are 13 times more effective than external auditing. So why wouldn't we want the SEC to be 13 times more effective? Lord knows, this agency needs to be more effective."

When I concluded my testimony, I was satisfied that I'd made all the points I'd intended to make. The only question I was asked that I hadn't been prepared for was, "Who's going to play you in the movie?"

Rather than fighting our way through the media horde lined up outside the hearing room, we went into the Democratic anteroom to watch the SEC's leadership testify. This was a good place to blow off some nervous energy, talk with my attorneys, have lunch—and watch the SEC get ripped apart by Congress.

The SEC had five representatives there to read its nonsensical opening statement. In real life it was actually worse than it had been on the printed page. It was basically a recitation of the SEC's mandate that could be read on its web site. They made no attempt to explain what had happened, to apologize, or even to admit why they were sitting there in the first place. It was disgraceful. Any doubts I might have had that Congress would allow them to get away with it were quickly dispelled by Chairman Kanjorski's angry response. As I heard him berating the agency I wanted to stand up and cheer. "In terms of hearing the testimony today of Mr. Markopolos, I have tentatively come to the conclusion that the Securities and Exchange Commission has been anointed by God to be all-righteous. I hope I can disabuse the members of this panel of that fact, because, quite frankly, we are about to decide in what nature and how the Securities and Exchange Commission should continue to exist. And the lack of cooperation shown in the last several weeks, and I think the abuse of authority, or the attempt to bring a protective shield over an executive agency or independent agency of this government is not acceptable. And if that is going to be the process, the easiest thing to do is follow Mr. Markopolos's advice and just do away with the entire regulatory system as it is presently constructed and start anew. . . .

"And as I have heard the testimony, I mean, you know, I like oatmeal, and that is about how I classify the testimony I heard today. . . . We did not call you up here for us to hear a traveler's guide of the Securities and Exchange Commission."

It got progressively worse and worse for the SEC. Linda Thomsen, the director of enforcement, claimed she could not respond to many questions because it might jeopardize prosecutions. When Chairman Kanjorski asked her how long those prosecutions might take, she replied, "I honestly don't know the answer."

Chairman Kanjorski erupted. "Well, if it is years, and you do not intend to say anything, if I listen to your statement and how your counsel structured the statement, there are three things. You cannot help if it is a pending criminal investigation; you cannot help if the inspector general is doing something; you cannot help if it is an ongoing violation. I mean, if there is a snowstorm in Washington, the SEC cannot help. That must be one of their conditions."

It only got more difficult for the SEC when the committee members finally got to ask their questions. Obviously these politicians knew there were a lot of angry and frustrated constituents watching them. And I don't think anyone was more angry than New York's Gary Ackerman. "I am frustrated beyond belief," he began. "We are talking to ourselves and you are pretending to be here. I really don't understand what is going on. The previous witness said that you guys as an agency act like you are deaf, dumb, and blind. I figured you were coming here and you were going to testify before Congress. Don't you dare tell anybody you testified before Congress. You are going to be subjected to violation of false advertising lawsuits.

"You have told us nothing and I believe that is your intention. I figured you would leave your blindfolds and your duct tape and your earplugs behind, but you seem to be wearing them today. And instead of telling us anything, you read from the preamble of your mission statement and broke it up into five segments. What the heck went on? You said your mission was to protect investors and detect fraud quickly. How did that work out? What went wrong? It seems to me a private— With all your investigators and all of your agency and everything that you all described, one guy with a few friends and helpers discovered this thing nearly a decade ago, led you to this pile of dung that is Bernie Madoff, and stuck your nose in it, and you couldn't figure it out."

I don't remember, but I'm pretty sure I smiled when I heard that. At times the questioning got so heated that Gaytri would walk out into the hearing room because she wanted to feel the tension. I just sat on a couch, eating a sandwich, savoring every single moment. There wasn't a moment, a second, I felt sorry for these people. I just hoped that the investors they had failed to protect were watching. It wasn't much compared to what Madoff's victims had lost, but at least they would know that someone cared about them and that the SEC leaders were not going to walk away unscathed. Maybe it would never be payment in full, but it was a down payment.

Ackerman continued attacking. "You couldn't find your backside with two hands if the lights were on. Could you explain yourselves? You have single-handedly defused the American people of any sense of confidence in our financial markets if you are the watchdogs. You have totally and thoroughly failed in your mission."

When Linda Thomsen mumbled some response to his question, he interrupted her, asking, "Were you suspicious when the guy had a one man accounting firm investigating a $50 billion empire? And you keep saying alleged, alleged. This guy confessed on national television, you might have noticed. . . ."

Linda Thomsen tried to explain, saying, "We have an action pending in the Southern District of New York."

Ackerman pointed out, "You took action after the guy confessed. He turned himself in. Don't give yourself any pat on the back for that."

After Linda Thomsen again explained that "We cannot answer as to the specifics . . . " Ackerman said flatly, "You know, if anybody made the case better than Mr. Markopolos, and I didn't think anybody could, about you people being inept, you have made the case better than him." I just sat there, thinking silently, *Thank you, Congressman.*

It was a wonderful afternoon, just great. Obviously, members of Congress don't swear inside the hearing room, but while we were sitting in the anteroom they would come inside and let loose. They were livid; they were rip-roaring mad. I remember one member fuming, "If this is what our regulators are like, we don't need them. It's better the public knows they aren't protected than to think they have protection from these clowns."

New York's Carolyn Maloney was as angry as Ackerman. "Mr. Markopolos in his testimony earlier testified that he brought complaints five times in writing to the SEC, and these were detailed complaints. It wasn't, 'I think something's wrong.' These were detailed complaints that this is wrong. 'They are not trading. They are not doing this. Here are examples.' And it was a very specific complaint, not once, not twice, not three times, but five times to the SEC. . . . And how many more times would a whistleblower have to bring complaints to the SEC for them to have investigated the Madoff case? . . . Now, if you went in and just asked for the trade slips or proved that they were doing trades when whistleblowers were saying they weren't doing trades, then you could have shut him down in one-half hour. You could have shut Madoff down in one-half hour by just following up on one of the allegations."

"As to the specifics of the investigation," Thomsen replied, "I can't answer."

Eventually I started writing down questions they might ask, questions I knew these people couldn't answer. The hearing continued through the afternoon, and when it was over, the SEC had been exposed and embarrassed in front of the entire nation.

Two days after this hearing, the SEC's acting general counsel, Andrew Vollmer, was replaced. Five days later Linda Thomsen resigned; according to an SEC press release, she was leaving to "pursue opportunities in the private sector." Five months later, Lori Richards, the SEC's director of the Office of Compliance, Inspections and Examinations, resigned to pursue other growth opportunities. Eventually all but one of the SEC directors on that panel was replaced: The acting general counsel was replaced by David Becker, the head of enforcement by Rob Khuzami, and the director of compliance by John Walsh. It was nearly a clean sweep.

Gary Ackerman escorted us out of the building. He was still angry. We stood outside the Capitol in the freezing cold for more than a half hour as he explained what he intended to do next to make certain the SEC was reformed, and if it couldn't be reformed, it would be closed down.

I didn't even feel the cold.

Chapter 9

Soaring Like an Eagle Surrounded by Turkeys

The greatest irony was that by failing to pay attention to my submissions the Securities and Exchange Commission had succeeded in giving me a national platform—which I intended to use to either help create a new and functioning agency or put it out of America's misery. The SEC officials had created their own worst nightmare. They'd picked a fight with the wrong Greek.

After the agency had insulted a congressional committee by failing to prepare for its hearings and then refusing to answer questions because telling the truth might adversely affect an ongoing investigation, I had no doubts Barney Frank was going to do whatever was necessary to change the culture of the SEC.

But there were also a lot of dedicated people inside the SEC who wanted it to be better. Ed Manion and Mike Garrity weren't alone. After many phone conversations, both Gaytri and I felt that the SEC's inspector general, David Kotz, might be one of those people. Pat Burns had vouched for him, telling me he was the real deal. "Every time he does a report he kicks them in the balls multiple times," he said. Kotz emphasized that his report was going to be thorough and honest. But to accomplish that, he needed my cooperation. He just wanted to know what happened. So I had volunteered to meet with him in his office the day after my House testimony—inside the SEC building.

It had seemed like a good idea at the time.

I realized, perhaps too late, that I was going to be as welcome at the SEC as a wolf on a chicken farm. After I had shredded this agency on nationwide TV, I expected its employees to despise me. As I mentioned to Gaytri, it always makes me a little uneasy when the welcoming committee either is armed or has access to a rope. Actually, I really had no idea how we would be greeted, but for protection I asked my *60 Minutes* producer, Andy Court, if he'd allow Reuben Heyman-Kantor, his junior reporter, to stay another day in Washington and accompany us to the SEC with a handheld minicam. I was hoping to use the incredible power of a TV camera to help us balance the odds.

Gaytri and Phil Michael went with me to this meeting. As we approached the front of the building, I saw the SEC's general counsel lying in wait, standing next to another man, whom I didn't recognize. Maybe it was just a coincidence that they happened to be standing there when I arrived, and an equal coincidence that when they saw the camera they turned around and scurried to an elevator bank.

David Kotz was waiting for us on the far side of security. The *60 Minutes* reporter was permitted to film Kotz greeting us and escorting us into the building. As we were to learn, David is not shy. But after filming the introductions, our junior *60 Minutes* journalist was asked politely to leave.

The meeting was held in a large conference room. David Kotz was joined by four other people, among them his deputy inspector general, Noelle Frangipane; Senior Counsel Heidi Steiber; Senior Counsel Chris Wilson—and a transcriber. I'd assumed this was going to be an informal meeting in which I basically described my interactions with their agency over the intervening eight and a half years, but before we began I was asked if I minded testifying under oath.

It turned out that it was not going to be an informal chat, but rather a transcribed deposition under oath. Gaytri challenged them immediately: "What do you mean? You didn't say anything about that."

They explained, "Well, all of the SEC staff is testifying under oath, and they may say it's unfair if you don't, and we don't want to give them an out."

That made sense to me. I didn't mind taking an oath; I was going to tell the truth. And Phil pointed out that in this situation an oath was not even necessary. Whether or not I took it, making a false statement to the federal government is a crime punishable by up to five years in prison and a fine of $250,000. I raised my right hand and swore to tell the truth.

I had spent more than two decades dealing with the SEC, both while working in the financial industry and as a potential whistleblower, so I had seen up close how abysmally it was run. And I had the documentation to prove it. In addition, because I had been working with other, far more competent government agencies the past several years as a fraud investigator, I was in the advantageous position of being able to do the type of comparative analysis that nobody had done before. I wanted the SEC to be effective, and I believed I could help make that happen.

It became clear almost at the beginning that the purpose of this investigation was much deeper than simply solving problems inside the agency. David Kotz began by telling me right off the bat that he was conducting a criminal investigation. Now, that was odd, because I knew that the SEC has no criminal investigative power. By law, it handles only the civil portion of securities cases; criminal matters have to be referred to the Department of Justice. I remember wondering if the Department of Justice had appointed David Kotz as a special assistant U.S. attorney with criminal investigative authority. Phil Michael nudged me with his elbow to make sure we were on the same wavelength.

So, this was a criminal investigation. Well, I knew for sure I wasn't a criminal, and I was pretty sure Gaytri and Phil weren't suspects; so the only people he could have been investigating for illegal activities were members of the SEC's own staff. I had no objection to that. That certainly raised the stakes, and it was obvious that the rest of the day was going to be chock-full of surprises.

As the meeting progressed, I felt more and more comfortable. David explained that he had watched the congressional hearing, and he was stunned and ashamed that his people could perform so badly. The fact that he would criticize his own agency broke the ice. In fact, very early in the meeting I mentioned that after Madoff had surrendered I had been afraid that the SEC might come into my house and confiscate my computers and my documents to prevent me from making my case against the agency. I knew the SEC didn't have subpoena power, I said, but with careers at stake I was afraid people might dummy up a subpoena to get them into my house.

One of the SEC attorneys in the room couldn't resist laughing. "You were afraid of our agency?" she asked with incredulity. "After you saw how incompetent and slow moving we are? You saw how long it takes us to make a decision, and you actually believe we were capable of organizing a plan that quickly?" She glanced at her colleagues, who were also laughing and slapping their knees while doing so. "Wow!" As a trained Certified Fraud Examiner I knew this was not on the approved list of interviewing techniques. We're trained to never show weakness during witness interviews. But I have to admit that the SEC inspector general's unorthodox questioning techniques were effective. They knew how to make a friendly witness feel comfortable and gain total cooperation.

David Kotz and each of his staff members were well prepared for this meeting. You can tell from the questions how serious the people asking them are, and the inspector general's office was serious. Rather than simply responding yes or no, I was giving lengthy, detailed answers to those questions. I wanted to shed light on this entire investigation. The people who had things to hide were in his agency, and I didn't want to leave any dark corners for them to hide in. Kotz's people didn't challenge my answers; they were probing to find out why the SEC had failed, who was responsible, and what should be done to make certain that nothing like this ever happened again. I began to feel like we shared common objectives. I went through my red flags with them. They had a whiteboard in the room, and several times I got up and showed them the math. The inspector general brought in a camera and took pictures of each of my formulas, explaining that they intended to hire a forensic accounting firm to review my math for accuracy. That seemed like the best way to handle it.

At one point late in the morning, Phil Michael took the unusual step of asking Kotz if he could step in and take over the questioning. He said, "I want to run by some points that we're not hitting." Phil had spent decades involved in criminal investigations and he knew the entire story, so he made sure we got out the pertinent information. After finishing his questions, he left the meeting to get a midafternoon train back to

New York. As soon as he walked out the door, I knew there was going to be a problem. Somehow it seems that every time Phil leaves a meeting something dramatic happens. This time was no exception.

We had been working late into the afternoon when David Kotz asked me to explain how the total damages could be assessed and calculated. That actually was a difficult question because it had several answers. There were several different formulas that could be used to determine that, I explained, and all of them were correct. It was really a question of what counted as a loss. Is it simply the actual dollars handed over to Madoff minus the money he returned? What about the interest that supposedly was accruing—does that count as a loss? This was a decision the SEC had to make. Then Noelle Frangipane asked me, "When you made your first submission to the SEC, how big did you estimate Madoff was?"

I said, "We had him at somewhere between three billion dollars and seven billion dollars."

"And how big was he when he finally turned himself in?"

"His number was fifty billion dollars."

"And so if the SEC had acted in 2000, when you made your first submission, how much money would have been saved?"

"We could have shut them down at under seven. So forty-three billion dollars."

"So forty-three billion dollars would have been saved if the SEC had listened to you in May of 2000?"

"Correct."

A split second later I heard a loud thud. I turned to Noelle. Her head was down on the table and she was sobbing uncontrollably. During my long pursuit of Bernie Madoff I'd seen a lot of strange things, but this certainly was one of the most unusual. It was an incredibly human moment, and I think we were all touched by it. Across the table from me was a gorgeous, talented deputy inspector general crying her eyes out, but I had no idea what it was all about. Again, I knew collapsing and crying were not on the approved list of interviewing techniques, at least not as I was taught. The investigator is definitely not supposed to have an emotional breakdown and cry in front of the witness. Gaytri responded, saying, "I'm taking my client outside for a sidebar." It was the only decent thing to do.

We walked down a very long corridor until we reached a public area, and sat down. "Harry," she said, "did you see the same thing I did? Noelle just collapsed."

I nodded. "Oh, yes, she did. What do you think that was all about?"

"It think it's a liability issue," she said. "Noelle is obviously a really sharp attorney, and she realizes that the government may have some culpability."

That didn't make sense to me. "No, you can't sue the government. It has sovereign immunity." The rule of law, you can't sue the king, prevents citizens from bringing legal action against the state.

Gaytri disagreed. "That's what most people believe. But the courts can make law, especially the Supreme Court. There's nothing to prevent people from suing. I guarantee you, there's going to be a lawyer out there who is going to file a lawsuit against the government, against the SEC. They know they're going to lose in federal district court; they're going to plan on losing in the circuit court on appeal; and then they're going to hope that the Supreme Court takes their case. The Supreme Court can make law or it can change law. Sovereign immunity may not hold up, because the SEC is clearly so negligent in this case the court could say, 'We are liable and the victims should get their money back.'

"And this certainly is an international case. Once all the national remedies have been exhausted, it wouldn't surprise me to see people trying to take it to the International Court of Justice. I'm sure the international community isn't that happy with the United States after this whole financial crisis. I think that's what Noelle is afraid of."

Maybe. It also could have been that, just like me, Kotz's staff had been working so hard for so long that they were all worn down, and Noelle simply had an emotional outburst—much like mine when Frank told me that Thierry was dead. Sometimes it just gets to be too much. Whatever it was, Noelle's response showed us how seriously she cared about reforming her agency. Ironically, it had a very positive effect on the rest of the afternoon's questioning. It removed any doubts that Kotz's team intended to follow the evidence wherever it led. This wasn't going to be a whitewash.

We all calmed down and the questioning continued, hour after hour. We were there for six hours. This was as much a military-style debriefing as testimony. Kotz's questions made it obvious that he was trying to discover whether his agency was simply incompetent or it was also corrupt. He asked a lot of questions about possible interference in the investigation, ranging from asking me if I knew anything about the phone call supposedly made by Senator Schumer—I didn't—to the possibility that Madoff had bribed team members. Among the questions he asked, for example, was: "If a person with a hedge fund background was on the SEC's examination team that went into the Madoff operation, should he have been able to miss all the red flags you pointed out?"

That required only a one-word answer. "No." Actually, months earlier I had accepted the fact that the SEC was not corrupt. If it had been, my name would have come out and I might be dead. "No," the agency wasn't corrupt at the team and branch levels. Down at those levels they were incompetent, just incredibly incompetent. This wasn't a bad apples case; it was a systemic failure.

The meeting continued through the day into the late afternoon. By the time we left, I was exhausted. Whatever excitement I'd felt a day earlier had been thoroughly washed out of me. But we had bonded with Kotz's team and felt confident they were going to produce the thorough, honest report he had promised. Before we left, I warned the inspector general's team that this investigation was going to be a trip through the Twilight Zone, and that nothing they were going to see would make any sense whatsoever. In fact, I told them, if it made sense that's how you knew it wasn't part of this case, because nothing we had encountered had ever made sense. I told them that what they were going to discover would traumatize them—because they were about to see the worst sort of human behavior. I cautioned them that they were going to have two choices every day while investigating this case: They could either cry themselves into depression or laugh themselves silly. I urged them to laugh, because that was going to be the only way they were going to get to the other side of their investigation. In the months afterward I'd make sure to call with positive messages to boost the team's morale. I knew the debilitating effect the Madoff case would have on their team because I had seen what this case had done to my team.

■ ■ ■

David Kotz followed up by interviewing the three other members of my team, each of whom had his own important story to tell about his role in this investigation. Assistant Inspector General David Fielder and Senior Counsel David Witherspoon traveled to Boston to interview employees of the SEC's New England office, as well as Frank Casey in person and Neil Chelo on the phone. They met with Frank and Gaytri, who was there to provide legal guidance for Frank and Neil, in a conference room at McCarter & English. Frank was . . . frank. He took them through the entire story, from the day he discovered Bernie until Thierry's suicide. He told them how he learned to recognize Bernie's footprint in documents and then tracked down funds invested with him. He re-created the conversations he'd had with Thierry and others in the industry and his strange encounter with a victim's son-in-law. He gave them the European background, then brought them inside the financial services industry. He explained to them the accepted methods of conducting due diligence, which obviously the SEC should have known, and what Access International had done. But then he went further, speculating that the SEC's failure to stop Madoff was more than just incompetence. "The first two years after Harry submitted his initial report, I figured they were just complacent," he told the investigators. "The next two years I began to believe that they were structurally incompetent. But after that, given Harry's submission, there is very little doubt in my mind that they were somehow complicit."

Neil gave them a quant's point of view of the financial industry, providing a considerable amount of information that wasn't in our documents, including best practices and, unfortunately, the commonly seen worst practices. He discussed in far more detail than I had the numerous interviews he'd conducted with fund managers, in particular his long interview with Fairfield Greenwich's chief risk officer, Amit Vijayvergiya, and how he had validated my theories and discovered additional red flags. Just as I had done, Neil emphasized the fact that there are no incentives for people inside the industry to report unethical or illegal activities. In fact, there are disincentives. Many of the large institutional investors in Madoff were also Neil's competition. Neil was actually better off watching his competition make the horrendous mistake of investing in a Ponzi scheme. But for Neil, exposing Madoff was simply the right thing to do.

As Gaytri walked out of the session, she noticed a tall, lanky man waiting in the reception area. He turned out to be Grant Ward, the SEC's former New England director of enforcement—the person I'd sent my first submission to in 2000. It was ironic; the investigation had finally come full circle. Incredibly, during his sworn testimony that afternoon Ward told Kotz's investigators that he did not remember meeting me in 2000—a statement that later was directly contradicted by Juan Marcelino, the former regional administrator of the SEC's Boston office. Marcelino testified that he had spoken with Grant the day after I had appeared in front of Kanjorski's subcommittee, and Grant had told him he "remembered meeting with Markopolos but didn't feel he had done anything wrong." David Kotz eventually concluded that "Ward's testimony was not credible," and that he had "told Manion that he had referred the complaint to NERO [the SEC's Northeast Regional Office in New York] but never did."

Mike Ocrant was interviewed in New York by Kotz and Senior Counsel Heidi Steiber. He provided the reporter's point of view, telling them how meeting Frank in a Barcelona taxi led to his interview with Madoff, but he also told them about his many conversations with other knowledgeable people in the industry. It seemed to be the general consensus in the industry, he explained, that SEC investigative teams too rigidly followed a checklist in their search for paper violations, rather than digging deep and actually trying to figure out what was going on. A primary reason for that, he suggested, was that the investigators lacked experience and real knowledge of brokerage operations. Additionally, he pointed out that it was well known in the industry that the greatest desire of many, if not most, SEC employees was to obtain a job inside the securities industry. A stint at the SEC was simply an important addition to their resumes before moving on to join the industry that they were supposed to regulate.

Between the three of them, they provided a clear picture of the way the financial industry is supposed to function, the level of awareness inside the industry of Madoff's operations, and why almost no one other than us felt compelled to try to expose him.

Kotz's investigation would continue for several more months. On occasion he would call Gaytri or me with a specific question. It certainly looked like he was doing a Herculean job. I know that eventually he conducted 140 interviews—including a jailhouse interview with Madoff—and examined more than 3.7 million e-mails. This was to be the definitive report on what went wrong and how to correct it, and we all waited patiently to see what conclusions Kotz would reach. The inspector general's team knew they were writing a report not only to Congress and the victims but also for the history books. It was obvious even back in February that this would be the most widely read inspector general's report in many years.

■ ■ ■

I wasn't done telling my story. In early March I was invited to meet with the new head of the SEC, Mary Schapiro. Actually, Gaytri had set up this meeting. She had contacted Schapiro's office to see if the SEC wanted to participate and support the ideas of the Global Financial Alliance that were being formed to discuss how markets could better be regulated through international cooperation. During that conversation she asked Schapiro's assistant if she wanted to meet with me. I think we would have understood if that meeting was not exactly a priority for her, but in fact she responded enthusiastically.

Mary Schapiro had been in charge of the SEC for less than two months when we met. Prior to that she had had a long career in financial industry regulation. Under President Clinton she had served briefly as acting chairperson of the SEC. In 1996 she'd been appointed president of NASD Regulation, and in 2006 she became chairman and CEO of that organization, which had become the Financial Industry Regulatory Authority (FINRA). I hadn't been impressed by her leadership; at FINRA she had earned a reputation for avoiding big cases and failing to find fraud, and I hadn't found any reason to disagree with that reputation. My opinion was that FINRA served the needs of the industry rather than protecting investors from the predatory practices of the industry.

It promised to be an uncomfortable meeting. After my participation in the Madoff investigation became widely known, a considerable number of people in the media suggested that President-elect Obama name me the new head of the SEC. In the congressional hearings I had been asked if I would head an SEC whistleblowers division if it were created. My answer had consistently been thank you very much, but no thanks. I had a number of whistleblower teams taking risks in too many cases to even consider accepting any other job. They were owed my loyalty, and I couldn't leave them exposed without support. But the thought was out there and it certainly was possible it would make Mary Schapiro uneasy.

We met in her new office. It was large, comfortably decorated, and brightly lit. Rather than sitting at her desk or around a conference table, we joined Chairman Schapiro, her newly appointed general counsel, David Becker, and another attorney, Steve Cohen, in a casual seating area. It was sort of like a living room. It was a nice setting, but the atmosphere in the room was very tense. It wasn't exactly like signing a treaty of surrender on the deck of the *Missouri*, but there was an uncomfortable feeling in that office.

Mary Schapiro immediately made it clear that she intended to do whatever was necessary to restore public confidence in the SEC. The SEC that I had fought was out of business. It was going to be replaced by a tougher, more aggressive organization. If anything at all positive had come out of the Madoff disaster, this was it. Sitting there, I didn't feel like I had won anything. I certainly didn't gloat, but at least my overwhelming sense of frustration was gone. I liked Mary Schapiro's words, but until she followed up by making real changes, those words meant nothing. And if she was asking for my help in transforming the SEC, well, I was very pleased to offer it. As my team well knew, I did have an opinion about the SEC.

After a brief discussion about the Global Financial Alliance, we began talking about Mary Schapiro's desire to create a serious whistleblower program. I handed her a copy of the Certified Fraud Examiners' 2008 Report to the Nation on white-collar fraud that proved the effectiveness of whistleblowers. She picked up the report and quickly read through the whistleblower data. "We need to do more of this," she said. "We need to reach out to whistleblowers to get the big cases to show the public we're serious about fighting fraud."

Well, I certainly agreed with that. "Yes, you do."

The difficulty, she explained, was that the SEC received as many as 800,000 tips a year. Although the majority of them were along the lines of "I think my broker is stealing from me because my account was down 20 percent last month" while the entire market was down 20 percent, there was no standard for separating the frivolous from the Madoffs. There were just too many tips and not enough people to follow up. In response, Gaytri recommended at information technology (IT) solution using keywords to limit the number of leads the SEC staff should pursue. Mary Schapiro said she was in the process of hiring a consultant to try to find a workable technological solution.

That was impressive. Clearly she was in a crisis response mode. I recommended several people I knew who had successfully developed whistleblower programs. Obviously Pat Burns was at the top of that list. When I mentioned one woman whom I greatly respected, Mary Schapiro's face lit up and she told me, "I know her—she's actually a friend of mine."

Then I explained that the best way to attract those big cases is to create a whistleblower program similar to those of the Department of Justice and the Internal Revenue Service that makes the guilty companies pay the government back treble damages and pays the whistleblowers between 15 percent and 30 percent of the settlement amount. And those bounty payments should not come out of the government's pocket. They should always be paid by the bad guys.

Until that point the meeting had been going very well. She had agreed that the SEC needed to develop a whistleblower program and needed to offer an incentive for people to take the risks. But then I told her that I had developed several whistleblower cases involving securities, and given my history with the SEC I had decided to file them with the Department of Justice, the IRS, or other government agencies.

David Becker interrupted, "You're telling me you know about securities law violations and you're withholding evidence from a government agency?"

"No," I responded. "I'm just withholding them from the SEC. I'm a citizen and I turn in my cases to the agency I think can best handle them, and at this point that's not the SEC. The government has the information, but it's just with another agency. If they're not bringing you into the case they have their reasons. Maybe they've lost confidence in you, too."

Becker was visibly angry. Until that moment he hadn't said a word. I began to discuss the specific reason I hadn't brought a case to the SEC, and I used another case as an example. When I mentioned a key player in that case, Becker put up his hands. "I have to stop you," he said. "I can't talk about this because I may have a conflict here."

I heard him, but it didn't really register. This was a case I had nothing to do with. It had been reported on extensively. I thought maybe the problem was the way I had described it, so I tried again.

Becker stopped me again. "I've already told you, you really need to stop because I may have a conflict here."

Mary Schapiro didn't say a word. At that moment, and it turned out that Gaytri felt the same way, it appeared to me that David Becker was really the person in charge of this meeting. Gaytri spoke up, saying, "I'm not sure what the problem is. I think he's just giving you an example. This isn't anything we need to get involved in." She looked at me. "Harry, I think you should just go on to something else."

So I did—for a least a few minutes. The one thing on my mind was avoiding that topic, so naturally I stumbled onto it again. It certainly was not my intention, but I mentioned the key player's name again.

David Becker stood up. Until that moment I didn't realize how large he was. We were about five or six feet apart, separated by a coffee table, and Gaytri's first thought was that he was about to come right over that table and go for my throat. I didn't quite feel that way, but I did understand he was challenging me. It was an incredible moment. After everything we'd been through, after living in fear of a Madoff hit team coming for me, after all that, imagine the absurdity of being attacked by an attorney.

Gaytri stood up, too. "I don't know what's going on here. But this is completely uncalled for. It's certainly not productive for anybody. We don't have to talk about this."

He ignored her. "I don't know where you get off," he said. "I told you I had a conflict. This is a case I've been involved in. You can't come in here and tell us about ongoing cases and not give us enough details so we can get involved."

I didn't know precisely what had triggered Becker's response. Maybe he simply was insulted that I had called his agency incompetent, or maybe it had something to do with his involvement in the other case, but whatever the reason, he was furious. For a few seconds I really believed he was going to hit me. I tried to calm down the situation. "Listen, I'd love for the SEC to get involved. But you guys don't have a very good track record. So until you guys prove you're serious about prosecuting these cases, I'll take them to the DOJ, the IRS, and other competent government agencies. And when you prove you can do it, I'll bring them to you."

David Becker said evenly, "I'm general counsel. I can't hear this information and be put in this position where I can't do anything about it. And I've told you, I have a conflict."

Gaytri was still trying to bring peace and harmony to this meeting. "This was supposed to be an informational meeting," she said to Becker. "We didn't know you were going to be here. Truthfully, I don't even know what you're doing here, but I'm not going to let you attack my client. We were asked to come and speak with Mary Schapiro."

I don't remember Mary Schapiro saying a word.

It was never my intention or my desire to cause any problems. But maybe David Becker should have left the room for a few minutes while we discussed that particular case. He didn't budge, and he gave no indication that he was going to move, so there really was no alternative. Gaytri said, "I think we should adjourn at this point. Come on, Harry, we're leaving."

We shook hands with Chairman Schapiro and Steve Cohen, but not with David Becker. He made it pretty obvious he didn't want anything to do with us. I left that meeting not really confident that the changes in the SEC that I believed were necessary actually were going to be made.

It was time to go home. It was at the airport that I began to understand that my life from that point on was going to be very different than it had been. Because my meeting with Schapiro had not lasted as long as I had anticipated, I had a chance to make an earlier flight to Boston. When I went to the desk at USAir to change my flight, the staff recognized me from TV. The desk clerk extended his hand.

"I just want to thank you for what you've done, Mr. Markopolos," he said, actually pronouncing it correctly. "The next flight to Boston is leaving in 10 minutes. I can get you on that one. Don't worry, we'll get your suitcase on board; I guarantee it."

A member of the ground crew literally hand-carried my bag to the airplane. As I sat down in my seat and snapped my seat belt into place, I allowed myself to just relax for the first time in . . . I couldn't remember. But I certainly remember those words from the desk clerk. And those words I savored.

There was considerably more to come in the next few months. The media had become ferocious. The *60 Minutes* piece ran in early March 2009. It's probably accurate to claim that I was the first person from Whitman, Massachusetts, to be profiled on that show; *60 Minutes* correspondent Steve Kroft narrated the story. I was "The one person who knows the most and is willing to talk"—but only after being besieged—"Harry Markopolos, the man who figured out Madoff's scheme before anyone else."

I saw this piece for the first time sitting in my living room with my family. It's an odd feeling watching the edited version of the past nine years of your life; it's a combination of too much and not enough, exactly right and where did that come from? Mostly, though, they got it right. "Until a few months ago Harry Markopolos was an obscure financial analyst and mildly eccentric fraud investigator from Boston. . . ."

Mildly eccentric? Okay, as a quant I actually took that as a compliment. Maybe they thought they were being kind. Actually, I would have preferred being called "wildly eccentric" because that would have impressed my fellow quants, but I accepted "mildly eccentric."

". . . But today he enjoys an almost heroic status. . . ."

I laughed at that line. I have never thought of myself as a hero, unless being a hero has come to mean simply telling the truth, pursuing a criminal, and trying to protect investors and my country's reputation. Heroes are brave and I know that I wasn't brave, just frightened. I went forward with the investigation only because it was too risky to turn back or stop. The only way to safety was forward, hoping we could get to the other side in one piece. My team and I had taken too many risks and made a few mistakes in whom we trusted. If Madoff had learned about our pursuit, only bad things would have happened.

The *60 Minutes* story showed me speaking at a gathering, at which I began, "I stand before you, a fifty-billion-dollar failure. . . ." To me, that's much more accurate. I often say, "We saved no one," which is not quite accurate, as there were a few people we warned away from Madoff; but we saved very few people. The best way to make up for that, I felt strongly, was to make sure the SEC became the agency it should be.

■ ■ ■

During the next few months, as we all waited patiently for David Kotz's report to be published, Mary Schapiro began making significant changes to the structure and culture of the SEC. She began by sending over 400 examiners to participate in the Association of Certified Fraud Examiners training and certification program, which teaches them how to recognize the warning signs of fraud and the risk of fraud. In addition, she took steps to ensure that investment advisers be required to hire truly independent firms to provide the necessary oversight; restructured the Enforcement Division by creating specialized units to "help detect patterns, links, trends and motives"; and hired an independent firm to revamp the SEC's procedures for "collecting, recording, investigating, referring and tracking" the 800,000 tips it receives annually and for using risk analysis techniques to "reveal links, trends, statistical deviations and patterns" that might be noticed when individual complaints are examined.

Maybe even more important, as far as I was concerned, she asked Congress to provide funds to reward whistleblowers; changed the agency's examination procedures to proactively identify "firms or products that may pose a risk to investors or markets"; and began recruiting new staffers with specialized experience "in areas such as trading, operations, portfolio management, options, compliance, valuation, new instruments, portfolio strategies and forensic accounting," as well as experts capable of providing "other staffers with new information and perspectives to help them identify emerging issues and understand the way the industry is changing." She instituted many of the reforms that my team had suggested, including adopting methods to create examination teams in which "people with the right skill sets are assigned to examinations" to ensure that "the examination team includes those most expert in the subject of the examination."

Obviously, Mary Schapiro realized that the existence of the SEC as an independent agency was at stake. To demonstrate that the SEC was serious about finally fulfilling its responsibility, in the first half of 2009 it filed "more than twice as many emergency temporary restraining orders this year related to Ponzi schemes and other frauds as compared to the same period last year."

I think it is fair and accurate to claim that this restructuring never would have happened without the work done by my team, without Frank, Neil, Michael, and myself. I've gotten most of the credit in public, but in every respect we were a team. These three men used excellent cover stories to push forward the investigation at every opportunity. They warned others away from Madoff and sometimes succeeded. I was very lucky to have this team in the field for that long a period and have them in one piece at the end. Several other like-minded folks in the industry helped us along the way, proving that there are plenty of honest people out there willing to do the right thing. And every single person did it for free, proving that some things are just so important in life that you'll do something because it is the right thing to do.

Reading about these changes made me cautiously optimistic; on paper the SEC was making substantial changes in an effort to do its job. Of course Bernie Madoff had proved how little value reports on paper actually have in the real world. So it will take a long time to determine if those changes actually translate into an effective SEC.

While we waited through the summer of 2009 for David Kotz's report to be released I focused on my other cases. One of them, involving a custody bank that was cheating millions of government pension accounts via a currency trading fraud scheme, had been successfully filed as a False Claims Act case more than a year earlier and remained under seal—but we were optimistic the state of California would be intervening and making the case public early in the fall. I'd been waiting several years for my first case to be unsealed. I figured I could wait a few months more.

On Wednesday, September 3, 2009, the greatly abbreviated 22-page Executive Summary of David Kotz's 457-page report was released.

It included staggering evidence of the SEC's complete and total failure in this case. It was even better than I anticipated it would be, and believe me, I was already expecting a great report. "Embarrassing" doesn't come close to describing the actions of the SEC investigators.

David Kotz had written a damning document that castigated his own agency. This summary concluded that the SEC's failure to catch Madoff began as early as 1992, when the agency first discovered that the accounting firm Avellino & Bienes had raised hundreds of millions of dollars for Madoff by guaranteeing 20 percent annual returns. When the firm was unable to provide an audit, the SEC allowed it to pay back all the money—but did nothing to stop Madoff. That was the beginning, and it continued until Madoff successfully caught himself.

In this summary one SEC investigator involved in the 2005 investigation described Madoff as "a wonderful storyteller" and "a captivating speaker," who claimed to be on "the short list" to become the next chairman of the agency.

But when these investigators politely asked Madoff to produce specific documents he got so angry that "veins were popping out of his neck." Apparently that proved to be an effective defense because the SEC investigators did not press him and when they reported his response they were "actively discouraged from forcing the issue."

As an attorney, Gaytri was particularly incensed by the fact that two SEC lawyers were aware that Madoff had lied to them but didn't know what to do about it. One of them apparently told the other, "I don't think he's allowed to lie to us!" She just couldn't believe that the people in charge of the investigation were not aware that lying to officials of the federal government is a felony.

Every complaint we had made about the SEC was verified in this report. It turned out that some of the investigators "weren't familiar with securities laws." The only time investigators tried to verify that Madoff actually was making the trades he claimed, a letter was drafted to be sent to the National Association of Securities Dealers (NASD) to obtain the necessary trading records—but that letter was never mailed, because the investigators decided that it would have taken them too much time to actually compare those records with Madoff's so-called trades. In fact, if they had sent that letter, just the opposite would have happened—there were no trading records, because Madoff never actually traded. They wouldn't have spent 30 seconds trying to match orders.

Apparently none of that mattered to the SEC—for attorney Simona Suh's work in this investigation, Meaghan Cheung gave her the highest possible performance rating, and particularly cited her "ability to understand and analyze the complex issues of the Madoff investigation. . . . Simona's command of the laws, regulations and staff guidance was such that she was able to convince Madoff and his counsel that he needed to register" as an investment adviser.

I don't know which was worse: the fact that most of the time the SEC had refused to investigate Madoff or the fact that on several occasions it actually did investigate Madoff. According to this summary, at one time, in fact, two SEC offices were simultaneously investigating the same issues—and neither of them knew about the other one.

As I read this summary, I realized this agency was more like Keystone Accountants than any kind of professional organization. And this report also confirmed what I had already been told. The New York office didn't take my submissions seriously because they didn't like me. They questioned my motives, claiming I was "a competitor of Madoff" who "was looking for a bounty." And the enforcement team reported that I didn't "have the detailed understanding of Madoff's operations that we do, which refutes most of his allegations."

Frank was disappointed in the summary. In his opinion it was a whitewash. He just couldn't believe that any institution could be that incompetent. "Maybe I am wrong," he told me later. "Maybe they really were just that stupid."

And this was just the summary. I couldn't wait to read the entire 457-page report, which was supposed to be issued before the Labor Day weekend. Apparently, though, someone in the SEC was not quite as excited about it as we were. There were some rumors that its release would be "delayed." That apparently infuriated the House Capital Market Subcommittee's chairman, Paul Kanjorski, a Pennsylvania Democrat, who contacted the SEC and expressed his concern. And then we were told it would be available at 1 P.M. that Friday afternoon.

There is an old public relations trick. When you have to release potentially damaging information and you want the fewest people to learn about it, do it Friday night after people have left for the weekend. The fact that it was finally released about 5 o'clock the Friday afternoon of the Labor Day three-day holiday weekend probably suggests how much the SEC wanted people to be aware of it. In this particular case, the Friday afternoon release had an additional benefit for the agency; so many of Madoff's victims were members of the New York Orthodox Jewish community, and the Jewish Sabbath begins Friday night at sundown.

As soon as it was available, I sat down and read it. Even after all I knew about the investigation, this report astonished me. At least one-third of the entire document either was directly attributable to me and Neil, Frank, and Mike, or was based on information we had provided. It was as if we were reading the story of the preceding decade of our lives. Just reading the 17-page Table of Contents told the whole story:

The SEC's 1992 Investigation of Avellino & Bienes, "SEC Contacted Avellino and Suspected That Avellino & Bienes Was Selling Unregistered Securities and Running a Ponzi Scheme."

SEC Review of 2000 and 2001 Markopolos Complaints: "Markopolos Approached the SEC's Boston Office in May 2000 with Evidence That Madoff Was Operating a Ponzi Scheme . . . Markopolos Met with Grant Ward, a Senior SEC Enforcement [Official] . . . Ward Decided Not to Pursue the 2000 Submission."

Markopolos Made a Second Submission to the Boston Office in March 2001 . . . "NERO Decided Not to Investigate Madoff Only One Day After Receiving the 2001 Submission . . . Two Articles Were Published in May 2001 Questioning the Legitimacy of Madoff's Returns."

Markopolos Made a Third Submission to the Boston Office in October 2005 . . . "Markopolos and His Team Continued to Gather Information about Madoff . . . The Boston and New York SEC Offices Reacted Very Differently to the 2005 Submission . . . The Matter Was Assigned to a Relatively Inexperienced Team, Particularly with Respect to Conducting Ponzi Scheme Investigations . . . The Enforcement Staff Considered the Evidence of Little Value Because Markopolos Was Not a Madoff Investor or Someone Personally Involved in the Alleged Ponzi Scheme . . . The Enforcement Staff Questioned Markopolos'

Credibility Because of His Perceived Self-Interest . . . The Enforcement Staff Concluded That Madoff Did Not Fit the 'Profile' of a Ponzi Scheme Operator."

"In April 2008, Markopolos Attempted to Send a Version of the 2005 Submission to the SEC's Office of Risk Assessment, but It Was Not Received."

The Table of Contents outlined an astonishing record of failure: "Madoff Testified . . . Madoff Contradicted . . . Madoff Denied . . . Madoff Caught Lying." It outlined an indictment of the SEC: "SEC Enforcement Staff Was Not Suspicious . . . SEC Enforcement Staff Never Thought . . . SEC Enforcement Staff Halted Efforts . . . SEC Enforcement Staff Did Not Exhibit an Interest . . . SEC Enforcement Staff Effectively Stopped . . . SEC Enforcement Staff Officially Closed . . ."

There were several things in this report that surprised me, especially the fact that the SEC's director of risk assessment, Jonathan Sokobin, had never received my last-ditch attempt to expose Madoff—because I'd mistakenly sent a copy of my 2005 submission to the wrong e-mail address.

Among several things in this report that we didn't know was the fact that the SEC had received other warnings about Madoff and had ignored them, too. In 2003, for example, an unidentified fund of hedge funds manager alerted the SEC as to his suspicions about Madoff, explaining during a conference call that "he couldn't understand how [Madoff] was maintaining his performance" and "he couldn't figure out how he was . . . earning returns." This manager's firm had responsibly conducted due diligence on two Madoff feeder funds—apparently using Mike Ocrant's *MARHedge* article as at least a partial blueprint—and submitted its own list of red flags that, in many cases, pointed out many of the same problems we had tried to warn the SEC about. The SEC branch chief who handled this complaint pointed out that *MARHedge* was a respected industry publication, but "not one that she believed the Commission usually received." And just like all of our submissions, this was lost in the bureaucracy.

The fact that Madoff's scam was widely known in the industry and easy to rip apart was proved in 2004 by an SEC compliance examiner. As Kotz reported, while conducting a routine examination of Renaissance

Technologies LLC, this investigator discovered e-mails between executives of that fund that professionally analyzed Madoff's strategy and returns and concluded there was no way to explain Madoff's activities. As one of those executives told Kotz, "This is not rocket science." The reason they had not notified the SEC was that all the information they relied on to reach these conclusions was readily available to the SEC. "It's not like we needed a PhD in mathematics to do the . . . study on the OEX."

In 2005 the SEC received an anonymous tip from a former investor who had taken his $5 million out of Madoff. The informant claimed he was "deeply concerned that Madoff is running a very sophisticated fraudulent pyramid scheme," adding, "I know that Madoff [sic] company is very secretive about their operations and they refuse to disclose anything. If my suspicions are true, then they are running a highly sophisticated scheme on a massive scale. And they have been doing it for a long time." The SEC has no record of ever investigating this claim.

Reading this, it almost makes me wonder why the SEC believed Bernie Madoff when he claimed to be the mastermind of a $50 billion Ponzi scheme. If they had needed any more clues, they received an anonymous letter in March 2008, apparently mailed from the New York Public Library, which concluded, "It may be of interest to you that Mr. Bernard Madoff keeps two (2) sets of records. The most interesting of which is on his computer which is always on his person."

There is no stronger evidence of financial fraud than a second set of books. Nobody keeps a second set books for fun. But rather than investigating this detailed claim, which seemed to me to indicate some insider knowledge, Simona Suh responded, "[B]ecause the letter is anonymous and lacks detail, we will not be pursuing the allegations in it."

Kotz's conclusion was obvious: The SEC never took "the basic and necessary steps to determine if Madoff was operating a Ponzi scheme," and if it had it could have uncovered the scheme "well before Madoff confessed." Personally, after reading all 457 pages of this report I have great admiration for David Kotz. He took on his own agency and shredded it with the truth. As I said later, Kotz and his team reaffirmed my faith in government. That's how strongly I supported his report.

A lot of people disagreed with me—they were very disappointed with the report because it didn't assess blame. They wanted to see the people responsible for this debacle named and punished. And like Frank, they found it very difficult to believe that the failure of the SEC was due to inexperience and stupidity, rather than collusion or even corruption. But I was at the center of the storm, and I never caught even a whiff of corruption, only incompetence and arrogance.

David Kotz investigated what went wrong at the SEC and why, and the evidence he presented makes it obvious who should be blamed. It also wasn't his job to determine how Madoff actually was able to pull off this scam for decades. In our investigation we didn't go after that, either. I don't even remember discussing it. Who knew?

My team didn't even attempt to find evidence that anyone else, including his wife, his two sons, his brother, his friends, his landscaper, or any of the employees of his money management firm knew about the mechanics of his scheme and helped him pull it off. But I believe it was impossible for him to have done it without considerable help. My family couldn't even operate one Arthur Treacher's Fish & Chips franchise without assistance. This was a $65 billion international scam that operated successfully for decades. Madoff's Ponzi scheme was too large an operation for one person to have done it by himself—unless you're talking about Superman, of course. And truthfully, Bernie really wasn't that smart. He wasn't particularly sophisticated with the numbers. For example, the reports provided to investors every month had to be prepared, and whoever did that had to know that the numbers were based on fairy dust. There was no mathematical basis for them. But who knew and when they knew it may well take years to be settled.

One member of my team did hear a story from a potential Madoff investor who had met with Bernie only two months before his surrender. This man was a fund executive who was interested in making a substantial investment, but insisted on meeting Madoff personally. Madoff agreed, and spent more than an hour with this executive in his office, answering every question and carefully explaining his strategy. It was, according to this man, an impressive performance. But at the end of the meeting the man asked politely, "You know, Mr. Madoff, this all sounds good, but the fact is you're getting older—and what's going to happen to the company when you're no longer able to manage it?"

Bernie apparently waved his hands in the universal "no problem" gesture. "There's nothing to worry about," he explained. "I've been grooming my two sons to take over their whole life. If anything happens to me, they know what to do."

Who knows if that was true? But the executive shook hands with Bernie, promised to think about it, and left. As he got on the elevator, two other men joined just as the doors were closing. As the elevator started going down, they began making some small talk. One of them asked the other, "So how's business going?"

The other young man nodded, saying, "I got to tell you, even with everything that's going on, we're doing great. It's really amazing."

The curious executive couldn't help himself, and he asked, "Do either of you know Bernie Madoff?"

They both turned to look at him, and one of them responded, smiling, "Yes, he's my dad." They said a few more words before the doors opened. Later, when the executive thought about it, he believed this apparently chance meeting in the elevator seemed much too coincidental. He was supposed to overhear this conversation. The whole thing appeared to be orchestrated in an attempt to sway his decision. As a result, he decided not to invest in Madoff.

Among the people Kotz interviewed while preparing this report was Bernie Madoff himself. Kotz spent three hours in prison with him. It's impossible to know how much of what Bernie told Kotz that day is true. Bernie Madoff's entire life had been a complete lie for decades. Imagine that. We never stopped during our investigation to wonder what kind of human being Bernie Madoff actually was, what kind of insanity it must have taken to get through every day. In all that time there wasn't one day, one conversation, in which he could tell the truth. Every single word he said carried with it the risk of exposure. Every time he went to a synagogue or had dinner with friends or attended an affair, he had to look people whose money he was stealing right in their eyes and smile and humbly accept their gratitude—and all the while he was probably thinking, *You suckers*. And if you choose to believe Bernie, those people he was lying to also included his wife, his sons, his sister, and other members of his family. For Bernie, lying became his natural way of life. So when he told Kotz he sometimes wished he had been caught sooner because the stress was incredible, only he knows if he is telling the truth.

Unfortunately, the government wasn't quite done with me. I'd told my story and made my recommendations, and I had a tremendous amount of work to do in my False Claims Act cases. My whistleblowers were depending on me to get this work done. The anger I'd felt was gone; it was up to the proper authorities to make sure the SEC followed through on its promises and that legal action be taken against those people who deserved it. But after Kotz's report was issued, I was invited to appear in front of the Senate Banking, Housing, and Urban Affairs Committee to comment on the report. I knew I owed it to David Kotz to do that.

So when I was invited to support Kotz's report I agreed, and on September 10, 2009, I appeared before what was supposed to be the Senate Banking Committee. The stated purpose of this hearing was to examine the information contained in the inspector general's report. It was a strange hearing. David Kotz testified first, and the committee asked him a lot of very good questions. But after a period of time the committee adjourned temporarily to allow the senators to vote on the floor. Only Senators Chuck Schumer, who had made a phone call to the SEC, and Jeff Merkley, a Democrat from Oregon, returned. Schumer took over the questioning.

During the recess, Gaytri, Pat Burns, and I had gone for a walk. When we returned, the whole feeling in the hearing room had changed. The SEC had reserved all the seats in the room. With the exception of two senior officials from the Association of Certified Fraud Examiners who had come to Washington from Texas for this hearing, the entire room was filled with SEC staffers. Gaytri took one look around and whispered to me, "The fix is in." We were hoping the room would be full of victims, an audience we considered among our biggest supporters; but the victims had been shunted to a hearing room on the floor below us to watch the proceedings on closed-circuit television. We couldn't have picked a more adverse audience.

I was joined on the panel by Robert Khuzami, the new director of the SEC's Enforcement Division, and John Walsh, the SEC's acting director of Compliance, Inspections and Examinations. In my opening statement I praised David Kotz, explaining that if my three sons grew up to be men like him I would be very proud. As for the SEC, in my prepared submission for the official record I wrote, "Even a great fiction-writer like Stephen King couldn't have made up the nightmare that the SEC was pre-December 11th, 2008. The SEC's actions and inactions during the Madoff investigation were a comedy of horrors." But in my oral testimony I was a little more succinct, telling Senator Schumer, "In a nutshell, the SEC staff was not capable of finding ice cream in a Dairy Queen."

I was surprised that I was asked so few questions in this hearing. Senator Schumer seemed to focus on the other members of the panel. In fact, throughout the panel questioning Gaytri was handing me index cards with suggestions, but I really got very little opportunity to speak. Finally she started handing me cards urging me, "Jump in whenever you can."

The whole situation was unusual. The other senators had left after the first session and Schumer carefully controlled this panel. I'm sure he had his reasons. One question Senator Schumer did ask me was what my two strongest recommendations would be for the improvement of the SEC.

After explaining that in our investigation we saw only incompetence and no evidence of corruption, I replied, "The best tool that the SEC could use, in my opinion, is the pink slip. It's a piece of paper that every employee could understand. There need to be a number of them; I suspect about half the staff, perhaps more. The pink slip is when you get called into account and when you get fired for doing a bad job or not being competent on the job. I think many of these examiners and many of these enforcement attorneys lack competence at the basic skill level. There needs to be a skill inventory, a reduction of the staff. They need to take multiple-choice exams, and those who don't cut the mustard—let them go. Everybody's performance needs to be closely reviewed, and they basically need to start weeding out staff."

There. That seemed to me to be a pretty strong recommendation. Fire half the staff, more than 1,700 people. And if that didn't make the SEC a more effective force, there was still another half left to replace. Naturally the two SEC representatives appearing next to me disagreed. Naturally.

I actually had fun in the remaining few minutes of this hearing. Trying to make a long point in a brief statement, I resorted to the use of very descriptive metaphors, which everybody not working for the SEC seemed to enjoy. In response to the director's defense of the agency and its employees, for example, I pointed out, "It's very hard to soar like an eagle when you're surrounded by turkeys, and there're a lot of turkeys that need to be let go." When Schumer asked me to elaborate, I added, "Most of these attorneys at the SEC—I don't think they could find steak in an Outback."

As I left the hearing that day, all in all I thought it was probably a good thing that at that moment I was not going over to the SEC Building.

■ ■ ■

Officially, at least, that was it for me and Bernie. Madoff was in jail for the next 150 years, with good behavior perhaps 140 years; Thierry was dead; and the tens of thousands of people who had lost their savings will recover only a portion of it at best. The Madoff story was far from done, though, as a large posse of lawyers had ridden into town, armed with loaded briefcases. The litigation has barely even started as those lawyers try to figure out which people and what organizations may bear some responsibility for these losses. There certainly will be more civil cases filed, more criminal indictments, and even more deaths like that of Thierry de la Villehuchet and that of Jeffrey Picower, who had received $7 billion from Madoff and was found on the bottom of his swimming pool in late October 2009. The SEC already has made substantial changes in the way it does business, and there will be many more changes to come if it intends to survive as an independent agency. The federal government will also be instituting new regulations and procedures for overseeing government financial institutions. Some of those industries—unregulated hedge funds, for example—undoubtedly will be trying to police themselves in an effort to keep the government out. And Gaytri has become very active in helping establish the first international financial court through the Global Alliance to deal with cross-border financial claims.

And unfortunately, other financial frauds will be uncovered. Soon after the story of our investigation became public, each member of the

team began receiving letters and tips offering evidence of other financial frauds, including several Ponzi schemes. I've gotten a large pile of
them that allege frauds in a variety of industries. Unfortunately, I'm so
busy with active cases that I don't have time to even look at the mail
that comes my way.

What has become apparent to me and to Frank and Neil and Mike
and Gaytri is that there is an overwhelming desire among the majority
of people in the financial industry to clean up the mess. Most people who
work in the industry actually are proud to be part of it, and a scandal
like this one taints all of them. While a few people make money, scandals make the business harder for everyone else. So there is widespread
support for these suggested changes. For Neil's efficient markets theory
to function, it is essential.

■ ■ ■

On October 20, 2009, five years after I became a full-time fraud investigator, the very first whistleblower case that I developed became the first
of my cases to be unsealed. California's attorney general, Jerry Brown,
charged the State Street Corporation with a $56.6 million fraud against
the state's two largest pension funds, announcing that he hoped to receive
$200 million in overcharges and penalties. Brown said, "State Street
bankers committed unconscionable fraud by misappropriating millions of
dollars that rightfully belonged to California's public pension funds."

This amount was only the tip of what my team and I believe
was nothing more than a fraudulent iceberg. Basically, our complaint
alleged that the bank has executed more than $35 billion in currency trades
for the pension systems since 2001, and what foreign exchange traders
were doing was falsely claiming that buy trade orders were made at or near
the highest exchange rates of that particular day while sell orders were
executed at or near the lowest exchange rates of the day, allowing the
bank to pocket the difference. It remains to be seen whether the bank
will choose to go to a jury trial to prove its innocence or will settle the
matter before it goes to trial.

Two days after Brown unsealed the lawsuit, the bank's chairman
and CEO, Ron Logue, announced he would retire the following
March. There was no mention of the lawsuit in this announcement,
and if anybody had asked about the odd timing, certainly the answer

would have been that there was no link between the two events. And clearly that is possible. But it is quite a coincidence.

I have many other cases in the pipeline. There will be a lot more announcements and lawsuits just like this one to come in the future. In fact, I intend to be in this business until I can't find anymore financial or Medicare frauds—which makes me think I'm going to be in the whistleblower business for a long, long time.

Epilogue

Mr. Pinkslip Goes to Washington

'Ve seen the failures of the Securities and Exchange Commission (SEC) from both inside and outside the industry. I know how the agency was supposed to function, and by this time I certainly knew how it actually worked—or, more accurately, didn't work. So when I was asked numerous times to suggest ways in which the SEC could improve, I was able to offer a long and fairly detailed list of ideas.

SEC Commissioner Mary Schapiro has begun making the necessary changes. The agency is trying to get better and, for a government agency, it is moving at an enviable pace. But you have to crawl before you can walk, and you have to walk before you can run. The SEC has to learn how to crawl again. It has suffered through decades of sloth, abysmal leadership, underfunding, and benign neglect, and realistically it will take several years for it to begin functioning as the effective, efficient cop on the financial beat that both investors and industry professionals expect.

As I told Congressman Kanjorski's House subcommittee, the Senate Banking Committee, David Kotz, Mary Schapiro, and reporters for several newspapers and magazines, there are numerous concrete steps that need to be taken as soon as possible if the SEC is to be transformed into a respected agency.

First, banish the lawyers from the land. Currently the SEC, like most Washington agencies, is dominated by lawyers. In 2009 all five SEC

Commissioners were lawyers. Now, I have nothing against lawyers. I'm sure they are good to their children, and many of them contribute to charities. But putting them in charge of supervising our capital markets has been an unmitigated disaster. It would be like putting a political appointee in charge of the Federal Emergency Management Agency and expecting him to handle a flood. Very few SEC lawyers understand the complex financial instruments of the twenty-first century, and almost none have ever sat on a trading desk or worked in the industry other than doing legal work. A primary reason the SEC has reached this point is that historically the SEC Commissioners have been lawyers who may know where to find the best power lunches in Washington, D.C., but don't have a clue as to how the financial industry actually operates on a day-to-day basis.

Maybe lawyers know the difference between a tort and a tortilla, but there is a reason that most firms in the industry are run by businesspeople with capital markets or banking expertise—it's because they're experts. Obviously that didn't prevent the industry from barely surviving the 2008 crisis, but just about anything would be an improvement over lawyers attempting to lead an industry whose complexities they don't understand.

Of course there is a place for lawyers inside the SEC. They should be in charge of making sure the rules and regulations promulgated by financial experts are followed, and that those people who don't follow them get penalized. The director of enforcement should be a lawyer, but the other departments should be led by people knowledgeable about what they actually do in those departments. Lawyers need to be removed from most positions of senior leadership and replaced with people who understand the markets and institutions being regulated.

Anyone who doubts this should simply read David Kotz's report for evidence that the SEC's enforcement lawyers did not have a clue as to what Bernie Madoff was telling them about his trading strategy. As a basketball coach once scolded a poor shooting guard, "You couldn't hit the ocean if you were standing in it." Most lawyers couldn't recognize a Ponzi scheme if they were having dinner with Charles Ponzi. They couldn't recognize Madoff's obvious lies because none of them had the financial expertise to understand the capital markets. The typical SEC attorney would have trouble finding fireworks on the Fourth of July, so asking them to uncover financial frauds was well beyond their pay grade. There were a lot of financial experts who knew that Madoff was doing something illegal—even if they didn't publicly expose him. But at least we should put those people in position to stop these scams—and then make it worth it for them to do it.

The purpose of laws is to define the lowest form of acceptable behavior between people, but ethics are the higher standard that the SEC's securities lawyers have successfully ignored. For example, mutual fund market timing isn't illegal, so the SEC ignored it while individual investors lost billions of dollars to market timers and hedge funds engaged in the practice. But within the industry the professionals with a moral compass knew this activity was unethical, that it cheated investors and needed to be stopped. Lawyers are trained to follow the black-letter law and regulation the way Hansel and Gretel tried to follow the bread crumbs home from the forest. But the SEC has to do more than just follow the technical bar set by the rules; it has to lead in regulating industry behavior so that it embodies the highest standards of transparency and fairness for all.

There certainly is an important role for lawyers to play in the SEC, just not the part they've been playing. Securities laws are outdated almost as soon as they go into effect, because new financial instruments are created to skirt these new laws. Lawyers should focus on using regulations to establish a standard of behavior for the industry that is substantially higher than now exists. But it would be tough to do a worse job running the show than they've done, so we really should put professionals in charge. The lawyers should have a separate enforcement unit in which they can prosecute both civil and criminal cases of securities and capital markets fraud. Let lawyers prosecute, not investigate.

Second, smart is as smart does. The people who should fill the positions created when we clean up the SEC should have industry experience, not resemble a clown car filled with college degrees. These college green-horns couldn't find a steer in a stampede. This is actually a great place for reverse age discrimination. For the broker-dealer exam teams, the people who actually go into an office to conduct an investigation, we should be hiring experienced brokers with as many years of experience as can be found. These people know the tricks and the hiding places; they may even have used some of them themselves when they were on the other side of the investigation. So put veteran traders and veteran back-office personnel on these investigative teams to conduct trading floor exams. For the money management and hedge fund teams, hire experienced portfolio managers, analysts, and buy-side back-office personnel to conduct asset manager examinations. Hire experienced accounting professionals to examine required corporate filings.

Hire experienced leaders. Most people in the industry considered William Donaldson a capable chairman—and he came from the industry. He knew where the skeletons were buried, and he allowed his staff to dig them up.

There is a theme here: Hire people who know what they're doing, not college kids who know what they want to do—which is get a better-paying job at the companies they're investigating!

This is a true story: A woman I know with an undergraduate degree in economics and math, an MBA, and a CFA, with more than 10 years' experience in the industry, wanted to leave her job as a senior analyst at a large mutual fund in order to have a second child. She wanted out of the 70-hour-a-week rat race, so she applied for a job at the SEC. If she were hired, she would almost immediately become one of the most experience people on their staff. But during her interview she was told that she was overqualified with too much industry experience, that she was overeducated, and that it was clear she wouldn't be happy inspecting paperwork and would probably just quit anyway, so it made no sense to hire her.

Instead, the SEC hires unqualified, sometimes undereducated people without financial industry experience, apparently because those people won't get bored doing the boring work. All they want these people to do is check pieces of paper to make sure that a company's paperwork is in compliance with the outmoded securities laws that have to be followed. So is it any surprise, given the current quality of the SEC's staff, that major felonies go undiscovered and unpunished while paperwork violators are cited and fined? This is the regulatory equivalent of death by a thousand paper cuts!

No Child Left Behind tests students to determine if they're learning, yet we don't test those people given power to regulate our financial industry. So maybe we should hire the fifth graders who passed the test? Because it's clear that a significant portion of the SEC's professional staff—my guess is at least half and maybe more—need to be let go because they are not qualified to hold their positions. Certainly based on their performance in the Madoff investigation, quite a few employees of the New York regional office staff should be fired—unless they've had the good sense to resign. Fortunately, given the layoffs that have swept Wall Street, there are many extremely qualified industry professionals with a clear understanding of the capital markets who are currently at liberty and would be delighted to start tomorrow morning. The quality of the SEC's staff needs to be dramatically upgraded, and the people who are capable of doing that are incredibly available and ready to jump into that particular pool.

Before hiring an employee, the SEC should give applicants a simple entrance exam to test their knowledge of the capital markets. To me, it doesn't seem unreasonable that someone joining the agency that regulates the financial industry should have some knowledge of the industry he or she is being hired to regulate. Many SEC staffers, particularly the staff attorneys, don't know a put from a call, a convertible arbitrage strategy from a municipal bond, or an interest-only from a principle-only fixed income instrument. The Chartered Financial Analysts Level I exam covers the material that I would expect all of the SEC's professional staff to have mastered *before* being hired. But that's just me being Harry. I seriously doubt that 20 percent of the SEC's current staff would be able to pass this important exam.

There are several other tests that could be used to determine the proficiency of potential or active employees. SEC employees should be tested regularly, and if they perform poorly on those tests they should be required to attend classes until they prove their ability to conduct professional inspections.

Third, examine the SEC's examination process. I have survived an SEC inspection, although I didn't get the official T-shirt. I was a portfolio manager, then the chief investment officer at a multibillion-dollar equity derivatives asset management firm. My firm, Rampart, was considered high-risk only because we managed derivatives; therefore, we received SEC inspection visits every three years, so I know from my own experience how flawed these examinations are. Incredibly, the SEC never sent in a single examiner with any knowledge of derivatives. These examiners had no idea what they were looking at. Rampart was always honest, but we easily could have pulled a Madoff and they never would have caught us. These examiners were very young and had little or no industry experience. These examiners would come in with a typed list of the documents and records they wished to examine. They handed this list to our compliance officer, who escorted the examiners to a conference room where they could diligently inspect the piles of documents and records we provided to them. If we were corrupt—if any firm is corrupt—we easily could have kept a second set of falsified but pristine records, committing the equivalent of mass financial murder, and gotten away with it, just as long as the documents and records shown to the inspection team were in compliance.

Yes, it is that simple.

That particular inspection team wouldn't have been able to find a batter in the batter's box. First, it interacted only with the firm's compliance team, not the traders, not the portfolio managers, and not the client service officers; they didn't even speak to the people who ran the place, top management. The examiners sat there looking at papers, rather than taking advantage of the tremendous human intelligence–gathering opportunities who happened to be sitting a few feet away. They're called people, and you can't make a good pile of them, but they have a lot of information about those papers. The SEC examination teams should send their so-called experts onto the trading floors and into the portfolio manager's office to ask leading, probing questions. Here's an example of one of those questions: Is there anything going on here that is suspicious, unethical, or even illegal that I should know about? Are you personally aware of any suspicious, unethical, or even illegal activity at any competing firms that we should know about?

The SEC examiner should point out that it is a felony to lie to an official of the federal government—even without taking an oath—and then hand them a business card, making it easy to call an examiner if they should see any illegal activity. This isn't rocket science, it isn't brain surgery, and it isn't even supermarket bagging; these are basic internal auditing techniques. But the SEC staff is so untrained that for them it *is* rocket science, because these examiners are so inexperienced and unfamiliar with financial concepts that they clearly are either afraid or embarrassed to interact with industry professionals; instead, they choose to remain isolated in conference rooms looking at paperwork.

The current examination process is an insult to common sense—as well as a waste of taxpayer dollars. It is essential that examiners interact with industry professionals and talk to them about what's going on inside their firm and what they know about their competitors.

The examination teams should be made up of people with various types of expertise. You certainly need a subject matter expert on each team, at least one person who is familiar with the area being investigated. Then you need an investment professional, someone from the industry who knows precisely what to look for. And you also need an accountant on the team capable of combing financial statements until every flea shakes out.

Currently the SEC measures the performance of a regional office by the number of exams it conducts annually, a totally worthless statistic. The SEC's stated mission is to protect investors and to find or prevent fraud. As David Kotz's report has shown, conducting poorly planned and executed exams and then promoting staff based on the completion of those exams is not a deterrent to fraud. Incredibly, people involved in the Madoff examination were promoted. The goal should never be how many pieces of paper were inspected, but rather how much fraud was caught or prevented.

The success metrics the SEC should use to determine the value of its examination teams are income from fines, dollar damages recovered for investors, dollar damages prevented, and the number of complaints received from Congress complaining about the severity of those fines or the thoroughness of the agency's investigation. The way exams are currently conducted, they catch so little major fraud as to be worthless, unless someone actually believes that compiling minor technical violations stops fraud.

Until the SEC puts professionals on these examination teams and allows them to conduct thorough examinations, the odds of uncovering the next Bernie Madoff—and Bernie was not out there alone—are minuscule at best.

Fourth, money talks business. The only way the SEC is going to attract those qualified industry professionals it needs is to increase its pay scale and offer incentive compensation tied to how much in enforcement revenue each office collects. Make it financially worthwhile to do this job right. The SEC pays peanuts and then wonders how it ended up with so many monkeys. Firms in the financial industry pay a salary plus a bonus and to attract the best talent; the SEC needs to be competitive. Obviously SEC Commissioners would be setting the levels of fines for enforcement actions, but each SEC regional office should keep some percentage—I recommend 10 percent to start—which would form an office bonus pool.

If you want to motivate enforcement officers, a pile of bonus money will light that fire. Staff members should be given a proper incentive; believe me, if there is a bonus at stake and someone tries to stop a staff member from bringing a big case, the staffer will roll over the obstacle with a bulldozer to get that case in the door.

Regional enforcement teams that uncover a $100 million case should be compensated for that. And to prevent taxpayers from having to pay these multimillion-dollar bonuses, I would insist that the fines be triple the amount of actual damages and that the guilty firms pay the cost of the government investigation—so the SEC staff bonuses given out for uncovering fraud are paid by the people and companies committing those frauds.

In the financial centers like New York and Boston, where the cost of living is high, I believe base compensation should be $200,000. That's a salary level sufficient to attract the brightest and most experienced industry professionals. Compensation above that would need to come from each regional office's bonus pool and be tied directly to revenues from fines each office generates. People who don't bring in quality cases that settle eventually will be asked to leave to make room for other people who can produce solid cases and generate bonus revenue.

Fifth, relocate the SEC headquarters to New York City. New York, New York, it's a wonderful town. I love Boston, but the single thing the SEC can do to quickly upgrade the agency's talent pool is move its headquarters to New York City. Currently the SEC headquarters are in Washington, D.C., and Washington, D.C., is the place where you'll find a lot of politicians, but not very many qualified finance professionals. As New York is the world's largest financial center and Boston is the world's fourth largest financial center, moving the SEC to New York City or elsewhere in the New York–New England corridor makes a lot of sense. Put the SEC headquarters in the center of the financial industry, a place with easy access to New York and Boston. Go where the best people are instead of trying to lure the best people to where the politicians are.

Sixth, book 'em. If you walk into any substantial investment industry firm, you'll find a library stocked with professional publications for its staff to use as an important resource. Among those publications would be the *Journal of Accounting, Journal of Portfolio Management, Financial Analysts Journal, Journal of Investing, Journal of Indexing, Journal of Financial Economics,* even the *Wall Street Journal.* But if you walk into an SEC office, you probably won't see any of these publications—and you won't find an investment library. So where do SEC staffers actually go to research an investment strategy, or find out which formulas to use to calculate investment performance, or even figure out what a CDO-squared is? Apparently the SEC staff uses Google and Wikipedia—because both of them are free. Good luck to a man or woman attempting to figure out a complex financial instrument using free Web resources. The SEC makes sure its staff will remain uneducated—by not providing the educational tools they need.

Seventh, card 'em. Perhaps the easiest change the SEC can make is to supply every employee with business cards. If SEC employees want their own business cards, they have to pay for the cards themselves. It's very difficult to get a call back from someone you've met at an industry conference—assuming you are permitted to attend an industry con-ference—or from an employee of a firm who you've just suggested should "Call me if you run across a securities fraud" if you can't hand the employee your business card. If private industry provides business cards for its employees, then so should the SEC. It's common sense.

These business cards should include the list of professional credentials each SEC staffer has obtained. Credentials such as CAIA, CFA, CFE, CFP, CIA, CISA, CPA, FRM, JD, PhD, and any other initials earned should appear prominently on all business cards. And maybe at the bottom of each card the words "To report a securities fraud, call me" could appear. This would send the message that each SEC staff member is a fraud fighter first. And business cards should be given to secretaries and clerks, too, as a way of building internal pride in the agency as well as advertising that the SEC is in the fraud-fighting business.

When these staffers do receive that call reporting a potential fraud, they should immediately forward it to the proper person under the SEC's new standard operating procedure for handling whistleblower tips.

Eighth, go to events. The SEC should encourage its staff to participate in industry events. The thinking in not encouraging this, I assume, is to keep the staff away from the people they regulate. I believe the most important thing the SEC can do to increase the opportunities for uncovering fraud is to encourage staff members to socialize with industry professionals wherever and whenever possible. Interacting with industry professionals before and after industry functions is a great way to keep up to date with what's happening in the industry and obtain tips on possible frauds—especially when they are just beginning.

New York, Boston, and other major cities with robust financial centers have numerous financial analyst societies, CPA societies, securities traders associations, and economic clubs, which frequently hold the type of educational meetings the SEC staff needs; but the SEC generally doesn't allow its staff time off to attend these meetings, nor does it reimburse its staff for attending this type of industry meeting. It's rare to see SEC staff at these educational events—and we know that isn't because they already know everything—and they would be welcomed.

Ninth, establish a lessons learned database. The very first thing the SEC employees who received my submission should have done is gone directly to the SEC database on their computers to see if the red flags I raised were comparable to information learned about other Ponzi schemes. Unfortunately, that would have been impossible because there is no existing SEC database like that. The SEC should build a strong online knowledge center for its staff. In this case when staffers keyed in "Ponzi" they would have been able to find diagnoses of past Ponzi schemes and several checklists teaching them what to look for, what questions to ask, and how to most efficiently solve such cases. A Ponzi scheme is actually one of the easiest fraud schemes to detect because there is no underlying investment product and no trading, while the assets are being diverted to pay off investors. Yet this case was assigned to SEC staffers who had absolutely no experience and little knowledge of Ponzi schemes, and they really had no place within the SEC to go to learn about them.

To further increase the SEC's auditing effectiveness, I would create a Center for All Lessons Learned, a CALL center, similar to a database that has been used with great effectiveness for decades by the U.S. Army. CALL would collate and sort through every fraud uncovered by the SEC. These frauds would be analyzed to find both the common and the unique elements so that the odds of future similar frauds being undetected would be greatly reduced.

CALL would be a password-protected online Web-based resource for all SEC employees to use and, more important, for them to contribute information concerning their own investigations. The SEC needs to be able to learn at a faster pace than the bad guys they are pursuing, and the only way to increase the SEC's decision-making ability quickly is to demand that all levels of the organization pitch in and contribute to building this database. The traditional top-down, command-from-above approach, the way the agency does business, just doesn't work anymore and has to be abandoned if the SEC is to achieve greatness. That's possible. The SEC currently has a staff of more than 3,500, and every single one of those 3,500 brains needs to be turned on and contributing to this core knowledge base.

Ironically, most banks have set up or are establishing risk databases, putting the SEC investigators in the odd position of expecting to find this level of risk management within the organizations they regulate—but not within their own agency.

Tenth, give staff access to the tools of the trade. Another thing those SEC employees who received my submissions should have done was immediately turn on their Bloomberg terminals and analyze the actual OEX Standard & Poor's 100 index options trades that Bernie Madoff purported to trade on specific dates. If they had done that, they would have discovered that those trades never took place. But they couldn't do it, because they don't have easy access to Bloomberg machines and they have not been trained in how to operate them. That's like trying to prevent online identity theft without having access to a computer or knowing how to use one. If the staff had had this equipment, this case would have quickly been cracked open.

The Bloomberg machine is the key knowledge tool used in the finance industry, but admittedly it is expensive. Each machine costs more than $20,000 a year. Industry allocates one Bloomberg machine per trader, analyst, and portfolio manager so that they can efficiently and professionally conduct the business of finance. The SEC is lucky to have a single Bloomberg terminal in a regional office. Sending SEC teams into exams and enforcement actions without a Bloomberg terminal is like sending unarmed teams to the O.K. Corral and then wondering why they straggle back to the office in defeat each time.

When financial analysts are trying to determine whether to invest in a certain corporate stock, the first thing they do is go to a Bloomberg terminal and analyze the firm's capital structure, its financial statements, and its financial ratios. They look up the firm's weighted cost of capital and then start running a horizontal and vertical analysis of that firm's financial statements. A well-trained analyst will also use the Bloomberg machine to read all the news stories available on that company, look at the firm's SEC filings, and use the information collected to make a list of questions that have to be answered before committing funds to that company. The analyst will also obtain Wall Street's research reports on the company to see how those analysts interpreted all this data to make sure there was nothing they might have missed. Doing it correctly is a long process, made possible only by access to a Bloomberg.

The SEC staff examiners can rarely do any of this, either because they don't have access to a Bloomberg or because they don't know how to use it. I don't see how SEC compliance staff can function effectively without at least one Bloomberg available to each exam team for every exam it conducts. They just can't do a passable job without it. Bloomberg machines have become the lifeblood of the industry, and they make readily available almost all of the data an SEC staffer needs for conducting a basic fraud analysis. Not funding these machines saves money but costs a fortune.

Eleventh, as a policy, encourage whistleblowers. This is nearest and dearest to my heart and is the bottom line if the SEC intends to recover its reputation from this debacle. It has to open up an active Office of the Whistleblower to provide a central clearinghouse for complaints, which currently are handled ad hoc by 11 regional offices. According to the Association of Certified Fraud Examiners' 2008 Report to the Nation, whistleblower tips detected 54.1 percent of uncovered fraud schemes in public companies. External auditors (and the SEC exam teams would certainly be considered external auditors) detected a mere 4.1 percent of the uncovered fraud schemes. Let's examine that: 54.1 percent versus 4.1 percent. Whistleblower tips were 13 times more effective than external audits, which is why I believe the SEC should do more to encourage people to submit tips. There needs to be a single place to which people can submit those tips, anonymously if they choose to for protection.

Another interesting statistic from that ACFE report is that 57.7 percent of all whistleblower tips received come from employees. How easy would it be for the new and more efficient SEC enforcement teams to uncover a fraud after an internal whistleblower presented them with hidden books and records or information as to where they could be found? This would be sort of like informing the SEC that Bernie was keeping a second set on books—and kept the second set on his person! Customers provided 17.6 percent of whistleblower tips, vendors 12.3 percent, and shareholders 9.2 percent.

Whistleblower programs work. Among the most effective market watchdogs is the New York attorney general's office, which relies on whistleblowers. When a tip comes in they vigorously pursue it, unlike the SEC, which receives a tip and vigorously ignores it.

The best way to encourage people to become whistleblowers is to offer a reward, a bounty. The SEC needs to authorize a viable whistle-blower bounty program similar to those at the Department of Justice and the Internal Revenue Service. The IRS opened its Office of the Whistleblower in 2006 and in less than three years the staff grew to include 18 people—and as a result the IRS now receives larger and better-quality cases than ever before in its history. Consider the cost of 18 IRS employees and office equipment against the billions of dollars in additional tax revenue they are responsible for collecting for the U.S. Treasury. Whistleblowers need to be compensated for the risks they are taking; for many people, once it becomes known that they turned in a case, their careers are essentially over. They are blacklisted from the industry.

The key to the success of that program is the fact that the IRS offers bounty payments of between 15 and 30 percent to whistleblowers for cases that lead to successful recoveries for the Treasury. These payments don't come out of the IRS budget and they don't come from taxpayer dollars—all bounty payments are made by the defendants. This is a no-cost program that funds itself and allows the IRS to cherry-pick from cases that come in the front door. The investigators have the liberty, and the luxury, of selecting credible cases for immediate investigation.

It seems only logical that the SEC should expand and reinvigorate its almost never used whistleblower program. Section 21A(e) of the 1934 Act allows the SEC to pay a bounty of up to 30 percent to whistle-blowers—but only for insider-trading cases. The SEC can fine a person or company found guilty of insider trading triple the amount of its ill-gotten gains or its losses avoided for insider trading, and can award up to 10 percent of the penalty amount to the whistleblower.

Unfortunately, unlike the IRS's whistleblower program and the False Claims Act, the SEC's reward payments aren't mandatory. The SEC can simply refuse to pay these rewards and doesn't even have to explain why it isn't paying. If Congress would expand this program to encompass all forms of securities violations and make the reward payments man-datory, hundreds—maybe thousands—of new cases would be brought into the office. That would provide an incentive for the foxes out there in the field to bring cases against their firms with specific and credible allegations and documents—they would be able to provide the smoking e-mails! And this is the financial industry, meaning many of those cases would lead to huge settlements. If cases brought under the False Claims Act now lead to billions of dollars recovered annually, there is good reason to believe the SEC might also recover literally billions of dollars each year.

As each tip is received, it should be logged in and assigned a case number. For tips deemed credible, meaning those that come with real evidence, the whistleblower and the whistleblower's counsel would be put in direct contact with the SEC unit best able to investigate the complaint. This certainly would prevent anyone from having the same experience I did, in which over the years I kept submitting increas-ingly detailed complaints but got nowhere. The SEC just wasn't equipped to handle whistleblower complaints; there was no central processing unit, no one to delegate investigative authority, and no one to track it. Standardizing the treatment of whistleblowers to ensure that they are not ignored or mistreated should be a priority for the SEC. The agency should be required to report annually to a congressional committee all the whistleblower complaints it receives and the agency's follow-up actions.

Let me add one additional and very important point: the issue of self-regulation and whistle-blowing. I believe that several hundred finance professionals around the world knew or suspected that Bernie Madoff was a fraud—but none of these people contacted the SEC with their suspicions and identified themselves. Nor was there any system in place to encourage these professionals to communicate with the SEC. Unfortunately, my team and I may have been the only ones.

Getting rid of the shysters, fraudsters, and banksters is in every American's best interest. It is imperative that we do so if we intend to restore worldwide trust in the U.S. capital markets. If I'm the CEO of an honest firm and I hire a new employee who worked at a competing firm and find out from that person that my competitor is dishonest, it's in my economic self-interest as well as good public policy to turn that firm in to the SEC. If self-regulation is ever going to work, we need to find ways to advertise it, reward it, and measure it. And the SEC has done none of these.

Twelfth, reform the SEC or create a new super-regulatory agency. There is, of course, another option. If the SEC does not reform itself, it should be disbanded. Just zero out its budget and put every one of those 3,500 staff members on the streets, because right now they do not offer us any real protection. This would be harsh, I know, but anything short of a bottom-to-top reorganization of the SEC will not be sufficient to fight the financial frauds that plague our system.

The federal government has to get involved, too. The SEC is an agency of the government and has to abide by the rules and regulations, and the budget, set by Congress. So Congress also has a responsibility to ensure that changes are made to the way we govern our financial markets. That's why I agreed to testify in front of both House and Senate committees. As I told them, there are several things that Congress can do to guarantee a fair playing field for investors. For example, David Kotz's report highlights the complete lack of coordination and even communication between the Boston, New York, and Washington SEC offices, which severely hindered the Madoff investigation. It actually was even worse than that. The examination team in the New York regional office that had just finished an investigation of Madoff's operations in 2005 wasn't able to coordinate effectively with the enforcement team from the same office that was just starting its own Madoff investigation. If regional offices from a single agency can't coordinate with each other, and if teams within one regional office don't coordinate with each other, it makes no sense to maintain all of our financial industry regulatory agencies—the Federal Reserve, the Office of the Comptroller of the Currency (OCC), the Federal Deposit Insurance Corporation (FDIC), the Commodity Futures Trading Commission (CFTC), and the SEC— as independent entities. It gets worse: Each of these five regulators would have its own internal computer system—and none of them would have the slightest idea what any of the other regulators were doing with respect to a specific company.

Our current regulatory system was cobbled together in the 1930s, and the financial industry of that period had absolutely no resemblance to what exists today. But regulators in many cases are still bound by the basic structure created at that time and just don't have the tools to deal with financial institutions magnitudes larger than those that existed decades ago. Unfortunately, these agencies have to confront gigantic "too big to fail—too big to succeed—too big to regulate" multinational corporations like Citigroup, Bank of America, American International Group, and all the others. While these companies once were vertically oriented (they operated within a certain narrow field), now they may have subsidiaries operating banks, insurance companies, mortgage lenders, credit card companies, money management arms, investment banks, and securities broker-dealers, and they're operating both domestically and internationally. Relying on several separate regulators working independently to spot problems is like trying to rein in a beehive with a chain-link fence. If the SEC can't coordinate two examinations within its own agency, there is little reason to believe that five separate agencies can successfully coordinate their examinations.

It seems to me that the existence of so many financial regulators leaves gaping holes for financial predators to engage in what I called regulatory arbitrage. They find those regulatory gaps where no agency is looking or there is some question about which agency has the oversight responsibility, and they exploit them. I've seen corporations in which employees have two very different business cards. One card identifies them as a registered investment adviser, which falls under SEC regulation, while the other card has their bank title, which falls under the control of banking regulators. It's a very clever ploy: When the Federal Reserve comes in to question them, they claim to be under the SEC's jurisdiction, and when the SEC shows up, they explain they're under the Fed's jurisdiction. If both the Fed and the SEC were to show up to search for fraud in the company's pension accounts under management, that company could claim, "I'm sorry, but those are Employee Retirement Income Security Act (ERISA) accounts and they fall under the Department of Labor, so unfortunately you don't have jurisdiction." Obviously this structure allows firms to play regulators against each other, and literally to choose to be regulated by that agency least likely to pose any problems.

The objective should be to combine regulatory functions into as few agencies as possible to prevent regulatory arbitrage, centralize command and control, ensure unity of effort, eliminate expensive duplication of effort, and minimize the number of regulators to whom American corporations must respond.

It seems logical to me that one super-regulatory agency be formed, perhaps called the Financial Supervisory Authority (FSA). It should have all of the security and capital markets and financial regulators underneath it. To simply command and control, to ensure unity of effort and eliminate expensive duplication, I would place under its command the Fed, the SEC, a national insurance industry regulator, and some form of Treasury or Department of Justice law enforcement entity with a staff of dedicated litigators responsible for carrying out both civil and criminal enforcement for those three combined agencies. All banking regulators should be merged into the Fed, so that only a single national banking regulator exists. Pension fund regulation should be moved from the Department of Labor to the SEC. The Commodity Futures Trading Commission should be brought into the SEC, which would then become the sole capital markets regulator.

To ensure the highest degree of coordination, this super-agency would maintain a centralized database, a super-duper CALL center so that the details of any enforcement action by one agency would be online for all the other agencies to see and utilize. Spread the knowledge, share the experience, be bigger than the biggest bad guys. Bernie Madoff got caught for the first time in 1992, but apparently none of the investigators after the turn of the century knew about it. Cross-functional teams of regulators from the SEC, the Fed, a national insurance regulator, and the Treasury or Department of Justice should be sent together on audits whenever possible to prevent regulatory arbitrage. The SEC, the Fed, and the national insurance regulator would be responsible for the inspections, while the Treasury or Department of Justice would be responsible for taking legal action against offenders. American businesses need and deserve a simple, easy-to-follow set of rules and regulations, and they deserve to have competent regulation. Financial institutions currently pay high fees to support regulation, but neither they nor the public are getting their money's worth.

Thirteenth (lucky thirteen), take away the "Get out of jail free" cards. Right now there is no accountability in government. None. Following the accounting scandals that led to the demises of Enron, Global Crossing, WorldCom, Adelphia, and the others, Congress passed very strict laws that held corporate CEOs and CFOs accountable for their companies' financial reporting. Under the Sarbanes-Oxley Act (SOX), these leaders can no longer claim that they don't know what is happening in their companies. If a CEO and CFO has signed off on a company's books, he or she has assumed responsibility for the numbers; if those books are materially inaccurate, this officer faces a 10-year prison sentence. (That has gotten their attention.) And if they have been willfully cooking their books, they face a 20-year sentence.

I propose that Congress pass legislation that holds agency heads responsible for the successes or failures of their agency under their watch. If an agency fails to enforce laws passed by Congress, then the head should be referred to the Justice Department for criminal prosecution. It is a disgrace that the regulators charged with overseeing the financial industry have gotten away scot-free. At the SEC a few of the department heads were allowed to resign "to pursue other growth opportunities," called "pogo-ing out," often to well-paying positions in private industry. It would be satisfying to see a few of these people sent to prison for their willful blindness in allowing our nation's financial system to collapse; unfortunately, there are no laws on the books that make that possible. Entire government agencies can remain comatose, letting the industries they are charged with regulating commit crimes without any fear of being penalized for it.

A similar SOX making agency heads responsible for the failures of their staff would also go a long way toward eliminating so-called regulatory capture, a situation in which the regulators become beholden to the industries they supposedly are regulating. The mission of the SEC is to protect investors, but in reality it ended up serving the needs of deep-pocketed and influential industry firms.

Fourteenth, publicly censure the SEC. Clearly the SEC has been unofficially censured. Its reputation is in tatters, its employees have been shamed. Obviously no one can take pride in being an employee of the SEC. But maybe we should make that embarrassment official. One way to light a bonfire under agencies that are under-performing or non-responsive to Congressional oversight is to publicly censure them. Call them out. Identify them for what is, a national disgrace. Then force that agency to include that censure in every communication sent out by employees—for a predetermined amount of time or until the agency proves it has rectified its problems. This is a low-cost but effective means for Congress to publicly express its displeasure over the lack of regulatory action. No one, absolutely no one, enjoys playing on a losing team.

Fifteenth, regulate and give investors some guidelines. Bernie Madoff didn't just steal billions of dollars; he exposed the lack of government supervision of the financial industry to a public that had already been badly burned. Madoff is already a tragedy. It would be an even larger disaster if we didn't take the steps necessary to create fair and transparent markets.

For example, the over-the-counter (OTC) market is unregulated space. It's where the financial industry's cockroaches congregate, because it is a place where there is no light, only darkness. And perhaps not coincidentally, this is also where the industry's highest margins exist, so people will fight like Mike Tyson to protect their profit margins.

That needs to change. Laws should be passed to prevent American investors from trading OTC products offshore and still receive government protection in the form of bailouts. In other words, there should be no more trading through unregulated entities like AIG's London-based Financial Products unit, where the risk ends up getting transferred back onshore and U.S. taxpayers end up footing the bill. It seems only fair and logical that if American regulators don't have visibility into an OTC product traded offshore, then strict risk and capital limits should be placed on U.S.-based counterparties in order to avoid systemic risk.

You can't regulate common sense, but some sort of guidelines should be available to investors on the SEC's web site, pointing out that if you don't know how to model an OTC derivative yourself, then you, your company, or your municipality shouldn't be trading them. The SEC should closely investigate all disclosures in the OTC municipal derivatives market, because this sector of the marketplace is just rife with fraud. In many instances it is still a pay-to-play market with opaque disclosure documents and even more opaque pricing mechanisms, which only serve to defraud government entities.

I have seen the state of Massachusetts lose $450 million because no one in state government knew how to price interest rate swaptions. The Massachusetts Turnpike Authority was picked off by several Wall Street firms because they were lured into OTC transactions in which they didn't understand the pricing or the risks.

Once again, you can't regulate common sense, but we can regulate the OTC markets so they no longer remain outposts of lawlessness. More regulation can only come from the federal government. History has now taught us that we need to shed light on those dark places in our capital markets. Everybody deserves full transparency when they are dealing with investments, and it's up to the government to provide it.

Appendix A

Madoff Tops Charts; Skeptics Ask How

Michael Ocrant

M ention Bernard L. Madoff Investment Securities to anyone working on Wall Street at any time over the last 40 years and you're likely to get a look of immediate recognition.

After all, Madoff Securities, with its 600 major brokerage clients, is ranked as one of the top three market makers in NASDAQ stocks, cites itself as probably the largest source of order flow for New York Stock Exchange—listed securities, and remains a huge player in the trading of preferred, convertible and other specialized securities instruments.

Beyond that, Madoff operates one of the most successful "third markets" for trading equities after regular exchange hours, and is an active market maker in the European and Asian equity markets. And with a group of partners, it is leading an effort and developing the technology for a new electronic auction market trading system called Primex.

But it's a safe bet that relatively few Wall Street professionals are aware that Madoff Securities could be categorized as perhaps the best

This article was originally published in *MARHedge* magazine (No. 89) in May 2001. Reprinted with permission of Institutional Investor.

risk-adjusted hedge fund portfolio manager for the last dozen years. Its $6 –7 billion in assets under management, provided primarily by three feeder funds, currently would put it in the number one or two spot in the Zurich (formerly MAR) database of more than 1,100 hedge funds, and would place it at or near the top of any well-known database in existence defined by assets.

More important, perhaps, most of those who are aware of Madoff's status in the hedge fund world are baffled by the way the firm has obtained such consistent, nonvolatile returns month after month and year after year.

Madoff has reported positive returns for the last 11-plus years in assets managed on behalf of the feeder fund known as Fairfield Sentry, which in providing capital for the program since 1989 has been doing it longer than any of the other feeder funds. Those other funds have demonstrated equally positive track records using the same strategy for much of that period.

Lack of Volatility

Those who question the consistency of the returns, though not necessarily the ability to generate the gross and net returns reported, include current and former traders, other money managers, consultants, quantitative analysts and fund-of-funds executives, many of whom are familiar with the so-called split-strike conversion strategy used to manage the assets.

These individuals, more than a dozen in all, offered their views, speculation and opinions on the condition that they wouldn't be identified. They noted that others who use or have used the strategy—described as buying a basket of stocks closely correlated to an index, while concurrently selling out-of-the-money call options on the index and buying out-of-the-money put options on the index—are known to have had nowhere near the same degree of success.

The strategy is generally described as putting on a "collar" in an attempt to limit gains compared to the benchmark index in an up market and, likewise, limit losses to something less than the benchmark in a down market, essentially creating a floor and a ceiling.

Madoff's strategy is designed around multiple stock baskets made up of 30–35 stocks, most correlated to the S&P 100 index. In marketing material issued by Fairfield Sentry, the sale of the calls is described as increasing "the standstill rate of return, while allowing upward movement of the stock portfolio to the strike price of the calls." The puts, according to the same material, are "funded in large part by the sale of the calls, [and] limit the portfolio's downside.

"A bullish or bearish bias can be achieved by adjusting the strike prices of the options, overweighting the puts, or underweighting the calls. However, the underlying value of the S&P 100 puts is always approximately equal to that of the portfolio of stocks," the marketing document concludes.

Throughout the entire period Madoff has managed the assets, the strategy, which claims to use OTC options almost entirely, has appeared to work with remarkable results.

Again, take the Fairfield Sentry fund as the example. It has reported losses of no more than 55 basis points in just four of the past 139 consecutive months, while generating highly consistent gross returns of slightly more than 1.5 percent a month and net annual returns roughly in the range of 15.0 percent.

Among all the funds on the database in that same period, the Madoff/Fairfield Sentry fund would place at number 16 if ranked by its absolute cumulative returns.

Among 423 funds reporting returns over the last five years, most with less money and shorter track records, Fairfield Sentry would be ranked at 240 on an absolute return basis and come in number 10 if measured by risk-adjusted return as defined by its Sharpe ratio.

What is striking to most observers is not so much the annual returns—which, though considered somewhat high for the strategy, could be attributed to the firm's market making and trade execution capabilities—but the ability to provide such smooth returns with so little volatility.

The best known entity using a similar strategy, a publicly traded mutual fund dating from 1978 called Gateway, has experienced far greater volatility and lower returns during the same period.

The capital overseen by Madoff through Fairfield Sentry has a cumulative compound net return of 397.5 percent. Compared with the

41 funds in the Zurich database that reported for the same historical period, from July 1989 to February 2001, it would rank as the best performing fund for the period on a risk-adjusted basis, with a Sharpe ratio of 3.4 and a standard deviation of 3.0 percent. (Ranked strictly by standard deviation, the Fairfield Sentry funds would come in at number three, behind two other market neutral funds.)

Questions Abound

Bernard Madoff, the principal and founder of the firm, who is widely known as Bernie, is quick to note that one reason so few might recognize Madoff Securities as a hedge fund manager is because the firm makes no claim to being one.

The acknowledged Madoff feeder funds—New York–based Fairfield Sentry and Tremont Advisors' Broad Market; Kingate, operated by FIM of London; and Swiss-based Thema—derive all the incentive fees generated by the program's returns (there are no management fees), provide all the administration and marketing for them, raise the capital and deal with investors, says Madoff.

Madoff Securities' role, he says, is to provide the investment strategy and execute the trades, for which it generates commission revenue.

[Madoff Securities also manages money in the program allocated by an unknown number of endowments, wealthy individuals and family offices. While Bernie Madoff refuses to reveal total assets under management, he does not dispute that the figure is in the range of $6 billion to $7 billion.]

Madoff compares the firm's role to a private managed account at a broker-dealer, with the broker-dealer providing investment ideas or strategies and executing the trades and making money off the account by charging commission on each trade.

Skeptics who express a mixture of amazement, fascination and curiosity about the program wonder, first, about the relatively complete lack of volatility in the reported monthly returns.

But among other things, they also marvel at the seemingly astonishing ability to time the market and move to cash in the underlying securities before market conditions turn negative; and the related ability to buy and sell the underlying stocks without noticeably affecting the market.

In addition, experts ask why no one has been able to duplicate similar returns using the strategy and why other firms on Wall Street haven't become aware of the fund and its strategy and traded against it, as has happened so often in other cases; why Madoff Securities is willing to earn commissions off the trades but not set up a separate asset management division to offer hedge funds directly to investors and keep all the incentive fees for itself; or conversely, why it doesn't borrow the money from creditors, who are generally willing to provide leverage to a fully hedged portfolio of up to seven to one against capital at an interest rate of Libor-plus, and manage the funds on a proprietary basis.

These same skeptics speculate that at least part of the returns must come from other activities related to Madoff's market making. They suggest, for example, that the bid-ask spreads earned through those activities may at times be used to "subsidize" the funds.

According to this view, the benefit to Madoff Securities is that the capital provided by the funds could be used by the firm as "pseudo equity," allowing it either to use a great deal of leverage without taking on debt, or simply to conduct far more market making by purchasing additional order flow than it would otherwise be able to do.

And even among the four or five professionals who both express an understanding of the strategy and have little trouble accepting the reported returns it has generated, a majority still expresses the belief that, if nothing else, Madoff must be using other stocks and options rather than only those in the S&P 100.

Bernie Madoff is willing to answer each of those inquiries, even if he refuses to provide details about the trading strategy he considers proprietary information.

And in a face-to-face interview and several telephone interviews, Madoff sounds and appears genuinely amused by the interest and attention aimed at an asset management strategy designed to generate conservative, low risk returns that he notes are nowhere near the top results of well-known fund managers on an absolute return basis.

Lack of Volatility Illusory

The apparent lack of volatility in the performance of the fund, Madoff says, is an illusion based on a review of the monthly and annual returns. On an intraday, intraweek and intramonth basis, he says, "the volatility is all over the place," with the fund down by as much as 1 percent.

But as a whole, the split-strike conversion strategy is designed to work best in bull markets and, Madoff points out, until recently "we've really been in a bull market since '82, so this has been a good period to do this kind of stuff."

Market volatility, moreover, is the strategy's friend, says Madoff, as one of the fundamental ideas is to exercise the calls when the market spikes, which with the right stock picks would add to the performance.

In the current bearish environment, when some market experts think the fund should have been showing negative returns, albeit at levels below the benchmark index, managing the strategy has become more difficult, says Madoff, although performance has remained positive or, as in February, flat.

The worst market to operate in using the strategy, he adds, would be a protracted bear market or "a flat, dull market." In a stock market environment similar to what was experienced in the 1970s, for instance, the strategy would be lucky to return "T-bill like returns."

Market timing and stock picking are both important for the strategy to work, and to those who express astonishment at the firm's ability in those areas, Madoff points to long experience, excellent technology that provides superb and low-cost execution capabilities, good proprietary stock and options pricing models, well-established infrastructure, market making ability and market intelligence derived from the massive amount of order flow it handles each day.

The strategy and trading, he says, are done mostly by signals from a proprietary "black box" system that allows for human intervention to take into account the "gut feel" of the firm's professionals. "I don't want to get on an airplane without a pilot in the seat," says Madoff. "I only trust the autopilot so much."

As for the specifics of how the firm manages risk and limits the market impact of moving so much capital in and out of positions, Madoff responds first by saying, "I'm not interested in educating the world on our strategy, and I won't get into the nuances of how we manage risk." He reiterates the undisputed strengths and advantages the firm's operations provide that make it possible.

Multiple Stock Baskets

Avoiding market impact by trading the underlying securities, he says, is one of the strategy's primary goals. This is done by creating a variety of stock baskets, sometimes as many as a dozen, with different weightings that allow positions to be taken or unwound slowly over a one- or two-week period.

Madoff says the baskets comprise the most highly capitalized liquid securities in the market, making the entry and exit strategies easier to manage.

He also stresses that the assets used for the strategy are often invested in Treasury securities as the firm waits for specific market opportunities. He won't reveal how much capital is required to be deployed at any given time to maintain the strategy's return characteristics, but does say that "the goal is to be 100 percent invested."

The inability of other firms to duplicate his firm's success with the strategy, says Madoff, is attributable, again, to its highly regarded operational infrastructure. He notes that one could make the same observation about many businesses, including market making firms.

Many major Wall Street broker-dealers, he observes, previously attempted to replicate established market making operations but gave up trying when they realized how difficult it was to do so successfully, opting instead to acquire them for hefty sums.

[Indeed, says Madoff, the firm itself has received numerous buyout offers but has so far refused any entreaties because he and the many members of his immediate and extended family who work there continue to enjoy what they do and the independence it allows and have no desire to work for someone else.]

Similarly, he adds, another firm could duplicate the strategy in an attempt to get similar results, but its returns would likely be unmatched because "you need the physical plant and a large operation" to do it with equal success. However, many Wall Street firms, he says, do use the strategy in their proprietary trading activities, but they don't devote more capital to such operations because their return on capital is better used in other operations.

Setting up a proprietary trading operation strictly for the strategy, or a separate asset management division in order to collect the incentive fees, says Madoff, would conflict with his firm's primary business of market making.

Commissions Suffice

"We're perfectly happy making the commissions" by trading for the funds, he says, which industry observers note also gives the firm the entirely legitimate opportunity to "piggyback" with proprietary trading that is given an advantage by knowing when and where orders are being placed.

Setting up a division to offer funds directly, says Madoff, is not an attractive proposition simply because he and the firm have no desire to get involved in the administration and marketing required for the effort, nor to deal with investors.

Many parts of the firm's operations could be similarly leveraged, he notes, but the firm generally believes in concentrating on its core strengths and not overextending itself. Overseeing the capital provided by the funds and its managed accounts, he says, provides another fairly stable stream of revenue that offers some degree of operational diversification.

Madoff readily dismisses speculation concerning the use of the capital as "pseudo equity" to support the firm's market making activities or provide leverage. He says the firm uses no leverage, and has more than enough capital to support its operations.

He notes that Madoff Securities has virtually no debt and at any given time no more than a few hundred million dollars of inventory.

Since the firm makes markets in only the most highly capitalized, liquid stocks generally represented by the S&P 500 index, a majority of which are listed on the NYSE, as well as the 200 most highly capitalized NASDAQ-listed stocks, says Madoff, it has almost no inventory risk.

Finally, Madoff calls ridiculous the conjecture that the firm at times provides subsidies generated by its market making activities to smooth out the returns of the funds in a symbiotic relationship related to its use of the capital as a debt or equity substitute. He agrees that the firm could easily borrow the money itself at a fairly low interest rate if it were needed, and would therefore have no reason to share its profits.

"Why would we do that?"

Still, when the many expert skeptics were asked by *MARHedge* to respond to the explanations about the funds, the strategy and the consistently low volatility returns, most continued to express bewilderment and indicated they were still grappling to understand how such results have been achieved for so long.

Madoff, who believes that he deserves "some credibility as a trader for 40 years," says: "The strategy is the strategy and the returns are the returns." He suggests that those who believe there is something more to it and are seeking an answer beyond that are wasting their time.

Appendix B

The World's Largest Hedge Fund Is a Fraud

December 22, 2005 Submission to the SEC
Madoff Investment Securities, LLC
www.madoff.com

Opening Remarks:

I am the original source for the information presented herein having first presented my rationale, both verbally and in writing, to the SEC's Boston office in May, 1999 before any public information doubting Madoff Investment Securities, LLC appeared in the press. There was no whistleblower or insider involved in compiling this report. I used the Mosaic Theory to assemble my set of observations. My observations were collected first-hand by listening to fund of fund investors talk about their investments in a hedge fund run by Madoff Investment Securities, LLC, a SEC registered firm. I have also spoken to the heads of various Wall Street equity derivative trading desks and every single one of the senior managers I spoke with told me that Bernie Madoff was a fraud. Of course, no one wants to take undue career risk by sticking their head up and saying the emperor isn't wearing any clothes but. . . .

I am a derivatives expert and have traded or assisted in the trading of several billion \$US in options strategies for hedge funds and institutional clients. I have experience managing split-strike conversion products both using index options and using individual stock options, both with and without index puts. Very few people in the world have the mathematical background needed to manage these types of products but I am one of them. I have outlined a detailed set of Red Flags that make me very suspicious that Bernie Madoff's returns aren't real and, if they are real, then they would almost certainly have to be generated by front-running customer order flow from the broker-dealer arm of Madoff Investment Securities. LLC.

Due to the sensitive nature of the case I detail below, its dissemination within the SEC must be limited to those with a need to know. The firm involved is located in the New York Region.

As a result of this case, several careers on Wall Street and in Europe will be ruined. Therefore, I have not signed nor put my name on this report. I request that my name not be released to anyone other than the Branch Chief and Team Leader in the New York Region who are assigned to the case, without my express written permission. The fewer people who know who wrote this report the better. I am worried about the personal safety of myself and my family. Under no circumstances is this report or its contents to be shared with any other regulatory body without my express permission. This report has been written solely for the SEC's internal use.

As far as I know, none of the hedge fund, fund of funds (FOF's) mentioned in my report are engaged in a conspiracy to commit fraud. I believe they are naïve men and women with a notable lack of derivatives expertise and possessing little or no quantitative finance ability.

There are 2 possible scenarios that involve fraud by Madoff Securities:

1. Scenario # 1 **(Unlikely):** I am submitting this case under Section 21A(e) of the 1934 Act in the event that the broker-dealer and ECN depicted is actually providing the stated returns to investors but is earning those returns by front-running customer order flow. Front-running qualifies as insider-trading since it relies upon material, non-public information that is acted upon for the benefit of one party to the detriment of another party. Section 21A(e) of the 1934 Act allows the SEC to pay up to 10% of the total fines levied for insider-trading. We have obtained approval from the SEC's Office of General Counsel, the Chairman's Office, and the bounty program administrator that the SEC is able and willing to pay Section 21A(e) rewards. This case should qualify if insider-trading is involved.

2. Scenario # 2 **(Highly likely)** Madoff Securities is the world's largest Ponzi Scheme. In this case there is no SEC reward

payment due the whistle-blower so basically I'm turning this case in because it's the right thing to do. Far better that the SEC is proactive in shutting down a Ponzi Scheme of this size rather than reactive.

Who: The politically powerful Madoff family owns and operates a New York City based broker-dealer, ECN, and what is effectively the world's largest hedge fund. Bernard "Bernie" Madoff, the family patriarch started the firm.

According to the www.madoff.com website, *"Bernard L. Madoff was one of the five broker-dealers most closely involved in developing the NASDAQ Stock Market. He has been chairman of the board of directors of the NASDAQ Stock Market as well as a member of the board of governors of the NASD and a member of numerous NASD committees. Bernard Madoff was also a founding member of the International Securities Clearing Corporation in London.*

His brother, Peter B. Madoff *has served as vice chairman of the NASD, a member of its board of governors, and chairman of its New York region. He also has been actively involved in the NASDAQ Stock Market as a member of its board of governors and its executive committee and as chairman of its trading committee. He also has been a member of the board of directors of the Security Traders Association of New York. He is a member of the board of directors of the Depository Trust Corporation.*

What:

1. The family runs what is effectively the world's largest hedge fund with estimated assets under management of at least $20 billion to perhaps $50 billion, but no one knows exactly how much money BM is managing. That we have what is effectively the world's largest hedge fund operating underground is plainly put shocking. But then again, we don't even know the size of the hedge fund industry so none of this should be surprising. A super-sized fraud

of this magnitude was bound to happen given the lack of regulation of these off-shore entities. My best guess is that approximately $30 billion is involved.

2. However the hedge fund isn't organized as a hedge fund by Bernard Madoff (BM) yet it acts and trades exactly like one. BM allows third party Fund of Funds (FOF's) to private label hedge funds that provide his firm, Madoff Securities, with equity tranch funding. In return for equity tranch funding, BM runs a trading strategy, **as agent**, whose returns flow to the third party FOF hedge funds and their investors who put up equity capital to fund BM's broker-dealer and ECN operations. *BM tells investors it earns its fees by charging commissions on all of the trades done in their accounts.*

Red Flag # 1: *Why would a US broker-dealer organize and fund itself in such an unusual manner? Doesn't this seem to be an unseemly way of operating under the regulator's radar screens? Why aren't the commissions charged fully disclosed to investors? Can a SEC Registered Investment Advisor charge* **both** *commissions and charge a principle fee for trades?* **MOST IMPORTANTLY,** *why would BM settle for charging only undisclosed commissions when he could earn standard hedge fund fees of 1% management fee + 20% of the profits? Doing some simple math on BM's 12% average annual return stream to investors, the hedge fund, before fees, would have to be earning average annual returns of 16%. Subtract out the 1% management fee and investors are down to 15%. 20% of the profits would amount to 3% (.20 x 15% = 3% profit participation) so investors would be left with the stated 12% annual returns listed in Attachment 1 (Fairfield Sentry Ltd. Performance Data). Total fees to the third party FOF's would amount to 4% annually. Now why would BM leave 4% in average annual fee revenue on the table unless he were a Ponzi Scheme? Or, is he charging a whole lot more than 4% in undisclosed commissions?*

3. The third parties organize the hedge funds and obtain investors but 100% of the money raised is actually managed by Madoff Investment Securities, LLC in a purported hedge fund strategy. The investors that pony up the money don't know that BM is managing their money. That Madoff is managing the money is purposely kept secret from the investors. Some prominent US based hedge fund, fund of funds, that "invest" in BM in this manner include:

A. Fairfield Sentry Limited (████████████████████) which had $5.2 billion invested in BM as of May 2005; 11th Floor, 919 Third Avenue; New York, NY 10022; Telephone 212.319.6060; The Fairfield Greenwich Group is a global family of companies with offices in New York, London and Bermuda, and representative offices in the U.S., Europe and Latin America. Local operating entities are authorized or regulated by a variety of government agencies, including Fairfield Greenwich Advisors LLC, a U.S. SEC registered investment adviser, Fairfield Heathcliff Capital LLC, a U.S. NASD member broker-dealer, and Fairfield Greenwich (UK) Limited, authorized and regulated by the Financial Services Authority in the United Kingdom.

B. Access International Advisors; www.aiagroup.com; a SEC registered investment advisor, telephone # 212.223.7167; Suite 2206; 509 Madison Avenue, New York, NY 10022 which had over $450 million invested with BM as of mid-2002. The majority of this FOF's investors are European, even though the firm is US registered.

C. Broyhill All-Weather Fund, L.P. had $██ million invested with BM as of March 2000.

D. Tremont Capital Management, Inc. Corporate Headquarters is located at 555 Theodore Fremd Avenue; Rye, New York 10580; T: (914) 925–1140 F: (914) 921–3499. Tremont oversees on an advisory and fully discretionary basis over $10.5 billion in assets. Clients include institutional investors, public and private pension plans, ERISA plans, university endowments, foundations, and financial institutions, as well as high net worth individuals. Tremont is owned by Oppenhiemer Funds Inc. which is owned by Mass Mutual Insurance Company so they should have sufficient reserves to make investors whole. Mass Mutual is currently under investigation by the Massachusetts Attorney General, the Department of Justice, and the SEC.

E. Kingate Fund run by FIM Advisers LLP is headquartered in London at 20 St. James Street; London SW1A 1ES; telephone # +44 20 7389 8900; fax # +44 20 7389 8911; www.fim-group.com/. However, their US subsidiary, FIM (USA) Inc. is located at 780 Third Avenue; New York, NY 10017; telephone # 212.223.7321 or fax # 212.223.7592.

F. During a 2002 marketing trip to Europe ▮▮▮▮▮▮ ▮▮▮ FOF I met with in Paris and Geneva had investments with BM. They all said he was their best manager! A partial list of money managers and Private Banks that invest in BM is included at the end of this report in Attachment 3.

4. Here's what smells bad about the idea of providing equity tranch funding to a US registered broker-dealer:

A. The investment returns passed along to the third party hedge funds are equivalent to BM borrowing money. These 12 month returns from 1990 – May 2005 ranged from a low of 6.23% to a high of 19.98%, with an average 12 month return during that time period of 12.00%. Add in the 4% in average annual management & participation fees and BM would have to be delivering average annual returns of 16% in order for the investors to receive 12%. No Broker-Dealer that I've ever heard of finances its operations at that high of an implied borrowing rate (source: Attachment 1; Fairfield Sentry Limited

return data from December 1990 – May 2005). Ask
around and I'm sure you'll find that BM is the only firm
on Wall Street that pays an average of 16% to fund its
operations.

B. BD's typically fund in the short-term credit markets and
benchmark a significant part of their overnight funding to LIBOR plus or minus some spread. LIBOR + 40
basis points would seem a more realistic borrowing rate
for a broker-dealer of BM's size.

C. **Red Flag # 2:** *why would a BD choose to fund at such a
high implied interest rate when cheaper money is available
in the short-term credit markets? One reason that comes
to mind is that BM couldn't stand the due diligence
scrutiny of the short-term credit markets. If Charles
Ponzi had issued bank notes promising 50% interest
on 3 month time deposits instead of issuing unregulated Ponzi Notes to his investors, the State Banking
Commission would have quickly shut him down. The
key to a successful Ponzi Scheme is to promise lucrative
returns but to do so in an unregulated area of the capital
markets. Hedge funds are not due to fall under the SEC's
umbrella until February 2006.*

5. The third party hedge funds and fund of funds that market
this hedge fund strategy that invests in BM don't name and
aren't allowed to name Bernie Madoff as the actual manager in
their performance summaries or marketing literature. Look
closely at Attachment 1, Fairfield Sentry Ltd.'s performance
summary and you won't see BM's name anywhere on the
document, yet BM is the actual hedge fund manager with
discretionary trading authority over all funds, as agent.

Red Flag # 3: *Why the need for such secrecy?* *If I was the
world's largest hedge fund and had great returns, I'd want all
the publicity I could garner and would want to appear as the
world's largest hedge fund in all of the industry rankings. Name*

one mutual fund company, Venture Capital firm, or LBO firm which doesn't brag about the size of their largest funds' assets under management. Then ask yourself, why would the world's largest hedge fund manager be so secretive that he didn't even want his investors to know he was managing their money? Or is it that BM doesn't want the SEC and FSA to know that he exists?

6. The third party FOF's never tell investors who is actually managing their money and describe the investment strategy as: This hedge fund's objective is long term growth on a consistent basis with low volatility. The investment advisor invests exclusively in the U.S. and utilizes a strategy often referred to as a "split-strike conversion." Generally this style involves purchasing a basket of 30–35 large-capitalization stocks with a high degree of correlation to the general market (e.g. American Express, Boeing, Citigroup, Coca-Cola, Dupont, Exxon, General Motors, IBM, Merck, McDonalds). To provide the desired hedge, the manager then sells out-of-the-money OEX index call options and buys out-of-the-money OEX index put options. The amount of calls that are sold and puts that are bought represent a dollar amount equal to the basket of shares purchases.

7. I personally have run split-strike conversion strategies and know that BM's approach is far riskier than stated in 6 above. His strategy is wholly inferior to an all index approach and is wholly incapable of generating returns in the range of 6.23% to 19.98%. BM's strategy should not be able to beat the return on US Treasury Bills. Due to the glaring weakness of the strategy:

   A. Income Part of the strategy is to buy 30–35 large-cap stocks, sell out-of-the-money index call options against the value of the stock basket. There are three possible sources of income in this strategy.

      1) We earn income from the stock's dividends. Let's attribute a 2% average return to this source of funds for the 14½ year time period. This explains 2% of

the 16% average gross annual returns before fees and leaves 14% of the returns unexplained.

2) We earn income from the sale of OTC OEX index call options. Let's also assume that we can generate an additional 2% annual return via the sale of OTC out-of-the-money OEX index call options which leaves 12% of the 16% gross returns unexplained. On Friday, October 14, 2005 the OEX (S&P 100) index closed at 550.49 and there were only 163,809 OEX index call option contracts outstanding (termed the "open interest"). 163,809 call option calls outstanding x $100 contact multiplier x 550.49 index closing price = $9,017,521,641 in stock equivalents hedged.

3) We can earn income from capital gains by selling the stocks that go up in price. This portion of the return stream would have to earn the lion's share of the hedge fund strategy's returns. We have 12% of the return stream unexplained so far. However, the OTC OEX index puts that we buy will cost AT LEAST <8%> per year (a lot more in most years but I'm giving BM the benefit of every doubt here). Therefore, BM's stock selection would have to be earning an average of 20% per year. That would mean that he's been the world's best stock-picker since 1990 beating out such luminaries as Warren Buffet and Bill Miller. Yet no one's ever heard of BM as being a stock-picker, much less the world's best stock-picker. Why isn't he famous if he was able to earn 20% average annual returns?

Red Flag # 4: *$9.017 billion in total OEX listed call options outstanding is not nearly enough to generate income on BM's total amount of assets under management which I estimate to range between $20–$50 billion. Fairfield Sentry Ltd. alone has $5.1 billion with BM. And, while BM may say he only uses*

Over-the-Counter (OTC) index options, there is no way that this is possible. The OTC market should never be several times larger than the exchange listed market for this type of plain vanilla derivative.

B. Protection Part of the strategy is to buy out-of-the-money OEX index put options. This costs you money each and every month. This hurts your returns and is the main reason why BM's strategy would have trouble earning 0% average annual returns much less the 12% net returns stated in Fairfield Sentry Ltd.'s performance summary. Even if BM earns a 4% return from the combination of 2% stock dividends and 2% from the sale of call options, the cost of the puts would put this strategy in the red year in and year out. No way he can possibly be delivering 12% net to investors. The math just doesn't support this strategy if he's really buying index put options.

Red Flag # 5: *BM would need to be purchasing at-the-money put options because he has only 7 small monthly losses in the past 14½ years. His largest monthly loss is only <0.55%>, so his puts would have to be at-the-money. At-the-money put options are very, very expensive. A one-year at-the-money put option would cost you <8%> or more, depending upon the market's volatility. And <8%> would be a cheap price to pay in many of the past 14½ years for put protection!! Assuming BM only paid <8%> per year in put protection, and assuming he can earn +2% from stock dividends plus another +2% from call option sales, he's still under-water <4%> performance wise. <8%> put cost + 2% stock dividends + 2% income from call sales = <4%>. And, I've proven that BM would need to be earning at least 16% annually to deliver 12% after fees to investors. That means the rest of his returns would have to be coming from stock selection where he picked and sold winning stocks to include in his 35-stock* *basket of large-cap names. Lots of luck doing that during the past stock market crises like 1997's Asian Currency Crises, the 1998 Russian Debt / LTCM crises, and the 2000-2002 killer bear market. And index put option protection was a lot more expensive during these crises periods than 8%. Mathematically none of BM's returns listed in Attachment 1 make much sense. They are just too unbelievably good to be true.*

C. The OEX index (S&P 100) closed at 550.49 on Friday, October 14, 2005 meaning that each put option hedged $55,049 dollars worth of stock ($100 contract multiplier x 550.49 OEX closing index price = $55,049 in stock hedged). As of that same date, the total open interest for OEX index put options was 307,176 contracts meaning that a total of $16,909,731,624 in stock was being hedged by the use of OEX index puts (307,176 total put contracts in existence as of Oct 14th x $55,049 hedge value of 1 OEX index put = $16,909,731,624 in stock hedged). Note: I excluded a few thousand OEX LEAP index put options from my calculations because these are long-term options and not relevant for a split-strike conversion strategy such as BM's.

Red Flag # 6: *At my best guess level of BM's assets under management of $30 billion, or even at my low end estimate of $20 billion in assets under management, BM would have to be over 100% of the total OEX put option contract open interest in order to hedge his stock holdings as depicted in the third party hedge funds marketing literature. In other words, there are not enough index option put contracts in existence to hedge the way BM says he is hedging! And there is no way the OTC market is bigger than the exchange listed market for plain vanilla S&P 100 index put options.*

D. Mathematically I have proven that BM cannot be hedging using listed index put and call options. One hedge fund

FOF has told me that BM uses only Over-the-Counter options and trades exclusively thru UBS and Merrill Lynch. I have not called those two firms to check on this because it seems implausible that a BD would trade $20 - $50 billion worth of index put options per month over-the-counter thru only 2 firms. That plus the fact that if BM was really buying OTC index put options, then there is no way his average annual returns could be positive!! At a minimum, using the cheapest way to buy puts would cost a fund <8%> per year. To get the put cost down to <8%>, BM would have to buy a one-year at-the-money put option and hold it for one-year. No way his call sales could ever hope to come even fractionally close to covering the cost of the puts.

Red Flag # 7: *The counter-party credit exposures for UBS and Merrill would be too large for these firms credit departments to approve. The SEC should ask BM for trade tickets showing he has traded OTC options thru these two firms. Then the SEC should visit the firms' OTC derivatives desks, talk the to heads of trading and ask to see BM's trade tickets. Then ask the director of operations to verify the tickets and ask to see the inventory of all of the stock and listed options hedging the OTC puts and calls. If these firms can't show you the off-setting hedged positions then they are assisting BM as part of a conspiracy to commit fraud. If any other brokerage firms equity derivatives desk is engaged in a conspiracy to cover for BM, then this scandal will be a doozy when it hits the financial press but at least investors would have firms with deep pockets to sue.*

Red Flag # 8: *OTC options are more expensive to trade than listed options. You have to pay extra for the customization features and secrecy offered by OTC options. Trading in the size of $20–$50 billion per month would be impossible and the bid-ask spreads would be so wide as to preclude earning any profit whatsoever. These Broker/Dealers would need to offset their* *short OTC index put option exposure to a falling stock market by hedging out their short put option risk by either buying listed put options or selling short index futures and the derivatives markets are not deep and liquid enough to accomplish this without paying a penalty in prohibitively expensive transaction costs.*

Red Flag # 9: *Extensive and voluminous paperwork would be required to keep track of and clear each OTC trade. Plus, why aren't Goldman, Sachs and Citigroup involved in handling BM's order flow? Both Goldman and Citigroup are a lot larger in the OTC derivatives markets than UBS or Merrill Lynch.*

    E. My experience with split-strike conversion trades is that the best a good manager is likely to obtain using the strategy marketed by the third-party FOF's is T-bills less management fees. And, if the stock market is down by more than 2%, the return from this strategy will range from a high of zero return to a low of a few percent depending upon your put's cost and how far out-of-the-money it is.

    F. In 2000 I ran a regression of BM's hedge fund returns using the performance data from Fairfield Sentry Limited. BM had a .06 correlation to the equity market's return which confirms the .06 Beta that Fairfield Sentry Limited lists in its return numbers.

Red Flag # 10: *It is mathematically impossible for a strategy using index call options and index put options to have such a low correlation to the market where its returns are supposedly being generated from. This makes no sense! The strategy depicted retains 100% of the single-stock downside risk since they own only index put options and not single stock put options. Therefore if one or more stocks in their portfolio were to tank on bad news, BM's index put would offer little protection and their portfolio should feel the pain. However, BM's performance numbers show only 7 extremely small losses during 14½ years and these numbers*

*are too good to be true. The largest one month loss was only –
55 basis points (–0.55%) or just over one-half of one percent!
And BM never had more than a one month losing streak! Either
BM is the world's best stock and options manager that the SEC
and the investing public has **never** heard of or he's a fraud. You
would have to figure that at some point BM owned a WorldCom,
Enron, GM or HealthSouth in their portfolio when bad or really
bad news came out and caused these stocks to drop like a rock.*

8. **Red Flag # 11:** *Two press articles, which came to print well
   after my initial May 1999 presentation to the SEC, do doubt
   Bernie Madoff's returns and they are:*

   A. The May 7, 2001 edition of Barron's, in an article
      entitled, ***"Don't Ask, Don't Tell; Bernie Madoff is so
      secretetive, he even asks his investors to keep mum,"***
      written by Erin Arvedlund, published an expose about
      Bernie Madoff a few years ago with no resulting inves-
      tigation by any regulators. Ms. Arvedlund has since left
      Barron's. I have attached a copy of the Barrons' article
      which lists numerous red flags.

   B. Michael Ocrant, formerly a reporter for *MARHedge* visited
      Bernie Madoff's offices and wrote a very negative arti-
      cle entitled, "Madoff tops charts; skeptics ask how," that
      doubted the source of BM's returns. This article was pub-
      lished on May 1, 2001 and is attached [see Appendix A of
      this book]. Mr. Ocrant has graciously agreed to cooperate
      fully with the SEC and awaits the SEC's telephone call to
      arrange a meeting. The SEC should contact him directly.
      Michael Ocrant is currently serving as the Director of
      Alternative Investments; Institutional Investor; New York,
      NY 10001; Telephone # 212█████████ or 212█████████;
      Email: ███████████████████

9. Fund of funds with whom I have spoken to that have BM
   in their stable of funds continually brag about their returns
   and how they are generated thanks to BM's access to his

broker-dealer's access to order flow. They believe that BM has perfect knowledge of the market's direction due to his access to customer order flow into his broker-dealer.

Red Flag # 12: *Yes, BM has access to his customer's order flow thru his broker-dealer but he is only one broker out of many, so it is impossible for him to know the market's direction to such a degree as to only post monthly losses once every couple of years. All of Wall Street's big wire houses experience trading losses on a more regular frequency that BM. Ask yourself how BM's trading experience could be so much better than all of the other firms on Wall Street. Either he's the best trading firm on the street and rarely ever has large losing months unlike other firms or he's a fraud.*

10. **Red Flag # 13:** *I believe that BM's returns can be real ONLY if they are generated from front-running his customer's order flow. In other words, yes, if he's buying at a penny above his customer's buy orders, he can only lose one penny if the stock drops but can make several pennies if the stock goes up. For example, if a customer has an order to buy 100,000 shares of IBM at $100, BM can put in his own order to buy 100,000 shares of IBM at $100.01. This is what's known as a right-tail distribution and is very similar to the payoff distribution of a call option. Doing this could easily generate returns of 30%–60% or more per anum. He could be doing the same thing by front-running customer sell orders. However, if BM's returns are real but he's generating them from front-running there are two problems with this:*

    A. *Problem # 1: front-running is one form of insider-trading and is illegal.*

    B. *Problem # 2: generating real returns from front-running but telling hedge fund investors that you are generating the returns via a complex (but unworkable) stock and options strategy is securities fraud.*

Some time ago, during different market conditions, I ran a study using the Black-Scholes Option Pricing Model to analyze the value of front-running with the goal of putting a monetary value on front-running where the insider knew the customer's order and traded ahead of it. When I ran the study the model inputs were valued at: OEX component stocks annualized volatility on a cap-weighted basis was 50% (during a bear market period), the T-bill rate was 5.80%, and the average stock price was $46. I then calculated the value of an at-the-money call options over time intervals of 1 minute, 5 minutes, 10 minutes, and 15 minutes. I used a 253 trading day year. The SEC should be able to duplicate these results:

1 minute option = 3 cents worth of trade information value
5 minute option = 7 cents worth of trade information value
10 minute option = 10 cents worth of trade information value
15 minute option = 12 cents worth of trade information value

Conclusion: Bernie Madoff used to advertise in industry trade publications that he would pay 1 cent per share for other broker's order flow. If he was paying 1 cent per share for order flow and front-running these broker's customers, then he could easily be earning returns in the 30%–60% or higher annually. In all time intervals ranging from 1 minute to 15 minutes, having access to order flow is the monetary equivalent of owning a valuable call option on that order. The value of these implicit call options ranges between 3 – 12 times the one penny per share paid for access to order flow. If this is what he's doing, then the returns are real but the stated investment strategy is illegal and based solely on insider-trading.

NOTE: I am pretty confident that BM is a Ponzi Scheme, but in the off chance he is front-running customer orders and his returns are real, then this case qualifies as insider-trading under the SEC's bounty program as outlined in Section 21A(e) of the 1934 Act. However, if BM was front-running, a highly profitable activity, then he wouldn't need to borrow funds from investors at 16% implied interest. Therefore it is far more likely that BM is a Ponzi Scheme. Front-running is a very simple fraud to commit and requires only access to inside information. The elaborateness of BM's fund-raising, his need for secrecy, his high 16% average cost of funds, and reliance on a derivatives investment scheme that few investors (or regulators) would be capable of comprehending lead to a weight of the evidence conclusion that this is a Ponzi Scheme.

11. **Red Flag # 14:** *Madoff subsidizes down months! Hard to believe (and I don't believe this) but I've heard two FOF's tell me that they don't believe Madoff can make money in big down months either. They tell me that Madoff "subsidizes" their investors in down months, so that they will be able to show a low volatility of returns. These types of stories are commonly found around Ponzi Schemes. These investors tell me that Madoff only books winning tickets in their accounts and "eats the losses" during months when the market sells off hard. The problem with this is that it's securities fraud to misstate either returns or the volatility of those returns. These FOF professionals who heard BM tell them that he subsidizes losses were professionally negligent in not turning BM into the SEC, FSA and other regulators for securities fraud.*

Red Flag # 15: *Why would a fund of funds investor believe any broker-dealer that commits fraud in a few important areas – such as misstating returns and misstating volatility of returns – yet believe him in other areas? I'd really like to believe in the tooth fairy, but I don't after catching my mother putting a quarter underneath my pillow one night.*

12. **Red Flag # 16:** *Madoff has perfect market-timing ability. One investor told me, with a straight face, that Madoff went to 100% cash in July 1998 and December 1999, ahead of market declines. He said he knows this because Madoff faxes*

his trade tickets to his firm and the custodial bank. However, since Madoff owns a broker-dealer, he can generate whatever trade tickets he wants. And, I'll bet very few FOF's ask BM to fax them trade tickets. And if these trade tickets are faxed, have the FOF's then matched them to the time and sales of the exchanges? For example, if BM says he bought 1 million shares of GM, sold $1 million worth of OTC OEX calls and bought $1 million worth of OTC OEX puts, we should see prints somewhere. The GM share prints would show on either the NYSE or some other exchange while the broker-dealers he traded OTC options thru would show prints of the hedges they traded to be able to provide BM with the OTC options at the prices listed on BM's trade tickets.

13. **Red Flag # 17:** *Madoff does not allow outside performance audits. One London based hedge fund, fund of funds, representing Arab money, asked to send in a team of Big 4 accountants to conduct a performance audit during their planned due diligence. They were told "No, only Madoff's brother-in-law who owns his own accounting firm is allowed to audit performance for reasons of secrecy in order to keep Madoff's proprietary trading strategy secret so that nobody can copy it." Amazingly, this fund of funds then agreed to invest $200 million of their client's money anyway, because the low volatility of returns was so attractive!! Let's see, how many hedge funds have faked an audited performance history?? Wood River is the latest that comes to mind as does the Manhattan Fund but the number of bogus hedge funds that have relied upon fake audits has got to number in the dozens.*

14. **Red Flag # 18:** *Madoff's returns are not consistent with the one publicly traded option income fund with a history as long as Madoff's. In 2000, I analyzed the returns of Madoff and measured them against the returns of the Gateway Option Income Fund (Ticker GATEX). During the 87 month span analyzed, Madoff was down only 3 months versus GATEX*

being down 26 months. GATEX earned an annualized return of 10.27% during the period studied vs. 15.62% for Bernie Madoff and 19.58% for the S&P 500. GATEX has a more flexible investment strategy than BM, so GATEX's returns should be superior to BM's but instead they are inferior. This makes no sense. How could BM be better using an inferior strategy?

15. **Red Flag # 19:** *There have been several option income funds that went IPO since August 2004. None of them have the high returns that Bernie Madoff has. How can this be? They use similar strategies only they should be making more than BM in up months because most of these option income funds don't buy expensive index put options to protect their portfolios. Thus the publicly traded option income funds should make more money in up markets and lose more than Madoff in down markets. Hmm . . . that Madoff's returns are so high yet he buys expensive put options is just another reason to believe he is running the world's largest Ponzi Scheme. A good study for the SEC would be to compare 2005 performance of the new option income funds to Bernie Madoff while accounting for the cost of Bernie's index put option protection. There's no way Bernie can have positive returns in 2005 given what the market's done and where volatility is.*

16. **Red Flag # 20:** *Madoff is suspected of being a fraud by some of the world's largest and most sophisticated financial services firms. Without naming names, here's an abbreviated tally:*

    A. A managing director at Goldman, Sachs prime brokerage operation told me that his firm doubts Bernie Madoff is legitimate so they don't deal with him.

    B. From an Email I received this past June 2005 I now suspect that the end is near for BM. All Ponzi Schemes eventually topple of their own weight once they become too large and it now appears that BM is having trouble meeting redemptions and is attempting to borrow sizeable funds in Europe.

ABCDEFGH and I had dinner with a savvy European investor that studies the HFOF market. He stated that both RBC and Socgen have removed Madoff some time ago from approved lists of individual managers used by investors to build their own tailored HFOFs.

More importantly, Madoff was turned down, according to this source, for a borrowing line from a Euro bank, I believe he said Paribas. Now why would Madoff need to borrow more funds? This Euro Investor said that Madoff was in fact running "way over" our suggested $12-14 billion (Fairfield Sentry is running $5.3 BB by themselves!). Madoff's 12 month returns is about 7% net of the feeder fund's fees. Looks like he is stepping down the pay out.

    C. An official from a Top 5 money center bank's FOF told me that his firm wouldn't touch Bernie Madoff with a ten foot pole and that there's no way he's for real.

17. **Red Flag # 21:** *ECN's didn't exist prior to 1998. Madoff makes verbal claims to his third party hedge FOF's that he has private access to ECN's internal order flow, which Madoff pays for, and that this is a substantial part of the return generating process. If this is true, then where did the returns come from in the years 1991–1997, prior to the ascendance of the ECN's? Presumably, prior to 1998, Madoff only had access to order flow on the NASDAQ for which he paid 1 cent per share for. He would have no such advantage pre-1998 on the large-cap, NYSE listed stocks the marketing literature says he buys (Exxon, McDonalds, American Express, IBM, Merck, etc. . .).*

18. **Red Flag # 22:** *The Fairfield Sentry Limited Performance Chart (Attachment 1) depicted for Bernie Madoff's investment strategy is misleading. The S&P 500 return line is accurate because it is moving up and down, reflecting positive and negative returns. Fairfield Sentry's performance chart is misleading, it is almost a straight line rising at a 45 degree angle. This chart cannot be cumulative in the*

common usage of the term for reporting purposes, which means "geometric returns." The chart must be some sort of arithmetic average sum, since a true cumulative return line, given the listed monthly returns would be exponentially rising (i.e. curving upward at an increasing rate). My rule of thumb is that if the manager misstates his performance, you can't trust him. Yet somehow Madoff is now running the world's largest, most clandestine hedge fund so clearly investors aren't doing their due diligence. And why does he provide the S&P 500 as his benchmark when he is actually managing using a S&P 100 strategy? Shouldn't the performance line presented be the S&P 100's (OEX) performance?

19. **Red Flag # 23:** *Why is Bernie Madoff borrowing money at an average rate of 16.00% per annum and allowing these third party hedge fund, fund of funds to pocket their 1% and 20% fees based upon Bernie Madoff's hard work and brains? Does this make any sense at all? Typically FOF's charge only 1% and 10%, yet BM allows them the extra 10%. Why? And why do these third parties fail to mention Bernie Madoff in their marketing literature? After all he's the manager, don't investors have a right to know who's managing their money?*

20. **Red Flag # 24:** *Only Madoff family members are privy to the investment strategy. Name one other prominent multi-billion dollar hedge fund that doesn't have outside, non-family professionals involved in the investment process. You can't because there aren't any. Michael Ocrant, the former* MARHedge *Reporter listed above saw some highly suspicious red flags during his visit to Madoff's offices and should be interviewed by the SEC as soon as possible.*

21. **Red Flag # 25:** *The Madoff family has held important leadership positions with the NASD, NASDAQ, SIA, DTC, and other prominent industry bodies therefore these organizations would not be inclined to doubt or investigate Madoff*

*Investment Securities, LLC. The NASD and NASDAQ do not
exactly have a glorious reputation as vigorous regulators
untainted by politics or money.*

22. **Red Flag # 26:** *BM goes to 100% cash for every December
31ˢᵗ year-end according to one FOF invested with BM. This
allows for "cleaner financial statements" according to this
source. Any unusual transfers or activity near a quarter-end
or year-end is a red flag for fraud. Recently, the BD REFCO
Securities engaged in "fake borrowing" with Liberty, a
hedge fund, that made it appear that Liberty owed REFCO
over $400 million in receivables. This allowed REFCO
to mask its true debt position and made all of their equity
ratios look better than they actually were. And of course,
Grant Thorton, REFCO's external auditor missed this $400
million entry. As did the two lead underwriters who were
also tasked with due-diligence on the IPO – CSFB and
Goldman Sachs. BM uses his brother-in-law as his external
auditor, so in this case there isn't even the façade of having
an independent and vigilant auditor verifying the accounting entries.*

23. **Red Flag # 27:** *Several equity derivatives professionals will
all tell you that the split-strike conversion strategy that BM
runs is an outright fraud and cannot possibly achieve 12%
average annual returns with only 7 down months during
a 14½ year time period. Some derivatives experts that the
SEC should call to hear their opinions of how and why BM
is a fraud and for some insights into the mathematical reasons
behind their belief, the SEC should call:*
     ▪ Leon Gross, Managing Director of Citigroup's world-
     wide equity derivatives research unit; 3ʳᵈ Floor,
     390 Greenwich Street; New York, NY 10013: Tel#
     ▇▇▇▇▇▇▇▇▇▇ or ▇▇▇▇▇▇
     ▇▇▇▇ [Leon can't believe that the SEC hasn't shut
     down Bernie Madoff yet. He's also amazed that FOF's
     actually believe this stupid options strategy is capable of

earning a positive return much less a 12% net average annual return. He thinks the strategy would have trouble earning 1% net much less 12% net. ███████

███████████████████████████████████

███████████████████████████████████

███████████████████████████████████

███████████████████████████████████

███████████████████████████████████

███████████████████

b. Walter "Bud"Haslett, CFA; ██████████████████, LLC; Suite 455; ████████████████████ NJ 08065; Tel#: ██████████ or ████████████ ████████████ [Bud's firm runs $ hundreds of millions in options related strategies and he knows all of the math.]

c. Joanne Hill, Ph.D.; Vice-President and global head of equity derivatives research, Goldman Sachs (NY), ██ ████; One New York Plaza, New York, NY 10004; ███

███████████████████████████████████

███████████████████████████████████

███████████████████████████████████

███████████████████████████████████

████████████

24. **Red Flag # 28:** *BM's Sharpe Ratio of 2.55 (Attachment 1: Fairfield Sentry Ltd. Performance Data) is UNBELIEVABLY HIGH compared to the Sharpe Ratios experienced by the rest of the hedge fund industry. The SEC should obtain industry hedge fund rankings and see exactly how outstanding Fairfield Sentry Ltd.'s Sharpe Ratio is. Look at the hedge fund rankings for Fairfield Sentry Ltd. and see how their performance numbers compare to the rest of the industry. Then ask yourself how this is possible and why hasn't the world come to acknowledge BM as the world's best hedge fund manager?*

25. **Red Flag # 29:** *BM tells the third party FOF's that he has so much money under management that he's going to close his strategy to new investments. However, I have met several FOF's who brag about their "special access" to BM's capacity. This would be humorous except that too many European FOF's have told me this same seductive story about their being so close to BM that he'll waive the fact that he's closed his funds to other investors but let them in because they're special. It seems like every single one of these third party FOF's has a "special relationship" with BM.*

26. **Red Flag # 30:** BM's largest one month loss of –0.55% using index puts does not fit in with the prohibitively high cost of the extremely short-dated OTC OEX put options he would have to be buying to protect his portfolio from losses such that those monthly losses never exceeded –0.55% in any one month.

    A. Previously with Red Flag # 4, I mentioned that the cheapest possible put cost for BM would be 8%. That very conservative assumption assumes that he could get away with buying one OTC, at-the-money put per year. However, mathematically that one year at-the-money put would have a delta of .50, meaning that for each 1 point drop in the OEX index, the put's price would only increase .5 of half that amount or 50 cents. Therefore if the market dropped 1.1%, a .50 delta put would increase in price by 0.55%, resulting in a –0.55% loss for the fund.

    B. However, for all market drops greater than 1.1%, BM would experience a larger than –0.55% monthly loss and there were numerous instances of monthly market losses greater than –1.1% during the time period.

    C. Therefore, BM, in order to limit his losses would be forced to buy a series of shorter dated, higher delta put options with high gamma (a 2nd derivative term denoting that for each $1 change in index price, how much the

1st derivative term delta would change. Gamma is the change in price of Delta and Delta is the change in price of the Option with respect to the Index's Price). If you aren't intimately familiar with calculus, the English translation is that BM would need to be buying a continuing series of 1 day put options because these options and only these options would have the high gamma he would need to ensure that his delta changed rapidly enough to protect his portfolio enough so that he could never experience a greater than 0–0.55% monthly loss. If you've gotten this far, then if a one-year at-the-money OTC OEX index put option cost 8%, a continuing series of 253 (because that's how many trading days are in a year) one-day, at-the-money puts, would cost the square root of 253 or 15.9 times the cost of the one-year put. 15.9 times 8% the one year put's cost = 127.2% is the cost of a continuing series of one-day, at-the-money index put options if a one-year, at-the-money index put's cost is 8%. And this is a very conservative set of calculations! Consider that one would be carrying over stock positions in this strategy over weekends, so therefore you'd want 365 one-day, at-the-money put options and the square root of 365 is 19.1, so a truer cost of put protection would be 19.1 x 8% = 152.8%. That would mean BM's stock picking ability is not only the world's best but that he'd likely have to be an alien from outer-space to be able to pick stocks that went up over 152.8% per year + the 16% gross returns to the HFOF investors + an assumed 4% he's making in commissions. Therefore his stock picking ability would need to return 170% or so per year in order for him to be carrying out his strategy as he says he is in the HFOF third party marketing materials.

D. 170% per year from stock-picking is not likely for any human born on the planet earth so if BM's achieving these types of returns then he may be an alien species from another planet. A DNA test would be sufficient to determine whether this might be the case. However, if BM is an alien being possessing superior stock-picking skills of this magnitude, this would be seen as an unfair advantage in the marketplace and likely would panic the financial markets. Or maybe he's human and just a fraudster – take your pick.

E. Anyone capable of earning 170% per year from stock-picking would not need nor want any investors.

Conclusions:

1. I have presented 174 months (14½ years) of Fairfield Sentry's return numbers dating back to December 1990. Only 7 months or 4% of the months saw negative returns. Classify this as "definitely too good to be true!" No major league baseball hitter bats .960, no NFL team has ever gone 96 wins and only 4 losses over a 100 game span, and you can bet everything you own that no money manager is up 96% of the months either. It is inconceivable that BM's largest monthly loss could only be –0.55% and that his longest losing streaks could consist of 1 slightly down month every couple of years. Nobody on earth is that good of a money manager unless they're front-running.

2. There are too many red flags to ignore. REFCO, Wood River, the Manhattan Fund, Princeton Economics, and other hedge fund blow ups all had a lot fewer red flags than Madoff and look what happened at those places.

3. Bernie Madoff is running the world's largest unregistered hedge fund. He's organized this business as "hedge fund of funds private labeling their own hedge funds which Bernie Madoff **secretly** runs for them using a split-strike conversion strategy getting paid only trading commissions which are not disclosed." If this isn't a regulatory dodge,

I don't know what is. This is a back-door marketing and financing scheme that is opaque and rife with hidden fees (he charges only commissions on the trades). If this product isn't marketed correctly, what is the chance that it is managed correctly? In my financial industry experience, I've found that wherever there's one cockroach in plain sight, many more are lurking behind the corner out of plain view.

4. Mathematically this type of split-strike conversion fund should never be able to beat US Treasury Bills much less provide 12.00% average annual returns to investors net of fees. I and other derivatives professionals on Wall Street will swear up and down that a split-strike conversion strategy cannot earn an average annual return anywhere near the 16% gross returns necessary to be able to deliver 12% net returns to investors.

5. BM would have to be trading more than 100% of the open interest of OEX index put options every month. And if BM is using only OTC OEX index options, it is guaranteed that the Wall Street firms on the other side of those trades would have to be laying off a significant portion of that risk in the exchange listed index options markets. Every large derivatives dealer on Wall Street will tell you that Bernie Madoff is a fraud. Go ask the heads of equity derivatives trading at Morgan Stanley, Goldman Sachs, JP Morgan and Citigroup their opinions about Bernie Madoff. They'll all tell the SEC that they can't believe that BM hasn't been caught yet.

6. The SEC is slated to start overseeing hedge funds in February 2006, yet since Bernie Madoff is not registered as a hedge fund but acting as one but via third party shields, the chances of Madoff escaping SEC scrutiny are very high. If I hadn't written this report, there's no way the SEC would have known to check the facts behind all of these third party hedge funds.

Potential Fall Out if Bernie Madoff turns out to be a Ponzi Scheme:

1. If the average hedge fund is assumed to be levered 4:1, it doesn't take a rocket scientist to realize that there might be anywhere from a few hundred billion on up in selling pressure in the wake of a \$20 – \$50 billion hedge fund fraud. With the hedge fund market estimated to be \$1 trillion, having one hedge fund with 2% – 5% of the industry's assets under management suddenly blow up, it is hard to predict the severity of the resulting shock wave. You just know it'll be unpleasant for anywhere from a few days to a few weeks but the fall out shouldn't be anywhere near as great as that from the Long Term Capital Management Crises. Using the hurricane scale with which we've all become quite familiar with this year, I'd rate BM turning out to be a Ponzi Scheme as a Category 2 or 3 hurricane where the 1998 LTCM Crises was a Category 5.

2. Hedge fund, fund of funds with greater than a 10% exposure to Bernie Madoff will likely be faced with forced redemptions. This will lead to a cascade of panic selling in all of the various hedge fund sectors whether equity related or not. Long–short and market neutral managers will take losses as their shorts rise and their longs fall. Convertible arbitrage managers will lose as the long positions in underlying bonds are sold and the short equity call options are brought to close. Fixed income arbitrage managers will also face losses as credit spreads widen. Basically, most hedge funds categories with two exceptions will have at least one big down month thanks to the unwinding caused by forced redemptions. Dedicated Short Funds and Long Volatility Funds are the two hedge fund categories that will do well.

3. The French and Swiss Private Banks are the largest investors in Bernie Madoff. This will have a huge

negative impact on the European capital markets as several large fund of funds implode. I figure one-half to three-quarters of Bernie Madoff's funds come from overseas. The unwinding trade will hurt all markets across the globe but it is the Private European Banks that will fare the worst.

4. European regulators will be seen as not being up to the task of dealing with hedge fund fraud. Hopefully this scandal will serve as a long overdue wake-up call for them and result in increased funding and staffing levels for European Financial Regulators.

5. In the US Fairfield Sentry ▮▮▮▮▮▮, Access International Advisors, Tremont and several other hedge fund, fund of funds will all implode. There will be a call for increased hedge fund regulation by scared and battered high net worth investors.

6. The Wall Street wire house FOF's are not invested in Madoff's strategy. As far as I know the wire house's internal FOF's all think he's a fraud and have avoided him like the plague. But these very same wire houses often own highly profitable hedge fund prime brokerage operations and these operations will suffer contained, but painful nonetheless, losses from loans to some hedge funds that go bust during the panic selling. As a result, I predict that some investment banks will pull out of the prime brokerage business deeming it too volatile from an earnings standpoint. Damage to Wall Street will be unpleasant in that hedge funds and FOF's are a big source of trading revenues. If the hedge fund industry fades, Wall Street will need to find another revenue source to replace them.

7. US Mutual fund investors and other long-term investors in main stream investment products will only feel a month or two's worth of pain from the selling cascade in the hedge fund arena but their markets should recover afterwards.

8. Congress will be up in arms and there will be Senate and House hearings just like there were for Long Term Capital Management.
9. The SEC's critics who say the SEC shouldn't be regulating private partnerships will be forever silenced. Hopefully this leads to expanded powers and increased funding for the SEC. Parties that opposed SEC entry into hedge fund regulation will fall silent. The SEC will gain political strength in Washington from this episode but only if the SEC is proactive and launches an immediate, full scale investigation into all of the Red Flags surrounding Madoff Investment Securities, LLC. Otherwise, it is almost certain that NYAG Elliot Spitzer will launch his investigation first and once again beat the SEC to the punch causing the SEC further public embarrassment.
10. Hedge funds will face increased due diligence from regulators, investors, prime brokers and counter-parties which is a good thing and long overdue.

Potential Fall Out if Bernie Madoff is found out to be front-running customer order flow:

1. This would be just one more black eye among many for the brokerage industry and the NYSE and NASDAQ. At this point the reputations of both the NYSE and NASDAQ are already at rock bottom, so there's likely little downside left for these two troubled organizations.
2. The industry wouldn't miss a beat other than for the liquidation of Madoff Investment Securities, LLC. Figure it will be similar to REFCO's demise only there won't be a buyer of the firm given that they cheated customers who would all be embarrassed to remain customers once the news they've been ripped off is on the front-pages. These former customers are more likely to sue for damages than remain customers. Unsecured lenders would face losses but other than that the industry would be better off.

3. At least the returns are real, in which case determining restitution could keep the courts busy for years. The Class Action Bar would be thrilled. A lot of the FOF's are registered offshore in places where the long arm of the law might not reach. My guess is that the fight for the money off-shore would keep dozens of lawyers happily employed for many years.
4. The FOF's would suffer little in the way of damage. All could be counted on to say *"We didn't know the manager was generating returns illegally. We relied upon the NYSE and NASDAQ to regulate their markets and prevent front-running therefore we see no reason to return any funds."*

Attachments:

1. 2 page Summary of Fairfield Sentry Ltd with performance data from December 1990 – May 2005.
2. Copy of the May 7, 2001 Barrons' article, ***"Don't Ask, Don't Tell; Bernie Madoff is so secretetive, he even asks his investors to keep mum,"*** written by Erin E. Arvedlund.
3. Partial list of French and Swiss money-managers and private banks with investments in Bernie Madoff's hedge fund. Undoubtedly there are dozens more European FOF's and Private Banks that are invested with BM.
4. 2 page offering memorandum, faxed March 29, 2001, for an investment in what I believe is Fairfield Sentry Ltd., one of several investment programs run by Madoff Investment Securities, LLC for third party hedge fund, fund of funds. I do not know who the source was who faxed this document since the fax heading is blank. The document number listed at the bottom of the page appears to read I:\Data\WPDOCS|AG_\94021597.

ATTACHMENT 1: Fairfield Sentry Performance Data

Fairfield Sentry Ltd

Fund Category(s):
Long/Short Equity

Strategy Description:

The Fund seeks to obtain capital appreciation of its assets principally through the utilization of a nontraditional options trading strategy described as "split strike conversion," to which the Fund allocates the predominant portion of its assets. This strategy has defined risk and profit parameters, which may be ascertained when a particular position is established. Set forth below is a description of the "split strike conversion" strategies ("SSC Investments"). The establishment of a typical position entails (i) the purchase of a group or basket of equity securities that are intended to highly correlate to the S&P 100 Index, (ii) the sale of out-of-the-money S&P 100 Index call options in an equivalent contract value dollar amount to the basket of equity securities, and (iii) the purchase of an equivalent number of out-of-the-money S&P 100 Index put options. An index call option is out-of-the-money when its strike price is greater than the current price of the index; an index put option is out-of-the-money when the strike price is lower than the current price of the index. The basket typically consists of approximately 35 to 45 stocks in the S&P 100. The logic of this strategy is that once a long stock position has been established, selling a call against such long position will increase the standstill rate of return, while allowing upward movement to the short call strike price. The purchase of an out-of-the-money put, funded with part or all of the call premium, protects the equity position from downside risk. A bullish or bearish bias of the positions can be achieved by adjustment of the strike prices in the S&P 100 puts and calls. The further away the strike prices are from the price of the S&P 100, the more bullish the strategy. However, the dollar value underlying the put options always approximates the value of the basket of stocks.

Contact Info		Fees & Structure	
Fund:	Fairfield Sentry Ltd	Fund Assets:	$5100.00million
General Partner:	Arden Asset Management	Strategy Assets:	$5300.00million
Address:	919 Third Avenue	Firm Assets:	$8300million
	11th th Floor	Min. Investment:	$ 0.10million
	New York NY 10022	Management Fee:	1.00%
	USA	Incentive Fee:	20.00%
Tel:	212-319-6060	Hurdle Rate:	
Fax:		High Water Mark:	Yes
Email:	fairfieldfunds@fggus.com	Additions:	Monthly
Contact Person:	Fairfield Funds	Redemptions:	Monthly
Portfolio Manager:		Lockup:	
		Inception Date:	Dec-1990
		Money Invested In:	United States
		Open to New Investments:	Yes

Annual Returns

1990	1991	1992	1993	1994	1995	1996	1997	1998	1999	2000	2001	2002	2003	2004	2005
2.83%	18.58%	14.67%	11.68%	11.49%	12.95%	12.99%	14.00%	13.40%	14.18%	11.55%	10.68%	9.33%	8.21%	7.07%	2.52%

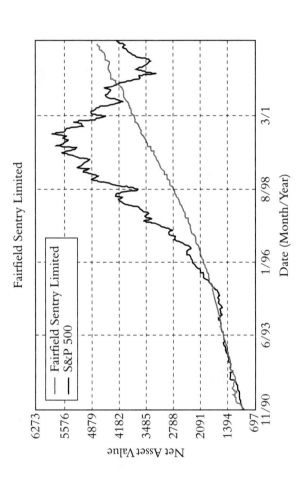

Fairfield Sentry Limited

Sharpe Ratio (Rolling 12):	2.56
Sharpe Ratio (Annualized):	2.55
Std. Dev. (Monthly):	0.75%
Std. Dev. (Rolling 12):	2.74%
Beta:	0.06
Alpha:	0.91
R:	0.30
R Squared:	0.09

Year To Date:	2.52%
Highest 12 Month Return:	19.98%
Lowest 12 Month Return:	6.23%
Average Annual Return:	12.00%
Average Monthly Return:	0.96%
Highest Monthly Return:	3.36%
Lowest Monthly Return:	−0.55%
Average Gain:	1.01%
Average Loss:	−0.24%
Profitable Percentage:	95.98%
Compounded Monthly Return:	0.96%
Longest Losing Streak:	1 mo.
Maximum Drawdown:	−0.55%

	Jan	Feb	Mar	Apr	May	Jun	Jul	Aug	Sep	Oct	Nov	Dec
1990	N/A	N/A	N/A	N/A	N/A	N/A	N/A	N/A	N/A	N/A	N/A	2.83% E
1991	3.08% E	1.46% E	0.59% E	1.39% E	1.88% E	0.37% E	2.04% E	1.07% E	0.80% E	2.82% E	0.08% E	1.63% E
1992	0.49% E	2.79% E	1.01% E	2.86% E	-0.19%	1.29% E	0.00% E	0.92% E	0.40% E	1.40% E	1.42% E	1.43% E
1993	0.00% E	1.93% E	1.86% E	0.06% E	1.72% E	0.86% E	0.09% E	1.78% E	0.35% E	1.77% E	0.26% E	0.45% E
1994	2.18% E	-0.36%	1.52% E	1.82% E	0.51% E	0.29% E	1.78% E	0.42% E	0.82% E	1.88% E	-0.55%	0.66% E
1995	0.92% E	0.76% E	0.84% E	1.69% E	1.72% E	0.50% E	1.08% E	-0.16%	1.70% E	1.60% E	0.51% E	1.10% E
1996	1.49% E	0.73% E	1.23% E	0.64% E	1.41% E	0.22% E	1.92% E	0.27% E	1.22% E	1.10% E	1.58% E	0.48% E
1997	2.45% E	0.73% E	0.86% E	1.17% E	0.63% E	1.34% E	0.75% E	0.35% E	2.39% E	0.55% E	1.56% E	0.42% E
1998	0.91% E	1.29% E	1.75% E	0.42% E	1.76% E	1.28% E	0.83% E	0.28% E	1.04% E	1.93% E	0.84% E	0.33% E
1999	2.06% E	0.17% E	2.29% E	0.36% E	1.51% E	1.76% E	0.43% E	0.94% E	0.73% E	1.11% E	1.61% E	0.39% E
2000	2.20% E	0.20% E	1.84% E	0.34% E	1.37% E	0.80% E	0.65% E	1.32% E	0.25% E	0.92% E	0.68% E	0.43% E
2001	2.21% E	0.14% E	1.13% E	1.32% E	0.32% E	0.23% E	0.44% E	1.01% E	0.73% E	1.28% E	1.21% E	0.19% E
2002	0.03% E	0.60% E	0.46% E	1.16% E	2.12% E	0.26% E	3.36% E	-0.06%	0.13% E	0.73% E	0.16% E	0.06% E
2003	-0.27%	0.04% E	1.97% E	0.10% E	0.95% E	1.00% E	1.44% E	0.22% E	0.93% E	1.32% E	-0.08%	0.32% E
2004	0.94% E	0.50% E	0.05% C	0.43% C	0.66% C	1.28% C	0.08% C	1.33% E	0.53% E	0.03% E	0.79% E	0.24% E
2005	0.51% E	0.37% E	0.85% C	0.14% C	0.63% C	N/A	N/A	N/A	N/A	N/A	N/A	N/A

Appendix C

Online Resource Guide for the Classroom and Beyond

The story of the Madoff fraud is far from over. Free downloadable resources are available for the general reader and for classroom use at www.noonewouldlisten.com, including:

- Victims' stories from news media
- Video clips
- Newspaper articles
- Research papers
- Written testimony
- The government's criminal prosecution of the case
- Civil case proceedings against the accountants, banks, board members, custodians, feeder funds, fiduciaries, hedge funds of funds, plan administrators, and others

Additional materials will be added as they become available, so be sure to check back often.

A Note for Educators: These resources are intended for use in business, business ethics, business law, and forensic accounting courses at the undergraduate and graduate levels.

A Note on Sources

This book is a first-hand account of my experience investigating the Madoff fraud from 1999 through 2009. Direct quotations are to the best of my remembrance. As noted in the text, several sources provided valuable insight into what went on at the government organizations and financial firms during this time. Those interviewed for the research of this book include Inspector General David Kotz, Sergeant Harry Bates, and each member of my investigation team—Frank Casey, Neil Chelo, Michael Ocrant, and Gaytri Kachroo.

Other books and articles have been written on the subject of the Madoff investigation. Those referenced in this book include Erin Arvedlund's article, "Don't Ask, Don't Tell," (*Barron's*, May 7, 2001, http://online.barrons.com/article/SB989019667829349012.html); her book, *Too Good to Be True: The Rise and Fall of Bernie Madoff* (Portfolio, 2009); Michael Ocrant's article, "Madoff Tops Charts; Skeptics Ask How" (*MARHedge 89*, May 2001, page 1)—also printed in full as Appendix A of this book; and Gregory Zuckerman and Kara Scannell's article, "Madoff Misled SEC in '06, Got Off," (*Wall Street Journal*, December 18, 2008, page A1, http://online.wsj.com/article/SB122956182184616625.html). Portions of an August 10, 2007 posting on Greg Newton's blog, *Nakedshorts* (http://nakedshorts.typepad.com/nakedshorts/2007/08/weekend-reading.html), are also referenced.

Publicly available court documents and transcriptions from my February 4, 2009, hearing before the House Subcommittee on Capital Markets and September 10, 2009, hearing before the Senate Banking Committee are quoted at length, and can be accessed through government web sites or through the links available at www.noonewouldlisten.com.

About the Author

Harry Markopolos attended high school at Cathedral Prep in his hometown of Erie, Pennsylvania. He received his bachelor of arts degree in business administration from Loyola University of Maryland and then went on to Boston College for his master of science in finance degree.

He received a reserve commission as a second lieutenant, Infantry, in the U.S. Army and is a graduate of several Army postgraduate schools, including the Infantry Officers' Basic and Advanced Courses, the Civil Affairs Officers' Advanced Course, and the U.S. Army Command & General Staff College. Mr. Markopolos has commanded troops at every rank from second lieutenant to major during 17 years of part-time service in the Maryland Army National Guard and Army Reserve.

He earned his Chartered Financial Analyst designation in 1996 and his Certified Fraud Examiner designation in 2008. From 2002 to 2003 he served as president and CEO of the 4,000-member Boston Security Analysts Society. He has also held board seats on the Boston chapters of both the Global Association of Risk Professionals and the Quantitative Work Alliance for Applied Finance, Education and Wisdom (QWAFAFEW), a quantitative finance lecture group.

He was assistant controller, assistant manager, store manager, and district manager for his family's chain of 12 Arthur Treacher's Fish & Chips restaurants before joining Makefield Securities in 1987. In 1988 he joined Darien Capital Management in Greenwich, Connecticut, as an assistant portfolio manager, leaving to become an equity derivatives portfolio manager at Rampart Investment Management Company in Boston, Massachusetts. In 2002 he was promoted to chief investment officer but decided to leave the industry in 2004 to pursue fraud investigations full-time against Fortune 500 companies in the financial services and health care industries. He brings fraud cases to the U.S. Department of Justice, Internal Revenue Service, and various state attorney generals under existing whistleblower programs.

The Madoff investigation, which he started in early 2000, was his first financial fraud case. He's been hooked ever since.

Acknowledgments

Many people contributed to this book, so it's hard for me to consider it a singular effort. To my friends and teammates Frank Casey, Neil Chelo, and Michael Ocrant for your willingness to risk it all over so many years under the very worst circumstances. You contributed so much to this story that you deserve as much credit as I do for exposing the Madoff fraud and the weaknesses of the Securities and Exchange Commission (SEC). Your dedication to our nation's core values speaks volumes about your character. I have led many whistle-blower teams over the years, but never one that faced danger like this team did; yet each of you pressed on regardless. And you did it for zero compensation because it was the right thing to do, proving that some things are just so important that you know you have to do them for free. This country needs to produce more good citizens like you, because right now the bad guys are winning. I hope this book inspires others to follow in your footsteps.

To my personal attorney, Dr. Gaytri Kachroo. Thank you for representing me pro bono and sharing your experiences about this case. You have always been able to see three steps into the future and outthink our opponents.

To my wife Faith for allowing me to work on this case even after realizing how dangerous it had become. I promise I will never do another case that puts our family at risk. If I had known how bad this case would get I would never have pursued it. No husband should ever have to ask his wife to defend the second floor armed with a pistol.

To David Fisher, who put up with the five of us and our too many edits and rewrites. No one knows organized crime better than you do, and that's what this was at its core—a criminal conspiracy that spanned the globe. It was a pleasure working with you. To Frank Weiman, our literary agent, whose patience we tried and tried again.

To the following partners at the Boston office of McCarter & English LLP, thanks for preparing me, pro bono, to testify before Congress: Burt Winnick, the Honorable Paul Cellucci, and Bill Zucker.

To Phillip Michael, my main *qui tam* attorney and confidant in working with so many brave whistleblower teams. Thanks for being a world-class enforcement attorney! Thanks also to the whistleblowers on Cases 81, 89, 92, 93, 94, 95, and 96. You are unsung heroes defending our nation's citizenry against those companies that would loot this nation's tax dollars. Thanks also to attorney Mike Lesser at Thornton & Naumes LLP for carrying on without me while this book was written.

To Pat Burns, Jeb White, and all the *qui tam* whistleblower attorneys at TAF.org for fighting the good fight against crooked corporations. Thank you for everything you've taught me.

Thanks to Joe Wells and Kevin Taparauskas at the Association of Certified Fraud Examiners for the excellent training and timely advice.

To Sergeant Harry Bates of the Whitman Police Department. Thanks for your help planning my personal security and keeping it a secret all these years. And my entire family thanks the townspeople of Whitman, Massachusetts, for being so protective and supportive after this case became public. I apologize for all the commotion this caused the town.

To my father Louie, thank you for teaching me to stand up and fight no matter the size of the opponent. You watched me lose and you were okay with it even while I was ashamed. To my mother Georgia for being a stay-at-home mom and superb educator.

To Colonel Michael N. Schleupner, my former battalion commander, thank you for the example you set for me. Your moral courage in always doing the right thing has always inspired me. Ditto for Colonel Ken Pritchard, Lieutenant Colonel James Berger, and Lieutenant Colonel Mike Tanczyn. I witnessed each of you stand up for what was right, and it hurt your military careers in the National Guard and Army Reserve but you did the right thing anyway. Moral courage is often the hardest to come by, and no one gives you a medal for having it; but without it the world quickly falls apart.

To some of the many good people in the financial services industry who helped me with this investigation: Dan diBartolomeo (Northfield Information Services), Andre Mehta (Cambridge Associates), Dave Henry (Carruth LLC), Nick Marfino (ConvergEx), Joel Kugler (Meridien Partners), Matt Moran (Chicago Board Options Exchange), Bud Haslett (CFA Institute), Tom Huber (Glenmede Trust), and Jeff Fritz (Oxford Trading Associates). Your help was invaluable in pursuing the case.

At Citigroup, thanks to Charlie Miles and Holly Robinson for your astute observations. To Leon Gross, thanks for your expert analysis; I wish the SEC had bothered to call you—things might have been different if they had. All of you were helpful at various points during my team's investigation, proving that plenty of honest people work on Wall Street.

I would like to thank the following people at Goldman Sachs for teaching me all about derivatives math: Dr. Joanne Hill, Dr. Emanuel Derman, Rebecca Cheong, Michael Liou, Jack Lehman, Mark Zurack, and Amy Goodfriend.

To the late John "Front Page" Wilke of the *Wall Street Journal* for your courage and inspiration on all those corruption cases you broke. Real investigative journalists are a rare breed, but you were one of the best. I miss you.

To Gregory Zuckerman of the *Wall Street Journal* and Ross Kerber of the *Boston Globe*, thank you for reporting the story when it first became public. You two went on faith and trusted me instead of the SEC as the case was breaking.

To Andy Court, Keith Sharman, and Reuben Heyman-Kantor at CBS News' *60 Minutes*, thank you for allowing me to explain to the victims what happened. Your investigative skills are unparalleled, and you discovered information that you wisely never reported because you know the difference between news and sensationalism.

To Diane Schulman for rescuing me in my time of need and to your husband John Davidow and Curt Nickisch of National Public

Radio's Boston affiliate for your in-depth reporting. To Eric King of *King World News*—thank you for teaching me how to interview.

To the men of Cathedral Prep in my hometown of Erie, Pennsylvania, thank you for your overwhelming support. Thanks especially to Chris Haggerty and my math teachers: Stanley Brezicki, Joanne Mullen, the late Sister Mary Denise, and the late Sister Mary DePaul.

To Ed Manion, thanks for believing me over the years and urging me to stay on the case well past the point of reason. To Mike Garrity, thanks for doing your best to get others in the agency to listen.

To SEC Inspector General H. David Kotz. You are my hero. I'd love my three young sons to turn out just like you. Your hardworking inspector general team restored my faith in government. Thanks to Deputy Inspector General Noelle Frangipane, David Fielder, Heidi Steiber, Christopher Wilson, and David Witherspoon. Your dedication to the truth won out. If the SEC really does adopt all of your recommendations, your work will have been worth it—otherwise it will be business as usual at the SEC, and our nation can't afford that.

To SEC Chair Mary Schapiro, thank you for having the moral courage to allow the SEC inspector general's report to be issued as written despite what must have been overwhelming pressure from the senior agency staff to heavily censor it instead.

To all of the FBI agents tirelessly working on this case in order to bring the guilty to justice. Personal thanks to special agents (first names only) Keith, Steve, Julia, Rob, and Paul. The case is in good hands now. Godspeed, keep your chins up, and go where the evidence leads you—because this case is surely the case from hell. No matter what you do, you'll never get them all. Just try to catch as many as you can. That's all anyone can ask of you.

And now I would like to make some very important acknowledgments on behalf of each member of the investigation team: Frank Casey, Neil Chelo, and Michael Ocrant, as well as my attorney, Gaytri Kachroo. This story would not be complete without them and their supportive friends and families.

Frank Casey wishes to thank his wife Judy and the late Major Peter W. H. Van Dine, who taught him the skills and responsibilities of leadership when he was a Reserve Officers' Training Corps (ROTC) cadet at Penn State.

Neil Chelo wishes to acknowledge his parents, Benjamin and Sevinc Chelo; brother John and daughter Sarah Chelo; as well as George Devoe Jr., CFA; Robert Ferguson, CFA; Scott Franzblau; and Jeremy Gollehon.

Gaytri Kachroo thanks her children, Kirin and Maya Kachroo-Levine; her brothers, Leeladher and Vidyadher Kachroo; her sister-in-law, Andrea Gauntlet; and her mother, Mohini Dhar Kachroo. Big thanks to Martha Minow; Mark Byers; Representatives Kanjorski, Frank, Arcuri, Ackerman, and Garrett and their incredibly helpful staffs; Mary Schapiro; David Kotz; Javier Cremades; and the executives of the Global Alliance.

Michael Ocrant thanks his wife Gail and son Max.

Last but not least, acknowledgments on behalf of David Fisher go to editors Meg Freeborn and Bill Falloon, who did such wonderful work under real pressure, as well as to Nancy Rothschild and the rest of the fine people at John Wiley & Sons. Thanks also go to Frank Weimann and Elyse Tanzillo of the Literary Group International.

David also wishes to thank Randall Arthur, Linda Yellin, George Cole, and Patricia Black of Wallin, Simon & Black; the entire Hicker family; his wife, Laura Stevens; sons Taylor Jesse and Beau Charles; Belle, their dog; and Buck, the Hall of Fame cat.

HARRY MARKOPOLOS

Index